ASPECTS OF TOURISM 4
Series Editors: Chris Cooper (*University of Queensland, Australia*)
and Michael Hall (*University of Otago, New Zealand*)

Natural Area Tourism

Ecology, Impacts and Management

David Newsome, Susan A. Moore and Ross K. Dowling

CHANNEL VIEW PUBLICATIONS
Clevedon • Buffalo • Toronto • Sydney

Library of Congress Cataloging in Publication Data

Newsome, D. (David)
Natural Area Tourism: Ecology, Impacts and Management/
D. Newsome, S.A. Moore and R.K. Dowling
Aspects of Tourism
Includes bibliographical references
1. Tourism. 2. Tourism–Environmental aspects. 3. Natural areas.
I. Moore, S.A. (Sue A.). II. Dowling, Ross K. III. Title. IV. Series.
G155.A1 N43 2001
338.4'791–dc21   2001042188

British Library Cataloguing in Publication Data

A catalogue entry for this book is available from the British Library.

ISBN 1-853150-25-3 (hbk)
ISBN 1-853150-24-5 (pbk)

Channel View Publications
An imprint of Multilingual Matters Ltd

UK: Frankfurt Lodge, Clevedon Hall, Victoria Road, Clevedon BS21 7SJ.
USA: 2250 Military Road, Tonawanda, NY 14150, USA.
Canada: 5201 Dufferin Street, North York, Ontario, Canada M3H 5T8.
Australia: Footprint Books, Unit 4/92a Mona Vale Road, Mona Vale, NSW 2103, Australia.

Typeset by Archetype-IT Ltd (http://www.archetype-it.com).
Printed and bound in Great Britain by the Cromwell Press.

Natural Area Tourism

Aspects of Tourism

Series Editors: Professor Chris Cooper, *University of Queensland, Ipswich, Australia* and Professor Michael Hall, *University of Otago, Dunedin, New Zealand*

Aspects of Tourism is an innovative, multifaceted series which will comprise authoritative reference handbooks on global tourism regions, research volumes, texts and monographs. It is designed to provide readers with the latest thinking on tourism world-wide and in so doing will push back the frontiers of tourism knowledge. The series will also introduce a new generation of international tourism authors writing on leading edge topics.

The volumes will be authoritative, readable and user-friendly, providing accessible sources for further research. The list will be underpinned by an annual tourism research volume. Books in the series will be commissioned that probe the relationship between tourism and cognate subject areas such as strategy, development, retailing, sport and environmental studies. The publisher and series editors welcome proposals from writers with projects on these topics.

Other Books in the Series
Dynamic Tourism: Journeying with Change
  Priscilla Boniface
Journeys into Otherness: The Representation of Differences and Identity in Tourism
  Keith Hollinshead and Chuck Burlo (eds)
Tourism Collaboration and Partnerships
  Bill Bramwell and Bernard Lane (eds)
Tourism in Peripheral Areas: Case Studies
  Frances Brown and Derek Hall (eds)
Tourism and Development: Concepts and Issue
  Richard Sharpley and David Telfer (eds)

Please contact us for the latest book information:
Channel View Publications, Frankfurt Lodge, Clevedon Hall,
Victoria Road, Clevedon, BS21 7HH, England
http://www.multilingual-matters.com

Contents

Preface

This book was born out of an individual and collective passion for the natural environment. We are all environmental scientists who have spent a great part of our lives travelling in, researching about, and teaching for, a greater understanding of the global environment. Therefore it was only natural that at some stage we should wish to share our knowledge of, and enthusiasm for, natural areas and this has manifested itself through tourism. One of us has been a tour guide to national parks and wilderness areas for 25 years, another has been a natural area manager for more than a decade, while all of us have led field trips to natural areas as part of our tertiary teaching. We love the environment and believe that through tourism to natural areas people will be stirred within to act positively for their own environment upon their return to the predominantly urban areas from which they came.

This book reflects some of our thinking on tourism in natural areas, especially in relation to its ecology, impacts and management. There are many existing environmental books that briefly address tourism impacts as well as a large number of tourism texts that have chapters on environmental impacts. This book dwells on the nexus that exists between the environment and tourism and unashamedly fosters a positive link between the two. It owes much to the earlier work of John and Ann Edington (1986), whose text *Ecology, Recreation and Tourism* is a classic in the field. While much lies unchanged over the past 15 years, much more has changed. This book then sets out to describe the settings, impacts and management related issues for tourism in natural areas in the new millennium.

The underpinning base of our approach to the subject is embedded firmly in our shared belief that it is only through a greater understanding of the environment that tourism in natural areas will evolve to a place where it can be truly synergistic. Too often in the past the relationship has been one-sided with tourism being the winner and the environment the loser. But it is our belief that with environmental understanding, informed management and an aware public, natural area tourism has the possibility of introducing people to the environment in an educative, ethical and exciting manner which will leave them with an indelible impression on the wonders of the natural world and the pivotal position that we humans have within it.

The book does not debate the concepts of ecotourism but instead deliberately chooses to focus on the wider field of natural area tourism. This is because it is the latter type of tourism which is more prevalent today and it is our desire to interact with this audience in a bid to introduce them to the essential core elements of ecotourism. Ecotourism is a narrow niche form of tourism in the natural environment which embraces the ideals of being conservation supporting, ecologically friendly and environmentally educative. It is our desire to lead natural area tourism developers, managers and tourists towards the central components of ecotourism. If this is fostered then the promise of the symbiotic relationship between tourism and the environment will begin to be achieved.

The book has been written for a broad audience including students pursuing university and training programmes, tourism industry professionals, planners and managers in natural area management, as well as government agency employees. As a general text, it should be useful to students in a range of disciplines including tourism, environmental science, geography, planning and regional studies. As a specific text it provides a practical guide for natural area managers, such as national and marine park managers, as well as tour operators. The applied approach to ecology and understanding of environmental impacts makes this book also suitable for those from business, communications and marketing backgrounds as well as those with more scientific leanings. The foundation of ecology and impacts is valuable, but of even greater value is the explanation of the practical aspects of managing natural area tourism. This includes planning frameworks for natural area tourism as well as a number of management strategies with special attention paid to interpretation and monitoring. Finally the book brings together the essential elements of ecology, impacts and management to address comprehensively the provision of sustainable natural area tourism.

Acknowledgements

Comments and suggestions by a number of people significantly enhanced the calibre and comprehensiveness of this publication. Valuable input to Chapter 2 was provided by Duncan McCollin, Karen Higginbottom, Richard Hobbs, Diane Lee, Daryl Moncrieff and Amanda Smith. Chapter 3 was refined using the ideas of Ralph Buckley, Doug Coughran, Michelle Davis, Kreg Lindberg, Daryl Moncrieff and Amanda Smith. Chapter 4 benefited from review by Kelly Gillen, Simon McArthur and Steve McCool. Chapter 5 was improved through comments by Terry Bailey, David Cole, Michael Hall, Tony Press, Wayne Schmidt and Peter Wellings. Chapter 6 incorporated insights from Rory Allardice, Kevin Keneally, Daryl Moncrieff and Amanda Smith. Chapter 7 received invaluable feedback from Richard Hammond, Luisa Liddicoat, Jeff Marion and Amanda Smith. The scope and production of the book owes much to the support of the West Australian Department of Conservation and Land Management, especially Daryl Moncrieff, Jim Sharp and Wayne Schmidt. Chris Cooper, David Fennell, Michael Hall and Dallen Timothy have also played important roles in producing a high quality publication.

Without the cartographic efforts of Alan Rossow, Colin Ferguson and Mike Roeger the diagrams and maps, which form the backbone of this book, would not have been possible. Noella Ross diligently entered and manipulated the references and formatted the text. Ross Lantzke provided illustrative plates and software assistance. Photographs provided by Steve McCool, the Parks and Wildlife Service Tasmania, Environment Australia, the Australian Antarctic Division and Trevor Hall added to the visual quality of this publication. Support in the field was provided to the first author by the Director of Kruger National Park, Wilhem Gertenbach, Teresa Whitehead, Rory Allardice and Richard Baker. We would also like to thank all those authors and publishers who kindly granted permission for us to reproduce copyright material, particularly the figures and tables. Full details of the sources are given in the reference list.

The first author acknowledges the patience and support provided by his family, Jane, Ben and Rachel. The second author gratefully acknowledges the support provided by Warren, Jessica and Samuel Tacey and the director, Maureen George and staff of the Murdoch University Child Care Centre. The third author thanks his wife Wendy for her constant support, accompanying him on field trips and tolerating long periods at the computer.

Without the enthusiasm and professionalism of the publishers, Mike and Marjukka Grover, and the team at Channel View Publications this book would never have become reality.

Chapter 1
Introduction

Introduction

The world we live in is an exciting place. From the surface of the moon the earth is viewed by astronauts as a pearl of bright colours in a sea of darkness. If we move closer to the earth we would see that it is made up of a number of natural environments. The area of life on earth is termed the biosphere which comprises the atmosphere (air), hydrosphere (water) and lithosphere (land). The biosphere and its elements contain all living organisms and the variations among living organisms is referred to as biological diversity or biodiversity (Figure 1.1).

The earth includes both terrestrial (land) and marine (water) environments. On land the earth's major environments are distributed primarily in accordance with temperature and precipitation. The earth's three major climatic zones are the polar, temperate and tropical regions. In the higher (polar) latitudes temperature is the more important whereas in the temperate and tropical zones precipitation determines differentiation. Within each of the major climatic regions are a number of different environments (or ecosystems). These include deserts, grasslands and forests. Tropical rainforests are rich in species and literally teem with life. Complementing the land is the water which covers 75% of the earth's surface. Marine areas can also contain a diverse number of species and coral reefs are examples of species rich regions.

Natural areas have always attracted people and with the advent of modern travel humans are now visiting places all over the planet. Indeed tourism to natural areas is booming and it has been estimated that it has risen from approximately 2% of all tourism in the late 1980s to about 20% of all leisure travel today (The Ecotourism Society (TES), 1998; Weaver & Oppermann, 2000). The World Tourism Organisation (WTO) concurs with this figure and suggests that natural area tourism is now worth US$20 billion a year (WTO, 1998a). Thus natural area tourism is undergoing explosive growth and as such it has the capability to change both natural areas as well as tourism itself. In this book we will explore this phenomenon from the standpoint that natural area tourism can be beneficial to individuals, regions and countries provided it is planned, developed and managed in a responsible manner.

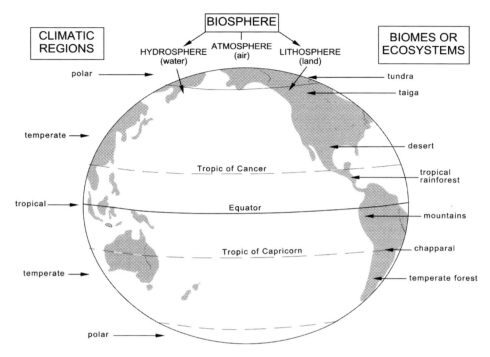

Figure 1.1 Conceptual diagram of the global environment

The growing concern for conservation and the well-being of our environment over the last two decades has moved far beyond the realms of a concerned few and into the wider public arena. At the same time there has been a corresponding upsurge in tourism all over the world leading to the phenomenon referred to as 'mass tourism'. With this unparalleled growth of the two it was inevitable that one day they would meet and interact. In natural areas, where tourism either exists or is proposed, there is the potential for both beneficial and adverse environmental and socio-cultural impacts to occur. Thus there are two streams of thought regarding the environment–tourism relationship. The first is that the natural environment is harmed by tourism and hence the two are viewed as being in conflict. The second is that the two have the potential to work together in a symbiotic manner where each adds to the other.

The environment–tourism relationship has been the subject of this debate for the last three decades. The International Union for the Conservation of Nature and Natural Resources (IUCN; now known as the World Conservation Union) first raised the nature of the relationship when its Director General posed the question in a paper entitled 'Tourism and environmental conservation: conflict, coexistence, or symbiosis?' (Budowski, 1976). Thirteen years later the question appeared to remain unanswered when (Romeril, 1989) posited the question 'Is tourism and the environment in accord or discord?'. Thus the environment–tourism relationship may be viewed from one of two standpoints: that it is either in conflict or symbiosis. Either point of view may be adopted and defended but it is argued here that no matter which standpoint is espoused the way to reduce conflict or increase compatibility is through understanding, planning and management which is grounded in environmental concepts and allows for sustainable development.

The environment–tourism relationship is grounded in the concepts of the sustainable use of natural resources as fostered by the World Conservation Strategy (IUCN, 1980) and the sustainable development strategy of the World Commission on Environment and Development (WCED, 1987). This environmental–development link often includes tourism as a bridge. The base of this partnership is resource sustainability and tourism must be fully integrated with the resource management process. This will require the adoption of resource conservation values as well as the more traditional development goals. Central to the goals of environmental conservation and resource sustainability is the protection and maintenance of environmental quality. To achieve this primary goal requires an awareness which is based on environmental protection and enhancement yet fosters the realisation of tourism potential.

Natural Areas

At its core the word environment simply means our surroundings. However, the environment is defined as including all aspects of the surroundings of humanity, affecting individuals and social groupings. At a broad scale the environment may be divided into two major divisions – the natural and built environments. These two different aspects of the environment are not exclusive and can be viewed as being interrelated by human influence. Natural environments are those areas that on the whole tend to retain their natural characteristics and are not modified to any large extent by human interference with the natural landscape or processes. Such areas include patches of natural vegetation that either are found naturally in the landscape or are more likely to be preserved in protected areas. On the other hand, built environments are human altered areas where the natural environment has been modified to such an extent that it has lost its original characteristics and has been transformed into human created places and spaces. Such areas include rural and urban landscapes that have modified natural areas to a lesser or greater degree.

Natural areas are regions which have not been significantly altered by humankind. Such areas include the geology, landforms, soils, water features, vegetation and animals. They contrast with other areas that have a significant human imprint on the natural environment either through past and/or present use. A natural area then is one where the natural forms and processes are not materially altered by human exploitation and occupation. Thus the landforms, wildlife and ecological processes are found largely in their natural state.

Generally the natural order of things is governed by both form and process. In natural areas these include both landforms and ecological processes. Natural areas comprise largely unmodified landscapes which preserve the integrity of the natural landforms and ecological processes.

Approaches to nature

People differ over how serious our environmental problems are due to their different perspectives of the world (Miller, 2002). Such views come in many forms but the two most common vary according to whether or not we put humans at the centre of things. These two are the human-centred or anthropocentric view that underlies most industrial societies and the ecocentric or life-centred outlook. Key principles of the human-centred approach are that humans are the planet's most important species and we are apart from, and in charge of, the rest of nature. It assumes the earth has an unlimited supply of resources to which we gain access through use of science and technology. Other people believe that any human-centred worldview, even stewardship, is unsustainable. They suggest that our worldviews must be expanded to recognise inherent or intrinsic value to all forms of life, that is, value regardless of their potential or actual use to us. This is a life-centred or ecocentric view in which humans believe that it is useful to recognise biodiversity as a vital element of earth for all life.

The ecocentric perspective believes that nature exists for all of earth's species and that humans are not apart from, or in charge of, the rest of nature. In essence it posits that we need the earth, but the earth does not need us. It also suggests that some forms of economic growth are beneficial and some are harmful. Our goals should be to design economic and political systems that encourage sustainable forms of growth and discourage or prohibit forms which cause degradation or pollution. A healthy economy depends on a healthy environment.

There are a number of major principles underlying the ecocentric or earth-centred view (Miller, 2002). These are interconnectedness, intrinsic value biodiversity, sustainability, conservation, intergenerational equity and individual responsibility. The first principle of interconnectedness focuses on the fact that humans are a valuable species. The second principle of intrinsic value is that every living thing has a right to live, or at least to struggle to live, simply because it exists; this right is not dependent on its actual or potential use to us. Part of this principle includes the notion that it is wrong for humans to cause the premature extinction of any wild species and the elimination and degradation of their habitats. This focuses on the need for the third principle – the preservation of wildlife and biodiversity.

The fourth principle focuses on sustainability and it means that something is right when it tends to maintain the earth's life-support systems for us and other species and wrong when it tends otherwise. Conservation is one principle most understood by people in general. It recognises that resources are limited and must not be wasted. The sixth principle of intergenerational equity suggests that we must leave the earth in as good a shape as we found it, if not better. Inherent in the notion is that we must protect the earth's remaining wild ecosystems from our activities, rehabilitate or restore ecosystems we have degraded, use ecosystems only on a sustainable basis, and allow many of the ecosystems we have occupied and abused

to return to a wild state. The seventh and final principle is one of individual responsibility. To carry this out we must ensure that we do not do anything that depletes
the physical, chemical and biological capital which supports all life and human
economic activities; the earth deficit is the ultimate deficit. All people should be
held responsible for their own pollution and environmental degradation.

Given this understanding then, sustaining the earth requires each one of us to
make a personal commitment to live an environmentally ethical life. By extension,
its application to natural area tourism is that governments, the tourism industry,
operators, tourists and the local communities should all play a part in not only
conserving natural areas but also in their enhancement. In doing this then the very
resource base which underpins the natural area tourism industry will be protected
and able to be utilised in a sustainable manner which fosters environmental, social
and economic well-being.

Types of natural areas

There are still many tracts of large natural areas on the earth. They include the
Antarctic, Arctic, Steppes, tropical rainforests, alpine environments such as the
Himalaya or Andes mountains as well as many marine areas such as parts of the
Southern and Indian Oceans. Some of these areas represent wilderness where the
earth and its community of life have not been seriously disturbed by humans and
where humans are only temporary visitors. According to Holden (2000) two main
perspectives on the meaning of 'wilderness' can be recognised. The first is a 'classical perspective', in which the view is taken that the creation of livable and usable
spaces, such as urban areas, is a mark of civilisation and progress. The second
approach is the 'romantic', in which untouched spaces have the greatest value, and
wilderness assumes a deep spiritual significance.

In addition there are many smaller enclaves of natural areas surrounded by
largely human altered environments. Such areas have generally been protected by
humans in an array of protected landscape categories. Protected areas are any
region of land and/or sea that have legal measures limiting the use of the wildlife
within that area (McNeely *et al.*, 1990). These include nature reserves, national
parks, protected landscapes, multiple-use areas, biosphere reserves, etc. The IUCN
(1994) nominates six categories of protected areas, including:

- Category I – Strict Nature Reserve/Wilderness Area
    Category Ia – Strict Nature Reserve
    Category Ib – Wilderness Area
- Category II – National Park
- Category III – Natural Monument
- Category IV – Habitat/Species Management Area
- Category V – Protected Landscape/Seascape
- Category VI – Managed Resource Protection Area.

The order of category does not constitute a hierarchy but reflects, in ascending
order, the degree of human use acceptable in each case. The values of protected

areas are to conserve nature and biological diversity as well as to offer humans opportunities for recreation, inspiration, education and understanding. It is this latter goal that fosters the enjoyment of natural areas for people in the form of recreation and tourism.

Tourism

It is important to distinguish between tourism, leisure and recreation. The interrelationships amongst the three have been discussed by Boniface and Cooper (1987). They define leisure as the time available to an individual when work, sleep and other basic needs have been met, and recreation as any pursuit engaged upon during leisure time. Their definition of tourism is based on that of Mathieson and Wall (1982) that tourism is the temporary movement of people to destinations outside their normal home and workplace, the activities undertaken during the stay and the facilities created to cater for their needs. They argue that if leisure is a measure of time, and recreation embraces the activities undertaken during that time, then tourism is simply one of those activities. Conversely, a central part of the tourism experience usually focuses on leisure and recreational activities. Tourism is usually viewed as being multi-dimensional, possessing physical, social, cultural, economic and political characteristics.

The tourism system has been described and modelled from several different perspectives. All include elements of demand and supply linked by the interconnecting strand of travel. Gunn (1988a) has proposed a simple approach called the Functioning Tourism System which consists of a number of interrelated components. Demand consists of the tourist market and incorporates people's interest in and ability to travel. Supply components include transportation, attractions, services and information/promotion. Transportation consists of the volume and quality of all modes of transport. Attractions are the quality resources which have been developed for satisfying visitors. Services include the variety and quality of food, lodging and other products, and information/promotion is essential to entice the tourist to visit the products offered. Other writers have described the components of the tourism system in a similar manner with only minor differences in functions. For example, Mill and Morrison (1985) combine attractions and services into a 'destination' component, whereas Pearce (1989) separates accommodation from services and replaces information/promotion with infrastructure. An origin-destination approach emphasises the interdependence of the generating and receiving environments (Leiper, 1981). Mathieson and Wall (1982) argue that tourism should be divided into three general components including a dynamic dimension (consisting of demand and travel), a static element (characteristics of tourists and destinations) and consequential component (impacts).

A tourism system model which embraces many of the elements of the existing models but which focuses on tourism's environmental aspects is outlined in Figure 1.2. It is based on the traditional view of a system incorporating inputs, processes, outputs and feedback. The inputs include elements of demand or markets, i.e. the

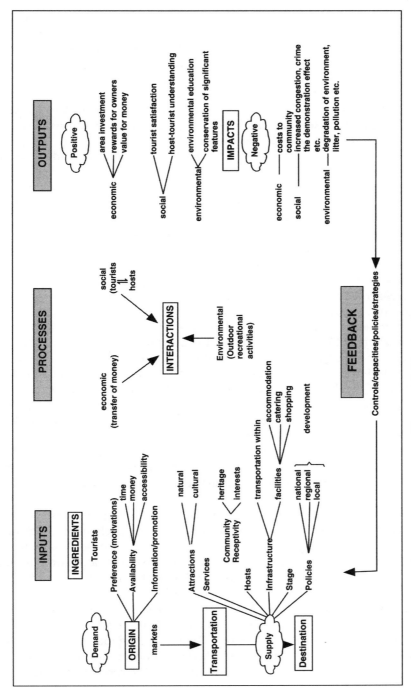

Figure 1.2 The tourism system

prospective tourist's motivation for and ability to travel, as well as supply, that is, the destination resource with its attractions, services, infrastructure and hosts. Processes include economic, social and environmental interactions which may have positive and/or negative outputs (impacts). Feedback allows for the planning of appropriate controls, capacities, policies and strategies for tourism growth whilst minimising adverse impacts.

Tourism is the fastest growing industry in the world and the fastest growing component of it is ecotourism. According to the World Travel and Tourism Council (WTTC) tourism is now the world's largest industry generating 12% of the global gross national product. It employs around 200 million people worldwide which is 8% of all jobs, or one in 12 workers. Overall the tourism industry is expected to double by the year 2005 (WTTC, 1995). The current growth rate of tourism is 4% with the 625 million international tourists in 1998 expected to grow to 800 million by the year 2005. However, it is natural areas tourism which is the most rapidly growing segment of tourism and the WTO estimates it generates approximately 20% of all international travel expenditures (WTO, 1998b).

Globally, tourism will continue strong growth of about 4% per year. International tourist arrivals are approximately 700 million per year. However, this is estimated to reach 1 billion by 2010 and 1.6 billion by 2020. A bigger proportion of the world's total population will go travelling, especially in developing countries, in the 21st century. People will holiday more often, maybe two to four times per year. Travellers of the 21st century will also journey further. One out of every three trips will be long-haul journeys to another region of the world. Long-haul travel is expected to increase from 24% of all international journeys now to 32% by the year 2020 (Neale, 1998). The year 2020 will see the penetration of technology into all aspects of life (Frangialli, 1998). It will become possible to live one's days without exposure to other people. WTO's study 'Tourism: 2020 Vision', predicts 1.6 billion tourists will be visiting foreign countries annually by the year 2020, spending more than US$2 trillion or US$5 billion every day (WTO, 1999). Tourist arrivals are predicted to grow by an average 4.3% a year over the next two decades, while receipts from international tourism will climb by 6.7% a year.

Tourism in the 21st century will not only be the world's biggest industry, it will be the largest by far that the world has ever seen. Along with its phenomenal growth and size, the tourism industry will also have to take on more responsibility for its extensive impacts – not only its economic impact, but also its impact on the environment, on societies and on cultural sites. The WTO indicates that tourists of the 21st century will be travelling further afield on their holidays. China will be the world's number one destination by the year 2020 and it will also become the fourth most important generating market. Other destinations predicted to make great strides in the tourism industry are Russia, Hong Kong, Thailand, Singapore, Indonesia and South Africa. Product development and marketing will need to match each other more closely, based on the main travel motivators of the 21st century, the three 'e's – entertainment, excitement and education.

Definitions of tourism share a range of common elements. However, in this book we have adopted the approach of Hall (1991) who suggests that tourism is the temporary, short-term travel of non-residents to and from a destination. It may have a wide variety of impacts on the destination, the transit route and the source point of tourists. Tourism may also influence the character of the tourist, and it is primarily for leisure or recreation, although business is also important.

Tourists

There have been many attempts at classifying tourists. Plog (1974) linked personality characteristics to particular types of tourist. His work is based upon the concept of psychographics and its application to tourism involves identifying the tourists' desires to choose a particular type of holiday or destination. Plog established a continuum of typologies ranging from what he termed 'psychocentrics' to 'allocentrics'. Psychocentric tourists are thought of as being non-adventuresome whereas allocentrics are more adventurous. Poon (1993) suggests that by the beginning of the 1990s a new type of tourism consumer had emerged. She suggests that they are more experienced, independent and environmentally aware than their predecessors. Poon adds that the new tourists are spontaneous and unpredictable, and not as homogeneous as the previous ones.

There is a marked absence of research into how tourists experience the environment. Holden (2000) draws on the earlier works of Ittleson *et al.* (1976) and Iso-Ahola (1980) to present a taxonomy of environmental experiences which includes a behavioural dimension (Table 1.1). This interaction demonstrates a gradation starting from little interest in the environment, beyond its providing the setting to indulge in a certain type of behaviour, to one of much greater interest and attachment. Given that tourists display different behaviour patterns, it is important for managing the environmental consequences of tourism that consideration is given in marketing strategies to attracting a type of tourist whose behaviour is likely to be compatible with the destination surroundings (Holden, 2000).

A consideration of the values, attitudes and behaviour of people is fundamental when discussing genuine forms of natural area tourism or trying to identify potential natural area tourists. It has been suggested that people are not necessarily such tourists just because they visit a natural area (Acott *et al.*, 1998). It has also been revealed that natural area tourists who have a more ecocentric attitude toward nature tend to prefer businesses that are environmentally friendly (Khan, 1997). Such tourists also expect knowledgeable personnel who are willing to instil a feeling of trust and confidence. This research found that natural area tourists showed a preference for service dimensions based on their attitude, behaviour, travel motivation and value.

According to Wearing and Neil (1999), research conducted in the USA suggests that natural area tourists have higher than average incomes and levels of education, and are also willing to spend more than the normal tourists. In terms of their psychographic characteristics, they report that these tourists possess an environmental ethic, and are ecocentric rather than anthropocentric in orientation. They

Table 1.1 The tourist experience

Mode of experience	Interpretation	Behaviour and environmental attitudes
Environment as a 'setting for action'	The environment is primarily interpreted in a functional way as a place for hedonism, relaxation and recuperation.	Conscious or subconscious disregard for the environment and a lack of interest in learning more about its natural or cultural history.
Environment as a social system	The environment is seen primarily as a place to interact with family and friends.	Physical setting becomes irrelevant as the focus of the experience centres on social relationships.
Environment as emotional territory	Strong emotional feelings associated with, or invoked by, the environment which provide a sense of well-being.	Sense of well-being and wonder at being in a different environment.
Environment as self	Merging of the physical and cultural environment with self.	Strong attachment to landscape and cultures that are perceived as being 'better' than the home society.

Derived from Holden (2000), developed from Ittleson *et al*. (1976), Iso-Ahola (1980)

have more leisure time and disposable income, and are serious travellers who know what they are looking for and their trips are not planned on the spur of the moment. There also seems to be slightly more female than male ecotourists.

Types of tourism

Tourism comprises either mass or alternative tourism (Figure 1.3). The former is characterised by large numbers of people seeking replication of their own culture in institutionalised settings with little cultural or environmental interaction in authentic settings. Alternative tourism is sometimes referred to as 'special interest tourism' or 'responsible' tourism and it is usually taken to mean alternative forms of tourism which place emphasis on greater contact and understanding between hosts and guests as well as between tourists and the environment (Smith & Eadington, 1992).

The development of the environmental movement in the 1980s coincided with the development of, and increase in, the availability and range of holiday types that inferred a greater level of awareness of the environment than is associated with mass tourism. Alternative tourism can be broadly defined as forms of tourism that set out to be consistent with natural, social and community values and which allow both hosts and guests to enjoy positive and worthwhile interaction and shared experiences (Wearing & Neil, 1999).

Cater (1993) notes that alternative tourism comprises small-scale, locally owned activities. She suggests that these contrast with mass tourism which is often charac-

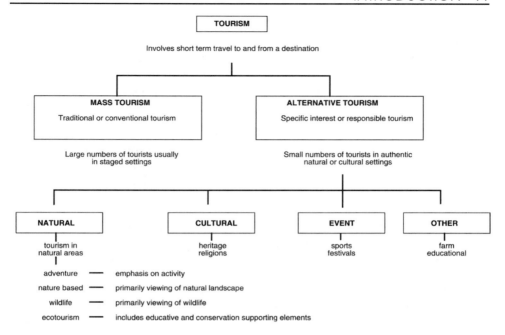

Figure 1.3 An overview of tourism

terised by large-scale multinational concerns typified by repatriation of profits to offshore countries. Other characteristics of alternative tourism include its minimal negative environmental and social impacts, links to other sectors of the local economy, and agriculture and the retention of economic expenditure by local people. Finally, alternative tourism also fosters the involvement of local people in the decision-making process and includes them in the tourism development process. Using these criteria, alternative tourism surpasses purely a concern for the physical environment that typifies green tourism, to include economic, social and cultural considerations. Thus alternative tourism can be viewed as being synonymous with the concept of sustainable tourism development (Holden, 2000).

Natural Area Tourism

One type of alternative tourism is natural area tourism, that is, tourism in natural settings. Examples can include nature-based tourism, in which viewing nature is the primary objective, and adventure tourism, in which the focus is on the activity, for example, white water rafting or scuba diving. Weaver (1991) states that alternative tourism is a generic term that encompasses a whole range of tourism strategies (e.g. appropriate, eco, soft, responsible, controlled, small-scale, cottage, and green tourism), all of which are supposed to be preferred alternatives to conventional mass tourism.

Fennell (1999) suggests that 'although mass tourism may be said to be predominantly unsustainable, more recently, new and existing developments in the industry have attempted to encourage more sustainable practice through various measures'. He adds that some of these include the controlled use of electricity, a rotating laundry schedule and the disposal of wastes. However, he notes that most forms of alternative tourism are theoretically sustainable. For him, the alternative tourism sphere comprises both socio-cultural tourism and ecotourism. Alternative tourism includes, for example, rural or farm tourism, where a large portion of the tourist's experience is founded upon the cultural milieu that corresponds to the environment in which farms operate. He describes ecotourism as involving a type of tourism that is less socio-cultural in its orientation, and more dependent upon nature and natural resources as the primary component or motivator of the trip. Fennell places ecotourism firmly in the division of alternative forms of tourism but expounds 'the belief that ecotourism is distinct from mass tourism and various other forms of alternative tourism'.

The all-encompassing term used in this book for tourism in natural areas is simply natural area tourism. This form of tourism is bounded and defined by its setting of the natural environment. There are a number of dimensions to tourism in the natural environment, categorised according to the relationship between specific tourism activities and nature. According to Wearing and Neil (1999) they include activities or experiences for which the natural setting is incidental, those that are dependent on nature, and those that are enhanced by nature. These three dimensions of natural area tourism equate to the environmental education equivalents of – in, about, and for the environment (Dowling, 1977, 1979). Thus by extension it is possible to characterise natural area tourism as:

- tourism in the environment – e.g. adventure tourism;
- tourism about the environment – e.g. nature based tourism and wildlife tourism;
- tourism for the environment – e.g. ecotourism (Figure 1.4).

Adventure tourism

Adventure tourism and nature-based tourism share similarities but are different aspects of tourism. Adventure tourism is tourism that is focused on the activity in a natural area. It involves physical challenge, education and contact with nature, and can be one of three types: small-scale, with many ecotourism characteristics (e.g. bird watching, scuba diving); medium-scale and sports oriented (e.g. canoeing and rafting); or large-scale, and an aspect of mass tourism (e.g. safaris). The Canadian Tourism Commission (1995, cited in Fennell, 1999) has defined adventure tourism as an outdoor leisure activity that takes place in an unusual, exotic, remote or wilderness destination, involves some form of unconventional means of transportation, and tends to be associated with low or high levels of activity. In this

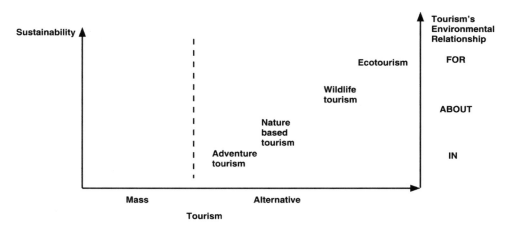

Figure 1.4 Natural area tourism and sustainability

definition adventure travel includes nature observation, wildlife viewing, as well as adventure pursuits on air, land and water.

Adventure travel, like ecotourism, is often divided into soft and hard dimensions. According to Christiansen (1990), soft adventure activities are pursued by those interested in a perceived risk and adventure with little actual risk, whereas hard adventure activities are known by both the participant and the service provider to have a high level of risk.

Nature based tourism

Nature-based tourism occurs in natural settings but has the added emphasis of fostering understanding and conservation of the natural environment. In addition it embraces viewing of nature as the primary objective. This focus is usually upon the study and/or observation of the abiotic (non-living) part of the environment, e.g. the rocks and landforms, as well as the biotic (living) component of it, e.g. fauna and flora. Essentially it is a form of tourism underpinned by the ecocentric philosophy so that the natural environment provides the platform for environmental understanding and conservation. Nature-based tourism also embraces the sustainable approach and fosters 'responsible tourism'. Harrison and Husbands (1996) describe responsible tourism not as a tourism brand or product but rather an approach in which tourism delivers benefits to tourists, host populations and governments.

Where it differs from wildlife tourism is that nature-based tourism has a broader focus than purely viewing wildlife. In nature-based tourism the whole landscape and surrounds is the primary focus for tours and it is more holistic in its embrace of the environment. It tends towards small-scale, but it can become mass or incipient mass tourism in many national parks (e.g. Yosemite). It is sometimes perceived as synonymous with ecotourism since one of its aims is to protect natural areas but it also differs in its lack of overt environmental interpretation and/or education.

Wildlife tourism

Often it is the quality of a natural area's living or biotic element, that is, the fauna and flora or wildlife that plays a primary role in attracting tourists to specific destinations. Wildlife tourists seek an experience that will enable them to explore, no matter for how short a time, a new ecosystem and its inhabitants. Some tourists are lifelong wildlife enthusiasts and others merely take day trips to a wilderness area from a luxury hotel base. Many such visitors seek to be informed and educated although others wish primarily to be entertained. There are many different kinds of wildlife-watching holidays, tourists can choose between a luxury hotel-based safari in Kenya, wilderness backpacking in the Rockies or an Antarctic cruise to watch penguins and killer whales (Shackley, 1996).

The growth in wildlife viewing in recent years has been phenomenal (Ceballos-Lascurain, 1998). For example, in the United States over 75 million people watch wildlife each year and it is now the country's number one outdoor recreational activity. In response to this growth, a national group of governmental agencies and conservation organisations created the Watchable Wildlife Initiative in 1990. Its goals are to promote wildlife viewing, conserve biodiversity, foster environmental education and generate economic opportunities based on ecotourism. California's Watchable Wildlife Programme was established in 1992 and is now the largest and most successful programme through its promotion of 'six steps to sustainable success' (Garrison, 1997). They include selecting sites based on regional diversity, biological sustainability and quality viewing as well as ensuring that each site provides adequate visitor services and resource protection. Another key goal is to provide 'seamless' recreational and educational opportunities focusing on quality products and a state-wide programme of visibility shared between all agencies. Other goals include establishing partnerships, identification of market segments, and the development of cooperative market strategies (Garrison, 1997).

Ecotourism

The primary goals of ecotourism are to foster sustainable use through resource conservation, cultural revival and economic development and diversification. On an individual level it should add value to people's lives through their learning about the natural world. Ceballos-Lascurain (1998) suggests that 'a lingering problem in any discussion on ecotourism is that the concept of ecotourism is not well understood, therefore, it is often confused with other types of tourism development'. Harrison (1997) argues that 'in recent years ecotourism has become something of a buzzword in the tourism industry. To put the matter crudely, but not unfairly, promoters of tourism have tended to label any nature-oriented tourism product an example of "ecotourism" while academics have so busied themselves in trying to define it that they have produced dozens of definitions and little else'. He goes on to suggest that if sustainable tourism development is to occur, trade-offs are inevitable and often nature will be the loser. He also notes that ecotourism cannot solve all the problems of mass tourism and may in fact generate problems of its own. Harrison continues that it should not be considered to be a stepping stone to large-scale tourism, though it often proves to be so. He concludes that ecotourism is an ideal, but one worth working towards, because at best ecotourism fosters environmental conservation and cultural understanding.

It has also been stated that ecotourism is often nothing more than a marketing tool. In theory it should be an economically and socially sound means to conserve biodiversity, and also to provide revenue to improve the lives of people living in or near biologically important areas. Ecotourism is the fastest growing segment of the tourism industry and is rapidly growing out of control. It really constitutes a niche market for environmentally aware tourists who are interested in observing nature. It is especially popular among government and conservation organisations because it can provide simultaneous environmental and economic benefits. In theory it should be less likely than other forms of tourism to damage its own resource base but this is only true if such tourism is managed with great care (Fennell, 1999).

Honey (1999) suggests that real ecotourism has seven characteristics. It involves travel to natural destinations, minimises impact, builds environmental awareness, provides direct financial benefits for conservation, provides financial benefits and empowerment for local people, respects local culture, and supports human rights and democratic movements. She defines ecotourism as 'travel to fragile, pristine, and usually protected areas that strive to be low impact and (usually) small scale'. She adds that it helps educate the traveller, provides funds for conservation, directly benefits the economic development and political empowerment of local communities, and fosters respect for different cultures and for human rights.

Thus ecotourism comprises a number of interrelated components all of which should be present for authentic ecotourism to occur. There are five key principles that are fundamental to ecotourism. They are that ecotourism is nature based, ecologically sustainable, environmentally educative, locally beneficial and generates tourist satisfaction. The first three characteristics are thought to be essential for a product to be considered 'ecotourism', while the last two characteristics are viewed as being desirable for all forms of tourism (Dowling, 1996). This book adopts all of these features as being essential for the development of natural area tourism.

Nature based

Ecotourism is based on the natural environment with a focus on its biological, physical and cultural features. Ecotourism occurs in, and depends on, a natural setting and may include cultural elements where they occur in a natural setting (Plate 1.1). The conservation of the natural resource is essential to the planning, development and management of ecotourism.

Plate 1.1 Tourists on a rainforest walk at O'Reilly's Guesthouse, Lamington National Park, South Queensland, Australia. Such self-guided interpretation walks form part of the essence of natural area tourism's educative focus. (*Photo*: O'Reilly's Rainforest Guesthouse)

Ecologically sustainable

All tourism should be sustainable – economically, socially and environmentally. The sustainability of natural resources has been recognised by many countries as a key guiding principle in the management of human activity. Ecotourism is ecologically sustainable tourism undertaken in a natural setting. The challenge to ecotourism in any country or region is to develop its tourism capacity and the quality of its products without adversely affecting the environment that maintains and nurtures it. This involves ensuring that the type, location and level of ecotourism use does not cause harm to natural areas.

The very incorporation of 'eco' in its title suggests that ecotourism should be an ecologically responsible form of tourism. Indeed if this is not the case then the natural attributes upon which the tourism is based will suffer degradation to the point where tourists will no longer be attracted to it. The scale of such ecotourism activities implies that relatively few tourists will be allowed to visit the site and consequently supporting facilities can be kept to a minimum and will be less intrusive. Cater (1994) argues that ecotourism, with its connotations of sound environmental management and consequent maintenance of environmental capital, should, in theory, provide a viable economic alternative to exploitation of the environment.

Ecotourism may bring considerable attention to how tourism as a whole may be made more ecologically sustainable. Certainly, converting all forms of tourism to ecotourism is neither realistic nor consistent with principles of sustainability. Ecotourism is perhaps best thought of as an achievable ideal for one segment of the nature-based tourism market, and setting an example in environmental management for much of the rest (Australian Department of Tourism, 1994).

This broadly defined travel orientated towards the natural environment is generally expected to respect and protect the environment and culture of the host country or region. However, according to Lawrence *et al.* (1997) it is this larger goal of protecting or enhancing the environment that represents both its strength and weakness. Its strength is that ecotourism differentiates itself from the more traditional consumptive forms of tourism while its weakness is inherent in the tension that often prevails between achieving economic goals at the expense of ecological aims. They add that the ecotourism industry faces the paradoxical situation that the more popular the product becomes, the more difficult it is to provide.

Environmentally educative

The educative characteristic of ecotourism is a key element that distinguishes it from other forms of nature-based tourism. Environmental education and interpretation are important tools in creating an enjoyable and meaningful ecotourism experience. Interpretation is the art of helping people to learn and it is a central tenet of ecotourism (Weiler & Davis, 1993). It is a complex activity that goes beyond making the communication of information enjoyable. Best practice interpretation requires a thorough understanding and integration of audience, message and technique (McArthur, 1998a).

Ecotourism attracts people who wish to interact with the environment in order to develop their knowledge, awareness and appreciation of it. By extension, ecotourism should ideally lead to positive action for the environment by fostering enhanced conservation awareness. Ecotourism education can influence tourist, community and industry behaviour and assist in the longer term sustainability of tourist activity in natural areas. Education can also be useful as a management tool for natural areas. Interpretation helps tourists see the big picture regarding the environment (Crabtree, 2000). It acknowledges the natural and cultural values of the area visited as well as other issues such as resource management.

Ecotourists expect high levels of ecological information. The quality of the environment and the visibility of its flora and fauna are essential features of their experience. They demand conservation (Chalker, 1994). Clear statements of the nature and aims of ecotourism need to be incorporated into literature and publicity material to educate and encourage active participation by stakeholders as well as the tourists themselves (Hall & Kinnaird, 1994). Lawrence *et al.* (1997) note that a dominant part of ecotourism is for tourists to learn about and appreciate the natural environment in order to advance the cause of conservation.

Locally beneficial

The involvement of local communities not only benefits the community and the environment but also improves the quality of the tourist experience. Local communities can become involved in ecotourism operations and in the provision of knowledge, services, facilities and products. These benefits should outweigh the costs of ecotourism to the host community and environment. Ecotourism can also generate income for resource conservation management in addition to social and cultural benefits. The contribution may be financial with a part of the cost of an ecotour helping to subsidise a conservation project. Alternatively it could consist of practical help in the field with the tourists being involved in environmental data collection and/or analysis.

Drumm (1998) points out that local communities view ecotourism as an accessible development alternative which can enable them to improve their living standards without having to sell off their natural resources or compromise their culture. In the absence of other sustainable alternatives, their participation in ecotourism is often perceived as the best option for achieving their aspiration of sustainable development.

There are many advocates of the need to integrate environmental conservation with tourism development in natural areas (e.g. Romeril, 1985; Wight, 1988; McNeely & Thorsell, 1989). According to Wight (1995), partnerships between tourism and conservation take many forms including:

(1) Donation of a portion of tour fees to local groups for resource conservation or local development initiatives.
(2) Education about the value of the resource.
(3) Opportunities to observe or participate in a scientific activity.
(4) Involvement of locals in the provision of support services or products.
(5) Involvement of locals in explanation of cultural activities or their relationship with natural resources.
(6) Promotion of a tourist and/or operator code of ethics for responsible travel.

The implementation of ecotourism as an exemplar for sustainable development stems largely from its potential to generate economic benefits (Lindberg, 1998).

These include generating revenue for management of natural areas and the creation of employment opportunities for the local population.

Wearing and Neil (1999) note that the current focus of the debate on tourism in protected areas is the extension of a long controversy that has existed since the conception of protected areas. They state that the imperative for conservation advocates becomes *how* to conserve rather than whether or not to conserve. They continue that in this way ecotourism, as a sustainable development strategy, is increasingly being adopted by protected area managers and conservation agencies as part of a political philosophy as a means of providing practical outcomes in the struggle to ensure a basis for continued protection for these areas.

Tourist satisfaction

Satisfaction of visitors with the ecotourism experience is essential to long-term viability of the ecotourism industry. Included in this concept is the importance of visitor safety in regard to political stability. Information provided about ecotourism opportunities should accurately represent the opportunities offered at particular ecotourism destinations. The ecotourism experience should match or exceed the realistic expectations of the visitor. Client services and satisfaction should be second only to the conservation and protection of what they visit.

Tourism's Impacts in Natural Areas

Impacts can be either positive or negative. In most of the current literature tourism's impacts on the natural environment have been related as being negative. Wall (1994) notes that ecotourism attracts attention to natural treasures, thereby increasing the pressures upon them.

Hvenegaard (1994) describes a litany of adverse environmental impacts caused by tourism in protected areas. They include overcrowding, overdevelopment, unregulated recreation, pollution, wildlife disturbances and vehicle use. These effects are more serious for ecotourism than general tourism because the former is more dependent on relatively pristine natural environments than the latter, in terms of attracting new travellers. In addition, since ecotourism impacts are often concentrated in ecologically sensitive areas, he argues that they must be controlled. Thus ecotourism is reliant on natural phenomena in relatively undisturbed sites such as protected areas (Hvenegaard & Dearden, 1998). Deming (1996) describes the adverse impacts of tourists on birds at Point Pelee National Park in Ontario, Canada, during the spring migration. The birders still continue to venture off the designated paths to view and photograph species despite being advised not to do this. In Kenya's popular Amboseli National Park, Masai Mara Game Reserve, and Nairobi National Park, hordes of camera-carrying tourists packed in minivans have impacted upon the cheetahs, which are now forced to hunt during the day at times when tourist traffic is light. The cheetah population in Amboseli has dropped to fewer than eight (World Resources Institute, 1993; cited in Honey, 1999).

However, the positive benefits of the natural area–tourism relationship have also been fostered for over two decades. Cooperation between conservation and tourism was advocated at a European Heritage Landscapes Conference held in 1985 by the Director of the Countryside Commission of the United Kingdom. He stressed their interrelatedness, pointed to the need for their future cooperation and argued that there were three reasons why conservation should seek the support of tourism. They were that tourism provides conservation with an economic justification, is a means of building support for conservation, and can bring resources to conservation (Phillips, 1985). The view that tourism can be a major agent for landscape conservation has also been endorsed by Leslie (1986) and Murphy (1986a).

At the same time the integration of the relationship has also been advanced for its benefits to both business (Murphy, 1986b) and regional development (Pearce, 1985). Other aspects of the relationship being examined, include biological impacts on the environment by tourists (Edington & Edington, 1986) as well as aspects of the environmental carrying capacity of tourism (Industry and Environment, 1986). More recently, Lindberg *et al.* (1996) have argued that natural area tourism can generate positive environmental impacts. For example, some tours involve cleaning trails or undertaking rehabilitation work. Also, ecotourism indirectly can generate positive impacts by increasing political and economic support for natural area conservation and management. Thus there is considerable support for the notion that tourism in natural areas can and does support conservation and therefore represents a sound symbiotic relationship. The question remains though how can this be achieved?

Planning and Management

The future of sustainable natural area tourism lies in its planning and management. Planning for natural area tourism enables developers and managers to foster tourism in these areas in such a way as to not only protect the natural environment but also to bring about a greater understanding of it. The key lies in the activity of planning for natural areas rather than solely planning in them. This is best carried out in an inclusive manner which embraces the interests of, and input by, key stakeholders. In addition such planning should be iterative and flexible so as to allow objectives and strategies to be achieved while still providing a means for consistent management.

There are a number of ways of managing tourism in natural areas some of which focus on site management whereas others focus on visitor management techniques. A key management strategy is zoning in which activities are separated by either space and/or time. Management is the strategies and actions taken to protect or enhance natural areas in the face of impacts from tourism activities. Strategies are defined as general approaches to management, usually guided by an objective, for example, reserving and/or zoning a natural area such as a national park. Actions are what must be done, for example closing a campsite for restoration.

Planning and management need to reflect a balanced approach to how natural resources are used and include local communities in the development process. A more 'sustainable' approach to tourism development is required and it is through natural area tourism that this may be achieved (Holden, 2000). While it is imperative that the earth's environmental elements are not perceived solely as attributes, the reality is that if natural areas are to survive they must be 'valued' more through developments such as tourism. Often it is only tourism that will provide the conservation of such areas. So while there is undoubted concern at the increasing demand for tourism to natural areas, this just may be the one activity that ensures their continued survival.

Outline of the Book

This book is intended to provide a review of natural area tourism as part of the new Aspects of Tourism series. It is designed as an introduction to the subject of tourism in natural areas so the reader can gain a feel for the scope of, complexities arising from, and possibilities of undertaking successful tourism developments in, natural areas. A key objective of the book is to overcome the existing perception that tourism developments in environmentally sensitive areas are inherently adverse. Rather it offers a view that with adequate foresight, planning and management such developments represent vehicles to bring about increased awareness and conservation. While built tourism developments in natural areas obviously change the naturalness of the area it is through design, interpretation and education that environmental awareness may be fostered and, more importantly, sustainability achieved.

This book offers a number of useful points for further research on natural areas and tourism. One underlying theme is that natural area tourism is an appropriate vehicle to bring about greater environmental understanding. For this reason such tourism separates itself out from other forms of tourism. If people seek to ascribe some form of legacy to the earth then one of the best ways of doing this is by gaining an understanding of our environment leading to its appreciation which inspires action for the environment.

This book reviews the environment–tourism relationship through the context of natural area tourism, a rapidly growing niche form of tourism. It involves the definition and clarification of terms and concepts such as mass tourism, alternative tourism, sustainable tourism, natural area tourism, ecotourism and wildlife tourism. The book focuses on the principles and characteristics of natural area tourism and illustrates these through the context of ecology, impacts and management.

Chapter 2 provides a synthesis of the ecological knowledge that is required to define the nature-based tourism resource, prevent its degradation and maintain its sustainability. This knowledge is based on the concept of 'ecological connectivity' in which all living things are viewed as being interconnected. It is an ecological axiom that all living and non-living parts of the environment are interdependent. Therefore the nature and characteristics of ecosystems are examined in relation to the structure of ecosystems, ecosystem function, ecological communities, ecological disturbance and succession and landscape ecology. This is followed by a review of tourism in a range of valued ecosystems including islands, coral reefs, tropical rain forests, savanna and modified ecosystems. Wildlife tourism then comes under our focus especially in regard to the disturbance of wildlife caused by tourism. The chapter concludes with the plea for humans to investigate the stability and resilience of ecosystems so that ecology and tourism can be better managed in future.

The third chapter provides an account of the environmental impacts of tourism and recreation in natural areas. The sources of impacts are reviewed including those caused by the development and operation of transport and travel, accommodation and shelter, and recreational activities. Impacts in selected environments are then described for water edges, mountains, caves and from observing wildlife. The chapter examines the landscape context in which tourism lies. An important conclusion is that tourism resources can be changed by other land uses and activities lying beyond the boundaries of a natural area. It also addresses the cumulative environmental impacts of tourism as well as a brief overview of tourism's social and economic impacts. Finally the biophysical impacts of tourism and recreation are illustrated in a case study of off-road vehicle driving in a range of environments.

Chapter 4 describes planning for visitor management in natural areas as a means of achieving efficient and cost-effective sustainable tourism management. The subjective nature of planning and the need to engage stakeholders throughout the planning process are emphasised. Reasons for planning are also given. A number of concepts central to visitor planning in natural areas, including carrying capacity, acceptable change and the recreation opportunity spectrum, are described before the planning frameworks central to the chapter are explored. Most important of the frameworks are the Limits of Acceptable Change and the Tourism Optimisation Management Model. Each framework is described using diagrams and examples. The chapter concludes with suggestions as to how to choose the 'best' planning framework.

The fifth chapter describes the enormous range of management strategies and actions available to assist in achieving sustainable natural area tourism. The management strategy of creating protected areas, such as national and marine parks, is outlined for both developed and developing countries. Other forms of protection, such as World Heritage designation, are also described. Zoning and joint management are recognised as other key management strategies. Two broad groups of strategies and associated actions – site management and visitor management – then dominate much of the remainder of the chapter. Site management actions seek to influence visitor use through manipulating the natural environment and facilities. Visitor management on the other hand relies on controlling visitor numbers, group size and education. Factors influencing the choice of actions by managers, such as cost and extent of impacts, are explored. Several means of managing/working with the tourism industry, including voluntary and regulatory approaches, are described. Voluntary approaches are particularly interesting and include codes of conduct as well as accreditation. A case study of Kakadu National

Park in northern Australia, with its application of a broad range of management strategies and associated actions to managing tourism in a large natural area is also presented.

Interpretation as a means of educating and communicating ideas to the natural area tourist is explored in Chapter 6. The principles and application of interpretation are considered in relation to providing minimal impact messages and thus fostering sustainable tourism. Interpretation's role in visitor impact management is described and it is also contrasted with environmental education and information. Examples of interpretive techniques are illustrated through publications, visitor centres, self-guided trails and guided touring. A case study is presented on dive tourism in Vanuatu which illustrates the contribution that interpretation can make in the protection of coral reef ecosystems.

Chapter 7 describes monitoring and argues it has been a long-neglected element of natural area management. It is defined and then principles to guide the development of monitoring programmes are suggested. Approaches to monitoring visitor impacts on natural areas as well as monitoring visitors themselves follow. Techniques for monitoring point features such as built facilities, campgrounds, campsites and water bodies are part of the focus on monitoring visitor impacts on natural areas. Techniques for monitoring linear features such as roads and trails complete the review of approaches to monitoring visitor impacts. Means for monitoring visitors themselves include counting them, questionnaires and interviews, observation and interactive techniques such as focus groups. Crucial to all these descriptions are accompanying details on sampling strategies, selecting indicators and standards and assessment procedures. Environmental auditing, a recent phenomenon and not yet widespread in natural area tourism management, is briefly introduced. A case study of Warren National Park in south-western Australia, illustrating an integrated approach to monitoring, concludes the chapter.

The final chapter, explores the future of natural area tourism from three perspectives. There is an assessment of the future links between natural area tourism and ecology, the types, scale and range of impacts caused by natural area tourism, and finally the trends and issues in management of natural area tourism. A number of key issues are addressed including the economic, social and environmental sustainability of natural area tourism, competitive threats to it, and marketing challenges. Some new directions are suggested by the authors and further research needs are identified.

Further reading

Weaver and Opperman (2000) provide a useful introduction to tourism and Miller (2002) does the same for the environment while Holden (2000) examines the link between the two. Hall and Lew (1998) explain the sustainable tourism approach from a number of different disciplinary perspectives. Weaver's (2001) *Encyclopedia of Ecotourism* provides a comprehensive overview of the subject.

Chapter 2
The Ecological Perspective

Introduction

Patches of natural vegetation, nature reserves, national parks, concentrations of animal life and larger wilderness areas are the focus of, and increasingly important as, tourism resources. Some of these areas are substantially natural as in the case of some deserts or arctic tundra. Other areas, such as many forests around the world, are more fragmented while some landscapes are almost entirely modified as in the case of the patchwork of woodlands and agricultural land in the British Isles. Even in already altered and semi-natural landscapes the continuing presence of people has the potential to bring about unwanted change to any remaining natural components.

Given the dramatic increase and interest in natural area tourism over the past decade Tyler and Dangerfield (1999) point out that the wider application of ecological knowledge has been largely neglected in predicting and managing tourism related disturbance in natural environments. In particular, they stress the importance of a holistic approach where the ecological system that supports a particular valued species is taken into consideration in the maintenance and management of sustainable tourism. A good diversity of reef fish for example requires an intact and healthy coral reef. Similarly the endemic bird life of many islands is dependent on specific plant communities. Furthermore, Tyler and Dangerfield (1999) also recognise that the nature of tourism itself complicates the ecological asessment of tourism impacts. These include the type, intensity, duration and spatial extent of various activities; accordingly examples and the specific nature of such impacts are the subject of Chapter 3.

The principal aim of this chapter, therefore, is to outline the important elements of ecology that can be applied to understand, predict and mitigate any change that might be brought about by tourism. For example, certain plant and animal species are especially prone to disturbance such as the endemic bird life of oceanic islands and species with colonial nesting habits. Roads, in particular, have the potential to act as barriers to movement and disrupt migration routes. In these cases an ecological definition of the physical requirements of living organisms, and the environment in which they live, can be used to predict the possible disrupting effects of tourist development and activity.

Managing visitors also requires an ecological perspective. Tourists may impact directly on wildlife and vegetation and may also change aspects of the physical environment, for example, through soil compaction and erosion. Knowledge of ecological sensitivity can help manage natural area tourism so it is sustainable over the longer term.

The interpretation of tourism destinations, such as landscapes and their biota, enhances and deepens the visitor's understanding of the natural environment. This is achieved by providing information on the biology of an organism, a story of how it survives and interesting facts on how it interacts with other organisms and the physical environment. Interpretation (Chapter 6) is also used as a means of protecting the natural environment especially when visitors are made aware of the fragility and sensitivity of some natural ecosystems.

For the purpose of exploring the ecological context of natural area tourism it is important to appreciate how ecosystems fit into the landscapes that form tourism resources. The ecological view in this chapter is therefore presented largely in terms of the composition and functioning of ecosystems. This view is justified because, for as in a car or clock, component parts are very important but we nevertheless need to appreciate how the whole fits together as a total functioning system.

Ecology is now a well-established discipline and its content is large and complex. It can be explored at the organism, population, community, ecosystem or landscape level (Figure 2.1). The treatment here is necessarily brief and our objective is to provide an ecological framework that first shows what ecosystems are made of and then briefly explain how they work. This is followed by a consideration of how various landscapes arise as a result of natural and human caused disturbance.

Because tourism takes place in many environments it is impossible to cover the full range of tourism situations from the ecological standpoint. We have therefore selected some of the most important natural area tourism destinations. For this purpose many tropical environments are important and some of their particular ecological characteristics are thus briefly described. Other specific environments are included in the remaining chapters of this book.

The purpose of including selected tourism destinations is to show a range of important natural area tourism situations and their differing ecological contexts. From these examples general principles, similarities and differences in ecosystem structure and function can be appreciated. Furthermore, in order to understand the ecological effects of tourism, this chapter also necessarily flags some of the discussion on impacts that are more fully covered in Chapter 3 as well as some management issues that are more fully explored in Chapter 5.

An Introduction to Ecosystems and Landscapes

Ecology is concerned with the structure and functioning of ecosystems and thus how plants and animals interact together and with the physical environment. Although most ecosystems are very complex and difficult to study as entire systems, their essential structure and function are well established.

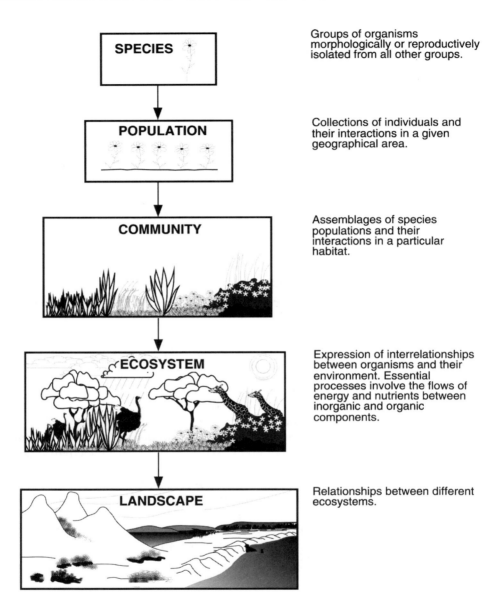

Figure 2.1 Levels of organisation within the science of ecology

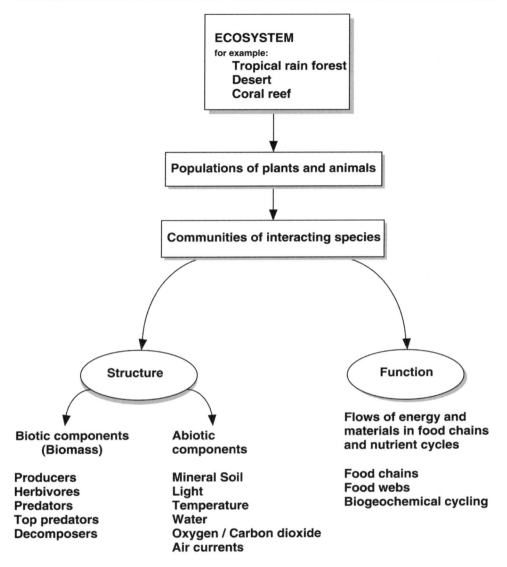

Figure 2.2 The components of an ecosystem

Ecosystems therefore comprise structural components such as living organisms (biotic components), soil and landforms and other non-living features (abiotic components), such as wind, rain and water flow. Energy and materials, such as water and nutrients, flow through this combined system resulting in ecosystem function (Figure 2.2). The purpose of the next two sections is to explain the connec-

Table 2.1 Major ecosystem types of the world

Aquatic ecosystems	Example of nature-based tourism destination
Ocean	Whale Shark tourism, Indian Ocean, Western Australia
Seashores	West Coast National Park, South Africa
Coral reefs	Great Barrier Reef, Australia
Mangroves	Bako National Park, Sarawak, Malaysia
Estuaries	Mawddach Estuary, Wales, UK
Streams and rivers	Igazu Falls National Park, Argentina and Brazil
Lakes	Lake Naivasha, Kenya
Freshwater marshes	Parc Natural Regional de Camarge, France
Terrestrial Ecosystems	
Chaparral/Mediterranean	Eucalypt forests and heathlands of south-west Western Australia
Grassland/Savannah	Serengeti National Park, Tanzania
Deserts	Mojave Desert, California, USA
Arctic/alpine tundra	Nordvest – Spitsbergen Nasjonal Park, Norway
Coniferous forest	Rothiemurchus Forest, Scotland, UK
Deciduous forest	Shenandoah National Park, Virginia, USA
Tropical forest	Reserva dela Biosfera del Manu, Peru

tions between the biotic and abiotic environment and also between plant and animal communities.

The structure of ecosystems

Ecology can be studied from the perspective of populations or communities of plants and animals or whole ecosystems (Figure 2.1). A population refers to the number of organisms of the same species, which inhabit a defined area, while a community consists of a group of populations of different species interacting with one another in a defined area. An ecosystem, on the other hand, represents a community of organisms interacting with the environment.

The scale at which an ecosystem can be identified ranges from the microbial community inside the gut of a cow through to a pond, the ocean, forests or the entire planet. Despite this issue of scale we can conveniently separate ecosystems into the two major divisions of terrestrial and aquatic ecosystems (Table 2.1). These can then be subdivided further according to the occurrence of specific plant and animal communities and the differing physical factors that determine their existence. On land for example differences in moisture and temperature give rise to different ecosystems in the form of forest, woodlands, grasslands and deserts. These comprise the major terrestrial biomes that can be further divided according to specific conditions of precipitation, temperature, the occurrence of fire and differences in soil conditions. An example of this can be seen in the global occurrence of forests which can be divided into tropical rainforests, tropical seasonal forests, temperate rainforests, temperate forests and northern coniferous forest or taiga. Despite such differences in detail it is possible to define the structure of any ecosystem according to its major biotic (living) and abiotic (non-living) components (Figure 2.2).

Biotic components

The biotic part of an ecosystem is its component plant and animal populations that make up the biotic community. In terrestrial ecosystems this comprises plants such as grasses, herbs and trees and associated populations of animals. The 'plant' component in aquatic ecosystems consists of rooted aquatic plants and phyto-plankton. The communities of plants and animals that make up different ecosystems are often centred around one or several dominant species.

In terrestrial ecosystems these are usually the larger plants such as trees and they exert a strong control over what other plants and animals comprise the biotic community. The community structure of terrestrial ecosystems can thus be charac-terised by the growth form of plants, as in the comparison between forests and grasslands. In aquatic ecosystems the massive growth forms of kelp beds and coral reefs helps to define community structure. Phytoplankton, however, which form the basis of most aquatic ecosystem food chains, do not accumulate obvious massive structures as the vascular plants do on land.

The biotic composition of an ecosystem also exists in a state of constant interac-tion. Organisms are dependent on one another and also compete for abiotic and other biotic resources. This relationship can be defined as the autotrophic-heterotrophic system (Figure 2.3). The autotrophic system consists of the photo-synthetic function of plants. This is where light energy is used in the conversion of carbon dioxide and water to carbohydrate and oxygen. Plant biomass is built in this way and converted into animal biomass as plant material is eaten, in the heterotrophic system, through a sequence of herbivory and carnivory. Different ecosystems have different capacities to do this according to prevailing abiotic conditions. For example, water, light and temperature are major limiting factors and where they are not limiting, as in tropical rainforests, the production of plant biomass is at its greatest relative to other terrestrial ecosystems on earth.

Abiotic components

The physical and chemical factors that affect the distribution and activity of plants and animals comprise the abiotic structure to ecosystems. At a fundamental level climate, geology and soils determine the different ecosystems around the world. These major physical environmental conditions significantly determine the kinds of organisms that are present and the degree to which they are organised into communities. Factors of latitude and altitude have resulted in a series of gradients between ecosystems around the world. For example, temperature gradients typify ecosystem change from the Arctic to the tropics.

Similarly moisture gradients determine the structure of vegetation within latitu-dinally determined climatic zones. The tropical climatic zone, for example, contains a range of vegetation formations that are determined by the amount of reliable rain-

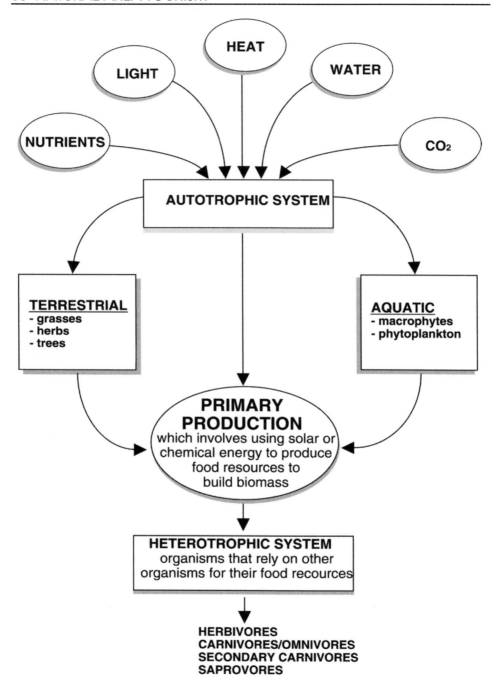

Figure 2.3 Interaction of the biotic component in ecosystems

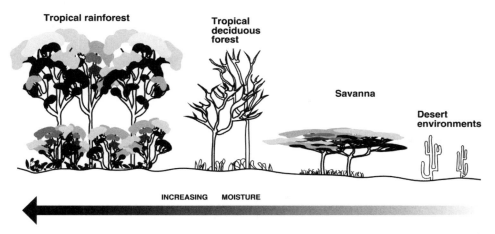

Figure 2.4 Moisture controls over the development of terrestrial vegetation in the tropical climate zone

fall (Figure 2.4). Mountain ranges also define temperature and moisture gradients either through altitude or aspect. These changes are often gradual as defined by the gradual moisture gradient in many terrestrial ecosystems. Sudden changes are, however, evident where aquatic and terrestrial ecosystems meet at an interacting edge known as an ecotone.

Ecosystem structure is thus made up of the biological community and the varying quantities and distribution of abiotic materials. It was noted earlier that some of these materials, for example water, act as limiting factors. Accordingly, the capacity of an ecosystem to produce biomass is primarily dependent on temperature, light conditions, water, supplies of nutrients and the efficiency with which energy and materials are circulated (Figures 2.3 and 2.5). For example, in cold environments mean annual temperature, duration of snow cover, water-logging in summer, wind speeds and soil rooting depth all act as controls over plant growth.

In aquatic ecosystems temperature and the availability of light and nutrients play a pivotal role in plankton biomass production. To this end, the amount of suspended solid material, water currents and the level of dissolved oxygen and salts can also influence aquatic ecosystem biota. The interaction of living organisms with these and other abiotic components constitutes in large the second major ecosystem property; that of ecosystem function.

Ecosystem function

The necessary components for ecosystem function are abiotic factors such as light, temperature, water, various minerals, oxygen and carbon dioxide, and biotic factors that comprise the living components. The sun, being the ultimate source of heat and light, is the driving force for all ecosystem function on earth. While it is

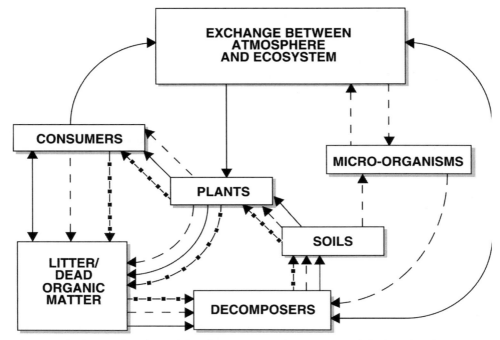

Figure 2.5 Generalised models of nutrient cycling ⟶ Global cycle of C, O and H. – –▸ Global nitrogen cycle. –▪–▪▸ Local scale nutrient cycle occurring at the ecosystem level, for example within a forest (P, K, Ca, Mg and micronutrients) (Derived from Etherington, 1975 and Krebs, 1985)

possible to see many of the structural elements of an ecosystem the processes of material and energy transfer cannot be directly observed. Ecosystem function operates through processes of nutrient and energy transfer. The transfer of organic matter, for example, occurs through biotic intake, growth, excretion, reproduction and death. Nutrients, any material that an organism needs (such as carbon, hydrogen, oxygen, potassium, nitrogen, phosphorus and sulphur), move through the biota in this way (Figure 2.5).

Flow of energy through ecosystems

Energy flows through all ecosystems but the amounts 'captured' by plants and other autotrophic organisms varies greatly between different ecosystems. Energy is then transferred from one organism to the next (eg. plant–caterpillar–bird–hawk) through food chains. There is a loss of heat at each stage in the process as energy is shifted from one level (trophic level) to the next (Figure 2.6). Because of physiological respiration and maintenance a large quantity of energy at any trophic level is not passed to the next level. The end result is that less energy becomes incorporated into biota at the next level and an ecological pyramid is formed.

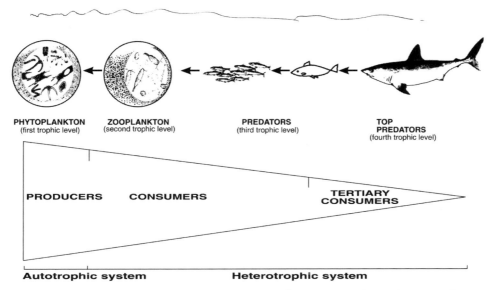

PHYTOPLANKTON
(first trophic level)

ZOOPLANKTON
(second trophic level)

PREDATORS
(third trophic level)

**TOP
PREDATORS**
(fourth trophic level)

PRODUCERS   **CONSUMERS**

**TERTIARY
CONSUMERS**

Autotrophic system   **Heterotrophic system**

Figure 2.6 Simplified marine ecosystem food chain and ecological pyramid

Looking at this another way, ecological pyramids are also formed because the primary producers outweigh the organisms that consume them. This is an essential relationship so that populations of organisms that are dependent on the primary producers do not exhaust the food supply that supports them. Thus there is always more energy available at the trophic level which supports the next (upper) trophic level. Herbivores that rely on primary producers, such as algae and plants, therefore must in turn outweigh the carnivorous species that are supported by them. This relationship explains why ecosystems are structured with a lesser mass of consumers (herbivores and carnivores) than producers (vegetation/algae). At the top of the food chain carnivores are naturally uncommon with secondary carnivores occupying the apex of the pyramid (Figure 2.6). The ecological pyramid is made up of a number of food chains, which are frequently interconnected, into a food web (Figure 2.7).

The universal food chain model consists of autotrophs (first trophic level), herbivores (second trophic level) and carnivores (higher trophic levels). It is thus through the process of herbivory and predation that energy moves along a food chain. Energy and materials are then eventually passed into the decomposer part of the ecosystem via death and excretion.

Ecosystems are thus essentially maintained by the shifting of energy and nutrients through them. Figure 2.8, a conceptual diagram of ecosystem function, encapsulates how ecosystems work. However, while energy is continuously being lost as heat, nutrients can cycle indefinitely through an ecosystem.

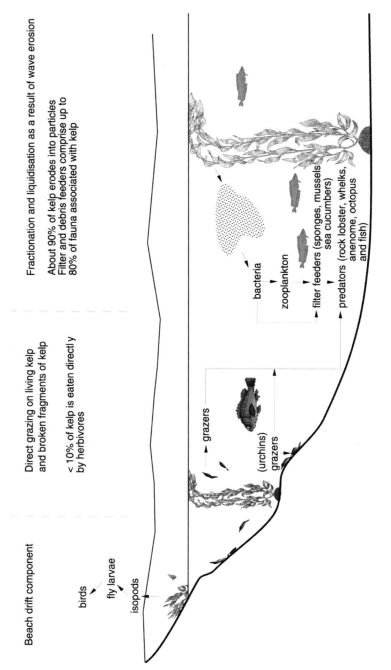

Figure 2.7 Food web dependence on kelp in marine ecosystems
(*Source of data*: Two Oceans Aquarium, Cape Town, South Africa)

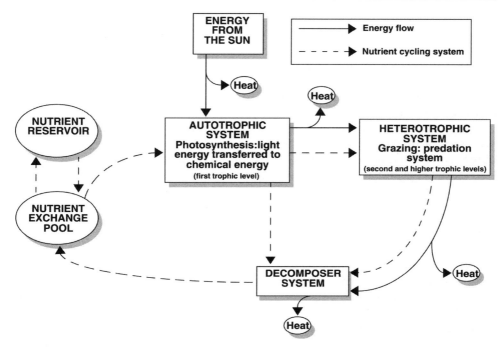

Figure 2.8 Conceptual model of ecosystem processes

Biogeochemical cycles

Nutrients are used to construct the bodies of living organisms and are the chemical elements and compounds essential to life. They occur in three categories as major, macro and micronutrients depending on the extent to which they are incorporated into the tissues of plants and animals.

There are a number of important nutrient elements which cycle between the abiotic and biotic components of an ecosystem as biogeochemical cycles. Nutrients such as carbon, hydrogen, nitrogen, phosphorus and calcium tend to be retained or recycled within the biota (Figure 2.5). Biogeochemical cycles operate at a global scale and at smaller scales within the various biomes. The forest biome, which includes a number of ecosystem types, will even contain nutrient cycles which operate at the local level of a river drainage basin.

Nitrogen is a particularly important nutrient as it is required by all organisms to manufacture proteins and the functioning of many ecosystems is limited by its availability. The reservoir for nitrogen is the atmosphere and in biota, but the main exchange pool is the soil. Soil bacteria determine its composition and concentration in the soil. Nitrogen enters land plants via the soil and decomposer part of terrestrial ecosystems (Figure 2.5). Animals obtain nitrogen by eating plants and a subsequent transfer along the food chain. Nitrogen is then returned to the reservoir and exchange pool through excretion and death of biota and thus used again and again.

Water in ecosystems

Of all the biogeochemical cycles the water or hydrological cycle is the most important (Box 2.1). In terms of the global water reservoir some 97% occurs in the oceans, but in terms of nutrient supply most of it is unavailable to terrestrial organisms because of its salt content. The biologically important freshwater component for land organisms is only a very small percentage of the total and its distribution on earth is not even.

Water movement through an ecosystem is driven by solar energy through the processes of precipitation, evaporation and transpiration that vary according to different world climates. Freshwater is stored in the atmosphere, soils and rocks, lakes and rivers and as snow, ice and permafrost. Freshwater in the form of ice or permafrost is 'locked' and not available for circulation. This means that < 1% of all water on earth is currently being cycled through the world's terrestrial ecosystems at any one time.

Furthermore, all terrestrial organisms have a minimum water requirement below which stress, dehydration and death will occur. Living organisms that occupy arid environments have evolved mechanisms to avoid water loss and/or conserve the water content in their bodies. Plants and animals have also become adapted to high water status environments such as lakes and other aquatic ecosystems. However, where there is an excess of water in otherwise relatively dry environments this can also present problems for organisms and particularly plants. This is because waterlogging leads to oxygen stress in soils and reduces the activity of other biogeochemical cycles. It also relates to the water cycle being closely connected with other cycles. Soil water, for example, contains dissolved nutrients

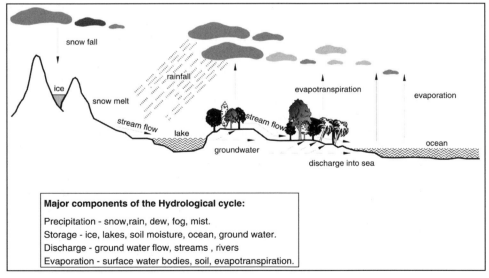

Major components of the Hydrological cycle:

Precipitation - snow, rain, dew, fog, mist.
Storage - ice, lakes, soil moisture, ocean, ground water.
Discharge - ground water flow, streams, rivers
Evaporation - surface water bodies, soil, evapotranspiration.

Box 2.1 Conceptual diagram of the hydrological cycle (local and global scale)

such as nitrogen, phosphorus and magnesium that circulate through living organisms. Plants therefore rely on soil water in order to acquire many nutrients by way of their root systems. Plants also shift water from the soil which is then moved into the atmosphere in gaseous form through the mechanism of transpiration. This is achieved through the pumping of water from the soil-root system to the atmosphere via the leaves. Box 2.1 shows the main stores and flows that comprise the global hydrological cycle.

Ecological communities

Community ecology is concerned with how plant and animal species interact with one another. The features of ecological communities that can be impacted by tourism development and activity include competition, predator–prey relationships, symbiosis, niche occupancy and keystone species. Competition is basically concerned with how the availability of resources, such as food and space which is utilised by various organisms, is reduced by other organisms.

Tourism and recreation can result in the transfer of plants and animals to locations where they do not normally occur. In these situations the 'alien' species are often at an advantage because the new environment is usually devoid of any natural controls that the 'invader' would have evolved with in its original environment. Alien plants compete with indigenous species for space, light, nutrients and water. The introduction of alien plants can result in the disruption and impoverishment of natural plant communities. This for example has occurred in South Africa where introduced Australian shrubs have and are degrading species rich fynbos plant communities in the Southern Cape region.

Predation in ecological communities

The predator–prey relationships of ecological communities need to be understood. Their importance relates to the potential impact of predators which are deliberately or accidentally introduced outside their normal environments. This problem is especially acute in island settings where a wide variety of naturally occurring predators and complex food webs may be absent. Island species are thus particularly susceptible to disturbance from the sudden arrival of a new predatory species (see 'Island ecosystems', p. 51).

A predator is an animal that kills and utilises another animal for food. Predators exert a significant control over herbivores. They also compete with one another and this has resulted in various behavioural and anatomical specialisations amongst the predators themselves. Predators will usually attack individuals that have been weakened as a result of disease and/or ageing. Moreover, this pressure has 'strengthened' prey species over time and has also resulted in the evolution of anti-predator detection, defense and escape mechanisms. Prey species have therefore evolved an entire spectrum of anti-predation devices such as toxins, camouflage, regimes of activity, spines and teeth for defence, flocking and herding for combined protection as well as various escape responses.

When 'alien' predators, such as dogs and cats are introduced into different ecosystems, such as islands, their impact can result in a severe reduction and even extinction of native species. This is because, in the absence of a co-evolved predation pressure, isolated and endemic island faunas have not evolved evasion and escape mechanisms. Island faunas then become easy prey for such introduced predators. This has happened on the Australian continent where introduced cats and foxes pose a severe threat to existing populations of native marsupials in national parks and nature reserves.

Symbiotic relationships

Symbiosis is another essential feature of ecological communities and is defined as a close association between two different organisms. Symbiotic relationships are widespread and occur as a number of specific relationships. Parasitism is one type of symbiotic relationship where one organism obtains its nutrition at the expense of a host. There are many types of parasites that live on or in another species. Perhaps the most significant from a tourism point of view is the potential for humans to transmit viruses and bacteria to animals that they visit in natural settings. An example of this is the sensitivity of gorillas to human diseases. Accordingly this issue is considered in more detail in Chapter 6.

Commensalism, on the other hand, is where one organism benefits from its association with another, such as where sea anemones provide protection for clown fish or where epiphytic orchids are attached to rainforest trees (see 'Tropical rainforests', p. 60). In these relationships, however, neither the sea anemone nor the trees appear to receive any particular benefit from the relationship.

Mutualism is where both species benefit, as in the case of the relationship between coral polyps and symbiotic algae (see 'Coral reef scosystems', p. 56). If this relationship is broken the coral will die as evidenced when coral is stressed due to coastal development and pollution. In terrestrial ecosystems an intimate association between plant roots and bacteria or fungi allows many species of plants to obtain additional nutrients under conditions of plant root competition, nutrient poverty and hostile substrates. Any disruption of this relationship will reduce a particular plant's capacity to obtain essential nutrients such as nitrogen and phosphorus.

Mutualism is also widespread in terms of plant–insect relationships. There are many examples of this, such as insect specific pollination of orchids and the widespread close plant–insect pollination systems in tropical rainforests. These features mean that a number of specialist, as opposed to generalist, species can be present in any particular ecosystem

Specialist and generalist species

Specialist species are particularly efficient in utilising their resources but in doing so have become specialised and adapted to a particular way of life. Such species are said to occupy a narrow niche (Box 2.2). An example of this would be the specialisation of fauna to specific feeding strategies in rainforest environments. Examples include narrow spectrum frugivourous (fruit eating) birds, specific flower adapted hummingbirds and insects which are certain plant specific herbivores. Such species

---

Box 2.2 Relation of organisms to their environment: habitat and niche

Habitat is the geographically located physical environment in which a species occurs. Occurring at various scales, habitats can be restricted areas such as a pool in a cave or within a bromeliad perched high in the tree canopy of a Costa Rican forest. Conversely, habitats can occur at much larger scales as in soil and be distributed at the continental level. The world's coral reefs, for example, are habitat to a wide array of marine organisms.

Niche refers to the role that species has in the community (the food it eats, its position in the food chain and the ways it competes for resources) in combination with how it interacts with its environment. In this sense each species has its own specific set of functions – its niche. Although niches might appear to overlap, no two species will occupy the same ecological niche.

---

are vulnerable to disturbance because of the tight relationship these animals have with their food supply. If the food supply situation changes then the animal, because of its specialisation, does not have an alternative source of food. It may then die out because its food supply has been lost or perish in the face of competition for food resources from other species. Generalist species, on the other hand, are more adaptable to such changes because they are not restricted to a particular food source.

Niche and habitat

Distinct abiotic and biotic needs and specific role in the ecological community define the niche of an organism. What these conditions amount to is how an organism lives and interacts with other species (Box 2.2). For example, up to six different species of monkey can co-exist in the West African rainforest because they all have a different niche (Mader, 1991). She points out that such diversity exists because the monkeys occupy different levels in the forest and have different diets. The Red Colobus *(Colobus badius)*, for example, lives in the forest canopy and feeds on leaves, flower buds and some insects. By contrast L'Hoest's Monkey *(Cercopithecus l'Hoesti)* lives mostly towards the forest floor and feeds on fruits, herbs, mushrooms and insects. In this way these species avoid direct competition for food resources and space by occupying slightly different habitats. While an organism's habitat is where a species can be found and involves some physical aspect of the ecosystem, the concept of niche also embraces feeding and breeding activity and the way the organism itself influences abiotic and other biotic components of the ecosystem.

Dominant and keystone species

A dominant species helps to determine the nature of the ecological community and its removal would result in a change in the community. In terrestrial ecosystems the dominants are trees and shrubs, but animals, for example some herbivores and carnivores, can also exert a dominant influence in communities. Trees are dominant in forest ecosystems in that they create microclimates and provide food and habitats for a range of other organisms. In the case of one dominant species declining or being lost it is possible for another to take its place. An example of this is in the situation of co-dominant trees or grasses. If the dominant is a keystone species, however, then the entire ecological community changes if this one species is lost.

Keystone species are plants and animals that exert an important controlling influence in the ecosystem. This is achieved by their presence determining the structure and or composition of the community. Such ecological changes being much greater than would be expected from the organism's overall abundance in the ecosystem.

Figure 2.9 illustrates this relationship in response to the reintroduction of the Wolf *(Canis lupus)*, a keystone predator, to Yellowstone National Park in the USA. The Wolf was formerly lost from Yellowstone primarily due to hunting pressure. The loss of this top carnivore resulted in a shift in the composition of the animal community. Following its reintroduction populations of herbivores are expected to decline resulting in less grazing pressure on vegetation. It is predicted that competition with the Coyote *(Canis latrans)* will result in less predation of rodents and there will be a consequent increase in prey species for other, smaller, predators such as the Lynx *(Felis lynx)* and Long-tailed Weasel *(Mustela frenata)*. Such changes, over time, have the capacity to increase overall animal biodiversity in the park.

A keystone role can also take place as a result of an animal physically modifying its environment. Naiman (1988) reports on how the disturbance of woody plants by increased numbers of African Elephant *(Loxodonta africana)* results in a large-scale reduction in trees and shrubs, which in turn impacts on the food supply and populations of other animals leading to an alteration in local biogeochemical cycling. Where a population of elephants is reduced, trees and shrubs able to re-establish in grasslands that, in the absence of elephants, would contain more woody species. Major structural components of the entire ecosystem are therefore dependent on the density of elephants.

Similarly, the holes made by the Red-naped Sapsucker *(Sphyrapicus nuchalis)* in the USA provide nesting habitat for two species of swallow and food resources (sap) for a suite of other species. These species are then in turn food resources for various predators (Daily *et al.*, 1993).

Disturbance and succession in ecosystems

Disturbance is the alteration of ecosystem structure and / or function arising from the loss of biotic components as might be caused by human activities such as clearing land, removing vegetation and accelerated erosion. Severe natural disturbances, usually infrequent but a normal part of ecological processes in landscapes, also bring about a similar effect, for example, in the case of wild fires, volcanism and severe storms. Succession is the process of ecosystem recovery following such disturbances.

Natural area tourism, that is, the intentional visits of humans to see and enjoy the natural environment, along with recreational activities and tourism centred devel-

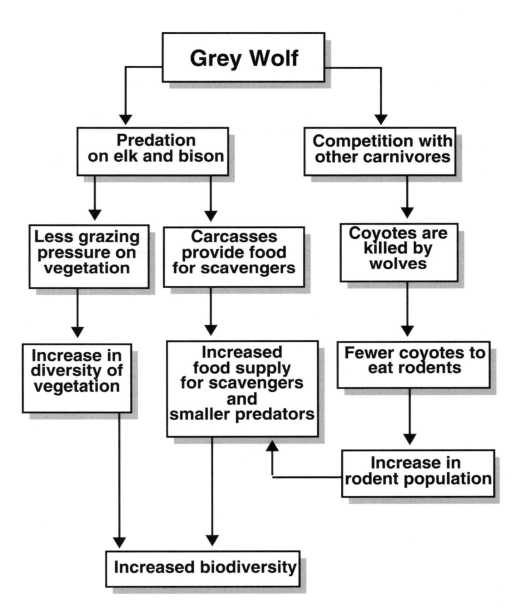

Figure 2.9 The potential role of the Grey Wolf as a keystone predator in Yellowstone National Park, USA

opment, also has the capacity to change ecosystem structure and function through disturbance (also see Chapter 3).

Disturbance: change in ecosystems

Plant cover is fundamental to the structure of most terrestrial ecosystems and when this is damaged or removed, the entire structure of the plant and dependent animal community can be changed. Loss of plant cover can also result in associated abiotic changes such as the loss of surface soils or an alteration in the physical and chemical properties of soils. Changes in ecosystem function as a result of disturbance can manifest as increased or reduced water availability and disruption to the normal pattern of nutrient cycling. The energy flux and microclimate of a particular site is also altered as a result of removing vegetation.

Disturbance, brought about by humans, plays a pivotal role in the creation of patches and corridors and thus landscape heterogeneity (see 'Landscape ecology', p. 45 and Figure 2.10). The edges of patches are more prone to wind acceleration, erosion, trampling and grazing. This increased frequency of disturbance results in the presence of generalist plants that can tolerate these conditions. An interesting aspect of edge habitats is that they can act as a sink for wildlife. An example of this is where herbivores preferentially graze and browse edge vegetation and this in turn attracts predators. The 'open' nature of edges thus provide good viewing for people who wish to view wildlife. Edges can also function as barriers where dense and spiny vegetation restricts access and thus reduces any source/conduit function arising from disturbance corridors.

Roads, tracks and hiking trails are corridors that are usually maintained in an altered state by continuous or repeated disturbance. Roads in particular show a central area of major disturbance with an outer edge composed of generalist species and usually an assemblage of exotic weeds. These road verge floras are subject to the influence of the conduit function of the road and tend to be more resilient to the additional wind, heat, particulate and pollutant imports from adjacent areas. Where tracks are subject to less frequent disturbance successional processes may take place.

Recovery from disturbance: succession

Ecological succession is where plant and animal communities change through time and comprise a recovery response following disturbance. Succession involves the replacement of species and changes in the availability of abiotic resources as the population structure of the community alters through time. The colonisation of disturbed ground, for example by pioneer species, contributes organic matter and also allows soil micro-biota to re-establish. As the vegetation community develops colonisation by larger plants changes the microclimate by providing shade and protection of the soil surface. Any disruption to nutrient cycling that has occurred can be restored in this way. Most succession involves the recovery of sites that previously supported vegetation and this process is termed secondary succession. In contrast primary successions are where vegetation gradually develops on a new land surface as in the case of recent glacial or volcanic deposits.

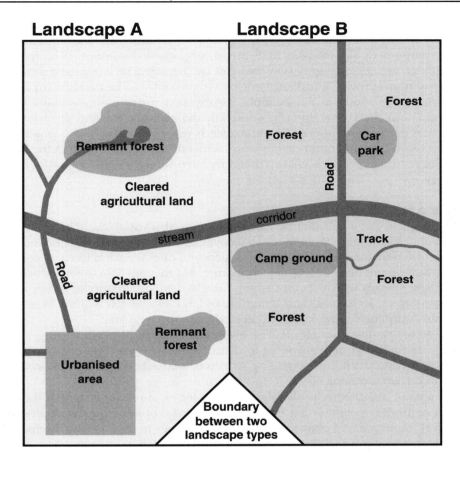

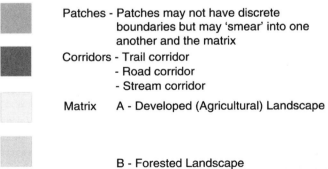

Figure 2.10 A comparison of patches and corridors in the landscape matrix. (A) Agricultural Matrix; (B) Natural Forest Cover Matrix

The way the succession develops (the successional pathway) is dependent on the intensity, timing and frequency of disturbance, area disturbed and the original state of the environment. The intensity of disturbance relates to the amount of biomass of a particular species or population that can be damaged or eliminated from an ecological community. Disturbance intensity therefore sets the baseline condition for succession to start from. For example, in Australian fire prone ecosystems, vegetation can burn at very low intensities and only the ground cover and shrub layer is affected. A particularly intense fire, however, is more damaging to the vegetation and can reach into the forest canopy and incinerate all of the foliage in the burnt area. The two different fire scenarios therefore have different implications for forest recovery.

The capacity for total recovery

The frequency at which disturbance can occur is also variable and has a bearing on how much time an ecosystem has to recover before the next disturbance occurs. An ecosystem that is subject to a high frequency of disturbance is likely to contain species that do not need a long time to mature and that are able to reproduce at a young age. Species which require a long time to develop, mature and reproduce (e.g. many trees, large birds and a number of large mammals) will not be able to maintain occupance under high frequency disturbance regimes.

The actual timing of a disturbance event can be critical in influencing which species are impacted or susceptible to disturbance as in the case of disturbance events occurring during the breeding season of seabirds which become concentrated at certain locations.

The area of disturbance is also significant in terms of recolonisation of the site. When a natural ecosystem is disturbed recovery can take place from the resprouting of underground parts of plants, dormant soil microbes re-establishing themselves and the arrival of propagules (seeds and spores) from adjacent areas.

The mobility of propagules and proximity to recolonisation sources exert control over the nature and speed of succession. Seeds and spores are more efficient in reaching a disturbed area if they are sourced in the immediate vicinity of the disturbance. Where natural areas are isolated, as in a matrix of agricultural land, then new sources of native seed may be limited. This situation is especially critical when an entire species is impacted by constant disturbance and where exotic weed species are widespread in the matrix.

The successional pathway can result in a return to the original ecological community, a structure that is only part of the original or a completely new community. The endpoint is strongly dependent on the previously considered factors and the original state of the environment. At the same time the process of disturbance and succession can result in species replacement, changes in the population structure of component organisms and an alteration in abiotic factors.

As already noted, the invasion of exotic species can result in competition for available resources and help to eliminate those species that are sensitive to disturbance. Changes in abiotic factors such as when soil is eroded can impact on plant productivity and nutrient cycling. A significant change in the ability of the abiotic environment to support vegetation can lead to loss of biodiversity and a reduced capacity for ecosystem function.

Disturbance and succession, however, are features of all ecosystems and each system, whether it is a forest, savanna, swamp, rocky shore or coral reef will have its own response and sequences of successional development. In addition to this some ecological communities exhibit more resilience to different disturbance regimes than others.

Landscape ecology

Landscapes are mosaics of different ecosystems and land uses. The landscape mosaic can be conveniently divided further into patches, corridors and matrix (Figure 2.10). The major issue in appreciating such a structural arrangement in landscapes is that there are boundaries to these various elements and these elements may be linked by flows of water, particulates, pollutants and organisms.

Patches in the landscape

Patches consist of uniform, non-linear areas of vegetation that differ from the surrounding landscape. Forman (1995) recognises five different types of vegetation patch, all of which clearly can vary in size and general shape. He sees vegetation patches comprising the following:

(1) Disturbance patches which usually occupy small areas within a large area of natural vegetation.
(2) Remnant patches are patches of vegetation which occur within a disturbed (e.g. agricultural) matrix.
(3) Environmental patches occur in situations where rock type or soils differentiate a patch.
(4) Regenerated patches reflect regrowth following disturbance.
(5) Introduced patches occur as urban, cultivated areas or plantations.

These vegetation patches change according to successional processes with large patches of natural vegetation often being the core habitat for important, tourist interest, species. Patches of vegetation that function in this way include remnant forest in Indonesia such as the Pangrango-Gede and Ujung Kulong National Parks in Java (Figure 2.11). Such large patches thus provide important landscape functions for tourism. This function is also achieved indirectly by protecting soils with stream networks from unsightly erosion and sedimentation as well as reducing the risk of flooding. In this way large patches act as a buffer against wider ecological degradation problems and help to promote wider sustainable land uses. At the same time small patches of natural vegetation, like Bukit Timah Nature Reserve in Singapore (Figure 2.11), additionally play a role in the provision of habitats for plants and animals. This is especially

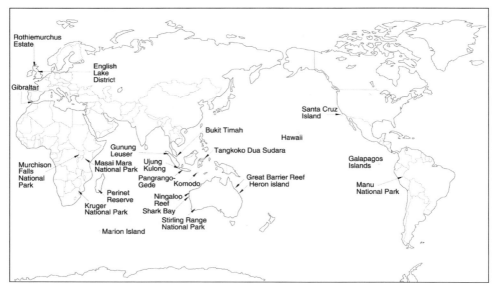

Figure 2.11 Location map of important nature-based tourism destinations referred to in this chapter

so when they are numerous and connected to one another by corridors of remnant vegetation.

Corridors in the landscape

Corridors can be viewed as differing from, and permeating the landscapes in which they occur. They vary in their width, length and in the nature and degree of activity that occurs along them and form strips that differ from the surrounding landscape (Figure 2.10). From a tourism perspective they are often key habitats, as in river systems, and sites where recreation can take place. Corridors can both separate and connect patches in the landscape. A disturbance corridor such as a road can act as a filter, thus preventing organisms moving from one patch to another. Conversely, the same road could act as a conduit for and source of organisms, allowing movement along the corridor and even dispersal into the matrix. The efficiency with which organisms can move from patch to patch will depend on the width of the corridor, as in the case of remnant vegetation, and its connectivity in the landscape. The more connected corridors are in the landscape the greater the conduit and source function is likely to be.

Corridors thus comprise different origins, for example strips of vegetation, roads, walking trails and rivers, are of different size and width and show variable degrees of connectivity. Forman (1995) also notes that corridors can change diurnally, as in the day/night movements of animals, according to seasonal cycles and in response to successional processes.

Ecological significance of disturbance corridors in landscapes

Forman (1995) provides a comprehensive overview of the role of corridors in the landscape. Five types of corridor are recognised: environmental (river with riparian vegetation); disturbance (trails and roads); remnant (strips of woodland / natural road reserves); regenerated (European hedgerows) and introduced (windbreaks). Of particular significance in natural area tourism are disturbance corridors such as roads, paths and trails. From a tourism perspective these corridors are useful attributes serving as a means of access to interesting sites and wildlife as well as being a focus of recreational activity. Some natural corridors, such as streams and rivers, are tourism resources in their own right and strips of natural vegetation along roadsides in Western Australia have become a significant wildflower tourism resource.

Because a large proportion of tourism centres on corridors it is important to understand the ecological functions of corridors. Five functions are recognised: these comprise corridor habitats, conduits, filters, sources and sinks (Forman, 1995). Disturbance corridors (roads, tracks and pathways) will provide a useful focus here as it is where many tourism and recreational impacts occur. Disturbance corridor habitats mostly comprise disturbance tolerant, edge and invasive species such as weeds. These species of course perform an ecological function in their own right in being able to tolerate the environmental conditions brought about by a change in the original habitat. Exposed soils can be stabilised in this way and these species can pave the way for the invasion of other species. If however the disturbance is continuous, as it normally is in these corridors, then a permanent community of disturbance specialists often persists.

Road corridors

In the case of roads and trails the open areas provide a conduit for the transfer of energy and wind. Plants can enter in the form of seeds and animals also use these corridors as a means of moving through the landscape. Disturbance corridors thus act as a source by which plants, animals and tourists can spread into a reserve or wilderness area (Box 2.3). At the same time a network of roads and / or trails can also act as a filter in that organisms can become separated into patches within a particular natural area. Propagules, sediments and animal life can accumulate in environmental corridors such as rivers. In major disturbance corridors, such as on many roads, the road becomes a sink because of the attraction of predators and scavengers to road kills.

The role of roads as disturbance corridors is in fact highly significant. Figure 2. 12 illustrates this relationship according to the five ecological functions of corridors mentioned above. By comparison, tracks and pathways, because of a general lack of vehicles and less hardened surface, tend to be less noisy, polluted and well defined. They are however, like roads, a significant source of ecological impact in the form of soil erosion, vegetation damage, weed invasion and disturbance to wildlife. The degree and nature of this impact is strongly connected with intensity of usage, extent and location of the trails and their management.

Box 2.3 The spread of an exotic fungus through tourism corridors in the Stirling Range National Park, Western Australia

This is a case study of the spread of an exotic fungus through tourism corridors. It highlights the significance of ecological linkages and demonstrates the potential ecological damage that can be brought about by apparently benign tourism activities.

The Stirling Range National Park (see Figure 2.11) is a large area (115,600 ha) of natural vegetation and a zone of exceptional biodiversity. It contains 1500 plant species of which 87 are endemic to the park. As with many national parks around the world the Stirling Range provides for tourism and recreation as well as the conservation of biodiversity. The mountainous scenery and rich array of wildflowers, visible from August to November, make the Stirling Range an increasingly popular tourism destination. Almost all visitors hike in the park with a significant percentage undertaking self-guided touring by car. Roads for tourist access were initiated at around 1920 and since that time further road improvements and the development of walking tracks has taken place (CALM, 1996). A number of mountain peaks provide for hiking, wildflower viewing and the appreciation of scenery.

Active management is necessary to maintain tourism facilities and prevent degradation such as path erosion. The long summer dry season gives rise to a bush fire hazard and this is managed according to a programme of prescribed burning and firebreak corridors (McCaw & Gillen, 1993). There is a risk of ecological degradation in

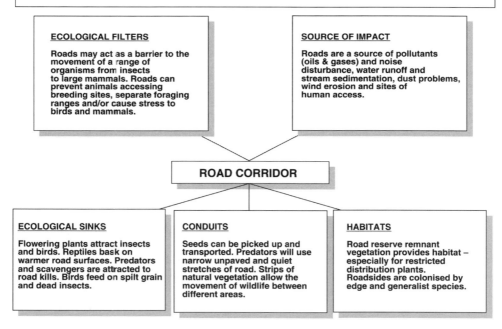

ECOLOGICAL FILTERS

Roads may act as a barrier to the movement of a range of organisms from insects to large mammals. Roads can prevent animals accessing breeding sites, separate foraging ranges and/or cause stress to birds and mammals.

SOURCE OF IMPACT

Roads are a source of pollutants (oils & gases) and noise disturbance, water runoff and stream sedimentation, dust problems, wind erosion and sites of human access.

ROAD CORRIDOR

ECOLOGICAL SINKS

Flowering plants attract insects and birds. Reptiles bask on warmer road surfaces. Predators and scavengers are attracted to road kills. Birds feed on spilt grain and dead insects.

CONDUITS

Seeds can be picked up and transported. Predators will use narrow unpaved and quiet stretches of road. Strips of natural vegetation allow the movement of wildlife between different areas.

HABITATS

Road reserve remnant vegetation provides habitat – especially for restricted distribution plants. Roadsides are colonised by edge and generalist species.

Figure 2.12 The ecological function of roads. (Derived from Foreman, 1995)

the form of edge effects from surrounding agricultural land. This includes increased fire hazard, weed invasion and the immigration of feral animals from adjacent farmland. Roads and tracks in the park are subsequently acting as habitats for weeds and conduits and sinks for introduced predators such as the European Fox (*Vulpes vulpes*). The single most serious threat to the integrity of the Stirling Range ecosystem, however, is an introduced fungus *Phytopthora cinnamomi*. (CALM, 1992; Wills, 1992; Newsome, 2001). The fungus is considered to have been introduced around 1960 when a number of roads, footpaths and fire management tracks were constructed (CALM, 1996; Gillen & Watson, 1993).

Phytopthora cinnamomi is a soil-borne fungus that enters the roots of susceptible plants. Vegetative reproduction produces sporangia which then release mobile zoospores which infect the roots of host plants. It can then spread by root-to-root contact, by soil being moved from one place to another and in water (Shearer, 1994). Widely dispersed infection can result from the movement of soil on footwear and the wheels of vehicles. Soil disturbing activities such as road building and the maintenance and construction of firebreaks would have been the initial mechanism through which the disease has spread through the park (Gillen & Watson, 1993; CALM, 1996). More recently, the fungus has also spread along walking trails as a result of infected soil being carried in the boot tread of hikers (Wills & Kinnear, 1993). There is a significant correlation between the distribution of the fungal infection and the more accessible tourist peaks (CALM, 1996). The presence of the disease in upland areas is of particular significance because of the potential for downhill spread of infectious zoospores in water through surface and subsurface runoff (Gillen & Watson, 1993; CALM, 1996).

Infected host plants are killed as a result of impaired root function followed by the death of photosynthetic tissues. A wide range of species, mostly in the plant families Proteaceae, Mytaceae, Papilionaceae and Epacridaceae, are susceptible (Wills, 1992; Shearer, 1994). These plant families comprise a very high proportion of the plants found in the Stirling Range. Moreover, the health of the wider Stirling range ecosystem is under threat from the total effect of *P. cinnamomi* on plant communities. The disease has a major impact on the species rich understorey that is an essential component of Mallee heath, and an important plant community in the park. Wilson *et al.* (1994) report that as many as 60% of the component species present can be destroyed following infection by *P. cinnamomi*.

Because the plant family Proteaceae contributes much of the floristic structure to many plant communities in the park their loss due to *P. cinnamomi* infection will cause a decline in species richness, changes in community structure and a reduction in plant biomass. Such observed and predicted changes to vegetation are illustrated in Figure 2.13. The resultant change in community structure and function degrades the vegetation and its capacity to provide suitable habitats and resources for fauna. Wilson *et al.* (1994) provides an overview of the likely impacts on wildlife. They point out the potential consequences for arboreal mammals and birds that rely on the canopy of dominant species, such as Banksia spp. for food and shelter (Figure 2.13). Widespread infection by *P. cinnamomi* therefore has the capacity to degrade the conservation and tourism value of the Stirling Range National Park.

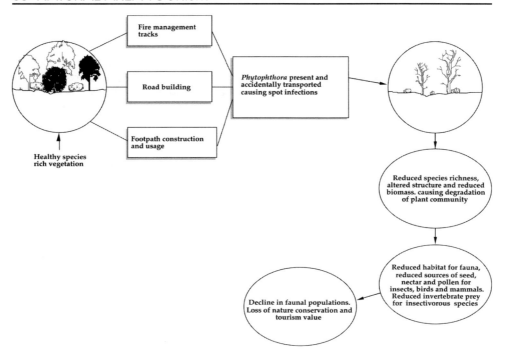

Figure 2.13 Predicted ecological impact caused by *Phytophthora cinnamomi* infection in the Stirling Range National Park, Western Australia. (Derived from Newsome, 2001)

River and stream corridors

River and stream corridors are of particular significance because of their tourism importance and hydrologic flow function. Water is a 'magnet' for tourists and recreational and other human activities have the potential to alter water quality. Polluted water, for example, can move easily along stream and river corridors from one ecosystem to the next (for example, see Box 2.4, p. 69). Additionally particulates, such as eroded soil sourced in the matrix, can enter, accumulate and be transported in stream corridors. River corridors also function as habitats for a wide variety of specialised and generalist species. Generalists often occupy the edges of streams and rivers where natural disturbance events take place due to fluctuations in water levels. Stream and river corridors also act as conduits for a wide spectrum of plants and animals.

The landscape matrix

In contrast to discrete patches and corridors the matrix is the background ecosystem or land use in a landscape mosaic. The important features of the landscape matrix are that it is usually an extensive area containing patches and corridors. The landscape matrix may be a cultural landscape comprising urban and agricultural land in which lie various corridors and patches of vegetation. Conversely it may consist of forest or some other vegetation type in which patches and corridors occur as a result of changes in soil type or manifest as disturbed areas (Figure 2.10).

Energy, materials and species flow between the various components of such a landscape mosaic. In this way different ecosystems can be inter-linked by the movement of water, particulates and organisms between them. Exotic species that invade native ecosystems are a particularly significant issue because of their capacity to degrade tourism resources and natural areas (see Box 2.3 and Figure 3.15, p. 131). Such invaders commonly include non-native weeds and feral animals, which profit from human disturbance. Opportunistic species such as non-native pioneer plants (weeds), that are adapted to and respond to disturbance, are able to proliferate in the absence of their usual diseases and predators.

Ecological Characteristics and Tourism in Different Types of Ecosystems

This section explores some of the specific ecological characteristics of selected ecosystems from around the world (Table 2.2). As mentioned previously, because of the large range of environments utilised for recreation and tourism it is impossible to survey all of them in one chapter. Instead some of the most highly valued tourism ecosystems (islands, coral reefs, tropical rainforests and African savanna) and some specific impacts are considered here. Tropical rainforests, although at this stage still not the subject of extensive tourism activity, are included because they are an immense nature-based tourism resource and the focus of increasing tourist attention. Specific ecological conditions, impacts and management problems at tourism destinations such as other forest ecosystems, the polar regions, deserts, mountains, lakes and rivers and caves are not covered here but are, however, periodically explored in the remaining chapters in this book.

Island ecosystems

Islands are highly desired as recreation and tourism destinations for a number of reasons. In the first instance special social values are attached which are associated with access, remoteness and 'tropical romance'. A boat trip can conjure up a sense of adventure and this is particularly so if the island is uninhabited or there is an element of danger as with island volcanoes. In contrast to this, the palm-clad beaches of the humid tropics attract visitors especially from north-western Europe and the USA. People who visit these sites are often in search of the 'recreational beach' life for a few weeks. This latter type of tourism can however occur in sensitive natural environments. Examples include coral reefs, turtle nesting beaches and seabird breeding areas. Management based on ecological knowledge is therefore crucial.

Many tourists wish to see wildlife. As a consequence of this islands all around the world have become the focus of wildlife centred tourism. Examples of these include

Table 2.2 Comparison of some important ecological characteristics of selected ecosystems

Selected ecosystem property	Ecosystem type		
	Coral reef	Tropical rainforest	African savannah
Major structural components	Growth of soft corals. Sediments stabilised by algae. Coral polyps build calcareous skeletons which accumulate as reef structures.	Four major levels of vegetation dominated by large trees.	Grassland with scattered trees and shrubs.
Aspects of ecosystem function	Warm ocean waters are low in mineral nutrients. Photosynthetic activity driven by zooanthellae. Blue-green algae fix nitrogen. Nutrients conserved by algae.	Nutrient stored mostly in vegetation and recycled via the soil. Insects are major grazers, consume large quantities of plant material and support complex food webs. Termites important in the recycling of woody materials.	Food chains based largely on grasses. Large nutrient store in herbivore biomass. Termites are key organisms in the recycling of plant litter.
Components creating habitat and niche	Architectural complexity and diversity of corals.	Complex vertical structure of woody vegetation. Epiphytes. Forest floor microclimate. Diversity of trees.	Diversity of grasses. River channels and surface water. Scattered trees and shrub patches. Topographical complexity.
Keystone organisms	Coral polyps. Coral feeding fish.	Large fruit bearing trees such as fig trees. Important fruit dispersers such as bats.	Elephants.

marine mammals such as seals and sea lions. Also, tourists can snorkel with Australian Sea Lions (*Neophoca cinera*) at Seal Island near Perth in Western Australia. The presence of seabird breeding colonies and other birds that occupy many islands are also a focal point of tourism in Australia (e.g. North Stradbroke and Moreton Islands); USA (e.g. Santa Cruz and Pribilof Islands); UK (e.g. Shetland and Farne Islands); Norway (Lofoten Archepelago); Peru (Ballestas and Chincha Islands) and Indonesia (e.g. Bali and the Banda Islands) and at many other island locations around the world.

Island tourism also embraces the desire to see unusual endemic species. Classical examples of these are the Galapagos Island Marine Iguanas (*Amblyrhynchus cristatus*) and Giant Tortoises (*Testudo elephantopus*), the Komodo Island Dragons (*Varanus komodoensis*) and rare and endangered birdlife on Hawaii. Penguins and seals are attracting an increasing number of visitors to South Georgia, the South Orkneys and the South Shetland Islands in the Antarctic region. ✓

The vulnerability of island biota and the problem of invasive species

Many island ecosystems are ecologically fragile due to their relative small size and unique evolutionary development (see later). At the same time some of this fragility is also related to the isolated nature of plant and animal populations as any renewal of species that are lost is dependent on external sources from beyond the island itself. Uniqueness and especially small endemic populations are thus major contributing factors to the sensitivity of island biotas. It should be noted that the accidental or deliberate introduction of non-native plants and animals to islands could occur as a result of tourism visitation and development.

Exotic plants can be transported to islands attached to visitors' clothing and as seed in soil stuck in the tread of footwear. Small mammals can be accidentally transported on boats and then reach land either by swimming a short distance or being carried in luggage or boxes of food. The house mouse (*Mus musculus*) can be readily transported in this way. The significance of such an introduction depends on how the 'invader' interacts in the local island ecosystem. For example, on Marion Island in the sub-Antarctic (Figure 2.11) the house mouse competes with Lesser Sheathbills (*Chionis minor*) for terrestrial invertebrates as a source of winter food. The reduced availability of food resources, due to this competition, is considered to be the cause of population decline in Marion Island Lesser Sheathbills (Huyser *et al.*, 2000).

Larger, especially herbivorous, species of animal have usually been introduced as part of an islands history of colonisation and development. Species deliberately transported in this way include food species such as rabbits, goats and sheep. The ecological significance of introduced herbivores is in their impact on plant community structure and on any fauna that particularly rely on plants that are being preferentially consumed. For example on Santa Cruz Island, California (Figure 2.11) the alteration of plant community structure has changed habitat structure, resulting in the loss of several endemic subspecies of ground nesting birds (Van Vuren & Coblentz, 1987). Similarly the loss of Mamane Forest on Hawaii (Figure 2.11), due to sheep grazing, has impacted on endemic Hawaiian birds. Mamane Forest, for example, is the main food supply of the Palila (*Loxioides bailleui*) and its loss threatens the bird's survival (Snowcroft & Griffin, 1983).

Many island plants are thought to be vulnerable because their populations have evolved in the absence of mammalian herbivores. Bowen & Van Vuren (1997) have recently demonstrated this on Santa Cruz Island, California. They investigated the morphological and chemical defences of the same species of plants, which occurred on Santa Cruz Island and mainland California. Some of the island species were found to have reduced defences against herbivory. The significance of these findings was tested in a feeding trial using sheep. The sheep were observed to consume a greater biomass of the island populations of four out of six species of plant tested. It was concluded that the island populations are more vulnerable to herbivory because they lacked the better-developed defences of their mainland counterparts. Bowen and Van Vuren (1997) emphasise that, because of this, island populations of mainland species and endemic plants are particularly sensitive to the introduction of exotic herbivores.

The evolutionary effects of isolation on animal life include flightlessness in insects and birds, gigantism and fearlessness. These three features combined give rise to a high sensitivity to disturbance. Many island endemic birds have evolved flightlessness in the absence of mammalian predators. Examples of this include the Galapagos Cormorant (*Nannopterum harrisi*) and the Kiwi (*Apteryx australis*) and Kakapo (*Strigops habroptilus*) of New Zealand. Because there has been little or no evolution to reduce their vulnerability to predation such species can be easily killed by introduced predators such as domestic dogs and cats. Fearlessness, especially in birds, is a behavioural trait that has also evolved in the absence of mammalian predators. This feature in itself, however, has also become a tourist asset, allowing visitors to approach and photograph island wildlife.

Tourists are also attracted to islands that host examples of gigantism as in the case of tortoises (*Testudo elephantopus*) on the Galapagos Islands and the Komodo Dragons (*Varanus komodoensis*) on the island of Komodo in Indonesia (Figure 2.11). Highly valued species such as these are then subject to much attention and potential attendant tourism development. When such species become the subject of constant attention by humans they may become stressed or habituated (see Chapter 3 'The observation of wildlife', p. 124). In some instances handouts of food result in changes in the animal's natural behaviour which can manifest as aggression and/or disease for the animal concerned (see 'Disturbance of normal feeding patterns as a result of food provisioning', p. 74).

Some of these problems are evident on the Galapagos Islands (Figure 2.11) where tourism related disturbance to seabirds, food provisioning and increased aggression in sea lions has been reported (Roe *et al.*, 1997). Similarly concerns over the health impacts of artificial feeding of Komodo Dragons (*Varanus komodoensis*) has led to the practice of attracting dragons with bait being terminated. Artificial feeding was resulting in an abnormal concentration of dragons at the designated feeding site. The cessation of food provisioning for the dragons also means that they are now able to properly occupy their niche as a significant predator on Komodo Island. There is now a revised programme of dragon tourism where visitors are encouraged and assisted in observing the animals under more natural conditions. The issue is now more one of overcrowding and pollution in and around the visitation zones in the Komodo National Park during the peak season (Goodwin *et al.*, 1998).

Human visitation to islands can cause significant disturbance as a result of walking and trampling, for example through the collapse of burrows as in the case of breeding petrels and shearwaters (Great Barrier Reef Marine Park Authority, 1997). Seabirds use islands because they are safe from predators and the impact of feral animals can be severe on ground-nesting birds. Introduced herbivores can compete for scarce resources and alter ecosystem structure by preventing the regeneration of larger, woody plant species. Introduced rats (*Rattus rattus*) are well known as egg predators and their introduction to island ecosystems causes significant mortality on burrow and ground-nesting birds (Marchant & Higgins, 1990).

Seabird breeding Islands

Many islands that are currently the subject of tourist interest as well as islands with lower visitation, such as Christmas Island in the Indian Ocean, are likely to experience an increased interest in the tourism potential of their biota in the future. Moreover, because birds are a particular tourist attraction and with breeding colonies vulnerable to disturbance, some attention is here given to specific aspects of seabird island tourism.

Natural ecological factors that determine the success of seabird breeding fall into the following categories: variation in the abundance of prey; capacity of the birds to obtain food and adequately feed their chicks; nest disruption by other animals; predation by gulls and raptors; disease and parasitic infections and severe weather conditions such as storms (Nelson, 1980). Studies have shown that seabird response to human disturbance is variable and is highly dependent on a particular species behavioural ecology (Great Barrier Reef Marine Park Authority, 1997; Hockin *et al.*, 1992).

However, a number of tourism and non-tourism related disturbances can be recognised that have the potential to determine the success of seabird breeding in island settings. Fishing and mainland based coastal development can result in the indirect alteration of food supply for seabirds. The alteration of islands by commercial development and human habitation often results in siltation and pollution of waterways or directly impacts on seabird breeding habitat. The permanent tourism development that arises from this often means that people bring in pets while exotic plants and rats get introduced accidentally.

The disturbance caused by tourism activity can result in an increased risk of egg and chick predation, nest desertion, reduced hatching success and increased stress for the birds. Any combination of these responses to disturbance can lead to a decline in the population of seabirds and even a change in bird community species composition. It has also been observed that some birds will shift the location of the breeding colony in response to disturbance. This has been reported for albatross colonies on the Galapagos Islands and at Taiaroa Head, New Zealand (Great Barrier Reef Marine Park Authority, 1997; Roe *et al.*, 1997). Reproductive success may consequently decline as a result of breeding colonies being 'pushed' into less favourable sites for the birds.

Despite the fact that it is known that some species are reasonably tolerant of human activity, with some species even benefiting, it is important to manage and study tourism activity on seabird breeding islands to prevent loss in numbers and/or community structure. The importance of understanding the above is exemplified by Burger & Gochfeld (1993) who assert that visitors to seabird islands cannot be properly managed without adequate information available to managers about the impacts of tourism on birds. They studied the impacts of tourism on boobies in the Galapagos Islands. The study set out to determine the potential for disturbance to breeding habitat and breeding behaviour. The investigation posed whether tourists on walk trails changed the behaviour of nesting boobies, whether boobies avoided trails when nesting and whether boobies abandoned their stations when visitors passed.

The results of their work showed that Masked Boobies (*Sula dactylatra*) that were 2 m from the trail flew off when tourists passed by. Blue-footed Boobies (*Sula nebouxii*) and Red-footed Boobies (*Sula leucogaster*) in contrast simply moved away. However with repeated passages of tourists these birds were seen to be in an agitated condition for quite a long time. In all species there were fewer nests adjacent to walking trails reflecting an alteration in territory boundaries and available nesting sites. The greater sensitivity exhibited by the Masked Booby (*Sula dactylatra*) is thought to relate to the early stage that this bird was at in its breeding cycle when it is more prone to disturbance.

These findings clearly demonstrate that the birds are reacting to the presence of tourists. Furthermore, many groups of birds are more susceptible to disturbance if they are at the crucial initial stages of breeding such as display and courtship. The reaction exhibited by these birds means that disturbance could be reducing the time that boobies need for display and courtship and also for incubation and care of the young. There are implications here for tourism planning and management (Chapters 4 and 5) in terms of the pressure to open up further walk trails if birds move away from existing trails and the need for the creation and maintenance of no-go conservation zones.

Coral reef ecosystems

Coral reefs have a wide distribution in clear, warm, shallow seas and extensive coral formations can be found along the coastlines of the Caribbean, East Africa, south-east Asia, Western and Eastern Australia. Coral reefs also occur in shallow waters that surround isolated islands and island archipelagoes in the tropical zone. Coral needs light and a temperature range that lies between 20 and 28°C in order to survive. Because of the sensitivity of coral to temperature conditions coral systems tend to favour slightly warmer and more sheltered eastern coastlines. Their presence on western coastlines, for example the Ningaloo Reef in Western Australia (Figure 2.11), is due to a warm current that is derived from warmer tropical seas that lie further north.

Coral formation can be divided into three main types: coral reefs that occur close to the shoreline are called fringing reefs and become well developed where there is little or no sedimentation from local river systems; they are believed to evolve into barrier reefs through a combination of land subsidence with the coral growing upwards towards the light as the landward side of the reef sinks downwards, this process being accompanied by more rapid coral growth on the seaward side where the water is better oxygenated and ocean currents bring in nutrients. Over time the reef evolves into a barrier reef and occurs some distance offshore, separated from the coastline by a zone of deeper water. The Great Barrier Reef, Australia (Figure 2.11) which occurs from 35 to 100 nautical miles offshore, is a striking example of barrier reef development.

Many islands are surrounded by fringing reefs and barrier reefs can form extensive off-shore coral formations as with the Great Barrier Reef which lies off north and central eastern Australia. The third type of coral reef development is the coral atoll, which is a ring of coral enclosing an inner lagoon. Coral atolls can occur far out to sea in deep water and they form first as a fringing reef around an island but over time the island gradually sinks. The coral has however continued to grow upwards by the same process as described above.

The various species of coral colonies grow by forming a variety of structural forms; these include branches, rounded features, shelf and plate-like structures. This makes the reef architecturally complex and provides shelter, breeding sites and sources of food for a diverse array of marine organisms (Table 2.2). The coral reef itself is composed of the calcium rich skeletons of coral polyps. When the coral polyp dies these skeletons become the base for new living coral polyps which grow upwards towards the light. The dead coral material, which lies beneath, gradually becomes compacted forming coral rock. Coral reefs are eroded by wave action and subject to grazing by various species of fish, molluscs and echinoderms. It is through these activities that parts of the reef are converted to coral sand and rubble. This loose material is often moved around by currents and deposited to form the substrate for a new reef or coral island.

Diverse animal communities

Coral reefs are biologically rich and contain a significant proportion of the world's marine biodiversity. For example, from the Ningaloo Reef in Western Australia 250 species of coral, 500 species of fish and 600 different species of mollusc have been identified (Storrie & Morrison, 1998). Moreover the most diverse reef systems in the world occur in the Indo-West Pacific zone which ranges from the Australian Great Barrier Reef to the Philippines (Veron, 1986).

One fundamental characteristic of all coral reef systems is the symbiotic relationship between the coral polyp and single celled organisms called zooanthellae which occur inside the coral tissue (Figure 2.14). Because zooanthellae are photosynthetic light is essential. Zooanthellae utilise carbon dioxide which is given off by the coral while at the same time the coral polyp is able to obtain some of the products of photosynthesis. The relationship between the two organisms is so profound that if the partnership is disrupted the coral will die. The photosynthetic activity of coral reefs allows them to proliferate and grow under relatively low nutrient conditions.

Fringing reefs can be divided into two distinct ecological zones (Figure 2.15). The zone which lies under the influence of the highest and lowest tide levels is the reef flat and is, in part, subject to drying every time the tide recedes. The reef flat is a zone of relatively shallow water and is also influenced by wave action and inputs of freshwater as a result of rainfall. As a consequence of these environmental conditions only the more resilient coral species can be found here. These include rounded

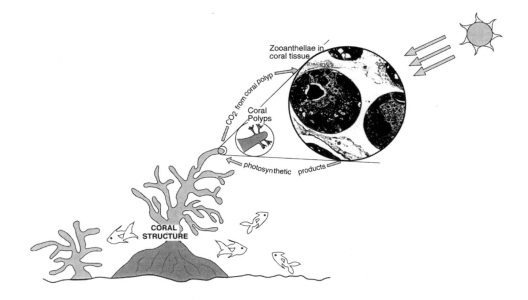

Figure 2.14 The coral polyp ingests a dinoflagellate which then becomes incorporated into the gastric endodermis forming a symbiotic relationship with the polyp

and flexible soft corals. The sand flats also provide a different habitat for animals; and burrowing echinoderms, crustaceans and molluscs can be found in this zone. Some species of fish specialise in utilising the reef flats by moving to and fro with the tide.

Further out to sea, and where the edge of the reef meets deeper water, two more zones can be distinguished – that of the reef crest and the reef slope (Figure 2.15).

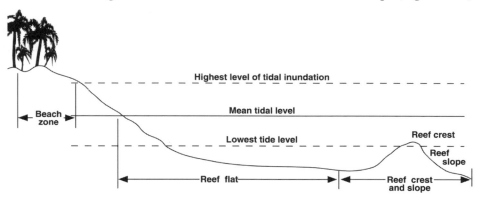

Figure 2.15 Ecological zones of a fringing coral reef

The reef crest is subject to wave action, which limits the presence of many species of coral; the reef slope, however, is always covered with water. Here occur corals, such as the staghorn coral that is intolerant of wave action and desiccation. The habitats of many species of invertebrate and fish can also be found here.

Coral reef tourism

The diversity of animal life, brightly coloured organisms and structural complexity of the coral attract many people to coral reef environments. Coral reef tourism is increasing in popularity, with some parts of the world showing dramatic increases in visitation in recent years. For example, Salm (1986) reports that resorts in the Maldives catering for divers had risen from three to 37 in the period 1972 to 1981. In Western Australia the town of Exmouth, which services tourism associated with Ningaloo Reef, recorded 49,000 visitors in 1995. This figure subsequently increased to 62,000 visitors in the following year (Storrie & Morrison, 1998).

Tourism in coral reef environments includes pressure to develop tourist facilities and accommodation. Visitor activity includes swimming, boating, snorkelling and scuba diving. In more recent times certain species have been the focus of tourism interest, for example swimming with Manta Rays (*Manta birostris*) at Coral Bay and Whale Shark (*Rhiniodon typus*) trips from Exmouth in Western Australia. Other associated problems can include fishing, pollution and the collecting of marine life as souvenirs.

Ecological consequences of coral reef tourism

Coral reefs are susceptible to damage and become stressed when there is too much sedimentation, high nutrient levels, high water temperatures and massive inputs of freshwater that alters optimum salinity conditions (Johannes, 1977). Whereas the first two of these problems can be caused by tourism development, the latter two are more associated with natural fluctuations in climate.

Siltation and eutrophication are common problems associated with tourism development. Sediments are derived from runoff when adjacent land is cleared of vegetation. Eutrophic conditions are brought about by the addition of nutrients into the ecosystem from sewage out-falls and/or fertiliser runoff, for example, from coastal golf course maintenance. Also of widespread significance are the problems brought about by visitor activity on and about coral reefs.

Research has demonstrated this latter problem in various parts of the world. Visitor impact problems on Australian coral reefs were recognised some 20 years ago by Woodland and Hooper (1976). They investigated damage caused by walking on exposed coral at Heron Island, Australia (Figure 2.11). They performed an experiment in which people walked on a designated transect and collected the broken coral. Woodland and Hooper (1976) found that there was an 8% reduction in coral cover after 18 traverses. A total of 607 kg of living coral was seen to be destroyed and 37.5% of this was broken off by the last eight traverses. Experiments such as this clearly demonstrate the potential for damage if there is intensive use of an area. More recent work detailing the impacts of recreation and tourism on coral reef systems is further considered in Chapter 3 'Use of water edges', p. 118.

The reason for coral being susceptible to damage is due to the occurrence of polyps in the outer layers of the coral structure. This living veneer will not tolerate constant trampling and breakage. The deposition of mud and silt on coral surfaces blocks out light needed by the zooanthellae. Similarly, the addition of extra nitrogen and phosphorus into the ecosystem leads to an excessive growth of epiphytic algae. The growth of these algae is normally limited by low concentrations of nutrients. The transport and input of additional nutrients by currents is therefore a significant ecosystem process and any changes can lead to disruption of the normal coral reef nutrient cycle. When nutrient levels are increased algae grow in greater profusion on the surfaces of the coral, blocking out light. This results in the death of coral polyps.

The loss of coral means a loss of habitat structure and food supply for dependent biota and therefore a reduced capacity to support associated animal communities. These changes have the potential to alter the ecological structure of the reef; that is, if large areas of the structural elements afforded by the coral are lost with a subsequent loss of animal diversity, disruption of symbiotic relationships and ecological function through the simplification of food chains will occur. Coral reefs that become heavily damaged will therefore support less diversity and be less appealing as tourism resources

Tropical rainforests

The tropical forest biome contains both wet and dry forests while an annual rainfall of >2500 mm defines a tropical moist forest. Within the moist forest classification there are tropical rainforests and tropical deciduous forests. The latter consist of the Asian monsoon forests, the seasonally dry forests of South America, West Africa and north-east Australia and various other sub-tropical forest formations. Tropical rainforests, however, are mostly distributed in the equatorial climatic zone (Figure 2.16) and receive between 4000 and 10,000 mm of rainfall per annum. Average temperatures range from a minimum of 23°C to a maximum of 32°C along with constant high relative humidity. Tropical rainforests that occur in

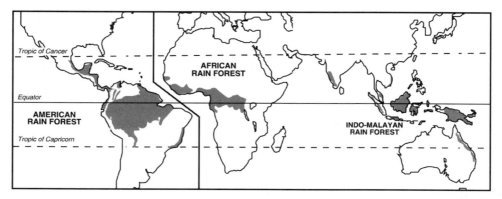

Figure 2.16 Global distribution of tropical rainforests

mountainous environments above an altitude of 1000–1500 m are referred to as montane rainforests and they are usually wetter and somewhat cooler than their lowland counterparts.

The world's tropical rainforests all exhibit the same basic structure. Because of the non-limiting inputs of solar energy and moisture there is abundant growth of vegetation and rainforest trees are able to attain heights of up to 50 m and sometimes 60 m. This is despite the fact that the soil nutrient content of many rainforest ecosystems is low due to the leaching effects of heavy rainfall. However, symbiotic relationships between rainforest trees and fungi or bacteria enhance the uptake of some nutrients. In many situations the decomposition of leaf, flower and fruit fall is rapid and the released nutrients are taken up from surface root mats and rootlets which grow into the leaf litter. Many rainforest species also have thick, unpalatable leaves to resist loss of nutrients through herbivory.

An essential feature of tropical rainforest is the closed nature of the canopy which results in reduced light penetration to the lower layers of the forest. Vertical differences in light intensity give rise to different zones of vegetation. Four to five zones can be recognised comprising the forest floor, lower layer, middle layer, subcanopy and the canopy with emergents (Figure 2.17). The main ecological feature of

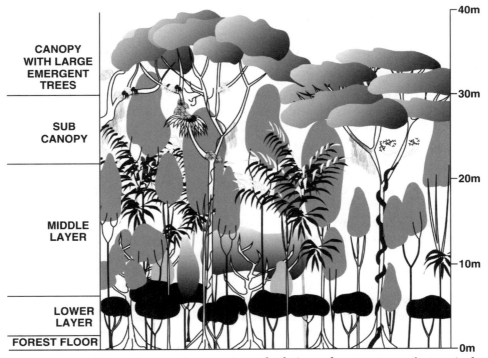

Figure 2.17 Different layers of vegetation which form the structure of a tropical rainforest

these various zones is a stratification of various habitats and the adaptations of plants and animals to live in these various zones. The forest floor receives the least light and maximum temperatures are a few degrees cooler (27–29°C). There is little air movement and the humidity is maintained at around 90%. Plants that occur here are much more shade tolerant than species which occur in the higher strata. In contrast to this the canopy can be up to 30% less humid, a few degrees warmer and is the site of intense photosynthetic activity.

Climbers and epiphytes reflect the struggle for light and typify tropical rainforest ecosystems (Figure 2.17). Epiphytes grow at all levels and comprise some 25% of all plant species in lowland rainforest ecosystems with some 15,500 species in tropical America alone (Collins, 1990). They provide additional habitats for insects, spiders and small vertebrates in the middle and upper strata by trapping, retaining, and localising water and organic matter. At the same time climbing plants germinate on the forest floor and then climb towards the canopy and, depending on the species, via spikes, thorns, tendrils, clasping roots or adhesive hairs. Many climbers produce woody stems and when these larger species mature and reach the canopy several tree crowns often support them. Buttresses or flanges typify the basal structure of many trees providing additional support for their shallow roots (Figure 2.17). Such structures most likely also give rise to more root space to optimise uptake of nutrients and assist in oxygen uptake in those regions where seasonal flooding of the forest floor takes place.

The complex structure of tropical rainforests therefore provides many niches. Niche differentiation is achieved through the separation of species according to diet, space or activity periods (Box 2.2). The forest floor provides a suitable habitat for organisms that favour more humid conditions. Other species are confined to and attracted to the concentration of flowering and fruit production in the canopy zone. Fig trees provide a source of food for many insects, mammals and birds. The fruits of strangler figs are mostly dispersed by frugivourous birds and germinate in notches and depressions in other rainforest trees. As they grow, aerial roots descend to the forest floor and establish growing points from which further branches ascend into the host tree. The development of many leafy branches that thicken and interlace act like a 'blanket' over the host tree and it eventually dies leaving the strangler fig standing in its place.

Tropical rainforests are typified by a diversity of tree species; for example, one hectare of rainforest in Malaysia contains up to 180 tree species (Collins, 1990). This, coupled with numerous insect-plant specific associations and the large range of animal niches, provides for the most structurally complex and biodiverse terrestrial ecosystem on earth. Furthermore, although plants and animals demonstrate a fundamental similarity in community structure, there is a wide variation in species composition between different geographic regions. For example, the tropical rainforests of South America are characterised by the tree family Lecythidaceae, species of *Cecropia* and bromeliads. Asian tropical rainforests, by contrast, are typified by the tree family Dipterocarpaceae, species of *Macaranga* and pitcher plants (*Nepenthes* spp).

Rainforest tourism

Tropical rainforests are a diminishing but important tourism resource. They are one of the most diverse biomes on earth and therefore of great biological interest. Widespread logging and the conversion of primary or virgin forest to secondary or regrowth forest is a major problem, and because of this forests of all kinds remain the subject of more environmental concern than any other type of vegetation. An increasing number of people are interested in the specific 'atmosphere' and structure of tropical rainforest ecosystems. Such features include distinctive botanical structures such as buttresses, epiphytes, lianes, strangler figs, cauliflory (flowers and fruits that grow directly from the trunks of trees) and palms. However, despite these unique features it is the animal life that still dominates tourism interest in tropical rainforests in many parts of the world. These include some spectacular, enigmatic and highly sought-after species. For example gorilla tourism in central Africa, Orang-utans in Indonesia and bird watching in South and Central America.

Ecological consequences of rainforest tourism

The endemic wildlife and diminishing forests of Madagascar are attracting a greater number of international visitors. Stephenson (1993) examined the impacts of tourism in the increasingly popular Perinet Reserve (Figure 2.11). Although established walkways are in place visitors were still straying from established paths in order to maximise their opportunities to photograph wildlife. Besides path erosion and the presence of litter it was found that additional trails were being created and the trampling of native vegetation favoured the invasion of herbs, weeds and rats. The altered structure of natural vegetation in turn caused a reduction in the number of small endemic mammals. Stephenson's work is a clear example of the ecological consequences of corridors and how the alteration of plant community structure results in wider ecological changes.

Furthermore, Stephenson (1993) also found that there was direct interference with wildlife such as small mammals, reptiles and the Indri (*Indri indri*) which is the largest lemur in Madagascar. It is often difficult to observe wildlife in forested environments due to visibility problems and the shy nocturnal habits of many species. Visibility is likely to be guaranteed by searching for animals. In the case of Perinet Reserve several species of reptile and small mammals are regularly caught so that tourists can directly observe them. The shy and easily disturbed Indri was also the subject of daily forest searching. Stephenson (1993) posed the question as to what the impact of these activities might have on wildlife.

Some answers to the above question are perhaps afforded by the work of Griffiths and Van Schaik (1993) in Gunung Leuser National Park, north Sumatra (Figure 2.11). Gunung Leuser is one of the largest complexes of lowland and montane rainforest in the world. The park contains a rich array of wildlife including the Tiger (*Panthera tigris*), Clouded Leopard (*Neofelis nebulosa*), Sumatran Rhinocerous (*Didermocerus sumatrensis*) and Orang utan (*Pongo pygmnaeus*).

Griffiths and Van Schaik (1993) set out to study the impact of human traffic on the activity and abundance of wildlife by comparing a pristine site with a site that was heavily travelled by humans. They found that animals such as the Tiger, Clouded Leopard and Sumatran Rhinocerous avoided heavily travelled areas. The Tiger also changed its activity period from diurnal to nocturnal activity. Other species, however, remained unaffected in that wild pigs (*Sus scrofa*) would only flee a short distance from humans. Macaques (*Macaca nemestrina*), on the other hand, became habituated (see Chapter 3 'The observation of wildlife', p. 124).

Griffiths and Van Schaik (1993) considered some of the wider ecological implications of these changes. It was suggested that habituated species, such as macaques, could increase in numbers but at the same time reduce their foraging range by staying in one place. A reduced foraging range could also lead to an altered pattern of seed predation and dispersal, which in turn could impact on the local dispersal of tree species. As many plant species rely on mammals for their seeds to be transported some distance from mature parent trees this type of impact, if sustained, could be significant in changing the species composition of trees in a particular area of rainforest.

Wild primates are a major tourist attraction and this is reflected by tourism interest in the Crested Black Macaque (*Macaca nigra*) of Sulawesi, Indonesia. Kinnaird and O'Brien (1996) examined the tourism impacts on these animals as part of a wider study in the Tangkoko Dua Sudara Nature Reserve (Figure 2.11). The interaction of tourist groups with three different groups of Crested Black Macaques habituated to humans was monitored and recorded. The results of their work (Figure 2.18) show that the macaques reacted to the visitors by running, screaming and retreating into trees. The degree of response, however, varied according to different groups of visitors and between different groups of Macaques (Figure 2.18). It was found that the most significant negative response was to groups of about five or more people who talked loudly and pursued macaques off the trail. Continuous disruption of this nature is likely to disrupt the daily activities of these animals and reduce foraging and feeding activity. Moreover, it was considered that if unsupervised tourists were allowed to feed the macaques, significant habituation could take place resulting in bold and aggressive behaviour towards tourists.

The implications of tourist visits and behavioural changes in primates have recently been reported from Belize (Marron, 1999). Howler monkeys (*Alouatta* spp.), considered to be an important component of the Belize nature-based tourism industry, have been the subject of long-term monitoring studies. The data show that howler monkey groups that are visited by a large number of tourists have fewer females and young than monkey groups with much lower tourist visitation rates.

Valentine and Cassells (1991) highlight a number of tourism/recreational management issues in tropical rainforest ecosystems. First, the potential of tropical rainforest tourism is still not realised and many tropical rainforest reserves around the world remain as untapped tourism resources. Furthermore, as seen in Australia, tropical rainforest itself appears to be incidental to a number of recreational activities such as through hiking, bike riding and picnicking. This leads to a second issue, that of appropriate use. There is a need therefore to engage the visitor through education and interpretation so that the tropical rainforest ecosystem itself

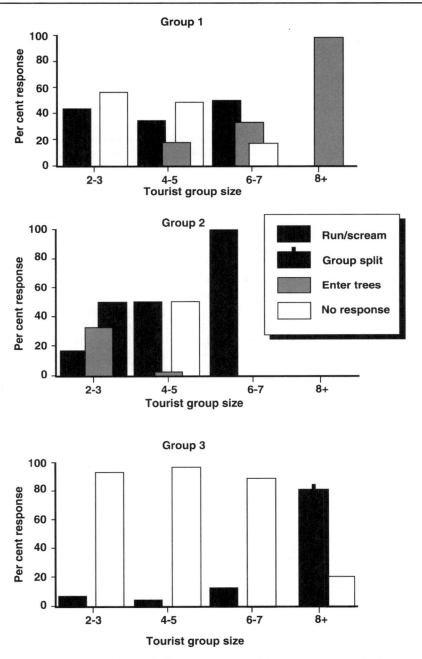

Figure 2.18 Response of three different groups of Sulawesi Crested Macaque to varying tourist group size. The data show differing responses from different Macaque groups. (Derived from Kinnaird & O'Brien, 1996)

is appreciated (Chapter 6). Thirdly, as recently highlighted by Henderson (2000), the impacts of trampling, erosion and disturbance to wildlife needs to be quantified so that such data can be fed into tourism monitoring and management. Finally, the development of tourism/recreation planning frameworks (Chapter 4) is essential for management of tropical rainforest tourism in the future.

African savanna

Savannah represents an ecosystem that lies somewhere between forest and grassland. It can vary from treeless plains through to densely wooded vegetation. Generally, however, it consists of open country charcterised by drought-resistant trees with a grass understorey. Savanna is a widespread and typical vegetation formation in East and Southern Africa.

There are five major physical or abiotic determinants of savanna. First is the amount and seasonality of rainfall in which a prolonged dry season (four to seven months) allows a fire risk to develop. This, coupled with seasonal aridity, has a strong controlling influence over the development of woody vegetation. Secondly fire which mostly occurs at the end of the dry season prevents the growth of young plants and colonisation by woody invaders. The occurrence of fire is dependent on the build-up of fuel loads that are derived from dead and dry grasses. Where savanna is less dominated by grasses fires are less frequent and more limited in extent. Thirdly, adverse soil characteristics, either through shallowness, salt levels or hardpans, prevent the growth of woodland and forest. Allied to this are geomorphological factors in which well-drained and dry slopes support grassland while wetter and waterlogging prone low lying areas enable the development of woody vegetation. Finally, frost is also a physical determinant where savannas occur in upland areas because of its role in eliminating frost sensitive woody species.

The major biotic determinant in savanna ecosystems is grazing pressure. Millions of years of prolonged grazing has resulted in the co-evolution of vegetation and herbivores which now means that grazing pressure is now essential for the maintenance of savanna ecosystems. The action of grazing stimulates storage of plant root assimilates which in turn stimulates continuous plant growth under grazing pressure.

In Africa there is a wide variety of herbivores and their evolution is connected with the wide spectrum of plant species that are available. The fact that different mammal species specialise in different plants or parts of plants also results in a dispersal of the grazing pressure. An example of such niche differentiation is the case of reduced competition for food between Impala (*Aepyceros melampus*), which eat acacia leaves, and wildebeest *(Connochaetes taurinus)*, which eat short growing species of grass. In order to maximise seasonal feeding opportunities many of these herbivores occur in large herds. Seasonal migrations in response to rainfall and growing seasons mean that the vegetation can recover between visits of herbivores.

National parks, which are often surrounded by fencing or agricultural land uses, are now the only safe refuge for large concentrations of wildlife in Africa. Here, because of the lack of natural migration systems, animal densities can be unnaturally high. The resultant constant grazing pressure means that there is no capacity for the savanna to recover, thus there is potential for an increase in the abundance of unpalatable species. Such plants would normally be controlled by fire but the over-grazing reduces fuel loads and thus capacity for grass fires to develop. Overgrazing also reduces plant cover, exposing soils to erosion. Woody shrubs are also more likely to invade because of a reduction of water usage by grasses; the surplus water becoming available to deep-rooted shrubs because more of it penetrates into the deeper sub-soils.

Tourism in the Masai Mara Game Reserve, Kenya

Ceballos-Lascurain (1996) reports on the potential impacts of viewing and photography on big cats in the Masai Mara (Figure 2.11). Tourist activities consist of vehicle congregation, encirclement and close positioning in order to get good photographs. It was found that leopard (*Panthera pardus*) would walk or run away when approached at a distance of <5 m. Moreover, encirclement by vehicles would prevent cats from getting away altogether. This type of disturbance can reduce the feeding activity of diurnal hunting cats and has been observed to be a particular issue for the cheetah (*Acinonyx jubatus*). In heavy tourism periods/zones cheetahs are often forced to feed in the middle of the day when the tourists have left and not at their preferred feeding time of early morning. Cheetahs that are subject to constant attention of this sort become stressed and less able to raise their young and compete with other predators. These observations show that the simple activity of viewing has the capacity to cause stress and interfere with prey searching, seeking cover and even mating. The lion (*Panthera leo*) is less affected because it largely hunts and feeds at night and is mostly at rest during the day.

Because seasonally dry grasslands, such as the Masai Mara, are at risk of deserti-fication Onyeanusi (1986) set out to examine the erosion risk caused by off-road driving. In the Masai Mara tourists are allowed to go off-roads and tracks, where the terrain is dry and grassy, to view and photograph wildlife. In order to quantify any ecological damage, Onyeanusi (1986) investigated the impacts caused by an off-road vehicle on experimental strips. The results showed that there was loss of vegetation cover and damage to underground plant structures, especially from the action of turning vehicles. It was concluded, however, that the total ecological impact in the park was small due to the rapid regrowth and recovery of grasses. Although the Masai Mara grassland appears resilient to off-road vehicle damage there remained the problem of informal tracks being converted to permanent tracks. Moreover, the development of further tracks and such off-road driving remains an issue in relation to disturbance to wildlife.

Tourism in the Kruger National Park, South Africa

The Kruger National Park (Figure 2.11) contrasts with the Masai Mara-Serengeti complex in terms of road access, the presence of boundary fencing and the nature of ongoing tourism and wildlife management. These differences also highlight a number of ecological issues that are concerned with tourism. For example, much of the extensive road network in the Kruger National Park is sealed. Although potentially detracting from a wilderness or 'natural' experience such roads reduce the impact of vehicles on soils and vegetation, help to confine visitors, minimise disturbance to wildlife and are cheaper to maintain in the long run.

The recreation, tourism and conservation function of Kruger National Park was recognised some 80 years ago and over time a series of boundary fences have been erected to protect adjacent human farming activity as well as wildlife in the park. Today this is an even greater issue because much of the Kruger National Park is surrounded by human modified landscapes, principally rural–agricultural landuses (Box 2.4). These boundary fences, however, bring their own problems by acting as barriers to natural migration systems and also preventing any in-migration of wildlife. Because natural migration patterns cannot take place wildlife cannot leave the park in times of drought or when populations of herbivores increase in good years.

The Kruger National Park is therefore managed according to principles of wildlife carrying capacity that is assessed according to the condition of the savanna grassland ecosystem. Culling has taken place in the past because migration has not been an option during drought years when the population of elephant, buffalo and hippopotamus has been high. Culling prevents sudden population crashes and prevents the mass death of wildlife due to natural causes when populations have increased due to restricted migration.

Increases in the elephant population are particularly significant in this regard because of their keystone function. Elephants also dominate waterholes under drought conditions and prevent other species from drinking. The problem is that tourists find the shooting of elephants very distasteful. Because of this the control of elephant populations in the Kruger National Park remains controversial and various other control strategies such as the use of contraceptives are being researched (Bannister & Ryan, 1993; Whyte *et al.*, 1998).

The provision of additional waterholes serves the function of preventing deaths in drought years and also concentrates wildlife for tourists during the dry season. Nonetheless, recent work has shown that the decline of the Roan antelope (*Hippotragus equinus*), which occurs in the northern part of the Kruger National Park, can be traced to the provision of artificial waterholes. Harrington *et al.* (1999) report that these waterholes attract a number of other herbivores, such as wildebeeste (*Connchaetes* spp.) and zebra (*Equus burchelli*) during drought conditions. These animals in turn had attracted predators such as the lion (*Panthera leo*) which have also preyed on the Roan antelope. Numbers of this locally endangered antelope started to recover when 50% of artificial waterholes were closed in the northern part of the park.

There is also loss of vegetation and accelerated soil loss around water holes. More significantly, trampling and heavy grazing pressure during the dry season eliminates herbaceous plants from around these areas. Thrash (1998) found this to occur in a 250 m radius around the watering points. Because of a subsequent loss in fuel loads these areas are not likely to burn and woody perennial species will then be able to invade the less trampled, over grazed areas over time. The subsequent lack of dense grass constitutes a reduction in habitat diversity and is likely to impact on those herbivores that require dense grass as cover for the protection of their young. Thrash (1998) suggests that a uniform spread of waterholes extend this type of impact over a wider area. His recommendation was to cluster the watering points in specific areas of the park to reduce trampling and overgrazing.

Tourism in modified and semi-natural ecosystems: the British countryside

This example differs from the previous ones in that the natural environment of Britain has been substantially modified in the presence of humans for thousands of years. The end result is that hardly any of the present day landscape can be consid-

---

Box 2.4 The Kruger National Park in the landscape mosaic

The Kruger National Park also serves to illustrate some important ecological impacts associated with river corridors that were considered earlier under 'Landscape ecology,', p. 50. As mentioned previously, the Kruger National Park is juxtaposed against a number of activities, such as irrigated crop systems, forestry and industrial development. This is especially so along the western border and the park is influenced by fires, erosion and pollution that are sourced beyond its boundaries. The ecological function of environmental corridors becomes significant here in that a number of rivers flow west to east through the Kruger National Park (Figure 2.19).

Much agricultural activity takes place in the upper reaches of these rivers that flow through the park (Deacon, 1992). The dependence of plants and animals in the Kruger National Park on these natural corridors is significant as reflected in the problem of reduced water volume due to water abstraction upstream, especially in the Crocodile River catchment. The loss in water volume can cause hippopotamus (*Hippopotamous amphibius*) to concentrate in areas of deeper water that in turn leads to localised overgrazing of riverine vegetation. Poor flushing of the river systems also results in an increase in stagnant water which can in turn provide suitable habitat for malarial mosquitoes which can then impact on the human population.

The conduit function of natural stream and river corridors is exemplified by the downstream transport of weeds which have colonised the banks of the Crocodile River in the Kruger National Park (Deacon, 1992). Land clearing along the western boundary has also resulted in soil erosion and downstream sedimentation in the Olifants River (Figure 2.19).

Fish kills have been directly associated with sedimentation events which in turn reduce the prey available for fish-eating birds. The death of fish in the Kruger National Park river systems has also been linked to eutrophication caused by nutrient inputs sourced from sewage derived from rural areas directly outside the park. Pesticides, originating from intensive farming activities, and known to impact on the breeding success of bird life, are also entering the park through these natural corridors (Bannister & Ryan, 1993).

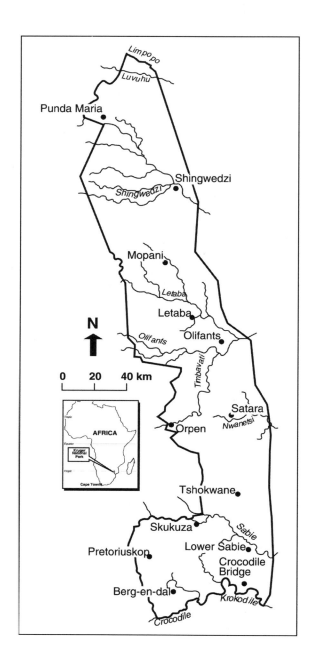

Figure 2.19 Kruger National Park, South Africa

Plate 2.1 Rural landscape in Leicestershire, England. The landscape consists of many patches and corridors comprising crops, grazing land, hedgerows, woodland remnants, roads and tracks. (*Photo*: David Newsome)

ered as pristine in the ecological sense. There is a long history of agricultural land use and in particular grazing. Moreover, intensive agriculture and the grazing of marginal lands are largely responsible for the vegetated landscapes that are evident today (Plate 2.1).

Once virtually entirely covered by forest and woodland these natural plant communities only remain as small semi-natural remnants or, in the case of the English New Forest, one of the few larger areas of forest cover. Many vegetation types represent various successional stages following disturbance by clearing or grazing. Interestingly enough these plant communities have become valued for their specific characteristics and biodiversity and are now managed to prevent them reverting to woodland as a result of natural succession.

The landscape mosaic described above is typical of many areas in Britain that are highly valued tourism resources. One such example is the English Lake District (Figure 2.11), a national park that comprises mountains, moorlands, lakes, streams, woodlands, agricultural land, grasslands and human settlements in the form of farms, small villages and tourism facilities. In contrast to wildlife or the other specific ecological attributes described previously, places like the Lake District attract visitors because of a 'sense of wildness', views of the landscape and out of geological interest. Some of these values are borne out of the fact that mountainous areas confer a more natural element to the landscape coupled with the need for people to escape city environments that are substantially devoid of 'natural' elements. The Lake District landscape mosaic thus provides for hiking, mountain top viewing, birdwatching and general nature study, rock climbing, boating, pleasure driving and other recreational activities.

The Rothiemurchus Estate in Scotland caters for both domestic and international tourism in a mountainous setting, amongst lakes and semi-natural pine forest (Figure 2.11). Tourism facilities consist of roads, car parks, walkways, nature trails, picnic sites, camping and caravan sites and tourism information centres. Part of the tourism experience also includes fishing, off-road driving, orienteering, cycling, mountain-bike riding and boating. Clearly this is a different type of tourism when compared to more remote and less intensively developed locations with fewer activities such as rainforest treks in Malaysia or wildlife viewing in Africa. The Rothiemurchus Estate certainly provides for a different tourist experience in a less natural setting.

Despite the fact that tourism in Britain takes place in largely modified environments there is still scope for detrimental ecological effects. Indeed it could be argued that any potential ecological effect is more significant because many ecological qualities have already been lost from the landscape and what remains is in special need of protection. Loss of biodiversity and a reduction in bird populations, for example, are ongoing problems in Britain and tourism can put additional pressure on what remains. Important remnant populations of plants and animals occur in areas that are visited by tourists. Moreover, some natural communities and wild animals are present and protected largely because of tourist interest in them and or their habitats.

The intensity of visitation is high in many parts of 'natural' Britain and as a result important remnant vegetation and wildlife remains under threat from development pressures and pollution. Sensitive mountainous areas are particularly at risk of further damage (see also 'Recreation and tourism in mountainous areas', p. 118, and 'Cumulative impacts', p. 134) and the sheer congestion that arises during peak holiday periods constitutes a social impact of overcrowding and possible visitor dissatisfaction. This can lead to negative attitudes about the area concerned or even result in irresponsible activities such as camping in undesignated zones and walking in untracked or restricted areas. As already noted, sites can become eroded, vegetation is at risk of damage and wildlife may be disturbed. An appreciation of ecology, environmental sensitivity and informed management is therefore important in all situations whether it be a national park in Madagascar or bird reserve in Britain. In doing so sustainable tourism can be achieved and different natural environments around the world can be enjoyed.

Wildlife as a Specific Component of Ecosystems

Evidence has already been provided that island tourism and the observation of animals in rainforest and savanna settings provide scope for disturbing reptiles, birds and mammals which are important biotic components of ecosystems. Furthermore, the alteration of predator–prey relationships, disturbance to keystone species and human assisted increase in some animal populations can result in reduced biodiversity and threaten the valued ecological resources that tourism is centred upon. Because wildlife is an increasingly important, and sometimes highly specific, component of natural area tourism it important to appreciate the main causes of disturbance to wildlife and have some understanding of the ensuing biological and ecological effects. Wild animals can respond to human attention according to the widely recognised behavioural responses of avoidance, attraction and habituation. Various ecological aspects of these responses are considered here while the nature of the psychological responses of animals is considered further in Chapter 3 under 'The observation of wildlife', p. 124.

A physiological response of ecological significance: stress

In many species the avoidance of humans starts with alarm behaviour and alertness followed by agitation and then escape to a safer distance. This is the obvious behavioural response to stress caused by the presence of humans. These reactions are frequently associated with physiological responses in the form of hormonal changes that result in increases in heart and respiration rates, elevated blood sugar levels and a rise in body temperature. Gabrielsen and Smith (1995) state that these responses are more intense when wildlife is nesting or caring for their young, when humans are visible while walking and when people move off existing trails. Some species, as in the case of many birds, have the opportunity to take immediate flight but others will not move until absolutely necessary, for example in the case of camouflaged birds sitting on eggs or during incubation at penguin rookeries. Fowler (1999) notes that although some birds, such as penguins, appear unperturbed by the presence of humans, physiological reactions such as increased heart rate have been detected.

The stress responses that are invoked can have detrimental health effects for the species concerned and could be particularly significant for those species existing under naturally stressful environmental conditions. Antarctica, for example, is becoming an increasingly important tourist destination. Some 100,000 people have now visited the Antarctic region and it is estimated that as many as 1.5 million people may be visiting the area every season by 2010 (Giese, 2000). Of particular note is that only 2% of Antarctica is utilised as breeding areas for seabirds and these are also the sites of tourist interest. The fact that penguins are reluctant to move in the presence of tourists means that visitors are able to get very close to birds which are incubating eggs.

Regal & Putz (1997) have shown that penguins exposed to human disturbance exhibit stress as manifested by increased stomach temperatures that result in additional energy expenditure by the birds. The conservation of energy is critical in cold environments and any unnecessary, and especially continuous, losses will result in reduced vigour and breeding success. Such disturbance may result in changes that

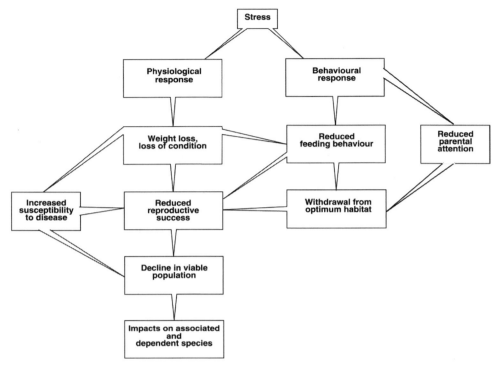

Figure 2.20 Potential ecological implications of stress caused by disturbance to wild animals

have implications at the population level which could ultimately translate into a loss in biodiversity (Figure 2.20).

Disturbance of normal feeding patterns as a result of food provisioning

There is a real danger of wildlife becoming accustomed to and dependent on humans for food in tourism areas. This could have serious health (obesity, loss of condition and tooth decay) and behavioural implications, particularly for a rare species or species with a restricted population. For instance, disturbance in the form of food provisioning can result in lower levels of foraging behaviour as demonstrated by Barbary Macaques (*Macaca sylvanus*) which occur in Gibraltar (Figure 2.11). Macaques normally spend at least 50% of their time foraging, but those receiving human foods have been recorded as only spending 7% of their time foraging (Fa, 1988). Predictable sources of food might reduce the home range of an animal and result in reduced learning behaviour in searching for food and thus a reduced capacity to find food in the wild.

Besides the potential risk of visitors being bitten, food provisioning may lead to aggression between members of the same species and social grouping. Brennan *et al.*

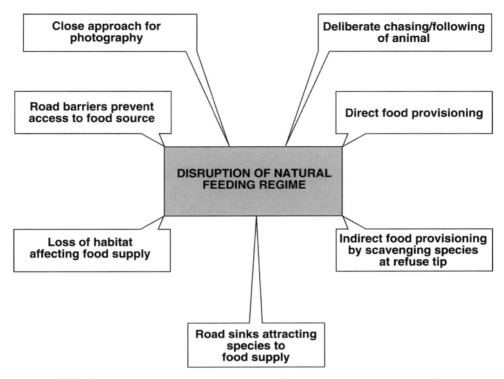

Figure 2.21 Ways that tourists can impact on the natural feeding activities of wildlife

(1985) reported that Vervet Monkeys (*Cercopithecus aethiops*) that had access to human food had more evidence of physical injury (scars, torn ears, hair loss) than their wild counterparts. The reason for this is that food provisioning leads to abnormal concentrations of animals competing for the same resource, resulting in aggression.

An increase in the population of opportunistic, scavenging and predatory species, due to food provisioning, can also have undesirable effects. Increases in various species of gull and crow, in tourist car parking areas and accommodation sites, can impact on less robust species of bird through the predation of eggs and their young. This can reduce diversity at a local scale and threaten the survival and recovery of any endangered species. The ways that natural feeding behaviour can be disrupted is summarised in Figure 2.21 and considered further below in relation to opportunistic predation.

Tourist activity resulting in the avoidance of optimal resting and feeding areas

Animals need to rest and secure protection from predators or conflict with the same species. Particular problems can arise when the peak tourist season corresponds with a period of restricted or preferred food availability for a particular animal. Roe *et al.* (1997) provide the example of the Giant Otter in Manu National Park in Peru (Figure 2.11). Here tourists have been observed chasing otters around lakes in order to get good views. Such lakes are optimal feeding areas for the otters and this, coupled with disturbance from trails that are located close to the lake shoreline, reduces the chance of otters maximising opportunities in obtaining food. Disturbance of this nature, through the effects of stress and disrupted feeding activity, has the capacity to reduce the density and diversity of species in a particular location.

Disturbance to feeding and the problem of opportunistic predation

Tourism can displace predatory birds and mammals from hunting and capturing their prey. Additionally, night driving and vehicle noise may interfere with the hunting strategy of an animal that relies significantly on hearing in order to detect its prey. A recent study carried by Wilson (1999) provides some insight into the potential effects of spotlighting on nocturnal mammals in Australia. She found that spotlighting disrupted the social and foraging behaviour of possums. Avoidance behaviour had resulted in a decline in the numbers of possums sighted at night. It was suggested that the animals may need a up to 30 minutes to recover their night vision following a spotlighting session.

Increased vulnerability to predators is recognised by many as an issue where human disturbance occurs on seabird breeding islands. Predatory birds such as gulls and skuas attend breeding colonies of Puffins (*Fratercula arctica*), Razorbills (*Alca torda*) and Guillemots (*Uria aalge*) in the Northern Hemisphere and penguin rookeries are attended by skuas, petrels and sheathbills in the sub-Antarctic. Displacement of adult birds from nests increases the opportunity for predatory birds to attack unattended nests and exposed chicks.

The eggs of reptiles are also subject to predation. Edington and Edington (1986) report on the increased mortality of crocodile eggs due to tourism in the Murchison Falls National Park, Uganda (Figure 2.11). The close approach of tourist boats to river banks, which are breeding sites for the Nile Crocodile (*Crocodylus niloticus*), causes the crocodiles to enter the safety of water but in doing so their unprotected nests are at risk to predation. It was found that while undisturbed sites suffered a predation rate of 0–47%, the disturbed sites were being predated at the rate of 54–100%.

Disturbance of reproduction and maternal care

As discussed earlier the reproductive success of an animal is likely to be affected by stress and poor body condition (Giese, 2000; Regal & Putz, 1997). Fa (1988) also reports that in the case of the Barbary Macaque in Gibraltar the feeding of high calorie foods can potentially distract monkeys from their normal breeding activity that may lead to a decline in breeding activity.

Problems that can arise in cases of disturbance at the courtship stage have been discussed by Burger and Gothfeld (1993) and in the case of nesting birds and during stages when young are vulnerable to predation by Anderson and Keith (1980) and Yalden and Yalden (1990). The disruption to parent–offspring caring and learning stages can also lead to offspring mortality. This has been recorded at the Monkey Mia dolphin feeding site, Shark Bay, Western Australia. In this case there was the loss of a young dolphin to a shark because of a non-attentive, food provisioned, mother (Mann & Barnett, 1999). Further issues surrounding the response of wildlife to tourists and tourism are discussed in Chapter 3 under 'The observation of wildlife', p. 124.

The Philosophy of Ecosystem Tourism

Recreation and tourism can alter the composition of biotic communities through habitat loss, the introduction of exotic species and pollution. Disturbance caused by trampling and erosion can reduce plant productivity and biomass at a particular site. Humans can also alter the structure of a community by directly or indirectly affecting dominant and/or keystone species. Indeed the structure of many ecological communities is a direct product of human disturbance and this also includes recreation and tourism.

The focus of this chapter has been on the importance of understanding ecology in terms of maintaining nature-based tourism resources. Various potential problems and impacts have been documented so that we are in a better position to anticipate tourist pressures in natural areas. At the same time understanding ecology also deepens our appreciation of nature by helping us to understand how plants and animals 'solve' their own problems of survival in various ecosystems. Accordingly, from a human standpoint this helps in the conservation of nature and enhances our quality of life.

Many natural areas around the world are, however, subject to intense tourism pressure and there is a need for studies of ecological impact and especially thresholds of change so the appropriate management can be instigated. Graham and Hopkins (1993) highlight the need for knowledge of ecology in understanding recreational activity in tropical rainforests, especially in terms of a forest's capacity to absorb various impacts. They emphasise that ecological information is fundamental to the accurate prediction of disturbance effects and at present the ecological determinants of many rainforest organisms remain poorly understood.

Furthermore, Tyler and Dangerfield (1999) emphasise that, in understanding how a natural area might respond to tourism and recreational activities, the emergent properties of ecosystems need to be taken into account: these include concepts of stability and resistance. Stability is the capacity of an ecosystem to remain unchanged, whereas resistance is the capability of an ecosystem to 'absorb' impacts. Understanding this requires knowledge of ecology. For example, as already noted, the sensitivity of coral reefs means that they are susceptible to damage and therefore have much less resistance to tourism impacts than other aquatic ecosystems such as estuaries. Tyler and Dangerfield (1999) provide savanna as an example of a resistant terrestrial ecosystem because significant disturbance is required to cause degradation. This can be contrasted with the sensitivity of the Stirling Range ecosystem and the potential damage that is predicted to be caused by the accidental introduction of an exotic fungus (Box 2.3).

As a result of this, Tyler and Dangerfield (1999) propose that effective ecological management of tourism depends on an understanding of key ecological processes along with some assessment of ecosystem resistance to change. Some progress has been made in assessing the sensitivity of various environments to impacts (see Liddle, 1997; Whitford *et al.*, 1999) but much work remains to done. The landscape ecology perspective also needs to taken into consideration as evidenced by the significance of environmental and disturbance corridors already mentioned.

The effective management of the ever increasing interest in natural area tourism will depend on an understanding of ecosystem structure and function, measurements of resistance to change, the effective use of key indicators of impact and the development of suitable monitoring systems.

Further reading

More detailed treatments of general ecology can be found in Colinvaux (1993) and Begon *et al.* (1996). Dickinson and Murphy (1998) have recently completed a useful introductory text on the ecosystem approach in environmental science. Bush (1997) provides a readily accessible account of ecology that focuses particularly on environmental issues.

A good explanation of global nutrient cycles is contained in Furley and Newey (1983). Further details on disturbance and succession can be also found in Dell *et al.* (1986) and Huston (1994). The work of Forman (1995) provides a comprehensive overview of landscape ecology.

Further information on coral reefs and marine biology can be found in Barnes *et al.* (1986), Van Woesik (1992), Veron (1986), Wallace *et al.* (1986), Williams *et al.* (1986) and Levinton (2001). Recent work on islands, their environmental characteristics, evolution and conservation issues is contained in Whittaker (1998). Particular issues concerning the problems faced by isolated and endemic populations of birds on islands can be found in Stattersfield *et al.* (1998).

Jacobs (1981) and Mabberley (1992) cover the ecology of tropical rainforest environments. More detailed accounts of savanna ecosystem processes are contained in Huntley and Walker (1982) and Solbrig *et al.* (1996).

Chapter 3
Environmental Impacts

Introduction

Natural areas are visited to 'get away from it all' and this involves many recreational activities that take place within natural ecosystems. People also see and 'use' nature differently, the consequences of which are that recreation and tourism tend to blur into one another. The increase in natural area tourism is punctuated by the wide availability of travel guides, natural history periodicals, websites and a plethora of travel magazines which focus on nature experiences.

Some people will simply undertake a 'country' drive and picnic in a semi-natural landscape while others require the challenge and solitude of more inaccessible wilderness areas (Plate 3.1). Some visitors to natural areas are generally interested in seeing wildlife as part of a walk amongst natural vegetation, along river banks or in mountainous areas. In contrast to this, birdwatchers will target specific species and make every effort to see that species whether it be in a remote area or at a city sewage farm. Others wish to see dangerous, rare or spectacular assemblages of wildlife. The immense range of environments available means that recreation and tourism spans forests, grasslands, lakes, rivers and marine ecosystems and is focused on wildlife that occurs in a wide range of cold, hot, temperate and humid countries around the world.

With increasing numbers of people visiting a spatially diminishing and continually degraded natural world there is much scope for negative impact. It is important however to realise that not all tourism has the potential to cause problems. Indeed there are many examples of sustainable tourism operations and positive impact occurring. Degraded and disturbed areas are repaired, nature reserves created and national parks expanded as a result of actual and anticipated interests in natural area tourism. However, impacts do occur and the nature and degree of impact can be complex and variably significant depending on the situation. Impact significance can depend on the type and source of impact, environmental sensitivity, other cumulative pressures and the effectiveness of any management that is in place. Moreover what is a well-recognised and significant impact in one country or environment may not be a problem elsewhere. Accordingly this chapter attempts to

Plate 3.1 Valley leading to the Jostadalen Ice Cap and Tungsbergdalsbreen Glacier, Norway. Few people visit this remote area that is accessed across snowfields, which are present throughout the northern summer. Beneath the snow are fragile and slow-growing lichen communities that are easily damaged by trampling. (*Photo*: David Newsome)

provide an overview of some of these issues and includes a range of examples from around the world.

The scope of this chapter

In Chapter 2, as part of an exploration of the importance of understanding ecology, we considered the role that disturbance plays in creating landscape heterogeneity. Many of these disturbances constitute natural fluctuations within ecosystems and mostly result in a temporary change in ecological conditions. The type of disturbance brought about by recreation and tourism is multifaceted and reliant on a number of factors and, depending on their nature, can be permanent. Human caused disturbance within a tourism/recreation–natural environment situation constitutes a biophysical impact. Moreover, because aspects of the physical environment (abiotic factors) can be changed there is the possibility of their translation

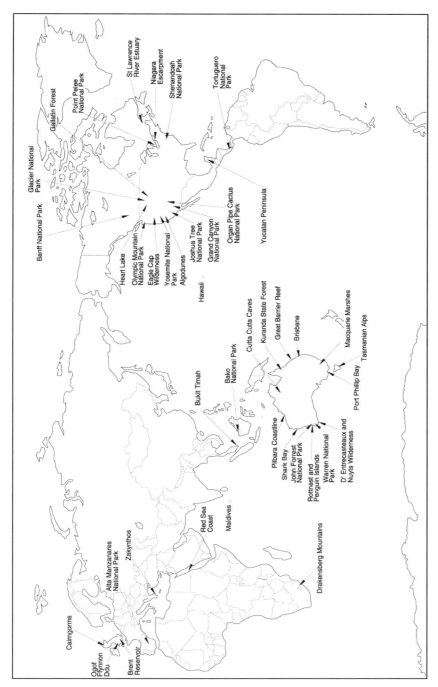

Figure 3.1 Location map of important nature-based tourism destinations referred to in this chapter

Figure 3.2 Signs informing visitors of prohibitive activities at the Boulders Penguin Colony near Cape Town, South Africa. This signage clearly indicates that visitor impacts are real and need to be controlled. (Adapted from National Parks Board Visitor Permit, The Boulders, Cape Peninsular National Park, South Africa)

into indirect ecological impacts. A number of such impacts have already been explored in Chapter 2.

Because of the importance and sensitivity of a large number of ecotourism destinations (e.g. Figures 2.1 and 3.1) it is vitally important that the potential for, and nature of, any environmental impact is properly understood and anticipated (Figure 3.2). As already noted by Tyler and Dangerfield (1999) we must attempt to understand the ecosystems that we are dealing with. To this end we also need to appreciate the sources and nature of potential impact on the tourism resource.

This chapter builds on the concepts explored in Chapter 2 and especially surveys the range of impacts associated with recreation and tourism in the natural environment. Here the focus is on potential biophysical changes that can be brought about by various recreation and tourism activities. Clearly there are also social and economic impacts associated with recreational activity and tourism development. General aspects of these impacts are also briefly considered in this chapter under 'Social and economic perspectives', p. 135, so that the full spectrum of potential impact can be appreciated.

Our main objective, here, is to provide on overview of biophysical impact problems and report on some important recent work in this area. There is an extensive literature that covers a wide range of environmental impacts. Recent syntheses of data and reviews can be found in Hammitt & Cole (1998), Kuss *et al.* (1990) and Liddle (1997). These publications contain a large amount of information that spans many years of work. Accordingly, this chapter constitutes a survey of the main elements of this work and this is examined according to major sources of biophysical impact. A global view has been taken but many examples are drawn from the large database of research that has been carried out in the USA. For further details of methodology, assessment and the study of specific user impacts the reader should consult the relevant cited work and further readings that are suggested at the end of this chapter.

Sources of Impact

There are various ways of categorising the potential environmental impacts of tourism. Buckley and Pannell (1990) divide these into transport and travel, accommodation and shelter, and recreation and tourism activities in the natural environment. In terms of tourism and recreational activities common sources of impact include boating, off-road vehicles, hiking, camping, mountain bike riding, horse riding and caving. In some cases all three-impact categories may occur together leading to a cumulative impact situation. The degree of biophysical impact, however, will depend on the location, diversity, intensity and duration of the activities themselves. Accordingly the following major sources of environmental impact – trampling and wear, and then more complex assemblages of impacts such as access roads, permanent overnight dwellings, walking trails, focal points of activity such as rivers, lakes and wildlife habitats – will be examined. Environmental response, on the other hand, will vary according to individual species / ecosystem resistance and resilience.

Tourism sites may be perceived to be at low levels of risk of biophysical damage where there are only few trails, little access and few visitors. This situation often fits in with the concept of wilderness tourism. A number of studies of recreational impacts, nevertheless, show that significant impacts can occur at recreation sites after only short periods of time and low levels of use (Hammitt & Cole, 1998). This work has also shown that there is a rapid increase in impacts at first which then increase slowly during subsequent years that the site is used (Figure 3.3). At the same time, Hammitt and Cole (1998) point out that some impacts, such as campsite expansion and damage to trees at campsites, do not occur rapidly but instead show a gradual deterioration over time.

A high and continuous impact potential may exist where there are many trails, roads, facilities and infrastructure. This situation comprises a spatial network of linkages and nodes. Networks include trails and roads, while nodes encompass car parks, campgrounds, river access points and scenic lookouts (Hammitt & Cole, 1998). Concentrations of use mean that, although intense and severe impacts may occur at a node or along a linkage, only small parts of large areas such as national parks are impacted. In relation to this, Cole (1981a) estimated that only around 0.5% of two drainage basins in the Eagle Cap Wilderness Zone, USA (Figure 3.1) were significantly impacted by recreation. In contrast to this, small recreation areas such as some nature reserves, as in the case of Bukit Timah Nature Reserve in Singapore

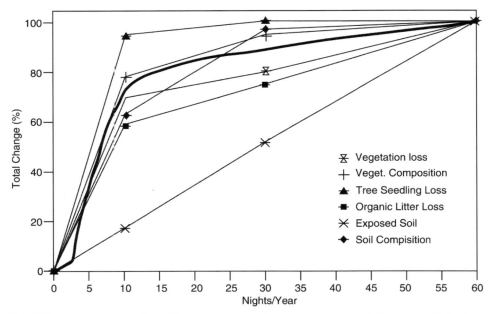

Total Change represents the difference between indicator measures taken on undisturbed control plots and on campsites with 60 or more nights of visitation annually. Thus, approximately 70% of the vegetation loss that occurs on campsites receiving 60+ nights/ year has already occurred after only 10nights/year.

Figure 3.3 Change in campsite impact parameters under low to moderate levels of annual visitation, Boundary Waters Canoe Area Wilderness (Derived from Hammitt & Cole, 1998; Leung & Marion, 1995)

(Figure 3.1), are much more at risk of a larger percentage of the resource being damaged by recreational activity.

Trampling

Vegetation

Trampling is a universal problem and damage to both soils and vegetation can take place as a result of visitors leaving established trails and pathways to take photographs or when a particular animal is pursued because people want to see it (Figure 3.4). Trampling can also occur at sites of concentrated use or where visitor activity is not confined to trails. Consequently, the following common tourism/ recreational activities are sources of trampling damage to vegetation: camping and firewood collection, use of bush/informal toilets, horse riding, off-road vehicles, walking and hiking, wildlife viewing and photography, off-road bikes, trail/motor-cycling, access to river banks and viewing points and boat launching activities.

Liddle (1997) provides a comprehensive overview of the impacts of recreation on vegetation and notes that the type and distribution of visitor activity, amount and

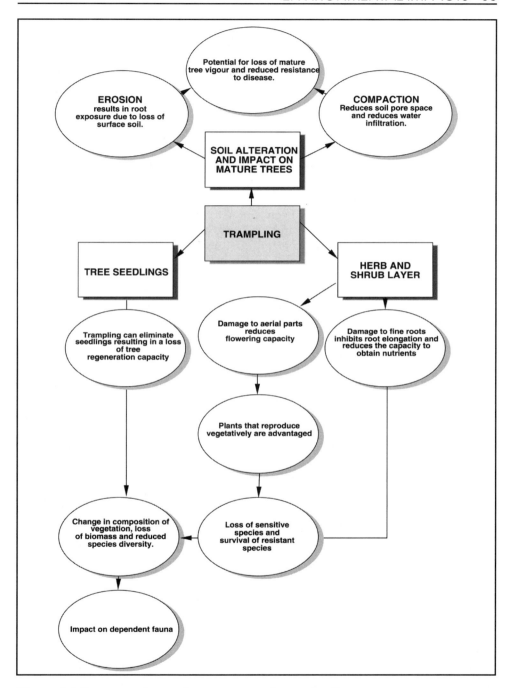

Figure 3.4 Impacts of trampling on vegetation and soils

type of use, density and relative fragility of vegetation influence the degree of impact. Vegetated surfaces can be altered through the development of flattened vegetation or narrow trails, at one end of the scale, through to a situation where extensive areas are denuded of plant cover and dominant plants, such as trees, are lost.

Changes to vegetation as a result of wear consist of a reduction in plant cover which is measured according to losses in percentage plant cover, reduced height of vegetation and reduced biomass of the original undisturbed vegetation. Phillips (2000) investigated the trampling impacts of horse riding in D'Entrecasteaux National Park in south-west Western Australia (Figure 3.1). Such findings confirm that of many other trampling studies (e.g. Hylgaard & Liddle, 1981; Sun & Liddle, 1993a) which show a reduction in vegetation height and loss of percentage plant cover (Figure 3.5).

Different vegetation types have been shown to respond differently to trampling impact. Liddle (1997) provides a useful summary of the resistance of different plant communities to trampling by walkers (Figure 3.6). The importance of this data is in its depiction of the different sensitivities of the different vegetation types. There is a marked contrast between two vegetation types which occur around Brisbane, Australia (Figure 3.1). While a sub-tropical grassland can tolerate 1412 passes before the vegetation is reduced by 50%, a eucalypt woodland can only tolerate 12 passes before the same percentage of vegetation cover is lost.

The reasons for such differences lie in the features of plants that confer resistance to trampling damage. Critical plant features are a low growth habit, growing points that are not easily damaged, flexibility and toughness. The latter structural aspects are conferred by the presence of lignified tissues, but too much lignin makes a plant inflexible and prone to snapping when trampled (Liddle, 1997). Grasslands are frequently more resistant because of their general low growth habit and growing points present just at the soil surface. Onyeanusi (1986) has illustrated this in an investigation of off-road vehicle damage in the Masai Mara in East Africa (see 'African savannah', p. 67).

Although many grasslands are, in terms of vegetation height and relative percentage cover, resistant to trampling, changes can occur in the species composition of the plant community. In a study of trampling impacts in the Alta Manzanares Natural Park in Spain (Figure 3.1) Gomez-Limon and de Lucio (1995) found that plant diversity decreased at popular weekend recreation valley grassland sites. An interesting aspect of this work is the finding that changes in soil and plant composition were occurring before any detectable loss of vegetation cover. Loss of species diversity was linked to soil compaction. Gomez-Limon and de Lucio (1995) suggest that a resistant species, *Spergularia rubra*, noted to increase as a result of trampling could be used as an indicator of high impact areas.

The disturbance associated with the edges of trails and pathways frequently gives rise to 'disturbance' communities. Changes in the species composition of a plant community is the result of sensitive species decreasing, more resistant species increasing and the possible arrival of invasive plants such as weeds (Liddle, 1997).

Such changes, as already noted, can result in a decrease in plant diversity with

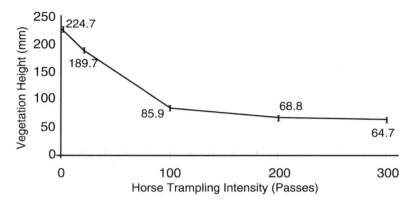

(a) Vegetation height averaged across the central 30-75cm of a treatment transect cross sectional profile after various intensities of horse trampling

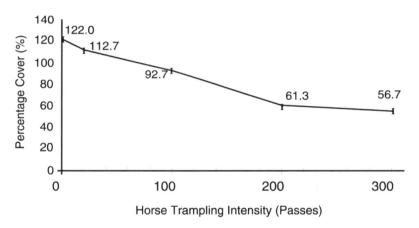

(b) Percentage of vegetation cover averaged across the central 30-75cm of a treatment transect cross-sectional profile after various intensities of horse trampling

Figure 3.5 Results of a field experiment to quantify the environmental impact of horse riding in D'Entrecasteaux National Park, Western Australia. (Derived from Phillips, 2000)

sensitive native and/or endemic species being replaced with more aggressive native colonisers and/or exotic species. In some cases, however, this can lead to an increase in plant diversity as demonstrated by Hall and Kuss (1989) in the Shenandoah National Park, Virginia, USA (Figure 3.1). In this case plant cover and diversity was found to decrease away from the trails. Hall and Kuss (1989) considered that resistance to trampling and competition for light were factors controlling

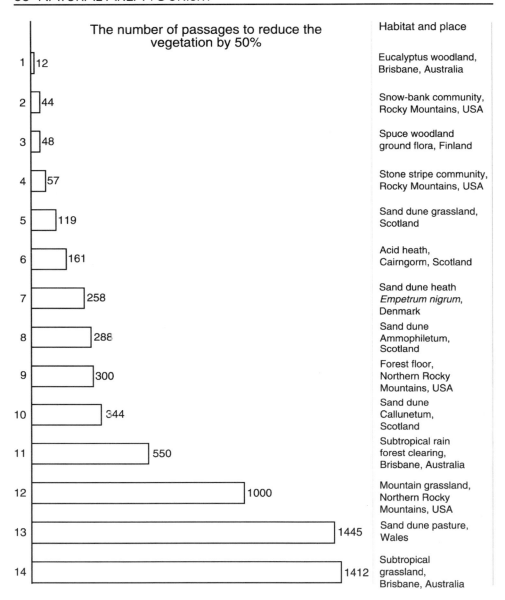

Figure 3.6 Resistance of different plant communities to trampling. (Derived from Liddle, 1997)

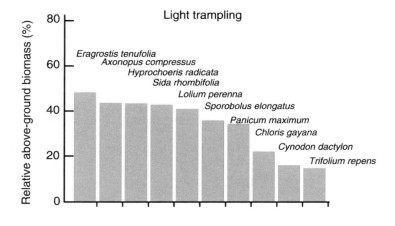

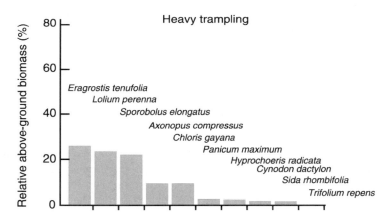

Figure 3.7 Change in relative biomass for different species of plant according to intensity of trampling. (Derived from Liddle, 1997; Sun & Liddle, 1993b)

the relationship. Trail side plants were characterised by more trample resistant growth forms (e.g. low growth habit) which would have benefited from the lack of competition for light afforded by the undisturbed vegetation.

The level of change also depends on the nature and intensity of disturbance as illustrated by Sun and Liddle (1993b) who found that grassy tussock species afforded resistance to trampling while woody and erect herbs were more suscep-tible. They also showed that a reduction in both root and above ground biomass were both greater under a heavy, as compared to a light, regime of simulated tram-pling. Moreover, there was a change in relative biomass survival for different species depending on whether they were heavily trampled or not (Figure 3.7).

Liddle (1997) points out that the ultimate survival of vegetation depends on the morphological and physiological characteristics of individual species that comprise a plant community. This issue is readily illustrated by a comparison of two different ecosystems. In the first case, reported by Boucher *et al.* (1991), the recovery of trailside vegetation following trampling at a tropical rainforest site in Costa Rica was rapid with substantial recovery after two years. Such recovery is related to the rapid growth ability of many tropical rainforest species under conditions where most of the important abiotic factors are not limiting. Boucher *et al.* (1991) also suggest that a rotating system of trail access and closure would mimic the light gap mosaic that is created when a large tree falls and allows light to penetrate the forest floor.

In contrast, environments where abiotic factors are limiting, as in the case of arctic-alpine environments (Plate 3.1), recovery from trampling damage can be slow (Liddle, 1975). Here plants are adapted to cold and dry conditions and the physiological response to this is slow growth and therefore recovery from distur-bance is slow. A recent study by Whinam and Chilcott (1999), in the alpine zone of central Tasmania (Figure 3.1), supports these conclusions. Shrubs were found to be most susceptible to damage and most of the trampled vegetation died within 42 days of the trampling period. The data show that vegetation continued to die even after the trampling had ceased. It is pointed out that the resting of tracks, as compared to the Costa Rica study, will not work due to the very slow recovery rates of Arctic-alpine vegetation. In this case other management strategies would need to be employed in these environments.

Biological crusts and microbes

Bacteria, fungi and related organisms play a key role in ecosystem function. They are instrumental in the functioning of key biogeochemical processes such as in the case of the nitrogen and phosphorus cycles. Moreover, soil micro-organisms can determine the nature of plant communities by affecting the ability of plants to obtain nutrients (as in the case of soil mycorrhizae), or by giving certain species competitive advantage (via mutualistic relationships) in colonising and surviving on disturbed sites and new substrates.

An investigation into how trampling impacted on soil microbial communities in a sub-alpine campsite at Heart Lake, Montana, USA (Figure 3.1) was carried out by Zabinzki and Gannon (1997). They found that there was a loss of microbial activity in the upper 6 cm of soil in areas disturbed by camping activity. Such a decrease in microbial activity is likely to be due to the corresponding loss of vegetation that in turn leads to a decreased availability of root exudates and organic matter as sources of energy for microbiota. As noted by Wardle (1992) any simultaneous loss of soil pore space which causes changes in aeration and water holding capacity is also likely to have an adverse effect on soil microbes. The loss of microbiota, such as symbiotic mycorrhizae, can translate into less favourable soil conditions for plants and impact on nutrient cycling at the local scale.

In arid and semi-arid ecosystems biological or microphytic crusts play a significant role in ecosystem processes. Based on a comprehensive review of the literature, Eldridge and Rosentreter (1999) list five important ecosystem functions of microphytic crusts: (1) soil surface stabilisation and the reduction of erosion; (2) regulation of water flow into soils by absorbing and retaining water; (3) production of nitrogen and organic carbon at the soil surface; (4) sites for the establishment of higher plant seedlings; (5) act as refugia sites for soil invertebrates.

Cole (1990a) investigated the impacts of trampling on microphytic crusts in the Grand Canyon National Park, USA (Figure 3.1). Experimental work showed that after only 15 passes human trampling had reduced the microphytic crust cover by 50%. Cover was subsequently reduced to zero after 250 passes. Monitoring data showed that it took five years for the crust to establish itself to a level similar to the pretrampled condition. Cole (1990a) also concluded that the crusts were highly susceptible to damage but moderately resilient if trampling ceases and recovery can take place. In situations where random and dispersed trampling takes place there is the potential for widespread and more permanent damage to the crusts.

Because of the role microphytic crusts have in stabilising the soil surface their loss in arid landscapes could lead to increased soil erosion. The associated loss of soil nutrients, sites for the establishment of higher plants and attendant invertebrates, is likely to lead to degradation in the biological condition of affected areas.

Soils

In terrestrial ecosystems soils comprise a complex mix of abiotic and biotic components, provide a medium for the growth of vegetation and form the exchange pool for major nutrient cycles. Soils thus exert a major control over the growth of plants and play a pivotal role in determining the nature of vegetation communities on land. Soil components, when eroded, can also be moved through the landscape from one ecosystem to the next. Any loss of, or damage to, soil therefore has major implications for the ecological integrity of nature based tourism destinations.

Many studies have documented damage to soil arising from tourism and recreation (e.g. Liddle, 1997) and a summary of the major impacts are shown in Figures 3.4 (trampling), 3.10 (camping) and 3.16 (use of off-road vehicles). Soil compaction is a common impact on soils and is measured according to bulk density and penetration resistance. For example, data collected by Smith (1998) as part of a study on campsite impacts in Warren National Park, Western Australia (Figure 3.1) show significant increases in bulk density and soil penetration resistance in the high impact zones of camp grounds (Figure 3.8). Smith (1998) noted that the reduced infiltration capacity of the soil, caused by compaction, resulted in flat areas becoming saturated and boggy which increased the need for visitors to excavate trenches around tents in order to facilitate drainage.

Of major importance is the degree of erosion that is occurring, and is likely to occur, in various recreational settings. Many soils can be inherently at risk from erosion and this is dependent on a number of important soil properties. Soil texture is a fundamental soil property and controls cohesion (ease with which soil particles resist detachment), soil structure (ability of the soil to form aggregates) and the infil-

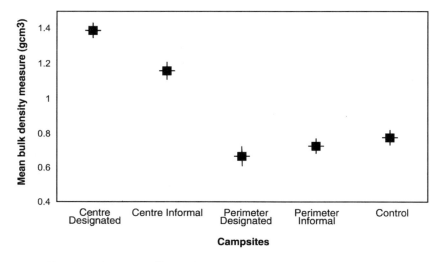

Mean bulk density (gcm3) and standard error for campsites in Warren National Park

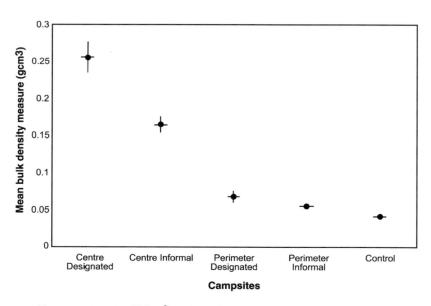

Mean penetrometry (kN/cm2) and standard error for campsites in Warren National Park

Figure 3.8 Mean bulk density and penetrometry (plus standard errors) for campsites in Warren National Park, Western Australia. (Derived from Smith, 1998)

tration of water into the soil profile. Soils dominated by sand and gravel are less cohesive than those with moderate to high clay content. The infiltration of water into the soil profile, on the other hand, is much higher in coarse textured (coarse sand and gravel) than in fine textured (clay and silt dominated) soils.

The formation of soil aggregates is dependent on the soil not being dominated by any particular size fraction. The presence of organic matter and 'cementing' agents such as calcium and magnesium also assist in the formation of stable soil aggregates. Such soil aggregates resist the splash impact of raindrops (see Box 3.1) which, in the absence of soil structure, have the capacity to detach particles. Larger soil aggregates are more resistant to the detaching force of raindrops and their large size can increase the roughness of the ground which acts to slow down any water that is moving downslope (Greeves *et al.*, 2000).

Those factors that decrease the infiltration capacity of the soil promote the risk of surface runoff which in turn can transport detached soil particles and erode the soil. These factors include: fine textured soils, poorly structured soils, hard surficial crusting and very shallow soils. Additionally the presence of sub-surface impermeable layers can slow down and reduce the drainage of soil profiles and increase the risk of surface runoff (Greeves *et al.*, 2000).

Water erosion is a commonly reported problem and especially results when raindrops strike bare soil. Aggregates are broken down by raindrop splash and detached soil particles can be transported by overland flow in thin sheets (sheet wash) or result in rill (small channels) and gully (large deep channels) development. Soil conditions that increase the risk of water erosion include low soil organic matter, poor soil structure (no or very little aggregate development), fine texture (especially silt and fine sands) and the impeded infiltration of water.

Other factors include the length and steepness of slope and climatic factors. A critical aspect of climate is the amount, distribution, frequency and intensity of rainfall. Sudden heavy downpours on unvegetated, steep sloping, surfaces have considerable erosive potential.

Vegetation plays a significant role in protecting the land surface from erosion. Initially foliage dissipates the kinetic energy of raindrop impact and the resultant interception of rainfall means that less water hits the ground. Second, the root networks of vegetation stabilises the ground surface by binding soil, enhancing the infiltration capacity and adding organic matter, which contributes to the development of soil structure. Different vegetation types have different capacities to counter the erosion risk. Kirkby (1980) demonstrated that forest was best at protecting soils from erosion, although as Liddle (1997) points out, the degree of protection from erosion is dependent on canopy continuity and height as well as the density of root mats and groundcover density. Rain falling through an open canopy or dripping off tall trees can erode soil in the absence of ground cover (Liddle, 1997).

The Universal Soil Loss Equation (Box 3.1) developed in the USA to assess water erosion on agricultural lands has been applied in a recreation context by Kuss and Morgan (1984) and Morgan and Kuss (1986). The equation is used to predict soil loss based on an assessment of rainfall characteristics (e.g. high intensity rainfall), soil

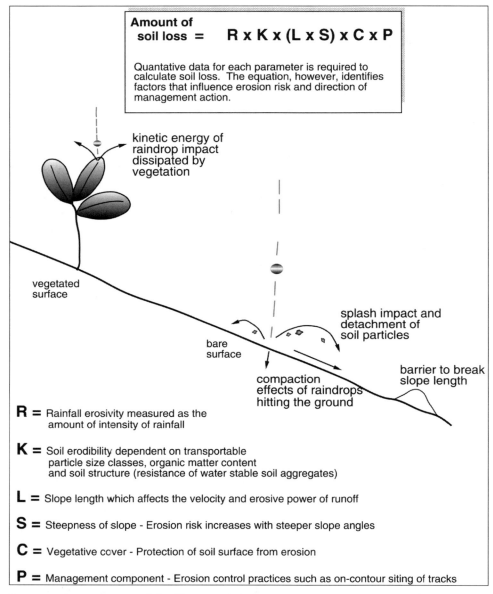

Amount of soil loss = R x K x (L x S) x C x P

Quantative data for each parameter is required to calculate soil loss. The equation, however, identifies factors that influence erosion risk and direction of management action.

kinetic energy of raindrop impact dissipated by vegetation

vegetated surface

splash impact and detachment of soil particles

bare surface

barrier to break slope length

compaction effects of raindrops hitting the ground

R = Rainfall erosivity measured as the amount of intensity of rainfall

K = Soil erodibility dependent on transportable particle size classes, organic matter content and soil structure (resistance of water stable soil aggregates)

L = Slope length which affects the velocity and erosive power of runoff

S = Steepness of slope - Erosion risk increases with steeper slope angles

C = Vegetative cover - Protection of soil surface from erosion

P = Management component - Erosion control practices such as on-contour siting of tracks

Box 3.1 Components of the Universal Soil Loss Equation. (Equation developed by Wischmeir & Smith, 1978)

erodibility (low organic matter, poor soil structure, sodic subsoils), slope characteristics (length and steepness), vegetation cover and land management factor (e.g.
cleared land).

Kuss and Morgan (1984) predicted that erosion, and thus a reduction in recreational carrying capacity, would occur if there was a decline to <70% of
groundcover under different forests and woodlands. Kuss *et al.* (1990) point out that
such an approach provides a basis for a interpreting the sensitivity of different soil
environments to degradation. Despite this, the applicability of this prediction
model outside of the USA has been significantly limited because of a lack of detailed
climate and soil data for many parts of the world.

Some soil environments are naturally fragile and easily damaged. Contributing
factors are aridity, very cold environments, shallow rocky soils, wet soils and new
substrates that become available for soil formation. For soil to develop, organic
matter needs to become mixed with the soil parent material (e.g. sand, coral debris,
volcanic ash). Disturbance and erosion result in the loss of organic matter and prevent
the accumulation of weathered soil and the development of a deeper soil profile.

Some soils take very long periods of time to develop especially when they are
developing from fresh rock as on the island of Hawaii (Figure 3.1). The colonisation
of such landscapes by vegetation is an essential process in gradually breaking rock
down as part of the soil formation pathway. Volcanic islands that have hostile
substrates, such as loose and friable lava, are subject to erosion damage from unre-
stricted hiking. Any damage to vegetation in these settings becomes significant
because of thin and poorly developed soils which do not allow the rapid colonisation of the landscape by vegetation. This in turn restricts the development of soil
that would eventually further promote the establishment of vegetation.

Soil formation is also a long process in arid and very cold environments. In the
Arctic tundra many soils are waterlogged during the brief summer period when
snow and ice melt. Wet soils tend to be soft and if trampled undergo rapid compaction. In temperate and tropical environments the compaction of wet soils results in
prolonged soil wetness which, if further trampling takes place, can result in a
permanent waterlogged trail or segment of pathway.

Arid landscapes are prone to wind erosion that occurs in situations of low soil
moisture, exposed surfaces and high wind speeds. Soils with a high content of silt or
fine sand are the most erodible. Situations where biological crusts are destroyed or
where off-road vehicles erode tracks into large networks can result in wind erosion
loss of organic matter, soil nutrients and reduce the depth of the soil profile (see p.
142 of this chapter under 'Biophysical Impacts'). The wind erodibility of arid and
semi-arid landscapes decreases as the size of the sand fraction and amount of clay in
the soil profile increases.

Access roads and trails

Roads and traffic

The major negative impacts frequently associated with roads and traffic include
clearing and road construction, sediment and pollutant runoff, weed invasion,

disturbance to wildlife due to noise and traffic and road kills (Figure 2.12). Roads however are an important means of access into and through natural areas and their ecological significance has been highlighted in Chapter 2, 'Landscape ecology', p. 45. Moreover, many species benefit from the presence of roads, especially generalist animals that are able to exploit the edge effect and in particular those plants that colonise open areas such as road verges.

In relation to wildlife related problems road mortality is generally recognised to be a significant issue. For example, in a study mostly carried out in the Organ Pipe Cactus National Park in the USA (Figure 3.1), Rosen and Lowe (1994) found that up to 4000 snakes were killed per 22.5 km of road per year. There was also evidence that certain species of snake were particularly affected.

In studies of the effects of roads on birds Kuitunen *et al.* (1998) point out that traffic induced mortality and road barrier effects are not significant as when compared to the mortality suffered by other vertebrates. Moreover a study carried out in Finland found that the edge effect created by roads favoured a number of species resulting in an increase in the breeding populations of birds (Jarvinen & Vaisanen, 1977).

Kuitunen *et al.* (1998), however, explored whether roads in central Finland impacted on the density of birds utilising roadside habitats. Their results showed that bird density was lower closer to highways. They considered that the reasons for such a decline could relate to traffic noise, gaseous pollutants from vehicles, some traffic-induced mortality and the road acting as a sink for predators. The role of traffic noise in disrupting defence of territories was considered to be the greatest problem for certain species. This conclusion is also supported by the findings of Reijen *et al.* (1995) who assert that noise is likely to be the most important factor in reducing bird densities close to roads.

The case with mammals is also a mix of positive and negative ecological impacts. For example, studies on the impacts of roads on the density, distribution and diversity of small mammals in the USA found that while five species did not prefer roadside habitats more species actually benefited from the presence of roads (Adams & Geis, 1983). In this case more generalist species were attracted to the edge effect caused by the road and that any road kills were not detrimental to small mammal populations.

The situation with larger mammals, however, is somewhat different, especially in the case of large carnivores. Gibeau and Heurer (1996) provide a useful summary of the issues surrounding large carnivore road mortality in North America. This work highlights the role of roads in causing direct mortality, displacement of species, barrier effects and as sinks for wildlife. Carnivores are particularly at risk because they have low reproduction rates, large territory and area requirements and low population densities. Table 3.1 shows road death data for six carnivores in and around Banff National Park, Canada (Figure 3.1). The high number of Coyote (*Canis latrans*) deaths results from the road acting as a sink with Coyotes being attracted to high densities of mice that occur in road edges. Gibeau and Heurer (1996) note these mortality figures are more typical of a harvested population rather than that of a

Table 3.1 Highway mortality of large carnivores in the Bow River Valley, Alberta, Canada 1985–1995

Species	Inside Banff National Park Highway	Outside Banff National Park Highway
Coyote	117	39
Black Bear	12	8
Cougar	1	2
Grizzly Bear	1	0
Wolverine	2	0
Lynx	0	4

Derived from Gibeau and Heuer, 1996

population occurring in a national park. Coyotes are also the fourth most killed mammal in Yellowstone National Park in the USA after Elk (*Cervus elaphus*), Mule Deer (*Odocoileus hemionus*) and Bison (*Bison bison*) respectively (Gunther *et al.*, 1998).

Although the figures for bear deaths are relatively low (Table 3.1) they are, in fact, significant because of the low populations of these animals in the park. Similarly the Cougar (*Felis concolor*) occurs at low population densities and has large home ranges within the park. Gibeau and Heurer (1996) also point out that, with Cougars, a road kill could result in the loss of the only male in a local breeding population. In contrast to Banff National Park road kills appear to be not as significant in Yellowstone National Park (Gunther *et al.*, 1998). Such differences may be due to a wide range of controlling features, such as road siting and configuration, vehicle speeds, pattern and extent of human visitation and ecological factors, illustrating the need to consider each case separately.

Road kills and the vegetation along quieter road edges are a source of food for Grizzly Bears (*Ursus arctos horribilis*). Roads, however, negatively impact on Grizzly Bears by acting as barriers, fragmenting habitats and reducing habitat effectiveness. Gibeau and Heurer (1996) reported on the low genetic diversity of Grizzly Bears in Banff National Park which in part can be attributed to and exacerbated by the barrier function of roads. Roadside fencing, which has been erected to reduce the road kill problem in Banff National Park, Canada, unfortunately is likely to enhance the barrier effect of roads by fragmenting existing populations of bears.

Many of the above problems occur on sealed roads but much recreation and tourism takes place in situations where access is only on unsealed roads and with the use of off-road vehicles. For example, four-wheel drive vehicles are often the only means of access into Arctic-alpine and many desert environments. Although off-road vehicle driving has the potential to cause damage in most environments its impact can be especially significant in situations where plants and animals are at the limits of tolerance to harsh environmental conditions. Accordingly the environmental impacts of off-road vehicle use, especially in sensitive areas, is explored as a case study later in this chapter.

Trails

Natural area tourism on land occurs mostly through corridors such as trails, pathways and sometimes informally along unsealed management tracks. Hiking trails form an important means of access and thus facilitate the recreational experience in many natural landscapes. Trails also serve to focus visitor attention, helping to prevent more dispersed and randomised soil erosion and trampling of vegetation. There is also an increasing demand for activity specific/combined trail use for horse riding and mountain bike (off-road bicycle) activities.

Leung and Marion (1999a) point out that the degradation of trail resources, through multiple treads, track widening, root exposure and soil erosion (track deepening) is an increasing problem worldwide. Monz (2000) notes that mountain regions throughout the world attract many hikers and are at risk of degradation due to steep slopes and harsh environmental conditions. Garland *et al.* (1985) reported that accelerated erosion from trails can be one of the most important biophysical impacts of visitors in wilderness areas. Trail erosion is now recognised as a major management issue and in addition to the localised problem of continuous erosion and unsafe trail conditions for users, there is the possibility of the wider problem of stream sedimentation in water catchment areas.

Weaver and Dale (1978) surveyed the complex relationships that determine trail degradation. These included the amount and type of recreational activity, steepness and roughness of slope, soil physical properties and moisture conditions, climate (rainfall characteristics) and vegetation type.

Environmental controls on trail degradation have been the subject of a review by Leung and Marion (1996) who presented a model containing climate, geology, user type and intensity of use as primary factors affecting trail degradation. Factors such as topography, soil, vegetation and user behaviour were identified as intermediate in importance. All these environmental factors would need to be taken into consideration in predicting and assessing trail degradation, particularly the widespread problem of soil erosion.

A study carried out by Wilson and Seney (1994) encapsulates many of the factors that need to be taken into account in understanding erosion on established trails. Wilson and Seney (1994) explored the relative impact of hikers, off-road bicycles, horse riding and motorcycles in the Gallatin Forest, Montana, USA (Figure 3.1). They found that horse riding and hiking caused more sediment loss than either off-road bicycles or motorcycles. In terms of environmental controls they confirmed soil erosion to be positively correlated with steepness of slope and where trails followed slope, rather than contour, water was readily channelled downhill. It was also stressed that sediment yield, the precursor to erosion, is detachment limited rather than transport limited. Thus the critical factor in initiating erosion is the ease with which soil particles are detached by the erosive force. Wilson and Seney (1994), however, like many previous authors, acknowledge that the complex interplay of rainfall events, soils, vegetation type and geomorphology often make it difficult to interpretate which is the most significant environmental control/s on trail erosion. Despite this difficulty Wilson and Seney

(1994) concluded that horses, by causing greater particle detachment, posed the greatest erosion risk and that sediment yield was greatest on prewetted trails. Moreover, of particular importance was the conclusion that these findings can be extrapolated to nearly all environments.

Many authors agree that horse riding causes the most damage to existing trails (eg. Dale & Weaver, 1974; Deluca et al., 1998). The high impact potential of horse riding is attributed to the large magnitude of stress imposed on the soil surface. A horse and rider can weigh up to 500 kg and the weight-bearing surface is concentrated on four steel horseshoes. The forces applied by horse hooves are much greater than that of hikers or tyres and horse traffic readily penetrates and deepens tracks. For example, Lull (1959) reported that horses exert a ground pressure of up to 2.8 kg/cm^2 as compared to 0.8 kg/cm^2 caused by hikers which was reported by Holmes and Dobson (1976).

The movement of horses along trails can be particularly effective in introducing exotic weed species into pristine environments. Weed species germinate from horse faeces in a ready supply of nutrients, and colonise the untrampled, disturbed edges of trails. The establishment of weed communities can, in the longer term, provide a source area for the invasion of exotic weeds into areas that experience natural disturbance events. Horses at the same time graze native species and can, in overnight stay and tethering areas, cause a reduction in the cover of vegetation.

Given the presence of existing trail degradation and the certain requirement for additional new trail networks in the future, the prediction and management of trail impacts lies in two main areas – trail condition assessment and path erosion risk assessment. Some of the latest perspectives on trail condition assessment can be found in Leung and Marion (2000) and Marion and Leung (2001) and are discussed further in Chapter 7.

In relation to the issue of developing trails and predicting user impacts the work of Garland (1990) provides a useful account of assessing the erosion risk from mountain trails in the Drakensberg Mountains, South Africa (Figure 3.1). Garland (1990) pointed out that access to the Drakensberg wilderness area is via thousands of kilometres of trails and that many of these trails are degraded by soil erosion. With the trend for greater use of trails and the high costs of rehabilitation Garland (1990) investigated a methodology for assessing the erosion risk before any new trails were opened up (Box 3.2).

Besides the erosion problem on existing trails there are a number of social issues that require mention. With increased visitation and usage of existing trails, and the public's requirement for a diversity of recreational experiences, user conflicts have arisen.

Research carried out in the Sierra National Forests, California, USA revealed that while 4% of horse riders disapproved of meeting hikers, some 36% of hikers did not like encounters with horses (Watson et al., 1994). Such findings are also mirrored by work recently carried out in Australia (Beeton, 1999).

The increasing use of off-road bicycles in the USA, Europe and Australia is also

Box 3.2 Assessing the erosion risk in the Drakensberg Mountains, South Africa

Garland (1990) built on previous research that had shown that the most important erosion risk parameters in trail erosion were rainfall, soil type and slope. Previous work by Garland (1988) had shown that hourly rainfall intensity correlated with soil losses from trails. In addition, 'the long term mean of the annual sum of all rain falling on the wettest day of each month' (MDR index) correlated strongly with levels of trail erosion.

The steepness of slope is a well-recognised factor in land stability and soil erosion. An assessment of the number of planned paths occupying various topographic slope classes (0–5°, 6–10°, 11–15°, etc) provides an indication of erosion risk. In order to assess the soil factor in trail erosion, soil maps and analytical data need to be available.

In the case of the Drakensberg Mountains, Garland (1987) showed surface runoff to be one of the most important causes of trail erosion in that it is the means by which detached particles can be moved. Soils which have different infiltration rates (see 'Soils', p. 91), as in the case of soils derived from the Karoo sediments and Drakensberg Basalts will be at differing risk of surface runoff during rainfall events. Furthermore, those soils, like the Drakensberg basaltic soils, which exhibit aggregate stability are more able to resist the pounding effect of hikers. These major risk factors in trail erosion were divided in to arbitrary classes and given scores (see Table 3.2). Despite its partially subjective nature Garland (1990) concluded that the method could be used in planning trail routes in the Drakensberg Mountains and flagged its applicability in other areas of extensive trail usage and development.

Table 3.2 Scores for erosion risk parameters

Score	MDR index (mm)	Lithology	Topographic slope (degrees)
1	<300	basalt/alluvium	<6
2	300–40	sediments/dolerite	6–10
3	401–500	–	11–15
4	501–600	–	16–20
5	>600	–	21–25
6	–	–	>25

Major land characteristics in each erosion risk class:

Class	Total score	Main characteristics
1 low risk	<4	sediments or dolerite only, sliping at <5°; MDR <300 mm
2 medium risk	4–6	any rock type; MDR <600 mm *and* slopes <20°
3 high risk	7–12	any rock type; MDR probably <400 mm and/or slopes probably >10°
4 very high risk	>12	any rock type; MDR >500 mm

Source: Garland, 1990

likely to cause similar problems. For example, in a recent appraisal of off-road bicycle user preferences, Goeft and Alder (2000) report that users of off-road bicycles prefer a variety of settings to cater for various degrees of riding difficulty, terrain and scenery. As in the case of horse rider–hiker conflicts most users of off-road bicycles preferred not to meet hikers or vehicles. Of particular interest were data collected from off-road bicycle users in Western Australia. When questioned as to how they perceived the impacts of off-road bicycles on trails most respondents did not agree that off-road bicycles caused damage. Given that there is a risk of impacts, such as soil erosion and that the use off-road bicycles frequently occurs in tandem with other recreational activities, these findings highlight the importance of education and interpretation (Chapter 6) in managing potential impacts.

Recent work by Kutiel *et al.* (2000) supports earlier findings by Weaver and Dale (1978) that motorcycles (trail bikes) effect a greater impact on vegetation than hikers. Nonetheless, in the majority of cases, motorcycle use of existing trails is not widespread but where allowed is more likely to cause noise and air pollution problems for other visitors and therefore user-conflict. Heavily used tracks are also likely to be subject to litter problems (see next section). This can be a particular problem for tourists visiting natural areas in those societies where the general public do not perceive littering to be an issue.

Use of built facilities and camp grounds

Environmental impacts associated with the construction and operation of built facilities

In many natural areas there is often a focus of intense visitation and impact such as a tourist resort, campground, picnic area or car park. Accommodation and shelter, in particular, provide continuous focal points of activity which range from simple overnight huts, campsites and caravan parks through to resort and hotel development (Buckley & Pannell, 1990).

The site clearance for a hotel complex may be substantial resulting in a complex node with corridors acting as sources of disturbance. This is particularly so if the development is situated entirely in a natural setting. More commonly, however, such developments are situated at the edge of a natural area/national park and form part of a modified/non-natural landscape matrix. Additionally, the widespread interest in beach areas has put coastal areas particularly at risk and mangrove systems, rocky shorelines and seagrass beds remain under threat from dredging, reclamation and the construction of boating facilities.

In many instances such planned developments would be subject to formal environmental impact assessment procedures as highlighted by Buckley *et al.* (2000). Ski resort development is a major issue in mountainous areas and the sorts of effects listed by Buckley *et al.* (2000) and others serve as a guide to the potential environmental impacts of tourist accommodation and resorts as well as their associated structures and facilities (Table 3.3). The degree and extent of any negative impacts, however, will depend on where the development is located, building design and adaptation to existing natural conditions, waste treatment systems, recycling and

Table 3.3 Environmental impacts of infrastructure and support facilities in the development of tourism

Activity	Possible impact
Land clearing	
Noise	Disturbance to wildlife
Light pollution at night	Disturbance to wildlife
Removal of vegetation	Loss of habitats Shift in species composition of area Smaller population of plants and animals Weed invasion Increased fragmentation of habitats.
Soil erosion	Soil loss Stream sedimentation and reduced water quality Sedimentation of coral reefs
Energy supply	Noise from generators Pollution from fumes and oil/reduced air quality Disturbance corridors
Water supply	Disturbance corridors Ground water abstraction/reduced water tables Construction of dams/disrupted stream flow
Waste disposal	Need for solid landfill or removal of waste off-site Liquid treatment facilities/odour, litter
Transportation infrastructure	
Roads	Nutrient, fertiliser, pesticide and oil run-off Road corridor impacts and noise from vehicles Barriers to animal movement
Airstrips	Noise
Boat landings	Damage to water margins

Derived from Buckley *et al.,* 2000

pattern of resource consumption as well as approaches to the recreational activities that take place in association with the development.

The permanent nature of hotel and resort type developments clearly also require access roads, ongoing water and energy supply plus waste disposal facilities. Infrastructure supply corridors frequently require regular maintenance and their open nature constitute disturbance corridors, especially where they occur in a natural landscape matrix. Electricity supply from generators creates semi to permanent sources of noise and the use of wood for fuel can result in coarse woody debris being taken from the surrounding natural environment. This latter issue can be particularly acute under conditions of poverty in mountainous environments where woody vegetation is already being removed for fuel. The provision of mountain village accommodation for travellers can put increasing stress on already depleted mountain forest resources.

Tourist facilities built in remote locations may also use local groundwater instead of scheme water piped from dams. The intensive use of groundwater supplies in more arid environments can result in water table draw down which in turn can result in the death of vegetation. Any loss of vegetation, such as trees, constitutes a major impact on the biotic environment. Water and power supply can also be a critical issue in island settings (Gajraj, 1988). Jackson (1986) reports that, historically, several Caribbean islands experienced water and power shortages that were directly attributable to tourist demand exceeding capacity. At the time it was estimated that the average tourist used twice the amount of water of local people.

As already noted (Table 3.3) various forms of environmental pollution can arise from the operation of permanent built facilities. This can range from visual pollution in the form of badly sited or designed hotels or ski complexes, solid and liquid waste disposal through to the ill-considered use of pesticides to control insect nuisance. The use of insecticides may be substantial in termite damage and malaria risk zones and can particularly impact on bird populations through direct acute toxicity or by the concentration of toxic compounds along food chains.

A major issue, however, is that of waste disposal and its effects and significance depend on the volumes produced, the application of recycling, waste prevention strategies and the nature of the receiving environment. The problem of waste disposal falls into the two main categories of solid and liquid wastes. Solid waste tips, depending on their location, typically attract opportunistic and scavenging birds such as gulls, crows, kites and vultures. Increased numbers of aggressive species like gulls have the capacity to displace and predate local populations of resident species. This has been reported from islands along the Great Barrier Reef where Silver Gulls (*Larus novaehollandiae*) predate the eggs and chicks of the Crested Tern (*Sterna bergia*) thus the breeding population of the terns is impacted upon by gulls attracted to tourist sites (Edington & Edington, 1986).

In a survey of the activity of animals around solid waste dumps Edington and Edington (1986) found that the presence of wildlife constituted two main problems for humans. The first comprises a direct threat to tourists from large and powerful species as in the case of Black (*Ursus americanus*) and Grizzly Bears (*Ursus arctos horribilis*) being attracted to refuse in the USA park system. Polar Bears (*Ursus maritimus*) are also considered to be a threat where tourism occurs in the Arctic region.

The second issue is that of disease transmission through the activity of gulls, rats and flies. Gulls in particular are attracted to refuse tips and can transmit disease when they also congregate at tourist sites such as picnic and bathing areas. Iveson and Hart (1983) demonstrated that wildlife can be a reservoir for diseases and reported the occurrence of Salmonella in mammals, birds, reptiles and frogs on Rottnest Island, Western Australia (Figure 3.1).

Edington and Edington (1986) have described the role of rats in transmitting Weil's disease. Rats transmit the pathogen *Leptospira icterohaemorrhagiae* which can enter water through rat urine. They also note that this becomes an issue where refuse tips are in close proximity to swimming areas. Refuse tips can also become

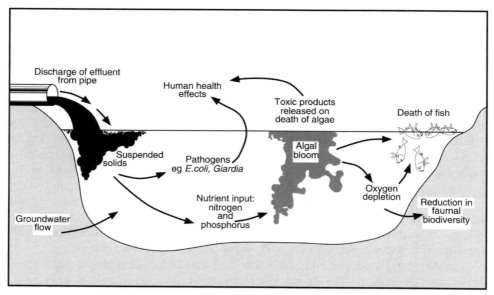

Figure 3.9 Conceptual diagram of the effects of sewage pollution in freshwater ecosystems

breeding sites for flies and mosquitoes and increased populations of these animals increases the risk of insect-borne disease.

Liddle (1997) has reported on the disposal of liquid wastes in recreational settings. Sewage enters natural areas from tourist developments, boats, chemical toilets and buried faeces. The general effects of sewage pollution in freshwater ecosystems are summarised in Figure 3.9. The relative impact of sewage disposal depends on volumes discharged, the degree of treatment, dilution factor and flushing regime of the water body. Those areas with poor flushing regimes, enclosed lakes and small bodies of water will be more susceptible. Moreover oligotrophic lakes, which have naturally low concentrations of nitrogen and phosphorus, are particularly at risk of ecological damage from organic effluent.

The changes that occur as a result of sewage entering rivers and lakes include increased levels of suspended solids and nutrients and decreases in the oxygen content of the water. These changes in abiotic factors provide different conditions for micro-organisms and invertebrates. The increased levels of nutrients give rise to dramatic increases in algal biomass and the resultant intense metabolic activity reduces the oxygen content of the water. Deoxygenation of rivers and lakes results in the death of fish and those invertebrates that are unable to tolerate low oxygen conditions. In severe cases of pollution only tolerant species, such as sewage fungus, tubifex worms and chironimid larvae can survive.

In marine settings the major risk is in the contamination of bathing areas by pathogens and the degradation of coral reef systems. Liddle (1997) points out that marine systems differ from freshwater environments in terms of water chemistry (often naturally low levels of phosphorus and nitrogen), the larger volume of water and in the presence of tidal cycles and wave action. Sewage impacts are much more pronounced where there is reduced flushing and the residence time of nutrients is measured in days or weeks. Various authors have documented organic pollutant damage to coral reefs as reflected by declines in species richness, a reduction in the size of coral colonies and significant decreases in coral cover (Liddle, 1997).

As reported by Morrison and Munroe (1999) the management of wastes is a critical issue in many island settings. Many islands around the world have already established tourism industries and others are developing. These same countries are faced with aesthetic impacts as well as land and water contamination problems arising from waste generation and its disposal. Both landfill (groundwater contamination, windblown debris, smoke and dust) and the management of wastewater varies from country to country. In the latter case treatment varies from effective facilities through to overloaded and outdated systems such as septic tanks and open latrines which pose the risk of disease.

Camping and campsites

Camping is one of the most popular of all recreational activities. Various workers have shown that, because of its highly concentrated use, camping has the capacity to result in significant localised effects which include impacts on soils, vegetation, wildlife, riparian zones, as well as social impacts (Cole, 1990b; Hammitt & Cole, 1998; Huxtable, 1987; Kuss *et al.*, 1990).

Litter and the disposal of human waste, in particular, comprise social and health issues and can impact on wildlife. Discarded items in the form of cigarette butts, food wrappings, drink cans, plastic cups and food debris are often a feature of moderately to heavily used trails and camping areas. Wild animals may eat or become entangled/trapped in discarded materials and subsequently die.

Because natural area tourism is clearly about appreciating nature under natural conditions, visitor experience can be spoilt by the presence of litter. Two recent studies demonstrate this. For example, 34% of visitors to Bako National Park, Sarawak (Figure 3.1) rated litter around the park as a serious problem (Chin *et al.*, 2000). In a study of recreation impacts in the Nuyts Wilderness in Western Australia (Figure 3.1) 71% of respondents rated the amount of litter as an extremely to very important factor in influencing the quality of their experience (Morin *et al.*, 1997).

Morin *et al.* (1997) also found that the inadequate disposal of human waste was rated to be extremely to very important (68% of respondents) or moderately important (15% of respondents) in affecting the quality of visitor experience. Human waste also poses a health risk as shown by the work of Temple *et al.* (1982). In the absence of pit toilets campers bury their faeces in shallow pits. Temple *et al.* (1982) demonstrated that pathogenic bacteria were able to survive in large numbers for several months and that *Salmonella* survived the northern hemisphere winter period. Areas without toilet facilities and with a high visitation rate are likely to have a high proportion of pits containing buried faeces in the vicinity of the campground. The long-term survival of bacteria also poses the threat of water contamination if such pits are located close to a water body.

Ongerth *et al.* (1995) examined the contamination of water by pathogens originating from human faeces in the Olympic Mountains National Park, USA (Figure 3.1). Their study sites comprised two remote pristine watersheds in which hiking and river-bank camping occurred. Ongerth *et al.* (1995) found that the more heavily used Hoh River had 1–3 *Giardia* cysts / 100 ml of water as compared to the much less intensively used Queets River which had 0.2–1 *Giardia* cysts / 100 ml of water. The presence of coliforms also peaked in accordance with human activity. Coliform bacteria were most abundant following the summer peak of tourist activity. The data also illustrate the importance of regional environmental conditions in influencing the numbers of bacteria. For example, the Queets River had only about five people / river km / month, but the faecal coliform count was as high as in the Hoh River which had around 70 people / river km / month. This relationship is explained by the latter river having lower water temperatures and higher stream flow than the Queets River.

The more obvious impacts on soil and vegetation are summarised in Figures 3.7 and 3.10. The overall biophysical problem is mostly soil compaction and damage to vegetation resulting in bare areas and changes in the composition of vegetation in and around campsites. Clearly where formal campsites occur there will be a permanent cleared area. Such areas are often hardened and can contain facilities such as fire rings and vehicle parking bays. Under these conditions the intensive use zone constitutes a permanent camping area of cleared vegetation. This can be contrasted with less frequently used and informal campsites. In these latter cases the impacts on soils and vegetation become much more of an issue especially where the camping takes place in 'pristine' riparian and fragile natural environments (see 'Use of water edges', p. 111).

Besides damage to soils and vegetation there is also the potential for disturbance to wildlife (see 'The observation of wildlife', p. 124). Wildlife can, however, be disturbed indirectly by camping activities through the activity of firewood collection. Dead wood or coarse woody debris is an important structural component and functional element in forested ecosystems and wholly or partly forms the habitat for a range of forest inhabiting organisms (Freedman *et al.*, 1996). Thus while soil compaction and damage to vegetation may not be a direct issue at permanent, hardened sites the collection of firewood could be. Firewood collection and secondary access track development are a feature of nearly all campsites. Informal access pathways are created when people need to excrete, search for firewood and access 'honeypot sites'. Although many permanent (official) campsites have toilets, designated tracks, and wood supplies provided to reduce the zone of impact the problem of firewood collection remains and deserves special mention. Accordingly this is discussed as a separate issue in the following sub-section.

Given that recreational demand for campsites continues to grow, the environmental impacts of camping are likely to increase in the future. Such a trend places importance on the assessment and monitoring of these impacts (Farrell & Marion,

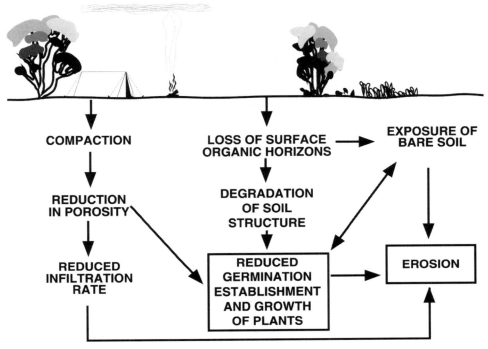

Figure 3.10 Campsite impacts on soils and ultimate effects on vegetation

2001; Leung & Marion, 2000). The work of Cole (1992) and Marion (1995) has especially set the scene for investigating campsite impacts in the heavily used and popular recreation/tourist sites in the USA. The major concerns for the future will involve expansion of formal campsites and the degradation of soils and vegetation at informal campsites.

Data need to be collected that provide resource managers with information relating to the design, location, management and campground rehabilitation requirements. For example, Smith (1998) found that although only about 1% of Warren National Park, Australia (Figure 3.1) had been impacted by camping this was a significant influence on visitor experience. When combined with walk trails and access tracks ecological and social impacts also become relevant, especially at the severely impacted designated campsites. Approaches to investigating campsite impacts (using examples from Africa, Australia and the USA) are therefore considered in more detail in Chapter 7.

Firewood collection

Both Cole (1990b) and Liddle (1997) have noted that where campfires are allowed there is a gradual depletion of coarse woody debris in the surrounding area. This activity can extend well beyond the immediate camping area. Such firewood gathering activities result in additional trampling, the creation of informal trails, an

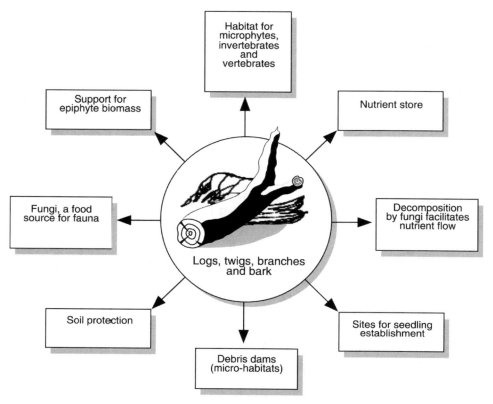

Figure 3.11 Ecological significance of coarse woody debris in forested ecosystems

extended zone of disturbance to wildlife and ecological impacts arising from the loss of coarse woody debris (CWD). Because of the work highlighting the importance of CWD in forested and other ecosystems our intention here focuses on the possible ecological impacts arising from CWD removal in campsite situations.

Harmon *et al.* (1986), for example, provide a comprehensive overview of the ecological significance of CWD in temperate ecosystems. Their extensive work on the subject includes amounts, decomposition and distribution of CWD. The ecological role of CWD is then described in terms of plant and animal habitats, nutrient cycling and geomorphic function. Some of the most significant functions that can be impacted by firewood collecting are depicted in Figure 3.11. Accordingly Harmon *et al.* (1986) point out that the removal of CWD is likely to result in ecosystem simplification leading in turn to a reduction in biotic structure and ecosystem function. Loss of CWD also results in the loss of habitats (shelter and food) provided by CWD, which in turn may lead to a reduction in local area biodiversity.

In the face of sustained and increased levels of camping activity, managers of natural area tourism need to understand the degree of firewood gathering impact and assess its significance. Firewood collection for campfires and recreational BBQs is widespread and a particular problem in Australia despite the fact that many recreation sites have electric or gas BBQ facilities (Box 3.3). Huxtable (1987) in a study of firewood gathering impacts at campsites in Innes National Park, South Australia, found that impacts extended well into the adjoining vegetation where there was a reduction in CWD and increased levels of tree damage.

Box 3.3 Assessing the loss of coarse woody debris around campsites in Warren National Park, Western Australia

As part of the campsite study carried out in Warren National Park, Western Australia, Smith (1998) also set out to obtain an overview of the firewood-gathering problem. The amount of CWD at each campsite was assessed using an adapted form of the line intersect technique (Figure 3.12) of Smith & Neal (1993) and Van Wagner (1968). CWD was categorised according to diameter classes of 25–70 mm, 70–300 mm, 300–600 mm and >600 mm. Quantities of CWD were determined at both the formal and informal campsites and in adjacent control areas. For CWD <70 mm diameter formal campsites recorded 93% less CWD than the control sites. Informal sites had 58% less CWD (Figure 3.13). The data also revealed that for CWD >70 mm diameter formal campsites recorded CWD at a level 64% lower than the control sites. Informal sites had 27% less CWD (Figure 3.13). This data was evident despite the gratis provision of firewood by park management and the possible complicating factor of natural/prescribed fire regimes. Smith (1998) concluded that the removal of CWD in the size class <70 mm diameter constitutes less of an ecological impact than the removal of larger size classes. This is likely to be due to the reduced water holding capacity, smaller nutrient store and reduced habitat potential relative to that afforded by CWD >70 mm diameter.

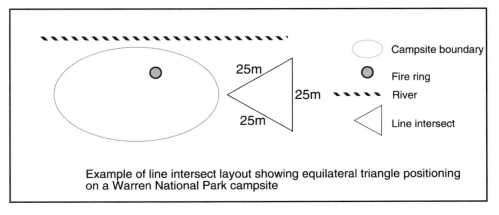

Example of line intersect layout showing equilateral triangle positioning on a Warren National Park campsite

Figure 3.12 Methodology applied in assessing the loss of coarse woody debris from campsites in Warren National Park, Western Australia. (Derived from Smith, 1998)

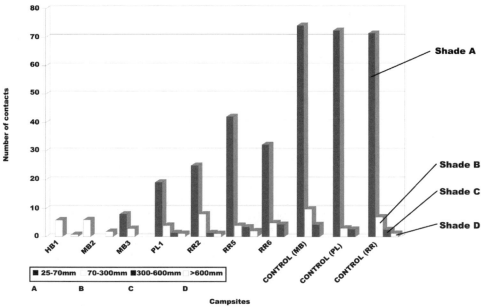

Number of contacts by diameter class for campsites at Warren National Park

Figure 3.13 Relative abundance of coarse woody debris at campsites in Warren National Park, Western Australia. (Derived from Smith, 1988)

In a study of the importance of CWD as fauna habitat Hecnar and M'Closkey (1998) investigated the effects of human disturbance on the Five-lined Skink (*Eumeces fasciatus*) at Point Pelee National Park, Canada (Figure 3.1). It was found that in areas of heavy human usage there was a corresponding lack of CWD and a reduced abundance of skinks. Because the skinks prefer to use large, but moderately decayed logs as habitat, the removal / accelerated disintegration of this CWD impacts on the skinks. An experiment in microhabitat restoration was conducted in which CWD was placed in areas in which previously there had been no CWD. Despite the presence of human disturbance the reptiles colonised the 'new' CWD. The experiment showed that the presence of large sized CWD was critical habitat for the skinks. Hecnar and M'Closkey (1998) also suggested that such CWD is also likely to be of benefit to at least eight other small vertebrates and a much larger number of invertebrates.

The above work is important in demonstrating that small vertebrates are dependent on the structure and invertebrate food (biotic factors) sources afforded by the microhabitat qualities of large size CWD. The extent to which rare and endangered invertebrates, other vertebrates, such as birds, and larger vertebrates (as in food chain relationships) are dependent on CWD in various different ecosystems remains to be demonstrated. The discussion presented here, however, strongly indicates that the removal of CWD for burning and other reasons is likely to lead to ecological impact.

Use of water edges

River banks

When utilising aquatic ecosystems, such as rivers and lakes, tourism and recreational activity can be more dispersed than in the well-defined 'confined' situation of a campground or walking trail. Despite this, there remains the tendency for visitor activity to be concentrated at specific sites or edges especially near beaches and at the most accessible parts of lakes and rivers. With rivers and lakes, the riparian zone, frequently consisting of specific plant communities, marks the interface between land and water. The importance of riparian vegetation lies in its protective function and through the influence of fringing vegetation on aquatic fauna.

Natural river channels demonstrate a balance between bank erosion and the deposition of sediment where the velocity of water flow decreases. Malanson (1993) reported on the protective function of riparian vegetation. The riparian fringe confers channel stability, especially under the erosive potential of flood conditions, and through root systems binding river bank sediments. The presence of river bank vegetation reduces the tractive force of water through sediment trapping and thus facilitates sedimentation. Malanson (1993) also considered the role of riparian vegetation in attenuating pollutants by trapping sediments with attached pollutants and intercepting nutrients, such as nitrogen, which may be transported by a river or stream.

The riparian fringe often also sits within a broader ecosystem context. Examples of this include river channels in the forested ecosystems of the USA, rivers running through savannah ecosystems in Africa and the intermittent flow river networks that occur in semi-arid Australia. In more arid settings the presence of fringing vegetation often constitutes important and prime habitat due to the presence of large trees, in an essentially treeless environment, in association with permanent pools of water that allow both aquatic and terrestrial organisms to survive the dry season. In this latter case such refugia pools remain cooler and receive additional inputs of organic matter when shaded by large trees. The shading, litter deposition, provision of CWD, river and terrestrial habitat function of riparian vegetation has also been reported by Hammitt & Cole (1998) and Kuss *et al.* (1990).

Tourism and recreation activities that take place along river banks and amongst riparian vegetation include accessing viewpoints, fishing, boat launching, camping and access for wading, tube floating and swimming. The major impacts arising from this are trampling and destruction of the line of riparian vegetation, loss of vegetation, bank erosion and pollution.

A consistent problem is trampling along the banks of rivers resulting in changes to and loss of vegetation. Depletion in the protective function of vegetation can lead to bank erosion. Such problems have been reported from Yosemite National Park (Figure 3.1) by Madej *et al.* (1994) who investigated bank erosion on the Merced

River. Madej *et al.* (1994) used historical photographs, air photograph interpretation and measurements of channel width and bank erosion to investigate river bank impacts. There was a strong association between poor bank stability and recreational activity. For example, bank erosion was significant in campground areas. One study area had more than 1000 camping sites located within 500 m of the river.

Smith (1998) also demonstrated the impacts on riparian vegetation resulting in erosion that was associated with river bank campsites (Plate 3.2). Trail networks leading from campsites to and along the Warren River showed severe bank erosion as a result of the loss of riparian vegetation (Table 3.4).

The loss of riparian vegetation also results in ecological impacts through diminished shading leading to increased water temperatures, reduced inputs of organic matter as sources of energy for aquatic organisms and increases in turbidity which may lead to changes in the populations of invertebrates and fish (Cole & Landres, 1995; Hammitt & Cole, 1998). Aspects of pollution from human wastes have already been dealt with earlier in this section.

Rivers, lakes and reservoirs

Recreation and tourism that focuses on rivers and lakes includes boating, sailing, swimming and bank/shoreline activities. Impacts on the riparian zone have already been considered and largely involve the destruction of fringing vegetation and bank erosion. Even the dry lake beds of inland salt lakes such as those that occur in semi-arid and arid Australia are not free of potential damage. When dry, visitors can cross them in vehicles leaving tyre scars and damaged shoreline vegetation at entry and exit points. This section, however, focuses mainly on the effects of boating activities on bodies of freshwater and draws from a comprehensive review undertaken by Mosisch and Arthington (1998) who provide a systematic discussion of the impacts of power boating on lakes and reservoirs.

Mosisch and Arthington (1998) divide the impacts caused by power boating into physical disturbances (wave action, turbidity, direct boat contact, noise and visual disturbance), chemical effects (various forms of pollution) and ecological impacts. Major physical impacts include the erosional effects of wave action on river banks and lake shorelines. According to Liddle and Scorgie (1980) waves and ripples generated by boats wash out the roots of emergent macrophytes and riparian vegetation. Many authors agree that this destabilises the bank and leads to bank erosion that then leads to a further decrease in vegetation.

Liddle (1997) notes that aquatic plants differ in their sensitivity to erosional impact. Data collected mostly in Europe showed that soft leaved species such as *Elodea canadensis* and *Rorippa amphibia* were very easily eroded; species such as *Potamogeton crispus* and *Sparganium emersum* were more difficult to erode with larger, tougher, more robust *Phalaris arundinacea* and *Phragmites communis* being the most difficult to erode. Poorly vegetated, exposed banks are particularly subject to direct erosional effects. These effects can also be caused by the destructive action of direct contact of boats with shoreline and river bank vegetation.

Direct contact also takes place in the form of propeller action that can cut and

Table 3.4 Mean width, depth, distance and erosion of main river bank access trails from campsites at Warren National Park, Western Australia

Campsite	Mean width (cm)	Mean depth (cm)	Distance (m)	Root exposure	Bank collapse	Gully development
HB1	191.0	55.0	6.2	Severe	Severe	Severe
MB2		Not applicable		Severe	Severe	Severe
MB3	209.4	86.0	15.5	Severe	Severe	Severe
PL1	69.7	0.7	37.9	Low	Negligible	Negligible
PL2	61.0	Flat	19.3	Low	Negligible	Negligible
PL3	63.0	6.8	15.5	Low	Low	Low
RR1	111.7	Flat	13.7	Negligible	Negligible	Negligible
RR2	180.1	Flat	14.3	Negligible	Negligible	Negligible
RR3	66.8	20.0	3.3	Moderate	Mild	Low
RR4	96.0	6.8	7.5	Low	Mild	Low
RR5	96.1	1.0	7.5	Moderate	Mild	Low
RR6	120.0	20.0	4.1	Low	Mild	Mild

Derived from Smith (1998).

Plate 3.2 Bank erosion showing scalloping, root exposure and loss of riparian vegetation adjacent to campsites in Warren National Park, Western Australia. (*Photo*: Amanda Smith)

damage macrophytes and disturb benthic organisms by stirring up sediment. Turbidity is caused by the stirring up and suspension of sediments in the water column. This can introduce nutrients stored on sedimentary particles into the water column and, depending on other limiting factors, give rise to an algal bloom. Continuous turbidity, nevertheless, obstructs light from reaching phytoplankton and can reduce algal productivity and limit the growth of submerged macrophytes. High levels of turbidity can also clog the gills of invertebrates and fish and reduce the feeding efficiency and food resources of fish-eating birds (Murphy *et al.*, 1995).

In their account of the biological impacts of power boating Mosisch and Arthington (1998) note that different species of fish appear to differ in their tolerance of the suspension and redeposition of fine particles. Power-boat activity has been recorded to cause some fish to leave nest guard duties leaving eggs at risk of predation. The stirring up of river and lake-bed sediments can also kill fish eggs. Murphy *et al.* (1995) report that fish populations can be reduced as a result of disrupted courtship and spawning and declines in the viability of fish eggs.

Recreational boating activity can also result in the spread of aquatic weed species as a result of propagules and fragments of vegetation being held on boat attachments such as propellers. In this way weed species can be transported from one lake to another. Johnstone *et al.* (1985), who investigated 107 lakes in New Zealand, found that the occurrence of five aquatic weeds could be traced back to recreational boating activity. The proliferation of weed species has the potential to alter ecological conditions and impact of the recreational value of a lake.

A number of studies have shown that the noise generated by boating causes water birds to seek refuge elsewhere on quieter stretches of water. At the same time visual effects and boat movement can also be important. In a study of the impacts of sailing on water birds utilising the Brent Reservoir in England (Figure 3.1) Batten (1977) observed that birds either temporarily left the site or congregated in refuge areas where sailing was not taking place. The importance of water bodies for over-wintering birds is also highlighted by Batten (1977) who found that Teal (*Anas crecca*) and Wigeon (*Anas penelope*) had stopped using the site as a winter refuge. The significance of such disturbance lies in the availability of other water bodies, quiet refuge areas and the intensity of recreational use. Tuite *et al.* (1984) note that local and short-term disturbance may cause changes in the distribution of birds and even more significant changes may occur at intensively used recreation sites (power boating and water skiing activities). The situation, however, can be ameliorated by the widespread occurrence of inland water bodies and reserved areas. In the UK the mobility of ducks and the fact that only low levels of recreational activity generally take place during the important over-wintering period also serve to reduce the level of impact.

Activities that lead to the disturbance of wildlife ranges from sailing and windsurfing, power boating and the use of jet skis through to tour boat visits to areas of wildlife occurrence. In relation to tour boat visitation Galicia and Baldassarre (1997) studied the effects on American Flamingos (*Phoenicopterus ruber ruber*) in the Celestun Estuary, Mexico. The Celestun Estuary is a coastal lagoon which lies parallel to the coastline in the north-western part of the Yucatan Peninsula (Figure 3.1). It is a biosphere reserve and a major site for one of the non-breeding populations of the American Flamingo. Tour boats carried 7488 tourists in 1992–3 and averaged 16 boat-viewing trips per day.

Activity budgets of both disturbed and undisturbed birds were assessed. Tour boat visits were seen to significantly increase alert time, but reduce the feeding time from 40% to 24% which translated into a loss of some 30 minutes feeding time per individual per day. Galicia and Baldassarre (1997) noted that on days of exceptional tourist visits (97 tour boats) feeding activity may be halted altogether. The biological significance of these findings relates to the possible impacts of reduced feeding time on the breeding activity of the flamingos. For example, if time spent in courtship reduces feeding time then flamingos need to acquire sufficient food reserves before such activity. An additional aspect of this study was the distribution of flamingos according to food supply in the estuary and that boat traffic could reduce their access to optimal feeding areas. Such impacts are additional sources of stress and may cause the decline of an important population of flamingos as well as threaten the viability of an important tourism resource.

The pollution of rivers and lakes is a consequence of boating activities and occurs mainly in the form of contamination from oils and fuel combustion products and in the liberation of motor exhaust fumes. Mosisch and Arthington (1998) report that between 380 and 600 million litres of outboard motor fuel are discharged into waters each year; how the oils and fuel enter the water and their chemistry are detailed in their review. Environmental impacts consist of reduced water quality through hydrocarbon contamination, the accumulation of pollutants (e.g. lead) in sediments, slicks of lubricating oils on the surface of the water and the deposition of unburnt oil on algae.

The presence of potentially carcinogenic hydrocarbons such as polynuclear aromatic hydrocarbons has been reported to correlate with peak power boating activity by Mastran *et al.* (1994). Contamination by these and other hydrocarbons has been found to be toxic to invertebrates and fish (citations in Mosisch & Arthington, 1998).

Coastal areas

Coastlines, consisting of beaches, mangroves, salt marshes, mud flats and rock pools, attract many people who engage in a variety of activities ranging from the typical 'beach holiday' through to more natural history centred activities such as searching rock pools and birdwatching on estuaries. Recreational fishing and the excessive collection of shells and organisms from rock pools can lead to a local depletion in fauna and faunal resources. Remote area coastlines that have only off-road vehicle access can attract the more adventurous tourist but this can also lead to the damage of important coastal ecosystems. This has been reported for the unique tropical arid climate, mangrove systems which occur along the north-west (Pilbarra) coast of Western Australia (Figure 3.1). In this area Gordon (1987) reports on the erosion of salt flats, destruction of algal mats and the restricted movement of tidal water as a result of recreational off-road vehicle activity.

The most significant issue in coastal tourism, however, is access to and use of beaches. Beaches are naturally dynamic systems and change according to tidal fluctuation. They are also subject to seasonal variations in sediment removal, transport and deposition. Beach sand is mobilised during stormy periods when the sea both moves the sand offshore as well as it being blown landward by strong winds. During calm conditions sand is mostly deposited on the beach, where onshore winds blow it inland to be trapped by vegetation to form sand dunes.

Sand dunes do not form where onshore winds are relatively weak as in the case of equatorial tropical beaches. In many parts of the world, however, strong onshore winds are a feature of the coastal environment and in some places extensive dune systems can develop as in the case of south-west Western Australia. In these cases the foredune systems act as a reservoir of sand and buffer against the penetration of erosive activity further inland. Coastal dune systems, however, are easily disrupted. Any disturbance to the natural cycling of sand has the capacity to alter the shape and position of a sandy shoreline. In particular the removal of vegetation can lead to the development of localised pockets of foredune erosion called blowouts, which reduces buffering capacity and can lead to the erosion of and transportation of sand further inland.

Recreational use of motorcycles and beach buggies and pedestrian access can destabilise coastal dune systems especially in cases where access is uncontrolled and a network of multiple access tracks develops. The resultant bare areas become focal points of erosion and blowouts can develop. Headlands can be especially susceptible due to the continuous presence of strong winds. Here the loss of sand can result in the exposure of underlying rocks.

Beach erosion that leads to the subsequent burial of once stable vegetation communities constitutes a major change in ecological conditions. Extensive burial of fixed dune vegetation can re-set the beach successional process in that only those species tolerant of burial will be able to survive and the new vegetation will approximate that of a foredune community. Such a loss of the fixed dune vegetation becomes especially significant if it contains rare and endangered species or critical habitat.

Sand dune systems are only poorly developed or absent from most humid tropical environments. In many of these areas, however, the beach itself is a critical habitat as they are used as breeding sites for turtles and seabirds. A combination of hunting for food and habitat degradation has decimated many turtle populations and viable nesting habitat is essential for their survival. There has been a widespread loss of turtle breeding beaches in the tropics and Mediterranean region encompassing North Africa and southern Europe. Poland *et al.* (1996) note that tourism comprising hotel sprawl, light pollution, human activity and obstacles on the beach and even building sand castles is a major threat to already stressed and reduced turtle populations on the Greek island of Zakynthos (Figure 3.1).

Many turtle egg-laying beaches have also become tourist attractions in their own right. For example, Tortuguero National Park in Costa Rica (Figure 3.1) hosts one of the largest nesting areas for the Green Turtle (*Chelonia mydas*) in the world. The impacts of tourism, as observed by Jacobson and Lopez (1994), on turtles at Tortuguero consisted of light disturbance from torches and flash photography, touching and blocking the progress of turtles, digging and movement around nests and the trampling and handling of hatchlings. The interruption of turtle activity also caused turtles to return to the sea without laying.

Jacobson and Lopez (1994) investigated the impacts of night-time viewing on the nesting activity of turtles. Data was collected on the number of turtle arrivals and nesting attempts along 7 km of beach. The amount of successful nesting activity was recorded and the data was then compared between low and high tourist activity zones. It was found that at times of high tourist concentration (weekends) 30% less turtles visited the beach. At the same time Jacobson and Lopez (1994) found that specific turtle behaviour such as successful nesting and females returning to the sea without nesting did not differ between the high and low tourist activity zones. A reduction in total nesting activity over time, however, could have repercussions for this turtle population.

Bathing, swimming and boating comprise major activities in coastal environments around the world. A number of studies have shown that these also carry potential impacts and can pose a risk for recreationists and tourists (e.g. see Liddle, 1997). A combination of sunbathing, picnicking and swimming can result in litter and human wastes which in turn can lead to water contamination. Contamination of water also takes place in the form of suntan oils, sun-screens, soaps and bacteria derived from human skin. Liddle (1997) cites several studies (e.g. Cabelli *et al.*, 1982) that demonstrate increased levels of pathogenic organisms and the risk of water-borne disease resulting from water-based recreation.

As discussed earlier, in the context of lakes, various boating activities and water sports can disturb wildlife. In the marine environment injuries to sea mammals can occur when an animal is suddenly surprised at the surface of the water by boats. The use of power-boats and water sport activities can increase the mortality of resident fauna as demonstrated by injuries to turtles in the Greek Islands and manatees in Puerto Rico (Mignucci-Giannoni *et al.*, 2000; Poland *et al.*, 1996). As already noted, motorised water sports produce noise and exhaust fumes. Furthermore, there is also the potential for the accidental release of oil and petrol and chemical pollution emanating from the weathering of anti-fouling paints.

Indirect impacts on marine wildlife can occur as a result of beach recreation and tourism. For example, the protection of popular Australian and South African swimming beaches with shark nets results in the death of many species of sharks and other vertebrate species. Sharks are declining worldwide and because of low fecundity have a slow capacity for recovery. Liddle (1997) shows data from various sources on the entanglement and mortality of large sharks, dolphins and small whales, birds, six species of turtle and large fish such as rays. In a number of cases such deaths are increasing the mortality of already depleted and stressed populations

Coral reefs

Some background to coral reef ecosystems and an account of some early work has already been covered in Chapter 2. This section follows on from this and provides further details on how recreation and tourism can damage coral reef ecosystems. Liddle and Kay (1987) employed several experiments in order to study the relative susceptibility to damage, survival and recovery of corals to reef walking on the Great Barrier Reef, Australia (Figure 3.1). It was found that the branching coral *Acropora millepora* was the least resistant to breakage and most resistance was offered by *Acropora palifera*. A study of trampling on the non-branching massive coral *Porites lutea* showed damage accumulated over time depending on how much trampling took place. Liddle and Kay (1987) also reported that corals differ in terms of survival and recovery from trampling impacts. The highest recovery rates were reported for *Acropora millepora*. Their work clearly established that the branching corals are more susceptible to damage and that some species are slower to recover than others.

Snorkelling also has the potential to impact on reef condition. Allison (1996), in a study carried out on Kaafu Atoll, a resort in the Maldives (Figure 3.1), found that remote parts of the reef were in good condition but coral breakage was apparent in the vicinity of a well-used snorkelling channel. There was a positive correlation between snorkelling activity and the presence of broken coral. A useful aspect of Allison's work was the observation of snorkeller behaviour. It was observed that snorkellers would kick and stand on the coral especially if the snorkeller was ill experienced or being dragged about by waves.

Hawkins and Roberts (1993) examined the impacts of snorkellers and scuba divers at the Sharm-el-Sheikh Resort on the Red Sea coast, Egypt (Figure 3.1). Two different sites were investigated. The 'Tower' site showed that trampling caused an increase in the amount of broken coral colonies, rubble and live loose coral fragments (Table 3.5). The impacts of trampling were also assessed at the 'Ras Umm Sidd' site and it was found that mean coral colony height was reduced where trampling occurred.

Recreation and tourism in mountainous areas

Mountainous environments comprise many of the 'classic' natural area tourism destinations around the world and can focus on single mountains such as Mt Kinabalu (Malaysia) and Kilamanjaro (Tanzania) or occur in entire regions such as the Cairngorms (Scotland) and the Himalayas (Nepal). Depending on the site and season activities range from hiking, camping, skiing, snowboarding, absailing, paragliding, rock climbing and mountaineering. There may also be the development and operation of tourist-dedicated built facilities on lower slopes and at the base of mountains.

Mountain environments are susceptible to disturbance due to steep slopes and thin soils and this is especially so in the high rainfall environments that span the tropics (Ahmad, 1993). The risk of negative impact also tends to be greater in mountainous areas because of the presence of slow growing and fragile Arctic-alpine

Table 3.5 Impacts of trampling and snorkelling on coral reef at Sharm-el-Sheikh, Egypt

(a) Impacts of trampling on corals occupying the reef flat at the 'Tower' site

	Tower	
Parameter	*Trampled*	*Untrampled*
Number of broken coral colonies	2.6	0.5
Number of live, loose coral fragments	1.0	0.1
Number of re-attached fragments of hard coral	0.1	0.0
Number of clams	0.3	0.2
Number of hard coral colonies	28.6	42.4
Number of species		
% hard coral	10.4	26.6
% soft coral	0.7	2.7
% bare substrate	87.4	70.5
% rubble	1.4	0.1

(b) Mean coral colony heights and diameters on the reef-flat according to tourist activity at the 'Ras Umm Sidd' site

Site, zone and treatment	*Mean colony height (cm)*	*Mean colony diameter (cm)*
Ras Umm Sidd		
Middle trampled	1.8	6.5
Middle snorkelled	1.9	6.6
Middle untrampled	2.6	9.0
Outer trampled	1.7	7.4
Outer snorkelled	2.2	8.2
Outer untrampled	3.1	13.1

Derived from Hawkins & Roberts, 1993

plant communities at high altitudes and in the colder temperate zones. Monz (2000) points out that this is of particular concern when rare, endemic and restricted distribution plant species are involved: for example, as in the case of potential recreational climbing damage to remnant Arctic-alpine vegetation in Snowdonia National Park, Wales (Edington & Edington, 1986).

Singh (1992) points out the wide spectrum of impacts arising from tourism and recreation in mountains. These embrace a complex array of ecological, socio-cultural and economic impacts. It is noted that the increasing demand for tourism in the developing world can result in an increased level of deforestation and loss of wildlife due to hunting as more people are attracted to tourist routes in search of employment. In global terms, significant biophysical effects include: disturbance to wildlife; camping impacts; trail degradation and erosion; damage to vegetation; water, air and noise pollution; litter and negative social conditions of crowding and congestion on popular routes. On the other hand Singh (1992) also points out that a number of positive impacts can flow from mountain tourism, including increased conservation efforts; changes from marginal agriculture; cultural preservation; up-grading of facilities; improved infrastructure and economic opportunities.

Many of the issues pertaining to mountain environments are already covered (see 'Trampling', p. 84, 'Access roads and trails', p. 95, and 'Use of built facilities and campgrounds,', p. 101) and the cumulative nature of the problem is explored on p. 134 ('Cumulative impacts'). Included here is recent work on some of the less obvious ecological effects of recreation and tourism in mountainous areas and where cliffs occur, namely that of the increasingly popular activity of rock climbing.

Rock ledges are reported by Giuliano (1994) to be important habitat components for cliff-nesting birds such as the Buzzard (*Buteo buteo*), Peregrine Falcon (*Falco peregrinus*) and the Golden Eagle (*Aquila chrysaetos*) in Europe. Birds that are typical of upland environments utilise rock ledges during the breeding season for nesting sites and fledging their young. Giuliano (1994) notes that disturbance by climbers may cause birds to desert their nests and the resultant exposure of eggs and young can lead to mortality. Similarly the disturbance of unfledged birds can cause them to fall from the nest area, risking injury and predation.

Other species of bird are also affected by rock climbing as shown by the work of Camp and Knight (1998) at Joshua Tree National Park, California, USA (Figure 3.1). In this study cliff and rock ledge bird communities were studied in the context of different levels of rock climbing. Camp and Knight (1998) found that birds at popular rock climbing sites, which had up to nine climbing routes on the cliff, responded by flying rather than staying at the site. When rock climbers were present birds tended to avoid the site. Birds were more likely to stay at unclimbed cliffs as evidenced by their perching behaviour. Camp and Knight (1998) also observed that rock climbers spent more time at the base of cliffs than hikers as they prepared for the climb. Varying lengths of time are spent on the cliff faces themselves. In some areas this can be as much as two days, as frequently occurs in Yosemite National Park during the peak climbing season which lasts from June to September.

In the Joshua Tree National Park study it was concluded that the birds appeared to be responding to rock climbing disturbance by adjusting their daily activities, habitat usage and spatial occurrence on the cliff faces. Such changes to preferred activity could increase stress on the affected birds through the disruption of feeding behaviour, breeding activity and increased avoidance of predators. The observed presence of aggressive, invasive species such as the European Starling (*Sturnus vulgaris*) at climbed sites could also lead to displacement of native bird species as a result of competition for nest sites.

In relation to disturbance to mammals White *et al.* (1999) studied the effects of mountain climbers on Grizzly Bears (*Ursus arctos horribilis*) in Glacier National Park, Montana (Figure 3.1). Grizzly Bears forage for Cutworm Moths (*Euxoa auxiliaris*) in the alpine zone during the summer period, a time when they are also likely to encounter mountain climbers. White *et al.* (1999) highlighted the potential disturbance to bears because of the many access routes through the mountains and in particular in the vicinity of moth sites. They noted that bears disturbed by climbers spent 53% less time foraging and 23% more time engaging in aggressive behaviour. It is suggested that such a reduction in feeding time and increased energy consumption could impact on the physiological status of the bears and reduce their reproductive success.

The relative sensitivity of mountain floras has already been considered. Studies on the impacts of rock climbing on cliff plant communities provides further insight into the potential damage that climbing can do in mountain environments. Kelly & Larson (1997), in a study of the impact of rock climbing on Eastern White Ceder (*Thuja occidentalis*) on the Niagara Escarpment, Canada (Figure 3.1), showed that the density of trees on cliff faces is lower where climbing occurs. In addition to this there was damage to trees in the form of rope abrasion, sawn branches and trees being cut down.

Farris (1998) emphasised the complexity in determining the effects of rock climbing on cliff vegetation. Importance is placed on comparison with suitable controls that can be difficult to find due to variation in the proportion of bare rock face, ledges and vegetation cover between sites. Of interest is the observation that degree of slope, micro-surface features and aspect are likely to influence the nature of vegetation and amount of disturbance that takes place. Farris (1998) investigated the impacts of climbing on Minnesota cliff system vegetation and found that complex upstanding lichens were readily damaged. Total plant cover was also found to be lower where climbing took place. This can be particularly significant where cliff edge vegetation exerts a control over runoff and soil erosion, and if weed invasion is taking place. Additionally, if a patch of cliff vegetation is an important source of seed and spores for the establishment of new vegetation in the area then its loss, and or replacement with weeds, also reduces site regeneration potential.

Recreation and tourism in and around caves

The unique features, archaeological remains and enigmatic wildlife of caves has resulted in many cave systems around the world becoming the focus of tourist activity. Cave recreation and tourism ranges from relatively easily accessible show caves (e.g. Jewel and Mammoth Caves in south-west Australia; Cango Caves in South Africa) and wildlife centred cave viewing (e.g. Niah and Mulu Caves, Sarawak, Malaysia) through to the more adventurous exploration of caves and cave diving (Huautla Caves, Mexico).

Baker and Gentry (1998) report that the numbers of people visiting caves has increased over the last few decades. For example, the British show cave at Poole's Cavern, Derbyshire, has around 40,000 visitors a year while some European caves receive up to 500,000 visitors a year. According to Gillieson (1996) the Mammoth Cave in Kentucky, USA, receives more than two million visitors per annum. He also

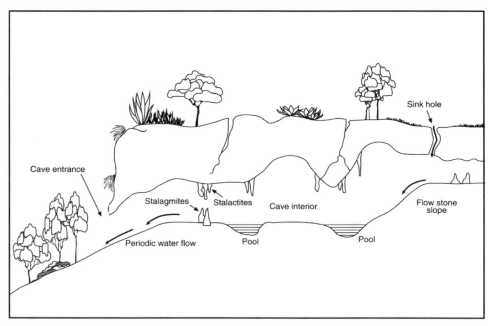

Figure 3.14 Conceptual diagram of cave habitats

notes that there are now some 650-tourist caves with lighting systems and an esti-mated worldwide total of 20 million visitors a year.

Sensitivity of cave fauna

The dark conditions and relative constancy of temperature and humidity has given rise to the evolution of distinctive cave faunas. Many organisms are adapted to the dark as shown by the loss of pigment and blindness. Cave faunas or troglobites have a very narrow ecological niche and thus are very sensitive to disturbance. Examples of these animals from Australian cave systems include the Giant Blind Cockroach (*Trogloblattella nullarborensis*), cave spiders (e.g. *Tartarus mullamullangensis*) and blind fish (e.g. *Anommatophasma candidum*).

Besides these specialised cave faunas a range of other animals use caves and cave entrances. These include various invertebrates, snakes, some birds and bats. Hamil-ton-Smith (1987) cautions that some cave entrance dwelling species are highly susceptible to disturbance as seen by the elimination of Weta (*Novoteettix naracoorensis*) from the Alexandra Cave in south-eastern Australia following the insertion of a draught-proof door to control desiccation. Besides the intermediate habitat of the cave entrance area the roof and cave walls provide resting areas for birds and bats. Various aquatic habitats can also be recognised comprising streams, flood pools, water percolation pools and flow stone pools (Figure 3.14).

The ecology of cave systems is dependent on inputs from outside the cave. Cave drainage systems such as streams and pathways made by large trees are natural corridors and a major source of organic debris. Wet surfaces, such as flow stone areas, trap organic debris which support bacterial mats. These, in turn, support colonies of crustaceans. Organic matter, derived from ecosystems outside the cave, enters the cave system in the form of guano deposited by birds and bats that roost in caves. The reliance on energy derived from outside the cave system makes cave fauna susceptible to changes which occur at the surface and beyond the cave system itself.

Sources of impact

Although deliberate damage and graffiti are rare the touching of cave features (stalactites and stalagmites) as a result of curiosity can result in breakage and discoloration. Besides speleothem deterioration, fauna such as bats may decline as a result of increased visitation to caves (Craven, 1999). Caves that receive large numbers of visitors are also subject to track degradation and pathways can become muddy when wet or liberate dust when dry. At the same time the habitats of cave faunas can be damaged by constant trampling and the stirring of sediment. Significant depletion of aquatic crustacean cave fauna has occurred in the Ogof Ffynnon Ddu Cave system in Wales (Figure 3.1) as a result of caving activity. Edington and Edington (1977) report that these aquatic crustacean fauna are only intact in pockets which lie outside the main caving routeway. Furthermore, entire populations of aquatic crustaceans can be lost due to chemical pollution caused by the careless dumping of torch batteries in pools.

Artificial lighting has been installed in many caves and may allow normally absent mosses and lichens to grow on and discolour cave features. The world famous Lascaux Cave paintings in France have been discoloured by algae as a result of artificial lighting and increased carbon dioxide (CO_2) levels derived from numerous visitors (Dellue & Dellue, 1984).

Respired carbon dioxide and heat derived from visitors and artificial lighting has the capacity to change the microclimatic conditions in a cave (Cigna, 1993). This is likely to occur and become significant where the cave system has limited air exchange with the outside environment. Those caves that experience naturally rapid air movements or have constant rapid water transit are less likely to be negatively affected by a fluctuating cave climate and increased levels of carbon dioxide.

Increased levels of carbon dioxide associated with localised increases in temperature under conditions of poor ventilation have been reported to increase the dissolution of speleothems (e.g. Craven, 1996). Kiernan (1987) notes that, under conditions of high humidity, a temperature increase of 1°C can increase the vapour capacity of the air by as much as 8%, increasing the evaporation rate and potentially resulting in the desiccation of speleothems.

Recent work by Baker and Gentry (1998) suggests that the calcium ion content of drip water is another critical factor. The calcium content of dripping water is pivotal in speleothem growth and any change in concentration will influence the growth of stalactites and stalagmites. Baker and Gentry (1998) advise that cave features may be at risk of damage where the calcium content of drip water become naturally low or where land use change alters the chemistry of cave system drip water. Kiernan (1987) reports that clearing vegetation from above cave systems may result in increased soil surface temperatures which could then facilitate biological activity and result in the increased generation of organic acids. More acidic waters, that dissolve and mobilise calcium ions, percolating into the cave system, could result in the dissolution of speleothems rather than incremental growth. Above ground impacts can cause water pollution, changes in water flow into the cave and soil erosion can lead to the sedimentation of cave passages.

Tourists also visit caves to see wildlife because caves are used as roosts and maternity sites by bats in many parts of the world and by swiflets (e.g. south-east Asia) and oilbirds (South America) in the tropics. Bats also use caves as rest areas when their normal food supply becomes scarce or during adverse weather conditions. Hibernating or over-wintering bats may be particularly prone to disturbance from large groups of people searching the roof-line of caves with torch light. In seasonal environments over-wintering bats rely on stores of fat built up from the previous summer. Disturbance can cause them to utilise important reserves of energy and if repeated can threaten their survival into the next season. Similarly during the breeding season many species of bat leave the young in-groups clinging to rock walls in the cave. Disturbance may cause the young to fall and frequent disturbance may increase the mortality of a population.

Techniques to manage visitor impact in caves have also resulted in population declines in bats. For example, Churchill (1987) reports that the application of a steel mesh grille to prevent illegal cave entry at Cutta Cutta Caves in northern Australia (Figure 3.1) caused a decline from a bat population of 5000 to just 350 bats within a 12 month period. The population subsequently recovered when the grille was removed. Five species of bat use the Cutta Cutta Caves and one species, the rare Orange Horseshoe Bat (*Rhinonicteris aurantius*), has strict microclimatic requirements in needing high humidity levels and temperatures of 28°–32°C at its roost sites (Churchill, 1987). This example highlights the importance of maintaining trees and vegetation adjacent to cave entrances as such action could alter temperature and humidity conditions inside the cave making it less suitable for fauna.

The observation of wildlife

Major wildlife experience destinations around the world include the Masai Mara Game Reserve and Serengeti and Kruger National Parks in Africa; Kakadu National Park in Australia; Chitwan National Park in Nepal; and the Galapagos Islands and the Pantanal Wetlands in South America. Spectacular and charismatic species are also the focus of specific tourism activity as seen in Gorilla tourism in Africa; Orang utan viewing in Indonesia; lemurs in Madagascar, swimming with Whale Sharks in Western Australia; observing Elephant Seals in the USA and Argentina and whale watching in Australia, New Zealand, South Africa and North America.

Besides those people who seek out specific species and concentrations of wildlife the presence and observation of wildlife plays an important part in the recreational experience of hikers, campers and other natural area users. Surveys of hikers in the

USA have shown that observing wildlife ranks high in their recreational experience. Likewise in the USA, 96% of campers stated that the opportunity to observe wildlife in natural settings added to their outdoor experience (Hendee & Schoenfeld, 1990). Further, in Western Australia, 70% of visitors to Warren National Park stated that viewing wildlife was an important reason for visiting the park (Smith, 1998). Additionally, much of the scuba diving that occurs in kelp beds and off rocky shores and around coral reef systems is centred around viewing animal life.

Given this sustained and increasing interest in seeing animals in the wild and the large number of different species involved there is a risk of negative impact occurring. A number of specific cases of disturbance to wildlife have already been covered in Chapter 2 of this book. In this section we provide an account of the general principles relating to wildlife response to disturbance and consider the specific case of sea mammals in Box 3.4.

Vulnerability to disturbance

The vulnerability of an animal to disturbance depends on its life-history traits and evolutionary strategies such as longevity, degree of parental care and reproductive effort (Hammit & Cole, 1998). Some animals, for example bears in the USA and elephants in Africa, are known to produce a more dramatic response to disturbance when caring for very young offspring. Tolerance levels can also vary with age, breeding season, time of year and habitat type. Furthermore, species with specialised food or habitat requirements are additionally more vulnerable than

---

Box 3.4 Sea mammal tourism

Observation of and interaction with sea mammals is an increasingly popular activity and particularly reflected in dolphin and whale watching tourism that now takes place in some 60 countries around the world. Colonies of seals and sea lions also attract tourist interest, for example Elephant Seal observation in California and Argentina and with more recent developments such as snorkelling with Australian Sea Lions at Penguin Island, Western Australia. All of these forms of tourism continue to be developed and interest continues to grow as seen in the dramatic rise in whale and dolphin tourism that has occurred in South Africa, Australia and North America during the last 10 years.

In a study on the effects of tourist boats on Beluga Whales, Blane and Jackson (1994) cited a number of examples identifying displacement from feeding areas, reduced feeding and disrupted social groupings as responses of whales to tourist boats. They examined Beluga Whale tourism on a population in the St Lawrence River estuary, Canada (Figure 3.1), which were already stressed by pollution hunting and heavy commercial boat traffic. The whales were observed to show avoidance behaviour, which was more pronounced when the number of boats increased. Such behaviour can reduce efficiency in locating food and maintaining social contact with the group. Given that at the time the study was carried out some 600 whale watching excursions were operating in the estuary the scope for significant and sustained disturbance was high. Recommendations put forward by Blane and Jackson (1994) included a restriction on the amount of whale watching that took place coupled with a controlled licensing system. Tour operator activity regulation coupled with interpretation was seen as ways to reduce disturbance to the whales.

There is also evidence of tourism impacting on dolphins. Weir *et al.* (1996) report that dolphins show evasive behaviour in response to disturbance but the actual response will vary according to individual dolphins, between different species and according to the specific circumstances. In their Port Phillip Bay (Figure 3.1) study, Weir *et al.* (1996) observed that the response of dolphins to swimmers delivered by boat varied according to the approach strategy used by the tour operator. A direct approach (operator moves towards dolphins, manoeuvres the boat in front of them and drops swimmers into the water) by the tour operator gave more active dolphin-swimmer interactions but at the same time culminated in much more avoidance behaviour from the dolphins. Weir *et al.* (1996) noted the invasive nature of such an approach which forced dolphins to react. Having to react requires additional energy expenditure and such losses on a sustained basis might be a significant factor in determining reproductive success and the survival of individuals.

Besides disturbance related stress Frohoff (2000) reports on deliberate harassment of dolphins which allow close contact and remain in the vicinity of humans. Examples of this include hitting and throwing various items at dolphins, feeding of non-edible items and attempts to hook and land them. In contrast to this there is also a risk to humans especially when people deliberately molest dolphins.

Apparently benign activities can however impact on dolphins. The Monkey Mia tourist centre is a major tourist attraction at Shark Bay in Western Australia (Figure 3.1). Here visitors can gain close contact with dolphins from the beach and are allowed to feed them under supervised conditions (Plate 3.3). IFAW (1996) listed the following impacts that have occurred as dolphin tourism has grown at Monkey Mia:

- Increased risk of dolphin disease, injury or death due to close contact, intentional harm or accidents with boats.
- Changed foraging and migration behaviour.
- Feeding with non-natural foods.
- Increased injury to humans from habituated animals.

IFAW (1996) distinguished the short-term impact of behavioural changes that are especially related to foraging behaviour as being caused by food provisioning. Despite management guidelines a longer-term impact of juvenile dolphin mortality was also identified because there is evidence that some adults were not training the juveniles to forage properly.

generalist animals. In contrast to this, species that live in large groups generally respond less to disturbances than solitary animals (Hammitt & Cole, 1998).

Species vary in their degree of tolerance to human intrusion. Some species, for example, are very shy and move away at the slightest detection of a human by sound, smell or eyesight. Previous experience, however, plays an important part in determining the response of a species to disturbance. For example, in Australia, Red-necked Wallabies (*Macropus rufogriseus*) will flee at the presence of humans in certain rural areas but those at picnic sites or golf-courses will tolerate a much closer approach by humans or may actually seek out humans in search of food offerings (Green, 1999).

Birds that occur in urban environments are much less wary than those that occur in more natural settings. Moreover, when disturbance does not result in negative effects birds will often cease reacting to humans as it is important for them to conserve energy for their normal daily activities (Burger *et al.*, 1995). Overall it appears that larger animals are affected more by the direct presence and activity of humans while smaller animals are more vulnerable to habitat modification or indirect impacts (Hammitt & Cole, 1998).

Many researchers have divided the effects of recreation and tourism on wild animals into direct and indirect impacts. Liddle (1997) divides direct impacts into a Type 1 or Type 3 disturbance. Type 1 disturbance is defined as 'an interruption of tranquility' and a Type 3 disturbance is where the animal is wounded or killed. Indirect impacts include habitat modification and impacts associated with infrastructure (Green & Higginbottom, 2000; Roe *et al.*, 1997). Liddle (1997) defines indirect impacts as a Type 2 disturbance incorporating those impacts that result from changes to habitat. The focus here is mainly on direct impacts, that is, a response to humans being present, as in walking, human-created sound and driving vehicles in a natural setting.

Behavioural responses of wild animals to humans

Tourists can have various attitudes towards wild animals. While some people enjoy and lobby operators for close sightings and even direct contact, members of the same tourist group may become alarmed if approached too closely by certain animals such as birds and bats. Some species appear to be universally acceptable and close contact is often desired, for example dolphins; while others, such as reptiles, invoke mixed feelings and are usually viewed from a distance. A tourist may be completely unaware of the effects they are having on a wild animal whether the contact is close, as in handling chameleons in Madagascar, or viewing from vehicles as in the case of African safari tourism.

How a wild animal responds to the presence of a human is dependent on the sensitivity of the animal itself, the animal's past experience and characteristics of the habitat in which it occurs. In addition to this, animal response is also dependent on the frequency, magnitude, timing and location of the disturbance (Hammitt & Cole, 1998; Liddle, 1997; Vaske *et al.*, 1995).

Three basic responses: avoidance, attraction and habituation

Three different types of behavioural reaction, namely avoidance, attraction and habituation, are recognised by Whittaker and Knight (1998) as being fundamental in understanding wildlife responses to humans. The ideas underpinning these reactions are the behavioural strategies that various animals employ in order to survive in the wild. For example, with attraction, an animal may associate humans with sources of food or shelter and be attracted to humans because of this. Such behaviour under natural conditions increases the chances of survival in the wild and has thus evolved as a natural survival strategy.

Whittaker and Knight (1998), however, emphasise that the attraction response is often confused with habituation. They see the difference between the two being that in attraction there is a positive reinforcement of stimuli while habituation refers to a 'waning of response to a repeated neutral stimuli'. This latter perspective is exemplified in the case of habituated gorillas that tolerate the presence of humans once the process of gradual deliberate habituation is complete.

Attraction, as Whittaker and Knight (1998) see it, would be where animals deliberately associate with humans in order to gain food. An example of this includes the many species of birds that are attracted to humans eating food as in the case of glossy starling attendance at dining and picnic areas in the Kruger National Park, South Africa. Many tourists see such close contact with colourful birds as an addition to the wildlife experience. Attraction for food can, however, cause problems as in the case where monkeys have totally lost their fear of humans and exhibit aggressive behaviour or elicit unwelcome close contact when they attempt to obtain food items from people.

According to Whittaker and Knight (1998) wild animals can become habituated to a wide range of human stimuli. Nonetheless, this can result in a negative impact on wildlife, for example, where wild animals are habituated to the sight and sound of traffic. Such animals, which do not move away from fast moving vehicles when crossing roads and are at risk of being hit resulting in a Liddle (1997) Type 3 disturbance (Green & Higginbottom, 2000).

Despite such potential problems habituation can be neutral to the animals concerned and a benefit for tourism. Shackley (1996) for instance, includes the example of macaws and capuchin monkeys that show tolerance to visitors in a Costa Rican Reserve. There appears to be no impact on the animals and visitors are able to gain good sightings. She warns, however, that habituation can also cause problems where it disrupts normal foraging and daily activity patterns.

The measurement and assessment of recreational disturbance to wildlife

Although wildlife tourism is a widespread and increasing activity there is dearth of 'hard' data on the nature and significance of tourism impact situations. A major reason for this is the absence of, and difficulties encountered in, researching animal behavioural responses to disturbance and relating this to tourism activity. Judgements regarding recreational impact on wild animals need to first consider total numbers in the animal population being studied, habitat requirements and the

Plate 3.3 Visitors interacting with wild dolphins at Monkey Mia, Shark Bay, Western Australia. (*Photo*: Jane Newsome)

natural distribution of the species of interest. Secondly, a profile of tourism activity and pressures need to be catalogued. Measures of impact can then be judged according to changes in the population, alterations in distribution and behavioural changes in the target species. A comparison between tourist/recreational sites with control (non-recreational) sites provides scope for the detection of impact.

The scientific approach to measuring impacts should include a knowledge of:

- Social behaviour.
- The animals' natural movements and use of various areas.
- Critical habitat requirements.
- An assessment of life history parameters (reproductive fitness and survival rate).
- Responses to tourism pressure and activity.

Various researchers have pointed out that impacts detected at the population level are likely to be significant in terms of reproductive success and long-term survival. Impacts on individuals or groups occurring at the local scale may be significant where local distributions are displaced or lost (e.g. Gales, 2000; IFAW, 1996).

The landscape matrix

The concept of landscape ecology was introduced in Chapter 2 'Landscape ecology', p. 45. Although this chapter is primarily concerned with impacts originating from recreation and tourist activities it is important to demonstrate that tourism resources can also be damaged by adjacent land use and activities. Furthermore, it needs to be appreciated that such situations can lead to combined stress on natural areas which may require additional management of a particular reserved area and / or attention given to source of impacts emanating from the landscape matrix. Clearly where natural areas such as reserves, national parks and other protected areas exist as a patch, within a matrix of agricultural or other land uses, there is capacity for the matrix to influence this patch. Such influences are also likely to be more significant if the natural patch is small and industrial or urban land uses occur as part of the matrix (Figure 3.15).

Cole and Landres (1996) point out that adjacent land use impacts include regulation of water flow, diversions of water and the siting of dams on watercourses, air pollution and the effects of particular land management regimes (e.g. intensive agriculture). Impacts derived from regulated river water flows and the impoundment of water up stream, highlight the role of river corridors as possible sources of impact on natural areas. The role of rivers, sourced beyond a reserved area, in influencing the ecology of a particular region is illustrated by the impacts of water abstraction, turbidity and pollution problems on segments of the Kruger National Park in South Africa (Box 2.4 p. 69).

Rivers systems in the matrix

Petts (1984) estimates that up to 75% of the world's rivers have their flow controlled by dams and regulation of their water flow. Such a scale of river system modification has impacted on a number of important natural areas as in the case of reduced water supply to the Everglades and Grand Canyon National Parks in the USA. These impacts also include the degradation of riparian landscapes, altered sedimentation regimes and changes in natural fish communities. These alterations are brought about by altered flow patterns, the introduction of exotic species and disruption to fish migration (Cole & Landres, 1996).

Recent work by Kingsford (2000) in Australia demonstrates the significance of river modification to actual and potential natural area tourism resources. Citing various authors he reports on the decline of wetland ecosystems around the world. Wetlands are indeed significant tourism destinations globally as indicated by important ecotourism resources such as the Pantanal in southern Brazil, Everglades in Florida, USA and Lake Tempe in Sulawesi.

Kingsford (2000) notes the high biological diversity of Australian floodplain wetlands as particularly reflected by the diversity and large populations of waterbirds. These floodplain wetlands consist of swamps, floodplain marshes and tributaries, river overflows, lagoons, lakes and waterholes, all of which are dependent on flood water from rivers. Many ecological processes in these wetlands are dependent on the arrival of floodwaters. Examples of theses include organic inputs providing energy for micro-organisms, stimulation of drought resistant zooplankton eggs to hatch, germination of plants from seed banks and the stimulation of breeding activity in frogs and birds (various authors cited in Kingsford, 2000).

The construction of dams can either submerge a wetland or substitute a variable flooding regime with a permanent one so that some wetlands never dry out with

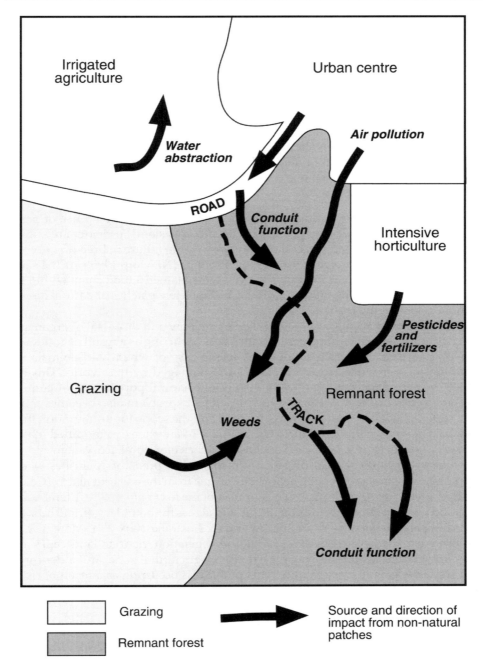

Figure 3.15 Potential impacts from non-natural patches in the landscape matrix

resultant ecological changes. Kingsford (2000) uses the Macquarie Marshes (Figure 3.1) as a case study in demonstrating the impacts of dam construction, water diversion schemes and water abstraction on an internationally important wetland for birds. These landscape level activities have reduced the extent of the marshes by up to 50%, caused a decline in the abundance and diversity of water birds, resulted in decreased breeding activity of colonial waterbirds and reduced the area of River Red Gum (*Eucalyptus camaldulensis*) by as much as 15%.

The natural corridor function of rivers has already been considered in Chapter 2 in the context of the Kruger National Park and adjacent land uses in South Africa. It has already been noted that eroded soils and toxic chemical components such as pesticides can be moved from one ecosystem to another in this way.

The agricultural matrix

In situations of a dominantly agricultural matrix the widespread use of pesticides could impact on adjacent patches of natural ecosystem. Pesticides are known to impact on birds through direct mortality, by causing failure in breeding success or indirectly by the removal of insect food supplies (Newton, 1995). At the same time it is possible that toxic materials which accumulate in a food chain within the matrix can cause breeding failure of predators that leave patches of natural habitat in order to feed in the matrix.

As pointed out by Cole and Landres (1996) the flow and dispersal of organisms from natural areas can be detrimental with losses occurring as a result of accidental road mortality or deliberate shooting as in the case of when wild animals kill domestic stock or when crops are grazed and damaged by herbivores. This can reduce the abundance and long-term viability of natural populations of animals confined to patches within a landscape mosaic. The problem also becomes much more significant where natural areas are small and the scope for in-migration from other source areas is limited, due to the presence of an extensive modified matrix and lack of connectivity, between separated patches of natural ecosystem.

In contrast to the dispersal of organisms out of patches, predators, parasites, weeds and pathogens can also enter patches of natural area from the adjacent matrix (Cole & Landres, 1996). An example of this is the spread of the fox (*Vulpes vulpes*), feral herbivores and weeds from adjacent agricultural land across the boundary of, and into, the Stirling Range National Park in south-western Australia (Box 2.3). Moreover, in Western Australia isolated reserves of natural vegetation, riparian landscapes and attendant wildlife, which occur in the extensive agricultural zone, are under threat from widespread landscape salinity. This problem is occurring as a result of rising saline water tables induced by the extensive removal of deep rooted woody vegetation which originally kept the water table at greater depths.

Sources of disease in the matrix

The Stirling Range case study (Box 2.3) demonstrates the potential impact of plant disease, derived from the wider landscape matrix, that entered the park mainly along disturbance corridors. Animal disease can enter a natural area in a similar way and even be derived from sources thousands of kilometres away. A pertinent case is that of Mountain Gorilla (*Gorilla gorilla berengei*). Gorilla tourism is seen as a reason for and means of conserving this endangered species (see also Chapter 6 'The case of reducing impacts on rare and endangered species', p. 249). Tourism visits to deliberately habituated gorillas has been established at five locations in central-east Africa. Despite the controls and strategies that have been put in place gorillas have been impacted on by human transmitted diseases. Gorillas are susceptible to human disease and tourists suffering from upper respiratory tract infections contracted in their source countries can transmit these illnesses to gorillas during a viewing session.

Urban encroachment and the need for land

The case of Mountain Gorillas also illustrates another landscape scale issue, that of agricultural and / or urban encroachment onto natural areas. Such developments increase the likelihood of detrimental impacts from the landscape matrix. In the case of the Mountain Gorilla agricultural encroachment has driven this species further and further up into the mountains and into less favourable habitat. With more people in the vicinity there is also a greater risk of disturbance and, where poverty is a factor, an increased threat of hunting and poaching.

Urban encroachment will be an increasing source of landscape level impacts globally in the future. In Australia, for example, some of the most popular natural areas, that also have increasing levels of recreation and tourism pressure, lie in the proximity of expanding urban areas. Housing development, for example, is expanding up to and alongside the borders of John Forrest National Park which occurs on the outskirts of the city of Perth, Western Australia (Figure 3.1). The close proximity of an urbanised landscape to the park increases the chance of fauna mortality should any out-dispersal take place. Furthermore, in a European study, Van der Zande *et al.* (1984) have shown that the density of breeding birds declines in association with high recreation intensities emanating from adjacent residential areas. The close proximity of urban areas means that there is a much greater chance of more people walking their dogs, damaging natural resources and utilising the area for a variety of reasons. Nearby urban areas can also act as sources of weeds and feral animals that may compete with or prey on native species.

Air pollution, recognised by Cole and Landres (1996) as a potentially significant impact originating from the landscape matrix, can take the form of acid rain, heavy metal contamination and photochemical smog. These forms of air pollution can be transported from urban areas into natural areas by local winds. Sigal and Nash (1983) report on premature leaf senescence, reduced growth and an increased susceptibility to disease in vegetation caused by air pollution damage in the Cascade Mountains in the western USA. The urban encroachment around John Forrest National Park, described above, could lead to pollution induced physiological stress on the vegetation. Non-point sources of pollutants flowing into the park could increase disease susceptibility; a critical issue in relation to the known presence of Jarrah Dieback Disease caused by *Phytopthora cinnamomi* that has already been accidentally introduced into the park (see Box 2.3).

Cumulative impacts

The problem of cumulative environmental impacts lies in a number of different smaller impacts which when combined result in a much larger and significant impact situation. An example from natural area tourism, say in the case of one national park, might include the combined impacts of tourist accommodation, infrastructure such as road linkages with attendant traffic, levels of resource consumption, recreation/tourism infrastructure such as campgrounds, trails and car parks plus the nature, location and intensity of various activities such as horse riding or rock climbing.

Clearly the extent and significance of such a cumulative impact situation will depend on the sensitivity of the environment, the scale at which sources of impact are developed and applied and the effectiveness of prevailing management systems. The larger the natural area is the more likely it will be able to 'absorb' various impacts. This is illustrated by the tourism situation in the Kruger National Park in South Africa which, despite an extensive road network and some 25 camps, remains largely a wilderness area. The Kruger National Park receives up to 800,000 visitors a year but the 1.9 million hectare park is able to accommodate such tourist pressure because of its size, the management systems in place and the fact that the major activity is viewing wildlife from the safety of vehicles. The major threats to the integrity of the Kruger National Park in fact reside in the landscape matrix in which the Park sits.

Cumulative impact situations are more likely to occur when both tourism and other factors come together. This can be seen at a prime natural area tourism location, the Cairngorm Mountains in the UK. This 500,000 hectare mountainous region is a major recreation/tourism site in Scotland with infrastructure such as ski areas, mountain resorts, ski roads and hotels. The recreational activities that take place include hiking, mountain biking, off-road vehicle driving and self-drive touring (Crabtree & Bayfield, 1998).

The negative environmental impacts associated with these infrastructures and activities include changes in site hydrology, visual intrusion, disturbance to wildlife, erosion, air pollution and the generation of solid wastes. It could be argued that these activities themselves, when combined, result in a cumulative impact situation. However, as mentioned previously, it is when some of the wider environmental issues are added to this list that cumulative impact is very apparent.

Crabtree and Bayfield (1998) state that the ecological sustainability of such a fragile mountain area is connected with the entire spectrum of land uses in the area. They report that significant environmental impacts are also generated by agriculture, forestry and estate management. Examples include high stocking rates on grazing land, farm intensification impacting on habitat diversity, drainage of wetlands and pollution. Superimposed on this situation are pollutants, such as acid deposition, derived from industrial landscapes beyond the Cairngorms. There are also positive economic impacts but, as Crabtree and Bayfield (1998) point out, it is mostly economic activity that has put the Cairngorms environment under considerable pressure. These problems will require wider social and economic solutions and a detailed consideration of this in the context of the Cairngorms situation is beyond the scope of this book. Nevertheless, such a complex set of land uses functioning on a regional basis is clearly governed by social and economic factors as well as aspects of landuse policy.

Social and economic perspectives

The emphasis of this book is on tourism's relationship to the natural environment and the planning and management principles of how to maximise the synergy between the two while minimising any adverse impacts. However, given the underpinning sustainable approach to the relationship it is also important to address tourism's role in impacting upon both social and economic components of natural area tourism. While these are now addressed briefly the authors wish to make it clear that both subjects could easily form the basis of entire books on their own. Therefore the brief summary that follows should be regarded as an introductory overview only.

Consideration of local communities in natural area tourism development has generally been a limited occurrence. However, some early studies have been made of such impacts including those of Cooke (1982), Smith (1977) and Mathieson and Wall (1982). Some communities have reported excellent host-guest interactions (e.g. Senegal – Bilsen, 1987) while others have noted adverse problems (Bhutan – Allan, 1988). Such differences have led one researcher to pose the question 'tourism for whom?' (Jafari, 1987) and others to advocate the necessity of conducting research into the attitudes of residents towards tourism and tourists (Marsh & Henshall,1987; May, 1990).

A survey and review of resident perceptions research on the social impacts of tourism indicates that although there is a sound description and knowledge base of tourism impacts, there is a need for further research of the central concepts in order to advance the conceptual and theoretical base (Ap, 1990). His survey concluded that the overall descriptive nature of the inquiries are indicative of a field of study at an early stage of development.

Liu *et al.* (1987) carried out a major study of resident perceptions on the impact of tourism on natural environments in Hawaii, North Wales and Turkey. The study illustrated the value of incorporating resident perception in evaluating the effects of tourism development for planning purposes. Residents of Hawaii and North Wales gave protection of the environment the highest priority. It was ranked higher than cultural benefits, social costs and even economic benefits. Liu *et al.* (1987) concluded that the 'protection of the environment is essential for the continued success of any tourist destination'. They added that there are two phases to tourism impacts and the picture is completed only when one phase supplements the other. These phases are what perceivers believe to be the case (a situation underlying policy decision) and the scientific monitoring of actual physical changes in the total environment.

Applied to planning the situation is obvious – to maintain environmental protection and tourism development there must be not only scientific evidence of cause and effect but also the public support for it.

Conclusions drawn from the study were:

(1) The impact of tourism on the natural and social environment is of universal concern.
(2) Different cultures view the ways environmental and negative impacts of tourism are perceived differently.
(3) Residents perceive many of the benefits brought by tourism such as the preservation of historic sites.
(4) It is important to incorporate resident perceptions in evaluating the effects of tourism development for planning purposes. Monitoring resident opinion is necessary in order to assess local sentiments which should be incorporated at the outset of the planning process.
(5) It confirms the necessity of adopting a holistic approach to tourism planning, since issues on the environment are not perceived as being entirely distinct from economic and social ones. (Liu *et al.*, 1987)

General public participation in natural area tourism planning is important for a variety of reasons. They include gaining attitudes and perceptions of residents' views on their environment, tourism development, their community aspirations and on the tourists themselves. Dasmann *et al.* (1973) suggested that 'the more local people benefit from tourism, the more they will benefit from a commitment to preserve the environmental features which attract tourism'. However, it should be noted that not all communities are in favour of tourism development. Therefore tourism development in natural areas should always be carried out in close collaboration with the local inhabitants who are most likely to be affected. De Kadt (1979) lamented that he knew of no country which evaluated alternative approaches to tourism for the purpose of selecting one that promised to maximise social benefits to hosts. He recommended community controlled, forward looking planning as opposed to typical remedial planning. Within a few years this emphasis on community participation for its own gain was echoed by Murphy (1985) and Getz (1986). A survey of four Austrian alpine communities found that although the residents viewed tourism positively they were also keen to ensure that their local community and environmental values were protected (Kariel, 1989). To do this they suggested the adoption of 'soft tourism' as a way of achieving a balance between preservation and development.

The preferences of tourists should be considered in the development of natural area tourism because without tourists there would be no tourism. Inskeep (1988) suggested that one major trend is the increasing fragmentation of tourist markets, especially as more tourists want to participate in a variety of sports, recreational, and cultural pursuits, as they seek new destinations, stay in residential, self-catering accommodation, and engage in special interest tourism such as natural area tourism. Therefore, it is essential to seek the views of tourists in order to accurately assess their opinions. Inskeep (1987) suggested that it is important to distinguish between capacity based on tourist acceptability and that predicated on environmental deterioration because the two may not be the same.

Tourism in natural areas also has the potential to provide a range of positive and negative economic benefits. Economic impact related to job creation in communities living near natural areas plays a critical role in the context of the debate over the development of tourism in natural areas. Probably the most beneficial economic role of ecotourism is its potential to generate employment opportunities, income and profit, often in areas where normally they are generally limited (Lindberg, 2001). In doing this the development of natural area tourism may reduce or eliminate traditional resource use. In addition, tourists, as consumers, may support the importance of tourism benefiting local residents (Eagles *et al.*, 1992). Finally, when residents receive benefits, the extractive pressure on natural resources is lessened, and residents are more likely to support tourism and conservation, even to the point of protecting the site against poaching or other uses.

The economic impacts of tourism in natural areas is generally measured by a range of indicators which includes fiscal impacts (taxes, fees, expenditures), the reduced access to resources, inflation, the effects on income distribution, revenue sharing and leakage. Tourism not only generates government revenue through business and other general taxes, but also through industry-specific channels, such as payment of occupancy and departure taxes. Conversely, tourism generates fiscal costs in the form of, for example, funding for infrastructure. At some ecotourism destinations, residents benefit from revenue sharing programmes that either provide cash payments or, more commonly, funding for community projects such as wells or schools.

Leakage is often viewed as a negative impact, but it should be seen more appropriately as the absence of a positive impact. Rather than causing economic harm, it simply does not provide the benefit of the forgone jobs. For example, Krakauer (1998) describes how increased fees and limitations on expedition numbers for climbing Mt Everest in Nepal led to a shift from Nepal to Tibet, thereby leaving hundreds of sherpas out of work. However, the shift turned out to be caused by the limitations, rather than the fee. A further increase in the base fee from $50,000 to $70,000 per group did not seem to deter groups from Nepal.

Though the diverse impacts of tourism are increasingly being recognised, the traditional positive impacts of jobs and income are the major economic benefits generated by tourism development in natural areas. Wagner (1997) estimates the economic impact of visitors for the Guaraqueçaba region of Brazil. Based on an estimate of 7500 visitor days per year in the region, natural area tourism was estimated to annually generate $244,575 in output (sales), $19,425 in labour payments (income), and 32 jobs (full-time equivalent). Smyth (1999) estimates that visitors to Glacier National Park generated $74 million in sales, $41 million in income, and 2531 jobs in 1990. This represented 4% of the region's income and 7% of the region's jobs.

Thus in the same way that tourism in natural areas impacts upon the natural environment in either positive or negative ways, it also has many social and economic consequences. The key to maximising the benefits of tourism for local communities is to encourage their active participation in the development of tourism (Ashley & Roe, 1998). When this occurs natural area tourism can bring about a number of benefits for the surrounding environment, local communities and local economies.

Biophysical Impacts: A Case Study of Off-Road Vehicle Driving

The use of off-road vehicles as a recreational activity

Access into natural areas has been facilitated by the proliferation and widespread use of off-road vehicles (motorcycles and four-wheel-drive vehicles) during the last 30 years. Many natural areas that were once mostly only accessible through an organised tour or expedition are now available to a greater number of tourists due to rising levels of wealth, personal off-road vehicle ownership and because of an interest in visiting more remote locations. Increased access and visitation rates have occurred in the Australian and North American deserts, Arctic tundra and in mountainous areas, forests and beaches at many locations around the world.

The use of off-road vehicles is obviously associated with roads and tracks but frequently involves driving across untracked areas where there are no roads, as in the case of viewing animals in savanna environments or beach driving. Furthermore, off-road vehicle access allows people to penetrate remoter areas (e.g. Australian deserts) or sites which many other people cannot access (off-road vehicle track only access sites). This also creates the potential for camping impacts, wildlife disturbance and pollution to occur at more remote and relatively unused sites. This case study explores a range of potential impacts caused by the use of off-road vehicles with examples drawn form arid, tundra and tropical environments.

The spectrum of environmental impact

The use of off-road vehicles has been found to impact on soils, vegetation, wildlife and social conditions. Webb *et al.* (1978) studied the impacts of off-road vehicle use on soil properties in a heavily used designated vehicle recreation area in California. Changes in soil properties included increases in bulk density, decreased levels of soil moisture, a reduction in organic matter and plant nutrients and accelerated erosion (Figure 3.16). Various studies have also reported damage to vegetation especially as a result of off-road vehicle use in beach environments. Broadhead and Godfrey (1977) observed the total destruction of above ground biomass of vegetation occupying dune systems at Cape Cod in the USA. Such loss of vegetation increases the risk of wind erosion and as also reported by Anders and Leatherman (1987) the degradation of foredunes especially under storm conditions.

Beach environments also reflect the composite nature of off-road vehicle impact. Steiner and Leatherman (1981) and Wolcott and Wolcott (1984) have noted the potential impacts on invertebrates such as crabs. The Ghost Crab (*Ocypode quadrata*)

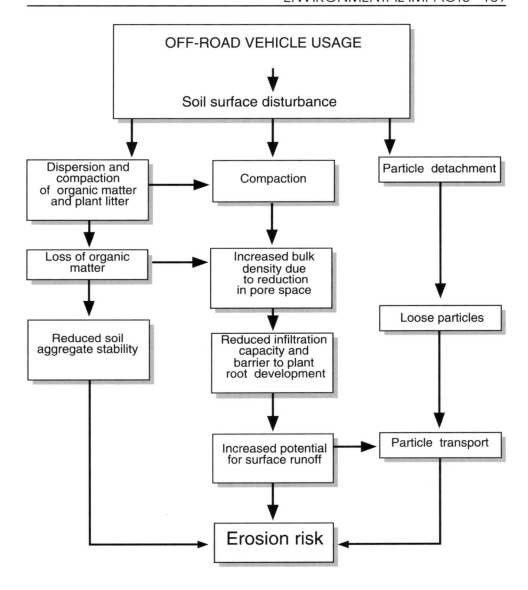

Figure 3.16 Impact of off-road vehicles on soils

appears to be particularly affected by the activity of off-road vehicles on coastal foreshores at night.

In contrast to the above biophysical impact studies the use of off-road vehicles can also lead to social conflict. Bayfield (1986) asserts that in the Cairngorms (Figure 3.1) the impact of off-road vehicles and their associated tracks is one of visitor

Table 3.6 Factors influencing the degree of impact caused by off-road vehicles

Environmental
Surface soil characteristics
Soil moisture content
Vegetation type
Slope
Climate
Operational and vehicular factors
Acceleration
Speed
Turning radius
Wheel track pressure
Wheel track configuration
Skill and attitude of the operator
Season the activity takes place

Derived from Rickard and Brown, 1974

perception. He goes on to state, in this case the ecological impact is limited, and that the impacts are social in nature. This is evidenced by a survey which showed that 72% of respondents thought vehicle tracks to be intrusive to their outdoor experience. It is also probably the case that associated biophysical impacts, such as noise, exhaust fumes and erosion scars, as a result of off-road vehicle activity also contribute to social discontent where hikers and off-road vehicles use the same areas.

In a study of off-road vehicle impacts on Arctic tundra Rickard and Brown (1974) consider aspects of environmental sensitivity and the factors influencing the degree of biophysical impact caused by off-road vehicles (Table 3.6). Although they have considered these factors in relation to the Arctic tundra many such factors also apply to off-road vehicle driving in other environments.

Rickard and Brown (1974) also consider a number of impacts in terms of increasing severity of disturbance in the Arctic tundra landscape. These are: aesthetic impacts, disturbance and damage to vegetation, destruction of plant cover and soil compaction leading to soil erosion and, finally, surficial peat disruption, subsidence of frozen ground and the ponding of water. They note that the latter two impacts are dependent on higher intensities of off-road vehicle activity taking place during the summer period.

Further specific effects of off-road vehicle activity in tundra environments will be considered in the remaining sections which examine different aspects of environmental impacts under contrasting environmental conditions.

Arctic-alpine environments

Temperature is a major limiting factor and the growing season for plants is short. Low levels of biological activity are reflected in the low biological diversity that typifies Arctic-alpine and tundra regions. Where the annual temperature regime is normally less than 0°C sub-surface permafrost, overlain by a thin layer of soil, is a feature of the landscape. Rickard and Brown (1974) report that the disruption of surficial organic layers and soils by off-road vehicles promotes thawing of the sub-surface permafrost. The resultant change in volume from ice to water then results in subsidence and the creation of ponded areas that are then susceptible to erosion.

Various authors also report on the slow recovery of tundra vegetation following disturbance by off-road vehicles (e.g. Forbes, 1992; Greller *et al.* 1974; Kevan *et al.*, 1995; Rickard & Brown, 1974). Furthermore it has been shown that different plant communities within the tundra ecosystem show different susceptibilities to damage. Greller *et al.* (1974) for example showed that the impact of snowmobiles was greatest on soil and rock lichens and rigid cushion plants. Those plants that resisted and tolerated the damage were found to have less height and a reduced woody biomass such as in the case of grassy species.

More recent studies of vehicle damage to tundra vegetation reiterate the findings of earlier researchers that the passage of vehicles in tundra ecosystems results in a reduction of woody species, loss of vegetation cover, subsidence of vehicle tracks and that recovery from damage is naturally slow (e.g. Forbes, 1992; Kevan *et al.*, 1995). As in many other tourism/recreation situations the spatial extent of these impacts is low but, as noted by Forbes (1992), there is an increasing demand for recreational access to tundra ecosystems which is likely to put additional pressure on these ecosystems in the future.

Tropical environments

As discussed previously a universal impact of off-road driving is damage to vegetation and the increased potential for soil erosion. The above examples have also highlighted the particular sensitivity of damage in some environments in which off-road driving takes place. While Arctic-alpine tundra is particularly sensitive to damage the vegetation that comprises savanna ecosystems in Africa has been shown to be less significant due to rapid recovery (resilience) of the vegetation (Onyeanusi, 1986; Tyler & Dangerfield, 1999). Other impacts, however, may be apparent as in the case of the aesthetic impact of numerous track lines that detract from the wilderness experience of visitors to the Masai Mara in Kenya.

Wildlife disturbance is also a possible problem associated with off-road vehicles in various settings around the world. This can occur directly as a result of road mortality or indirectly as a result of habitat alteration. An example of the latter case is afforded by unsealed roads that cater for off-road access. Goosem (2000) provides an account of how such roads can lead to changes in faunal composition in a tropical rainforest setting in Queensland, Australia. Roads that penetrate forested environments allow increased levels of light to reach the forest floor and this in turn reduces the normally higher levels of humidity which occur on the forest floor. The resultant microclimatic changes lead to a change in vegetation particularly towards disturbance adapted species. Such changes in the plant community change the prevailing conditions for resident fauna.

Goosem (2000) found that the small mammal community along a low traffic volume unsealed road in the Kuranda State Forest (Figure 3.1) was different to that of non-roaded forest. For example, *Rattus sordidus* and *Melomys burtoni*, non-rainforest mammals, had penetrated the forest by utilising the open habitat created by the presence of the road.

Studies such as this show the potential for the penetration of non-rainforest, and even exotic, mammals into areas of rainforest even along relatively unused and unsealed roads. Additionally such changes, over time, could lead to an alteration in the abundance and diversity of small mammals in the forest. This is an issue that applies to most forest environments that are dissected by roads.

Arid environments

The case of off-road vehicle activity in arid environments has been particularly investigated in the USA (e.g. Bury *et al.*, 1977; Webb, 1982; Webb & Wiltshire, 1983). To this end the wider implications of soil compaction have been discussed by Adams *et al.* (1982) who report that a reduction in the cover of annual plants was related to only low levels of off-road vehicle induced soil compaction. As also observed in other environments, the response of vegetation to disturbance varied according to plant species structure and growth habit. For example, Adams *et al.* (1982) found that large plants like *Erodium cicutarium* showed a greater loss of cover than grasses such as *Schismus barbatus*.

Cases of reduced biota with impacts on plants, invertebrates, reptiles and mammals has been reported from the Algodunes in California, USA (Figure 3.1) which is a popular recreation area for users of dune buggies (Luckenbach & Bury, 1983). Although such human use of a natural environment can, strictly speaking, be distinguished as recreation, as opposed to tourism, such studies are directly applicable to the tourism situation. This is because, as shown by Luckenbach and Bury (1983) and others, these impacts can be brought about only by low levels of access and activity.

Impacts on wildlife in arid areas are of particular importance because those animals that are adapted to arid zone and sand dune systems will be restricted to them. Furthermore, as in the Arctic tundra, there are environmental limitations that give rise to slow rates of recovery from disturbance.

Edington and Edington (1986) summarise the ecological consequences of off-road vehicles in desert ecosystems. Figure 3.17 depicts the impacts of off-road vehicles on ecosystem structure and function that leads to reduced biodiversity. Edington and Edington (1986) point out that there are many potential indirect impacts on animals. An example of such an indirect impact on fauna is the loss of food supply such as desert annual plants. This is because different species of rodents are dependent on the different sized seeds of various annual plants. In addition to this, the loss of shrubs means a loss of ecosystem structure which translates into reduced cover. This in turn reduces the scope for prey species avoiding predators; predatory species successfully ambushing prey; animals readily gaining shade under high temperature conditions and also

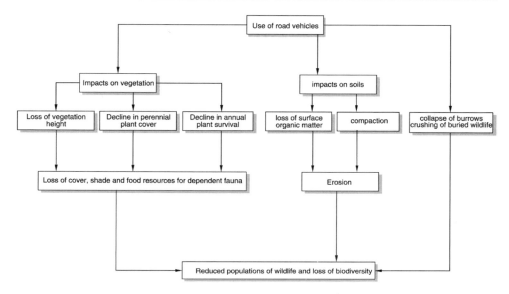

Figure 3.17 Environmental impacts of off-road vehicles in semi-arid and arid ecosystems. (Derived from Edington & Edington, 1986)

constitutes a reduction in the availability of breeding sites. Because vegetation is sparse and well spaced in desert ecosystems such losses can rapidly lead to a reduction in faunal populations.

The need for desert reptiles and mammals to gain shelter from the excessive heat and predators in a sparsely vegetated environment has led to the behavioural habit of small reptiles burying themselves and the widespread use of burrows by larger reptiles and mammals in sandy deserts. Kinlaw (1999) stresses that open burrows are also a major resource for many other species and their presence in semi-arid and arid environments contributes to increased species richness. Kinlaw (1999) cites various examples of this from the USA and from Southern Africa. In New Mexico, for example, Kangaroo Rat (*Dipodomys ordii*) burrows have been found to have 14 species of reptiles, 22 families of insects and 6 orders of other invertebrates associated with them. The 45% or more losses of mammals reported by Bury *et al.* (1977) and Luckenbach & Bury (1983) at heavy use locations is thus likely to translate into a wider ecological impact depending on how the associated burrow system fauna, as indicated above, is also impacted.

Conclusion

The purpose of this chapter has been to illustrate the possible consequences of recreation and tourism in a wide range of natural environments. Although it appears to paint a negative picture of natural area tourism the objective has been to highlight potential problems so that they can be anticipated and managed. Never before have so many people been interested in the natural world; moreover our social and political systems would not allow nature to be 'locked away' and left only for scientists and film makers. The future lies in making natural landscapes, flora and fauna available for people to experience and enjoy. Local communities and economies also need to benefit from natural area tourism; indeed this is usually the major justification for the protection of nature in both the developed and developing world. Impacts brought about by tourism, however, can spoil the resource and impact on visitor experience. This over time can lead to a decline or change in tourist interest in an area resulting in social conflict, economic impacts and environmental degradation.

The need for ecological understanding remains clear and being able to see how a natural area fits into the bigger landscape context is also critical in reducing impacts and protecting the resource. This is exemplified by the situation in the Kruger National Park which is being impacted upon by factors largely external to the park.

Although there is an extensive literature on the impacts of tourism there are many issues and specific cases that remain to be understood. As discussed by Sun and Walsh (1998) large gaps remain in our understanding of biophysical impacts. The data are just not available for many countries in the developing world and even in places like Australia which is a major nature-based tourism destination. Natural area tourism cannot be planned, managed and monitored without data on resource condition and environmental impacts. This chapter has provided an overview of a range of potential impacts and sets the scene for the planning, management and monitoring of various activities that fall under the umbrella of natural area tourism.

Further reading

Textbooks that contain substantive content on the environmental impacts of recreation and tourism include Edington and Edington (1986), Hammitt and Cole (1998), Hendee *et al.* (1990a), Kuss *et al.* (1990), and Liddle (1997).

For further information on the nature and properties of soils and details of soil formation, soil science texts such as those by Brady (1990) and Charman and Murphy (2000) should be consulted.

Disturbance to wildlife is a major issue in natural area tourism and has received much attention. For example, in recent years Hammitt and Cole (1998), Knight and Gutzwiller (1995), Liddle (1997), and Shackley (1996) have produced important accounts, case histories and discussion on recreational and tourism disturbance to wild animals.

For a classic treatise on the ecological, social and economic impacts of tourism, readers are referred to Mathieson and Wall, 1982. Sound coverage of the topic on community tourism is provided by Murphy (1985). For further practical information on the social and cultural opportunities of tourism development in natural areas readers are urged to consult two IIED Wildlife and Development Series publications. They are *Community involvement in wildlife tourism* (No. 11,

Ashley & Roe, 1998) and Case studies from Asia and Africa (No. 12, Goodwin *et al.*, 1998).

The economic aspects of tourism in natural areas are particularly well described and analysed by Lindberg and Huber (1998) and Lindberg (2001).

Chapter 4
Visitor Planning

Introduction

If natural area tourism and its potential impacts are to be managed in effective and cost-efficient ways, then planning is essential. This chapter focuses on recreation/tourism planning frameworks as a means of planning for visitor use of natural areas. The subjective nature of planning and the need to engage stakeholders thoughout planning processes is emphasised. The concepts of carrying capacity, 'acceptable' change and the spectrum of recreation opportunities are described because an understanding of them is essential before discussing the frameworks themselves. Details of six visitor planning frameworks follow, plus suggestions as to how to choose between them.

This chapter focuses on visitor planning. A variety of planning processes can be used to manage natural area tourism. Planning for and with the tourism industry is one such approach. Visitor and tourism industry management may also be part of a broader suite of issues considered in natural area management planning (also referred to, with slight variations in meaning, as protected area, heritage, and environmental planning). The Environmentally Based Planning (EBT) model for regional tourism development (Dowling, 1993) is another example of a broader approach to such planning. Planning for visitor use of natural areas desperately requires detailed attention given the rapid increases in visitation over recent years (Chapter 1) and the associated potential for increased impacts (Chapter 3). As such, it is the subject of this chapter.

Confusion continues to exist regarding the interface and overlaps between visitor planning frameworks and management plans for natural areas. Most often, these frameworks contribute to sections on visitor management in these plans. Management plans are usually much more broad-ranging than visitor planning frameworks, addressing management of ecological communities and especially rare species, wildlife, fire, introduced weeds and pests, adjacent land use and water bodies, in addition to visitors and the tourism industry (Dowling, 1993; Eagles, 1984). For reasons explored in this chapter, visitor planning frameworks have been infrequently used in management planning processes for natural areas. Their omis-

146

sion from such processes continues to compromise the quality of natural area management.

Much of the material here is drawn from the wealth of research and practice in recreation planning and management for wilderness areas and national parks worldwide. Planning activities in the United States, Canada and Australia were a particularly rich source of ideas. Most of the frameworks were developed and applied to individual, although often large, natural areas, with several having been applied more broadly across a region or to a group of natural areas.

Definition

Planning is a process of setting goals and then developing the actions needed to achieve them. For natural area tourism, it allows managers to define what experiences visitors will have, the experiences they want to produce, the visitors they want to attract, and the limits to environmental modification deemed acceptable. This type of planning focuses on managing to achieve desired outcomes. Planning helps achieve these outcomes in the face of changing internal conditions, such as funding and staff changes within management agencies. It also helps cope with external changes, such as swings in public opinion and changing demographics.

Planning has a number of distinguishing characteristics. For natural area tourism, these coalesce around the idea that natural areas used by tourists are products. Thus, the basic task of planning is to visualise the area, that is, the product, as visitors and managers wish it to be in the future. Planning is a process continuing over time, sometimes resulting in a written plan, but not always. It generally includes establishing goals and objectives, determining strategies and actions, and guiding implementation and review (Figure 4.1). Goals are general statements of desired future conditions, whereas objectives are specific, measurable and attainable. Strategies are management directions, for example, providing interpretive opportunities for visitors, and actions are specific details on what will be done, for example, providing a visitor centre in a specified place. Until implementation has

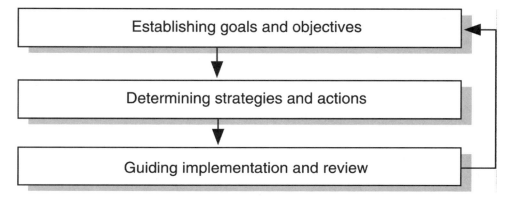

Figure 4.1 A generic planning process

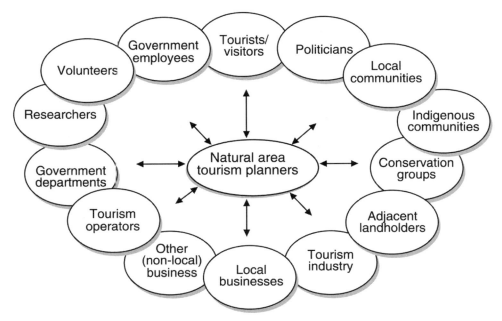

Figure 4.2 Possible stakeholders of natural area tourism. (Derived from Hall & McArthur, 1998; Sautter & Leisen, 1999)

occurred, planning is not completed. Hall (2000) described this process as strategic planning and emphasised its iterative nature. The process must be flexible, iterative and ongoing, allowing objectives and strategies to be adjusted while still providing a means for consistent management.

The last distinguishing feature of planning for visitor use of natural areas is its participatory nature. All the planning frameworks described in this chapter have provision for stakeholder involvement. Where and how involvement occurs depends on the framework. Stakeholders include those directly affected such as visitors themselves, plus others indirectly affected (e.g. local communities), as well as those managing or providing tourism opportunities such as land managers and tour operators. Those further afield, while not actively involved in or influenced by tourism use, may watch such activities with interest. They are also stakeholders. Hall and McArthur (1998) and Sautter and Leisen (1999) listed tourists/visitors, local communities resident in or near natural areas, indigenous peoples, conservation groups, local and other businesses, politicians, governments and their employees, and competitors as potential stakeholders (Figure 4.2).

Reasons for visitor planning

Planning for visitor use of natural areas is a relatively recent phenomenon, only emerging in the second half of last century. Such planning has been a response to dramatically increasing use of natural areas, worldwide, over the last four decades.

This increase is due to several factors including changing mobility. The advent of motor vehicles has placed many natural areas within easy reach of major population centres, while air travel means remote corners of the world are only a day away. Technology, and particularly lightweight camping and trekking equipment, has made extended stays in remote areas possible for increasing numbers of visitors. Also, at least in the 1960s and 1970s, people had increased leisure time to access, enjoy and become concerned about natural area management.

Other reasons for increased use of natural areas are related to changes in education levels, lifestyles and spirituality. Over the last few decades, people have become more educated, mainly through mass access to tertiary education. An increased appreciation of the natural environment is an outcome. Such an appreciation is also a product of the stresses of urban life with many urban dwellers relying on natural environments for relaxation and regeneration. Additionally, some people's spiritual practices depend on natural areas. Beliefs such as Gaia focus on the earth and the interconnectedness of all associated living and non-living matter. These relationships are perceived as most harmonious in natural areas. Other societal groups, such as the men's movement, rely on natural settings for ceremonies and rights of passage.

Several problems making planning imperative have arisen from this increasing use. The values that attracted visitors in the first place, whether they were spectacular landscapes, unusual plants or animals or high biodiversity, can potentially be degraded by human use. Conflict between users is also a possibility. For example, hikers often come into conflict with others enjoying the same area on horseback or in motor vehicles. Planning helps to avoid or at least minimise such conflicts. It can also help avoid problems created by successive minor decisions. Often, one decision leads to another and before long undesirable and even irreversible actions have been taken. This tyranny of small decisions can result in the values that drew visitors to an area being inadvertently lost.

For many natural area tourism destinations, such as protected areas in the United States, Canada, Australia, New Zealand, Indonesia, Thailand, India and Malaysia, managers have devoted their energies to acquiring and/or reserving land. In the face of limited staff and financial resources, acquisition has been the highest priority. The next steps for many managers are planning and management. Until recently, limited resources for these activities were accompanied by a lack of systematic and widely available planning approaches. Such approaches or frameworks have since been developed. The challenge now is to raise awareness of their existence and increase their use. Sustainability is the core goal of natural area tourism, the intention being to provide tourism resources for the future as well maintain biodiversity, avoid irreversible environmental changes and ensure equity within and between generations. Wearing and Neil (1999) identified recreation/tourism planning frameworks as crucial to managing protected areas for sustainability.

The last reason for visitor planning is a legislative one: planning for protected areas is mandated by legislation in many countries. For example, in countries such as the United States where management of protected areas is the responsibility of the federal government, planning is mandated by the Wilderness Act of 1964, the National Forest Management Act of 1976, and the National Environmental Policy Act of 1969. In other countries, such as Australia, where states/provinces are responsible for managing protected areas, legislation such as the Conservation and Land Management Act 1985 (WA) similarly requires planning. Such plans usually include visitor management.

Planning as a value-laden activity

In the previous section planning was defined as a process of setting goals and then developing the actions needed to achieve them. This is very much a rational, objective view of planning. Do value judgements have a place in such a process? The answer is a resounding yes, for two reasons. First, planning is about determining what should be as well as what is (Lipscombe, 1987). Making decisions regarding 'shoulds' always involves value judgements. Second, planning includes planning for visitors as well as recognising the concerns and interests of managers. As such, the value judgements of visitors, managers and other stakeholders have to be considered.

Stakeholder Involvement in Visitor Planning

Stakeholders in the developed world generally expect to have a choice regarding whether or not they become involved in visitor planning for natural areas. In contrast, in the developing world, citizens may not expect to participate. Planning may be perceived by local residents as the responsibility of government who then informs people of its decisions. An Indonesian government tourism planner interviewed as part of a recent survey commented that decisions should be made by government for the good of society (Timothy, 1999). Another interviewee commented that Indonesians' customary approach to authority based on respect and subservience may significantly inhibit grassroots involvement. Additionally, involvement may be curtailed by it being considered a luxury, people being more concerned with basic survival than long-term planning, and citizens' beliefs that they know too little to get involved. Not all stakeholders are excluded. Elites, such as influential business people and political figures, have long had access to governmental decision making (Timothy, 1999).

A range of very different intentions and possibilities can underpin the inclusion of stakeholders in visitor planning (Figure 4.3). Arnstein's (1969) ladder provides a useful summary of these possibilities, ranging from no opportunities for involvement (i.e. non-participation) through to stakeholders having complete control of planning and management of an area (i.e. citizen control). In the developed world, and specifically the United States, Canada and Australia, stakeholder involvement in planning for protected areas has relied on consultation and in some cases partnerships. Movement beyond partnerships is unlikely given that public agencies are legally responsible for managing most protected areas in these countries. As such,

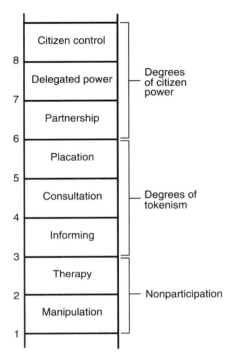

Figure 4.3 Ladder of citizen participation. (Derived from Arnstein, 1969)

devolution of responsibility for management through delegated power or citizen control is highly unlikely. Buchy and Ross (2000) noted the influence of tenure – who is responsible for managing an area – as a major influence on the level of stakeholder involvement. In the developing world, involvement is more likely located on the lower rungs of the ladder.

Benefits and costs

Involving stakeholders in visitor planning incurs both benefits and costs. Benefits may include better decisions, increased accountability, stakeholder acceptance, local community empowerment and clarifying visitor preferences (Bramwell & Lane, 2000a). Better decisions result from stakeholders providing and assessing collectively held information. Accountability of land managers is increased through stakeholder involvement as planning and associated actions are subject to scrutiny. Stakeholder and especially local involvement may help communities understand and then accept planners' proposals. Involvement may also empower local communities, through control over local resources and decisions becoming possible. And, most importantly, benefits from these resources may be accrued. Lastly, stakeholder involvement helps make explicit the values, norms and preferences of visitors. The success of a number of the visitor planning frameworks discussed in this chapter relies on these being made explicit. Stakeholder involvement in such processes also helps clarify the multiple goals and preferred futures associated with most natural areas (Krumpe and McCool, 1997).

Involving stakeholders also has disadvantages or costs. It requires more time and more staff. Not only are more resources needed to undertake consultation, such consultation also has indirect resource effects. For example, through consultation, communities are often able to exert pressure to have services extended beyond that originally planned, leading to increases in implementation costs. Other costs can flow from 'losing control' of a planning process. Land management agencies may lose control as communities struggle, either with them or other groups. Groups or individuals may seek control of the planning process or the process may inadvertently become part of broader community disputes.

Techniques

The objectives of stakeholder involvement in visitor planning range from providing information (the lower rungs of the ladder – Figure 4.3), through information receiving and sharing, to participatory decision making (the higher rungs) (Table 4.1). The planning frameworks discussed in this chapter work best with participatory decision making. Other techniques, as listed in Table 4.3, can be used

Table 4.1 Stakeholder involvement techniques in visitor planning for natural areas

Technique	Objective			
	Information giving	Information receiving	Information sharing	Participatory decision making
Information sheets	X			
Displays	X			
Media campaigns	X			
Draft plans	X			
Review of plans	X	X		
Discussion papers	X	X		
Telephone hotlines	X	X		
Stakeholder interviews	X	X		
Phone polling/surveys		X		
Focus group	X	X	X	
Public meetings	X	X	X	
Stakeholder meetings	X	X	X	X
Joint field trips	X	X	X	X
Advisory committees	X	X	X	X
Task forces	X	X	X	X
Workshop	X	X	X	X

Derived from Hall & McArthur (1998)

separately or in conjunction with participatory approaches. Information sheets are widely used to provide information, while reviewing plans is a means of disseminating and collecting information. Stakeholder meetings, information days and field trips are often used to share information. Different techniques are used at different stages of planning because each stage has different information requirements. Early on, information giving may dominate as planners inform stakeholders about the planning initiative. As planning progresses, this may change to information sharing as stakeholders describe existing visitor use and associated conditions. Later, participatory decision making is likely as desired future conditions are discussed and determined.

The choice of techniques depends on several factors, including the ability of land managers to share power with stakeholders and the desire of stakeholders to do so. If power sharing is possible and desired, then a task force or advisory committee can be used. Choice is also influenced by the complexity of the resource management problems and the levels of stakeholder interest (Smith & Moore, 1990). If the resource problems are simple or localised in a low use area, then minimal stakeholder involvement such as information giving (e.g. information sheet or display) and an opportunity for information sharing (e.g. plan review) may be sufficient. For a large natural area with many stakeholders, a range of techniques will be essential. If there are divergent values and preferences between these stakeholders participatory processes such as workshops will be necessary to explore and if possible resolve some of these differences.

Planning Concepts

An understanding of the concepts of carrying capacity, 'acceptable' change and spectrum of recreation opportunities is essential before progressing to the planning frameworks themselves. Over the years countless managers and researchers have attempted to determine a numeric carrying capacity for a natural area, generally without success. Yet the search continues. At least one of the following frameworks (e.g. Limits of Acceptable Change) was established to provide an alternative approach to the vexed issue of determining when the conditions of an area have become unacceptable. The concept of 'acceptable' change underpins this alternative approach. Providing a spectrum of recreation opportunities forms the basis of another framework (the Recreation Opportunity Spectrum) as well as underpinning most of the other approaches.

Carrying capacity

Carrying capacity is a fundamental concept in natural resource management. It is the maximum level of use an area can sustain as determined by natural factors such as food, shelter and water (e.g. three sheep per hectare). Beyond this limit, no major increases in the dependent population can occur (Stankey et al., 1990). The term has been applied in rangeland management worldwide and wildlife management in the United States. If the balance between animals and the range's capacity is upset, either by an increase in animals or a decline in the resource conditions, then problems will occur: fewer animals can be supported and in the worst case, irreversible environmental damage occurs.

In the early 1960s the concept of carrying capacity was carried across to recreation, and especially wilderness management, as wilderness conditions deteriorated in the face of rapidly escalating levels of use. Managers hoped to be able to determine a visitor carrying capacity below which the natural environment could be sustained. Wagar (1964) broadened capacity to include social as well as ecological capacity. Thus, recreation and tourism carrying capacity has two main components: an ecological capacity – the impact on the biological and physical resources (i.e. soils and vegetation) and a social capacity, that is, the impact on the visitor experience (Morin et al., 1997).

Continuing and growing impacts in natural areas fuelled research on carrying capacity as a way of helping make decisions about controlling impacts. By the early 1980s, more than 2000 papers had been published on the topic (Drogin et al., 1986, in Stankey et al., 1990). Why so many and where are we now regarding application and use of the carrying capacity concept? In reality, the carrying capacity concept has failed to generate practical visitor use limits. There are five main reasons (McCool & Patterson, 2000; Stankey et al., 1990):

- *Different recreation/tourism experiences have different carrying capacities*. Natural areas are used by many different people seeking many different experiences. Some want solitude, some want companionship. What are regarded as reasonable encounter levels by some are regarded as overcrowded or too isolated by others. Every person and form of use seems to have a different experiential carrying capacity.
- *Impacts on biological and physical resources do not help establish carrying capacity*. Any visitor use of an area produces some environmental change. And especially important, much of the biophysical impact observed at sites occurs at very low levels of use (Cole, 1985, in Stankey et al., 1990). Therefore, if a manager wants to minimise impacts absolutely, then excluding people is the only effective solution. Such an action is generally neither possible nor desirable.
- *A strong cause-and-effect relationship between amount of use and impacts does not exist*. Numerous studies have failed to link amount of use and impact. As mentioned in the preceding point, much of the biophysical impact observed occurs at very low levels of use. There may then be a period of time when no impacts are observable until levels of use become such that impacts become evident again. This relationship is anything but simple and linear, plus a variety of variables affect it. Type of activity is usually a better predictor of impact than intensity of use. For example, low levels of horse riding may have greater impacts on trail condition than large numbers or frequent use of the same trails by hikers. The season of use may also be more important in explaining impacts than amount. Hiking in wet, winter or monsoonal condi-

tions, for example, potentially has far greater impacts on trail condition than increases in use during the dry season.

- *Carrying capacity is a product of value judgements and is not purely a product of the natural resource base and therefore determinable through careful observation and research.* The idea of carrying capacity as a product of the natural resource base was taken directly from range management, where carrying capacity was a direct product of natural factors such as soils and rainfall. It was seen as a scientific idea whose identification was only constrained by the level of effort and ingenuity exerted by managers in measuring biophysical impacts (Stankey *et al.*, 1990). However, it became increasingly evident that carrying capacities are as much the product of value judgements as they are of science. These are the values of visitors and managers. Visitors' values influence the experience they are seeking and their perceptions regarding the acceptability or otherwise of impacts. This broadens carrying capacity from a solely scientific assessment into the political arena of stakeholder involvement.

- *Carrying capacity does not help determine the balance between protecting the pristine qualities of a natural area and allowing visitor use.* Managing visitor use of natural areas is inherently complex and must be based on recognising that allowing use leads to some degradation. Managing for protection and visitor use requires that protection is ultimately constraining but can be initially compromised (Cole and Stankey, 1997). Initially, protection and pristine conditions are compromised as visitor use impacts on the environment. Such use continues, accepting some level of environmental impact, until further change becomes socially unacceptable. Then, visitor use is managed to prevent further impacts. Protection becomes the constraining goal.

McCool and Patterson (2000) noted that research and planning have now advanced to the point where carrying capacity is recognised as 'a reductionistic, naive and inappropriate paradigm upon which to base actions that protect recreational settings or tourism dependent communities'. They suggested instead focusing on understanding what conditions are desired, what impacts are acceptable and unacceptable, and what actions will lead to accepted goals. Such a refocusing is clarified by rephrasing the question from 'How much use is too much? to 'How much change is acceptable?' or 'What are the desired conditions?' (Lindberg *et al.*, 1997).

'Acceptable' change

For many stakeholders associated with the natural environment, no change is acceptable. However, managers and other stakeholders are increasingly realising that changes inevitably accompany visitor use (Lindberg *et al.*, 1997). Thus, natural areas need to be managed to limit change to levels 'acceptable' to stakeholders. The value judgements made about acceptable levels of change reflect philosophical, emotional, spiritual, experience-based and economic responses. As such, few people will have identical responses, and therefore few will make identical value judgements. Thus, the task for managers is resolving fundamental differences between stakeholders to determine desired conditions and how to achieve them.

Spectrum of recreation opportunities

Not everyone wants the same experience or to be involved in the same activities when they visit a natural area. Also, not all activities can occur at the same site at the same time or conflict inevitably results. The opportunities sought by people range from easily accessible, highly developed areas with modern conveniences to undeveloped, primitive areas in remote locations and all the opportunities in between. The assumption that quality is best assured by providing a diverse array of opportunities underpins application of the recreation opportunity spectrum. The concept can be applied within a single natural area such as a national park or to a group of protected areas, for example, as a means of classifying national parks across a region (Watson, 1997).

Recreation/Tourism Planning Frameworks

Over the last two decades, a number of frameworks have been developed to plan and manage visitor use of natural areas. All aim to protect the natural environment while providing desirable opportunities for visitors (Cole & Stankey, 1997). The most widely discussed and applied, usually to an individual natural area, are the Recreation Opportunity Spectrum, Limits of Acceptable Change and Visitor Impact Management frameworks. Recently, the Tourism Optimisation Management Model has been developed specifically for tourism. It has been applied to both individual and groups of natural areas.

The following recreation/tourism planning frameworks are not mutually exclusive. As noted by Boyd and Butler (1996), this field has been evolutionary rather than revolutionary (Figure 4.4). Thus, a number of frameworks have common features and on first glance the differences between them may not be apparent.

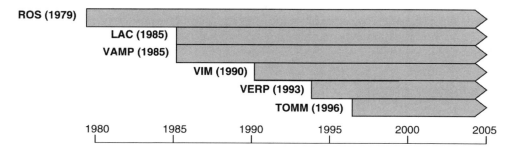

Figure 4.4 Chronological relationship between the recreation/tourism planning frameworks. (Derived from Nilsen & Tayler, 1997; acronyms are defined throughout the chapter)

Also, features of one framework may be subsumed within another. For example, the Limits of Acceptable Change framework includes most of the elements of the Recreation Opportunity Spectrum. To help tease out these differences the following sections include flow diagrams and examples, plus a section at the end on choosing between them.

Recreation Opportunity Spectrum

The Recreation Opportunity Spectrum (ROS) was developed in the 1970s by researchers associated with the United States Forest Service (Clark & Stankey, 1979; Driver & Brown, 1978). The 1960s and 1970s were a time of unprecedented growth in recreation use of natural areas and managers were very concerned regarding levels of use and maintaining the experience that drew users in the first place. ROS was offered as a means of identifying and determining the diversity of recreation opportunities for a natural area, based on the idea that the quality of visitors' experiences is best assured by providing diversity and helping visitors to find the settings providing the experiences they are seeking (Clark & Stankey, 1979).

Those who crafted ROS assumed that by providing diversity the adverse effects of increasing levels of use both on the natural environment and visitors' experiences would be mitigated. These effects would be reduced in large part by allocating high impact activities to more resilient sites and low impact activities to less resilient locations. The diversity recognised by ROS is usually categorised as a number of opportunity classes, ranging from primitive to developed (Figure 4.5, Table 4.2). Today, the term 'zone' is often used rather than opportunity class.

ROS spans places accessible only on foot with no facilities through to freeways

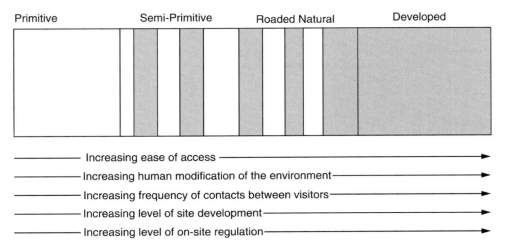

Figure 4.5 The Recreation Opportunity Spectrum. (Derived from Clark & Stankey, 1979)

Table 4.2 Recreation opportunity classes

Management factors	Classes			
	Primitive	Semi-primitive	Roaded natural	Developed
Physical				
Access	No motorised use	No motorised use	Motorised use and parking	High levels of motorised use and parking
Remoteness/ naturalness	Remote and completely natural	Completely natural	Appears predominantly natural	Natural background, site dominated by modification
Size	Large	Moderate	No size criteria	No size criteria
Social				
Contacts with other visitors	Few contacts	Low to moderate	Moderate along roads and tracks	High to very high along roads and tracks and at developed sites
Acceptability of visitor impacts	Not acceptable	Minor impacts accepted	Moderate impact in specific areas, such as campsites, accepted	Substantial impacts evident and accepted
Managerial				
Level of site development	No site development, no structures	Natural-appearing setting, structures rare and isolated	Roads, site facilities for comfort and security	Roads and site facilities for intensive use including resorts
Regulation	No on-site regulation, reliant on self-policing	On-site regulation if present, subtle	Moderate regimentation/ regulation via site design and signs	Controls obvious and numerous via design, signs and staffing
Example				
Natural area tourism site	'Wild' campsite in a wilderness area	Designated site for hikers in a national park	Campsite/ picnic area in most national parks	Built accommod-ation/interpret-ation centre/ resort village in or adjacent to a natural area

Derived from Clark & Stankey (1979); Leonard & Holmes (1987); McArthur (2000a)

and facilities with many comforts, such as resorts and lodges (Clark & Stankey, 1979). As such, it is as equally applicable to natural area tourism as to recreational use of wilderness areas, the focus of its initial development. Butler and Waldbrook (1991) used a similar approach in their tourism opportunity spectrum for ecotourism planning, although they paid more attention to the developed end of the spectrum.

ROS uses physical, social and managerial characteristics to describe and compare opportunity classes (Clark & Stankey, 1979). Physical characteristics include access, remoteness, naturalness (degree of human modification of the natural environment) and size. Social characteristics are contacts with other visitors and acceptability of visitor impacts. Managerial characteristics are the level of facility development and the amount of on-site regulation (e.g. site hardening, fencing, signs). One or more of these characteristics can be manipulated to provide a chosen recreation opportunity, ranging from primitive to developed (Table 4.2).

Steps in ROS framework

This framework has been used in various ways to plan visitor use of natural areas. The most widely used approach is given in Figure 4.6 (Stankey & Brown, 1981). It was developed for flexibility, not as a prescriptive set of steps. As such, every application is slightly different. Most importantly ROS is a process, dependent on collecting and analysing biophysical and social information, for making management decisions.

The first and most difficult step in ROS is determining the demand for recreation/tourism opportunities (Step 1). These opportunities are a product of the settings and experiences and to a lesser extent the activities sought. Existing demand is sometimes known from visitor surveys; however, often there are only informal records from field staff and in some cases nothing. Future demand can usually only be weakly predicted from current levels of use. Supply, the capability of the area to support various visitor uses and the opportunities currently provided, is easier to determine (Steps 2 and 3). Capability is based on factors such as an area's resilience to visitor use, remoteness, size, naturalness and landscape features appealing to visitors. Current opportunities can be mapped, giving particular attention to facilities such as campgrounds, roads and walk trails.

Determining the 'best' mix of recreation opportunities and allocation of land uses for a given area is not easy (Steps 4 and 5). Selection of opportunity classes and balancing recreation and other land use allocations draws on the preceding steps, considered within the constraints of budgets, statutory and non-statutory policy requirements, and other potential uses of the resource such as fire and wildlife management (Stankey & Brown, 1981). A number of options are usually considered, with maps of alternatives and costs and benefits compared. The last step is implementation, with management objectives given for each class (Step 6). An example of the application of ROS to planning at Mt Cole in south-eastern Australia follows (Box 4.1).

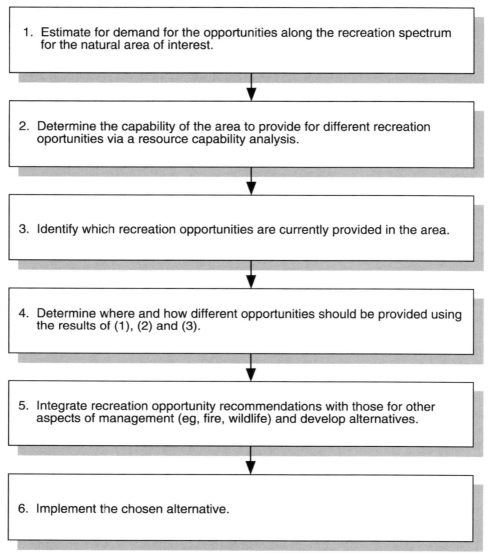

Figure 4.6 Process for applying the Recreation Opportunity Spectrum planning framework. (Derived from Stankey & Brown, 1981)

Application, strengths and weaknesses

ROS has been applied to recreation planning in the United States, Australia and New Zealand. By the early 1980s, it was being applied to about 30% of the United States' land area. In Australia, ROS has been applied to protected areas in five of the country's eight states and territories. Its longest-running and most effective appli-

---

Box 4.1 Applying ROS to Mt Cole Forest, Victoria, Australia

In the 1980s recreation use levels and associated conflicts in the Mt Cole forest, an area of some 12,150 ha in south-eastern Australia (Figure 4.7), were dramatically increasing. ROS was applied to help deal with these concerns (Leonard & Holmes, 1987). Recreation uses included camping, day use, hiking, trail-biking, off-road-driving and hang-gliding. The area supports rare fauna of great public interest including koalas, platypus and echidnas.

The Mt Cole project began by assessing the demand for various recreation opportunities (Figure 4.6, Step 1) and the recreation opportunities that could be offered, that is, supply (Steps 2 and 3). Demand was determined from information provided by field staff, booking systems and assessment of the physical effects of use. Most use was occurring in the middle part of the spectrum, in the semi-primitive and roaded natural parts rather than the primitive and developed ends. Supply evaluation included mapping and describing the biophysical environment, existing recreation features and opportunity classes, and reviewing the recreation opportunities that could be offered. Maps of landscape features such as streams and lakes, vista points and old sawmill sites likely to influence patterns of use were one output. Another was existing opportunity classes and associated site features such as walk trails and campsites.

The supply and demand information were used to determine where different opportunities classes should be provided (Step 4). Opportunity classes were allocated to provide choice and overcome conflicts between users. The next step was integrating recreation planning with other management concerns such as fire protection, timber production, water catchment values and fauna conservation (Step 5). Overlays of the various uses were used to 'adjust' the opportunity classes to avoid conflict and provide an equitable balance between various uses. Implementation, the final step in Figure 4.6, was sought via a 3–5 year plan. The plan details developments required, such as campgrounds and walk trails, ways of shifting a site from one class to another on the spectrum (e.g. from a roaded natural site to a semi-primitive one) and implementation costs.

---

cation has been in zoning natural areas (McArthur, 2000a). The most usual place to find the decisions resulting from ROS is in a zoning plan for recreation, usually included in a management plan, where the need to provide a spectrum of opportunities is recognised. It is unusual to find a document such as a management plan or strategy based solely on ROS.

Ensuring a range of recreation opportunities is considered in planning at local and regional levels is its greatest strength. ROS is also valuable as it allows visitor management to be integrated with other forms of planning (Nilsen & Tayler, 1997). Its weakness, as with other frameworks, is if agreement is lacking regarding opportunity classes and their characteristics, then decisions and implementation cannot follow.

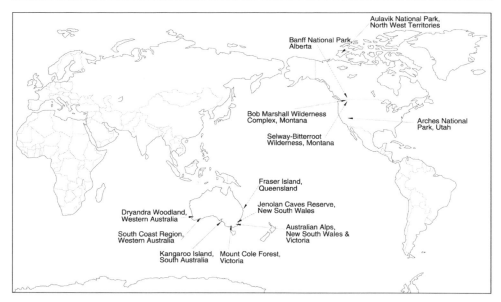

Figure 4.7 Location map of sites referred to in this chapter

Limits of Acceptable Change

The Limits of Acceptable Change (LAC) planning framework builds on and goes beyond ROS to set measurable standards for managing recreation in natural areas (Cole & Stankey, 1997). ROS is a process for recognising and designating opportunity classes with different levels of use. However, it does not provide guidance in setting of standards and their subsequent use in managing visitors and their impacts. LAC provides a process for deciding what environmental and social conditions are acceptable and helps identify management actions to achieve these conditions.

It represents a major alternative approach to the carrying capacity concept. Instead of asking 'How much use is too much?' and trying to link the number of visitors to environmental changes and failing, the LAC approach rephrases the question by asking 'How much change is acceptable?' (Prosser, 1986). Acceptability is a social phenomenon, and thus stakeholder involvement in the LAC process is essential. Stakeholders can provide judgements regarding the acceptability of impacts and in some instances can monitor to see if management is working. They can also provide a substantial amount of expertise on areas that are impacted and what management actions are likely to work. Also essential is the involvement of managers who have regular, if not daily contact with impacts and their response to management. For example, a ranger/field officer may drive or walk along an eroded track several times a week and will have views regarding its acceptability and likely responses to management actions.

LAC was developed by United States Forest Service researchers (Stankey *et al.*,

1985), in close collaboration with management staff, to address concerns regarding increasing levels of recreational use in wilderness areas and associated environmental consequences. Application to a large wilderness area in the north-western United States, the Bob Marshall Wilderness Complex (Figure 4.7), guided its development (Stokes, 1990). The description of LAC in this book has been broadened to include more developed environments such as tourism resorts and other built, intensively used facilities.

Steps in LAC framework

This framework, similarly to ROS, is a flexible process with managers expected to adapt and modify it using their and stakeholder's experience and knowledge of a given area. It is a process for making management decisions, not a prescriptive series of steps to be unthinkingly followed. It is universally described by nine interrelated steps leading to a set of standards and associated actions to achieve them (Stankey *et al.*, 1985) (Figure 4.8).

The first two steps describe the management issues for an area and the recreation opportunity classes (i.e. zones), providing the context for the remainder of the planning process. The opportunity classes are those managers wish to provide, not necessarily those currently available. Next, indicators are selected to measure existing resource and social conditions and acceptable standards determined (Steps 3, 4 and 5). Possible physical indicators are water quality, soil compaction and erosion, and air pollution. Biological indicators include vegetation cover and fauna. The number of people seen or heard is an indicator of social conditions. Chapter 7, 'Monitoring' has further details on possible indicators and associated standards.

Indicators must have the following attributes:

(1) Be capable of being measured in cost-effective ways at acceptable levels of accuracy.
(2) The condition of the indicator should reflect some relationship to the amount/type of use occurring.
(3) Social indicators should be related to user concerns.
(4) The condition of the indicator must be responsive to management control (Stankey *et al.*, 1985).

A number of indicators may be required to adequately cover the state of desired conditions.

Standards, a level beyond which further change is unacceptable, are selected for each indicator. A standard for an indicator will usually vary between opportunity classes (i.e. zones). In the most pristine zone the highest standard will be set with a lower standard in the most developed zone. For example, in the Selway-Bitterroot Wilderness in Montana (Figure 4.7), the standard for the maximum number of campsites per square mile was 1 for the most pristine opportunity class (Class 1) and 4 for the most developed (Class 4) (Ritter, 1997).

Standards may reflect the existing condition of an area or provide targets for rehabilitating an area where the level of change is no longer acceptable. Standards

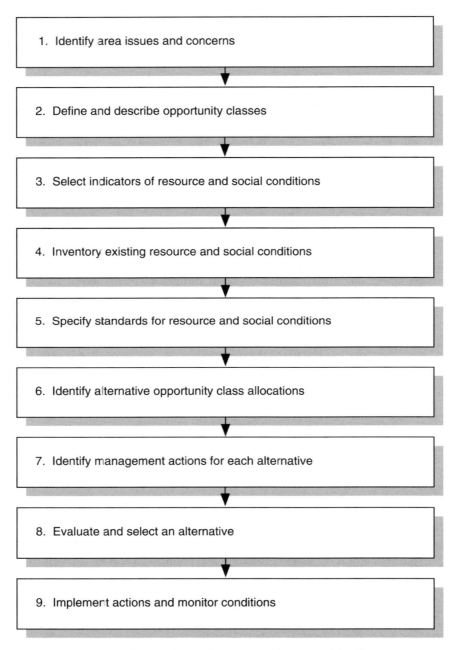

1. Identify area issues and concerns

2. Define and describe opportunity classes

3. Select indicators of resource and social conditions

4. Inventory existing resource and social conditions

5. Specify standards for resource and social conditions

6. Identify alternative opportunity class allocations

7. Identify management actions for each alternative

8. Evaluate and select an alternative

9. Implement actions and monitor conditions

Figure 4.8 Process for applying the Limits of Acceptable Change planning framework. (Derived from Stankey *et al.*, 1985)

are crucial in the LAC process because they determine the future character of an area. There is usually uncertainty about the accuracy of standards and in most places where LAC has been applied people have been hesitant to set standards in case they are wrong. This concern is unnecessary. Because monitoring and evaluation are the central component of the LAC system, standards and indicators can be revised as improved information becomes available.

Development of alternative zoning schemes and associated management actions and selection of a preferred scheme follows (Steps 6, 7 and 8). Implementation accompanied by monitoring is the last step (Step 9). Evaluating the effectiveness of management actions is also part of this last step (Morin *et al.*, 1997). An example of application of the process to the Bob Marshall Wilderness Complex in Montana follows (Box 4.2). Although this is an old example it is valuable because here the

---

Box 4.2 Applying LAC to the Bob Marshall Wilderness Complex, Montana, USA

The most often used example of LAC is recreation planning for the Bob Marshall-Great Bear-Scapegoat Wildernesses initiated in the 1980s and continuing today. This wilderness complex, straddling the Rocky Mountains in the north-western United States, encompasses 682,000 ha (Figure 4.7, Plate 4.1). The area provides opportunities for extended hiking and horseback trips and is renown for big-game hunting and river-rafting (McCool, 1986). It covers complete ecosystems from river bottom to ridge top on both sides of the North American continental divide (Forest Service, 1985). By 1980 there was increasing conflict among user groups and between some user groups and the managers, the US Forest Service. There was also a growing perception among users that the wilderness was deteriorating (Stokes, 1987, 1990).

A task force with representatives from local and national stakeholder groups and including land managers from the US Forest Service was brought together in 1982 and worked to prepare an action plan for recreation management (Stokes, 1987, 1990). Each of the following steps was undertaken consultatively by the US Forest Service and the task force. The first step was identifying area issues and concerns (Figure 4.8, Step 1). These included lake and range management, trail conditions, visitor encounters, level of regulation, wild and scenic river management, campsite numbers and condition, and management structures. Other issues raised but beyond the scope of the plan were use levels by commercial horseback tour operators ('outfitters') and wildlife management. Four existing opportunity classes were described, from unmodified natural environment with no facilities and very infrequent encounters with other visitors ('pristine') through to predominantly unmodified with facilities for resource protection and visitor safety and moderate to high levels of encounters with others (Step 2).

Once the opportunity classes were defined, indicators were selected (Step 3). Both biophysical and social indicators were selected because both were of concern to visitors and managers. Area of bare soil and number of damaged trees were the chosen environmental indicators of campsite conditions. Number of trail encounters and others camped within site and sound were the social indicators. To determine standards and set a baseline for ongoing monitoring, indicators were surveyed by stakeholders and the US Forest Service (Step 4). Standards for a given indicator varied between opportunity classes. For example, the standard for area of bare soil at a campsite ranged from 100 ft^2 in the most pristine class through to 2000 ft^2 in the most developed class. This was Step 5.

The task force then developed a number of alternative opportunity class allocations (i.e. zoning schemes) and selected a preferred alternative (Steps 6 and 8). One alternative reflected current conditions on the ground. Another provided additional recreational opportunities. Four alternatives were also developed by user groups. All were overlaid and a composite produced and debated. Some modifications to the composite were made and through consensus this modified version was adopted. The preferred alternative leaned toward pristine conditions, except along heavily used trail corridors.

Once the opportunity class allocations were made, the third-to-last step was determining management actions (Step 7). The task force agreed actions were needed where standards were currently exceeded or would be exceeded when the area was moved to another opportunity class. In many places the proposed standards were violated, for example, there were too many campsites in a given area or numbers of trail and campsite encounters were excessive. Information and education were popular proposed actions for all opportunity classes. The last ongoing step is implementation and monitoring (Step 9). These planning and management activities continue today as does the involvement of the task force.

Plate 4.1 Bob Marshall Wilderness Complex, United States. (*Photo*: Steve McCool)

LAC framework was developed in tandem with the realities of planning for visitor use, plus it continues to be used by managers.

Application, strengths and weaknesses

LAC has been applied predominantly in the United States with the next highest level of application in Australia. Watson and Cole (1992) in their review of indicators drew on at least six current applications of LAC in the United States. The Australian applications, to national parks, rivers and a world heritage area, have not been fully implemented (McArthur, 2000a). Efforts have recently been made to apply it to tourism in the Antarctic (Davis, 1999). Brunson (1997) suggested LAC could be broadened to applications beyond wilderness and Merigliano *et al.* (1997) outlined its possible application to non-recreation management issues in protected areas.

It is unusual to find a document, such as a management plan, with LAC as its central focus. If the LAC process has been used it generally manifests itself in the recreation section of a management plan as indicators and standards. The Bob Marshall Wilderness Complex Action Plan (Forest Service, 1985) is an exception (Box 4.2). More often, the processes of LAC rest behind a planning process and are not explicitly mentioned in the resultant management plan. Such a lack of transparency is unlikely to engender ongoing stakeholder support. Recent trends towards performance-based outcomes in natural resource management (Beckwith & Moore, 2001), may mean that indicators of 'performance' and associated standards become more visible products of visitor planning processes for natural areas.

The greatest strength of LAC is determining when 'enough' change has occurred. The two weaknesses of LAC have been selecting standards and gaining stakeholder support (McArthur, 2000a). Little information may be available to help choose a standard. Additionally, environmental changes rather than visitor activities may lead to fluctuations around a standard with these two very different causes often impossible to separate. Gaining stakeholder support has long been a concern in natural area planning. LAC and planning frameworks in general are doomed to fail if stakeholders cannot agree. In the case of LAC, agreement on indicators, standards and allocation of zones is crucial. This comment is based on recognising 'planning is a political process in politized settings' (McCool & Cole, 1997).

Visitor Impact Management

The Visitor Impact Management (VIM) planning framework was developed for national parks by researchers working for the US National Parks and Conservation Association (Graefe *et al.*, 1990). Similarly to LAC, VIM was developed as an alternative to carrying capacity; however, it was intended to be simpler, narrowing the focus to visitor impacts rather than broader concerns with opportunity classes. Its purpose is developing strategies to keep visitor impacts within acceptable levels. Recognising that effective management is part-science, part-subjective judgement is fundamental to its application (Graefe *et al.*, 1990). Also fundamental is recognising that use limits are only one possible way of managing unacceptable impacts.

Other management strategies, such as education and site design, may be more effective. Also, as carrying capacity research has shown, the relationships between overall use levels and impacts are weak. Controlling use alone may not reduce impacts.

Steps in VIM framework

VIM is described by eight steps (Graefe *et al.*, 1990) (Figure 4.9). Together, they lead the manager from reviewing existing data and management objectives, through selecting indicators and standards and using these to identify unacceptable impacts, to identifying causes and suitable management strategies. The first five steps are the problem identification phase of VIM. Step 5 requires observation of existing conditions for the indicators selected in Step 3. If the selected standards are exceeded then the causes need to be determined (Step 6). The challenge of Step 6 is isolating the most significant cause of the impact. This step may also require studies of the relationships between key impact indicators and visitor use patterns.

Having followed these steps, there is unfortunately no one 'right' management strategy. Graefe *et al.* (1990) recommended using a matrix for evaluating alternatives (Step 7). One side of the matrix lists possible management strategies and the other side criteria such as consistency with management objectives, difficulty in implementing, probability of achieving desired outcome, effects on visitor freedom and effects on other impact indicators. Achieving a balance among criteria is the basis for selecting a particular management technique (Graefe *et al.*, 1990). For example, a strategy such as enforcement may have good odds of reducing the impact but may cause even more problems through lack of visitor acceptance. The matrix helps make explicit these trade-offs. Similarly to the frameworks already described, VIM is intended as a guide rather than a prescriptive set of steps. The flexible use of VIM is evident from the following example, where several steps were adapted or combined with others (Box 4.3).

Application, strengths and weaknesses

VIM has been applied to at least 10 national parks/reserves/wildlife refuges in the United States, in three states of Australia, and in Canada, Argentina, Mexico and The Netherlands (McArthur, 2000a). In general, VIM has not appeared as a separate planning document, rather it has been used to develop strategies for localised impact problems, either directly for managers or forming part of a larger management plan. A useful exception is the report funded by the Australian Department of Tourism applying VIM to Jenolan Caves (Box 4.3) (Figure 4.7).

The main strength of this framework is its reliance on both science and subjective judgement to guide visitor management. It is particularly suited to smaller rather than larger sites as there is no recognition within the framework of different opportunity classes, making it is most useful where only one opportunity class exists. As such, one of its weaknesses is not making use of ROS. Another is addressing current rather than potential impacts (Nilsen & Tayler, 1997). Successful visitor management relies on dealing with visitor impacts before or as they occur, not afterwards.

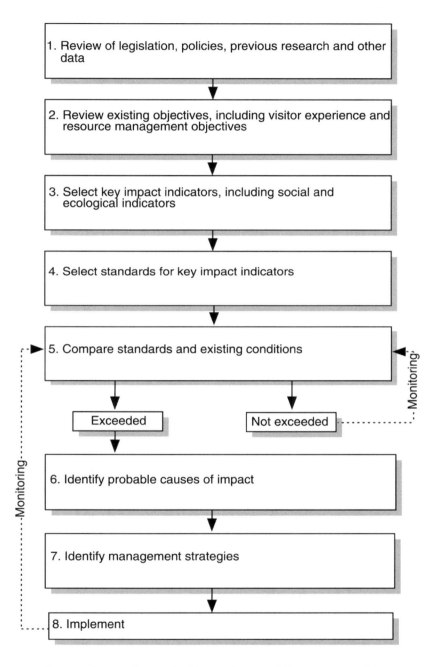

Figure 4.9 Process for applying the Visitor Impact Management planning framework. (Derived from Graefe *et al.*, 1990)

Box 4.3   Applying VIM to Jenolan Caves Reserve, New South Wales, Australia

Jenolan Caves in Eastern Australia is one of the country's best-known cave systems (Figure 4.7). By the 1990s, visitor numbers were increasing at 5–6% p.a. and resource degradation was an ongoing concern (Manidis Roberts Consultants, 1995). The study area is 2500 ha with 45 km of known passageways divided into about 350 caves. Of these, 16 caves are for public use. Infrastructure includes car parks, accommodation for guests and staff, and other amenities and service facilities.

A modified version of VIM was applied using a 3-day workshop of management staff, and physical and social scientists. Steps 1 and 2 (Figure 4.9) were subsumed within an issue identification stage. Issues included the need for clear objectives for the area and a better understanding of the needs of visitors. Also of concern were problems with traffic. The next steps were selecting indicators and standards for four resource management units (zones) (Steps 3 and 4). Carbon dioxide and water quality were two of the indicators for the developed caves management unit. Infrastructure capacity was an indicator for the developed above ground management unit. Visitor satisfaction was selected for all four units. Quantitative standards were selected for each indicator. For example, the desired condition or standard for visitor satisfaction was 90% of visitors rating their satisfaction as high to very high (Manidis Roberts Consultants, 1995). Subsequent to the workshop a monitoring programme has been initiated, with an annual State of the Environment report produced (Mackay, 1995). Collection of this data allows comparison of current and desired conditions (Step 5).

The workshop culminated with the determination of 'key limiting conditions' or issues for management attention. These were near-capacity vehicle parking, vehicle-pedestrian conflicts, overcrowding above and below ground, and hydrological disturbance to the caves from above ground developments. These limiting conditions were derived from probable causes of impacts (Step 6) as well as earlier steps in the VIM process (Figure 4.9).

Subsequent to the workshop, the Jenolan Caves Reserve Trust has, in addition to refining indicators and desired conditions, developed methods for and undertaken monitoring of indicators, and suggested causes of impacts and possible management responses (Steps 6 and 7). The Trust has expressed a high level of commitment to VIM and its ongoing implementation (Mackay, 1995).

Tourism Optimisation Management Model

The Tourism Optimisation Management Model (TOMM) was developed in the 1990s by the Sydney-based consulting firm Manidis Roberts, through application to Kangaroo Island off the coast of southern Australia (McArthur, 1996) (Figure 4.7). Unlike the frameworks discussed so far, it was developed specifically for tourism planning in natural areas. An important early step in this framework is describing the political, socio-cultural and economic context within which planning is occurring. Although it builds on the emphasis in LAC on monitoring, it differs in its broader regional application and its coverage of a number of land tenures, both public and private. Involving a diversity of stakeholders throughout the planning process is the final essential feature of this framework. The name TOMM was selected to take the emphasis away from limits that has led the tourism industry to equate LAC with anti-growth and anti-business sentiments (McArthur, 2000a).

Steps in TOMM framework

TOMM has three major parts – context description, monitoring programme and implementation (McArthur, 2000a) (Figure 4.10). Similarly to VIM and LAC, this framework leads the manager from describing the planning context, through selecting indicators and standards and using these to identify optimal conditions, to identifying causes and suitable management strategies. The description of the planning context includes current policies and plans, community values, product characteristics, growth patterns, market trends and opportunities, positioning and branding, and alternative scenarios for tourism in the region (Manidis Roberts Consultants, 1997) (Figure 4.10, Steps 1 and 2). Box 4.4 describes the Kangaroo Island application of TOMM.

Developing a monitoring programme is the heart of this planning process (Steps 3, 4, and 5). Included are identifying optimal conditions, indicators, acceptable ranges and benchmarks (Box 4.4). An optimal condition is a desirable yet realistic future. Indicators are then selected to measure these conditions. Indicators must be relevant to visitors and the associated data must be cost-effective to collect, available and accurate. The next step is developing an acceptable range and benchmark for each indicator. To-date, the value of an indicator at the start of monitoring has been taken as its benchmark. As data are collected from monitoring, optimal conditions, indicators and acceptable ranges can be refined.

The last major part is implementation, including the response by managers when an indicator falls outside its acceptable range (Figure 4.10, Step 6). Before acting, the manager needs to determine whether the result of concern is part of a longer-term trend or a one-off, and also its cause, which may be tourism or non-tourism related (Figure 4.11). The essential question is whether or not an indicator exceeding its acceptable range was caused by tourism (McArthur, 2000b). Many indicators are subject to effects from other sources such as ecological processes, the actions of local residents, initiatives by other industries, technological innovation, and national and global influences (Manidis Roberts Consultants, 1997). The last element of the implementation part of TOMM is taking action. A management response can be selected by brainstorming; thinking how the preferred response will affect other indicators and the likely results for the indicator of interest.

Application, strengths and weaknesses

As a relatively new framework, there are few applications of TOMM available as examples. It has been applied to Kangaroo Island and Dryandra Woodland in the wheatbelt of Western Australia (Figure 4.7) (McArthur, 1996; Moncrieff, 1997). It has been partially implemented in Canada at Lake Louise in Banff National Park and for Aulavik National Park (McArthur, 2000a) (Figure 4.7). In the case of plan-

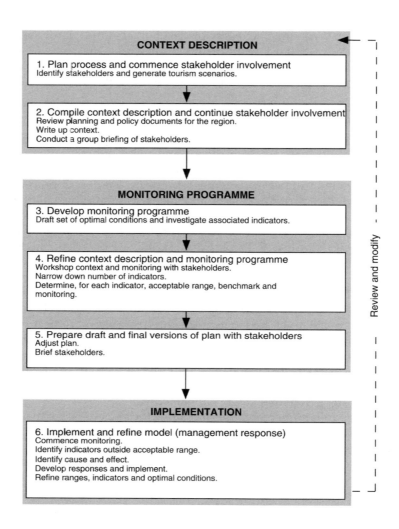

Figure 4.10 Process for applying the Tourism Optimisation Management Model. (Derived from Manadis Roberts Consultants, 1997; McArthur, 2000a)

Box 4.4   Applying TOMM to Kangaroo Island, South Australia, Australia

In 1996 TOMM was initiated for Kangaroo Island (Figure 4.7), lying 21 km off the mainland of southern Australia and with an area of 4500 square km, to facilitate tourism development and management. Most of the Island is private farms and residential properties, although about 24% is conservation reserve. The population of 4000 depends on agriculture and tourism. TOMM had three major parts – contextual identification, monitoring programme and management response. These equate directly to the three major parts in Figure 4.10. The following description is from Manidis Roberts Consultants (1997) and McArthur (2000a, 2000b).

1. Part One. Context identification (Steps 1 and 2)

This part involved identifying and describing the political and social context of planning. Also included was generating alternative management scenarios. A day-long briefing was held with the steering committee established for the project. The following aspects of the context were described.

Existing policies and political issues. Relevant policies included Commonwealth and State ecotourism plans and the Kangaroo Island Sustainable Development Strategy. Political issues included dealing with the negative and positive aspects of tourism and making sure that TOMM helped the tourism industry.

Community values included the natural landscape, wildlife and relaxed lifestyle.

The **tourist product** included:

- **Natural assets** such as a spectacular coastline and natural bushland; unique natural attractions, e.g. Seal Bay and Remarkable Rocks; wildlife, e.g. seals; cultural assets such as European maritime history; island industries, e.g. marron (freshwater lobster) and eucalyptus oil; parks such as Flinders Chase; and a healthy environment with low key development.
- **Activities** including nature-based activities such as sightseeing and viewing wildlife; recreational activities such as fishing, camping and swimming; and cultural activities such as farmstays and experiencing local produce.
- **Themes** including diverse coastline, wildlife, rural lifestyle and natural produce.

Growth trends. In 1995 the Island received an estimated 150,000 visits. The most popular site was Seal Bay, receiving 72–86% of total visits. Visitor numbers have grown at 8.8% per year from 1992 to 1997 with the majority coming from the nearby mainland (67%). This market segment is expected to have low to medium growth, with growth in the international market likely to be higher.

Market opportunities. Suitable markets are people who are environmentally aware and enjoy wildlife.

Positioning and branding. The Island will be positioned and branded to achieve excellence in nature-based tourism accommodation, low impact development, visitor infrastructure, interpretation and information, and local produce.

Ten scenarios were generated and examined including significant increases and decreases (15% p.a.) in tourism demand, a decrease in overnight stays and an increase in day visits. The benefits and costs of each were listed. The information needed to determine if there had been a benefit or cost was also identified. Generating the scenarios helped to make TOMM relevant to stakeholders as well as identifying information needs for future decision making.

Part Two. Monitoring program (Steps 3, 4 and 5)

Optimal conditions. These were desirable yet achievable conditions generated from planning documents and reworked at a stakeholder workshop. They were developed for economic, marketing, experiential and socio-cultural as well as environmental conditions. 'Major wildlife populations attracting visitors are maintained and/or enhanced in areas where tourism activity occurs' is an example of an optimal environmental condition.

Indicators. Indicators were selected so that conditions could be measured. They were identified through two workshops and further discussions with stakeholders. For example, an indicator of the optimal condition of a wildlife population was the number of seals at designated sites.

Acceptable range. Acceptable ranges for each indicator were developed using information from previous research, observations and estimations from those with experience. For the seal population, 0–5% decrease in numbers sighted per annum was the acceptable range. This step was really the most sensitive and difficult part of planning, as decisions were made regarding whether an indicator was outside its acceptable range.

Monitoring and benchmarking. A monitoring programme was developed to collect information on the indicators and especially how close each was to its acceptable range. A benchmark was set for each indicator based on the best information available in 1996. For wildlife, a benchmark was the number of seals at designated sites.

Part Three. TOMM management response (Step 6)

The management response involved identification, exploration and action (Figure 4.11).

Identification of poorly performing indicators. This involves annual measurement of indicators and then identifying those outside their acceptable range. For example, if number of seals is an indicator and the acceptable range was a 0–5% decrease and there was a sudden decrease of 10%, then this indicator has performed poorly.

Exploration of causes. For a poorly performing indicator, the next step is to work out if tourism was responsible. In the case of the seals, poor performance may be tourism or non-tourism related. A tourism-related cause might be increased numbers of visitors transgressing the boundaries of a designated viewing area leading to a decline in the number of seals hauling out on the beach.

Action. The third step is deciding on the action needed. For declining seal numbers at Seal Bay, if tourism were responsible, solutions might include closing the beach to tourists, advising tourists they will see fewer seals, and/or developing an alternative wildlife viewing opportunity. Brainstorming can be used as part of TOMM to determine the effects of proposed actions. For example, if beach access is closed what will be the effects on other indicators like native vegetation cover and the proportion of visitors experiencing wildlife in the wild?

ning for Kangaroo Island, the TOMM analysis is the planning document. For Dryandra, TOMM was applied after the management plan (CALM & NPNCA, 1995) had been completed and published. Further applications in Australia and Canada, from small sites through to regional groupings of conservation reserves, are being considered (McArthur, 2000a).

The strength of TOMM rests on its explicit inclusion of the political and economic environments in which use of natural areas occurs and of stakeholders throughout planning. Its main limitation is the amount of information needed, given it can cover a breadth of tenures across a region as well as including market, economic and socio-cultural as well as biophysical information. This limitation also means that data management and manipulation require a significant level of resources. Locating and working with stakeholders across large areas and a complexity of issues is also resource-intensive.

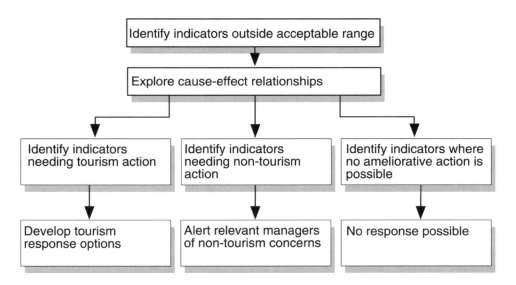

Figure 4.11 Using the Tourism Optimisation Management Model to take management action. (Derived from Manidis Roberts Consultants, 1997)

Other planning frameworks

Two other planning frameworks developed for natural areas also warrant mention. The Visitor Activity Management Process was created by Parks Canada in the 1980s to guide national park planning and management (Nilsen & Tayler, 1997). The Visitor Experience Resource Protection process was created by the US National Park Service in the 1990s for a similar reason (McArthur, 2000a).

Visitor Activity Management Process

The visitor activity management process (VAMP) is one element of a broad, integrated planning and management process. It is part of a whole-of-park approach to management. Other parts include a national parks management planning process and a natural resources management process (Figure 4.12). VAMP employs an overt marketing approach to integrate visitors' requirements with the resource opportunities provided by a given area (Nilsen & Tayler, 1997). It also provides a flexible framework for integrating social and natural science data (Lipscombe, 1993).

VAMP begins by establishing terms of reference and management objectives for an area (Figure 4.13, Steps 1 and 2). Next is creating a database of park ecosystems and settings, visitor activities and opportunities, and the regional context (Step 3). Analysis to produce alternative visitor activity concepts follows (Steps 4 and 5). The last two steps are creating a park management plan and implementation (Nilsen & Tayler, 1997).

VAMP has had limited application in its birthplace, Canada, and virtually none elsewhere. In Canada it has been used to establish a national park, assess the impacts of cross-country skiing, and for interpretation planning. Typical outputs include information on visitor activities and associated development options for assessment, or operational plans for visitor services or interpretation. As such, it can contribute to a management plan for a natural area or may appear as an operational plan for one aspect of visitor management, such as interpretation or visitor safety. By the late 1990s it had been abandoned in favour of ROS (McArthur, 2000a).

Its strength is recognising the demand as well as supply side of natural area management. This is also a weakness as it may be very difficult to shift managers from a product to market-centred approach (McArthur, 2000a). Another weakness is VAMP's failure to develop limits or acceptable ranges for impacts although ROS similarly does not include this level of detail in its planning framework.

Visitor Experience Resource Protection

The Visitor Experience Resource Protection (VERP) planning framework was developed by the US National Park Service as a means of addressing carrying capacity concerns in their national parks (Hof & Lime, 1997). Integral to this process, which is very similar to LAC, is determining the appropriate range of visitor experiences for a chosen area. Thus, zoning is a focus (Nilsen & Tayler, 1997). VERP underpins management plans by producing a series of zones for inclusion. An important premise underlying VERP is that zoning should be resource-related and not determined by the location of existing facilities (McArthur, 2000a).

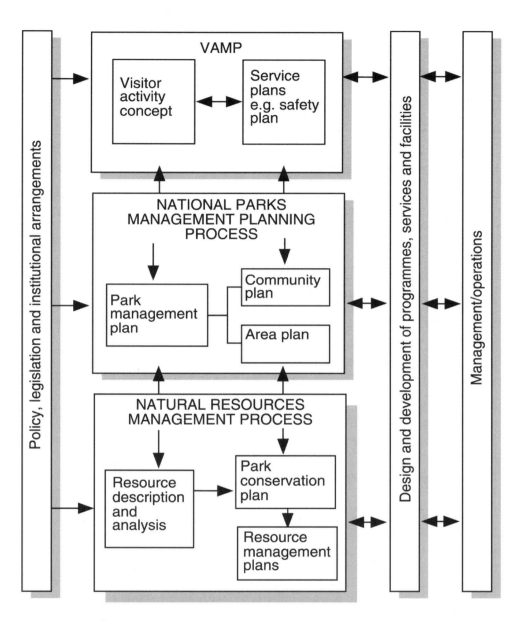

Figure 4.12 The Visitor Activity Management Process as part of national park management. (Derived from McArthur, 2000a)

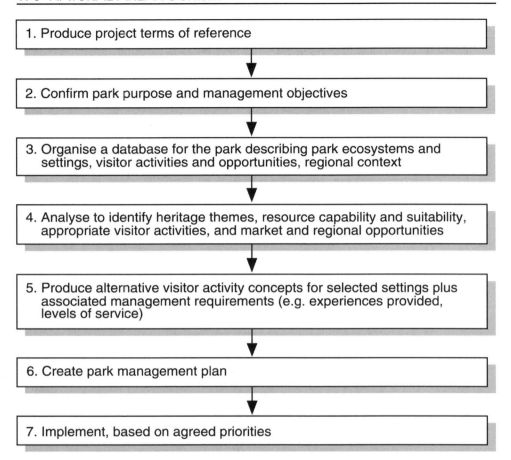

Figure 4.13 Process for applying the Visitor Activity Management Process. (Derived from Nilsen & Taylor, 1997)

The steps in the process include describing the context, analysing existing resources and visitor use, determining a potential range of visitor experiences and resource conditions and allocating zones, then selecting indicators and standards and monitoring. Specifying carrying capacities is avoided by providing desired ecological and social conditions. The last step is taking management action (Figure 4.14).

VERP has been applied at very few places, with an implementation plan only completed at Arches National Park in south-eastern Utah (Hof & Lime, 1997) (Figure 4.7). Two partial applications are known from Australia: in both cases an amalgam of frameworks was used. For Fraser Island off the eastern coast (Figure 4.7), VERP was combined with LAC. For the Australian Alps, elements of ROS, LAC, VIMM and VERP were used (McArthur, 2000a).

The strengths of VERP are its usefulness as a management planning framework

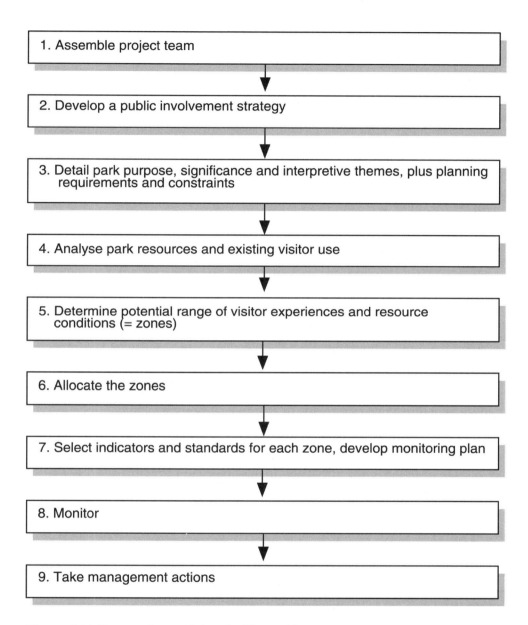

Figure 4.14 Process for applying the Visitor Experience Resource Protection planning framework. (Derived from Nilsen & Taylor, 1997)

and ready inclusion in management plans. Its weakness is shared with many of these frameworks – without implementation and monitoring the acceptability or otherwise of impacts cannot be determined and neither can the effectiveness of management.

Choosing a planning framework

Each of the frameworks discussed above builds on earlier ones (Figure 4.4) (Nilsen & Tayler, 1997). For example LAC, which appeared after ROS, similarly requires the identification of opportunity classes. More recent frameworks such as VAMP and VERP have translated and use opportunity classes as zones. All of the frameworks follow the steps of rational planning, that is, objective setting, data collection, collation and analysis, development of alternatives and a final plan, and recognition of implementation as a crucial last step (Hall, 2000).

All the planning frameworks also:

- focus on and manage human-induced change;
- rely on the natural and social sciences;
- depend on clearly articulated management objectives;
- recognise and use opportunity settings which are a combination of experiential, social and managerial conditions;
- base planning on a spectrum of recreation opportunities;
- require monitoring and evaluation (Nilsen & Tayler, 1997).

How then do we choose between these frameworks? Managers and planners continue to struggle to identify which they should use (Nilsen & Tayler, 1997). This question can be answered by considering six sets of choices (Table 4.3).

First, are managers planning regionally or locally? If managers want to establish management directions for a region or group of natural areas, ROS, VERP, VAMP and TOMM are the most useful. The essential feature of the first three is providing a range of recreation opportunities in optimal locations. ROS is particularly suited to regional planning and has been used to allocate national parks to different places on the recreation opportunity spectrum, for example, in the south coast region of Western Australia (Watson, 1997). TOMM can be applied across multiple land tenures although it does not explicitly cater for opportunity classes. Both LAC and VIM focus on site-level impacts so their application has tended towards individual protected areas. VIM is most often applied to a single site. Recently researchers have suggested that LAC can be applied more widely to where ever there are conflicts associated with resource use impacts (Cole & Stankey, 1997).

Second, do managers need information on the impacts of visitor use to implement management actions? If so, any of the planning frameworks relying on indicators and standards – LAC, VIM, VERP or TOMM – would be suitable. Two of the frameworks provide additional information on the likely causes of these impacts. VIM helps to identify causes of impacts and select suitable management strategies. TOMM also investigates the causes of impacts, seeking to differentiate tourism and non-tourism related ones.

Table 4.3 Choosing the 'best' recreation/tourism planning framework

Planning framework	Suitable for regional planning (i.e. for more than a single natural area)	Provides information on impacts of visitor use needed for management action	Makes explicit provision for inclusion of stakeholders in planning	Responsibility/ discretion for action left to managers	Readily integrated with other forms of planning (e.g. management or tourism plans)	Results in a publishable, stand-alone document
Recreation Opportunity Spectrum	XXX	–	–	–	XX	–
Limits of Acceptable Change	X	XX	XXX	XX	X	XX
Visitor Impact Management	–	XXX	–	XX	X	XX
Tourist Optimisation Management Model	XXX	XXX	XXX	XXX	X	XXX
Visitor Activity Management Process	XXX	–	–	–	XX	–
Visitor Experience Resource Protection	XXX	XX	XX	–	XX	–

XXX – matches criteria well; XX – partially matches criteria; X – poorly matches criteria; – does not match criteria

Third, what are stakeholders' expectations regarding their involvement? LAC was explicitly developed to include stakeholders throughout the planning process. Although, as mentioned earlier in the chapter, gaining stakeholder support and then agreement on indicators and standards continues to be problematic. This problem is not unique to LAC; it plagues all the planning frameworks. TOMM, similarly to LAC, was designed to make stakeholder involvement an integral part of the planning process. The TOMM process for Kangaroo Island had a steering committee and workshops held throughout the process. VERP has a single step directing the development of an involvement strategy while ROS, VIM and VAMP do not explicitly consider stakeholders.

Fourth, how much responsibility and discretion for independent action is to be left to managers? All the frameworks include elements of planning and management. The effectiveness of most depends on implementation, accompanied by the collection of data from monitoring. The latter is the responsibility of managers, although debate continues regarding whether it is the responsibility of managers or researchers.

Each framework gives managers a different amount of responsibility. All of the steps in the ROS process are completed by planners, although managers should be part of the planning group. Both LAC and VIM have increasing involvement by managers as the planning framework nears completion. Managers are expected to have a lead role in identifying management actions as part of LAC (Figure 4.8, Step 7) and identifying causes of impacts and designing management strategies as part of VIM (Figure 4.9, Steps 6 and 7). TOMM gives the greatest level of responsibility to managers and other stakeholders. Once the monitoring programme has been designed, responsibility for monitoring, identifying the causes of unacceptable changes to conditions and developing responses rests with them (Figure 4.10, Step 6). Both VAMP and VERP seem to have all the responsibilities resting with planners.

Fifth, how readily can the framework be integrated with other planning processes and documents? For those responsible for preparing management plans for natural areas or tourism plans for an area or region, great appeal lies in using a recreation/ tourism planning framework for the visitor management component of such a plan. Management plans for natural areas address visitor management as well as facets of the natural environment such as fire management and the protection of rare species. Tourism plans encompass managing visitors as well as the tourism industry.

None of the frameworks is exemplary in its ability to be explicitly integrated with other forms of planning. The principle behind ROS, of providing a range of recreation opportunities, implicitly appears in many management plans. Few of these plans, however, explicitly describe ROS and its application. Both LAC and VIM provide guidance to planners in preparing the visitor management part of plans but again, explicit mention is rarely made of them in planning documents. TOMM has been explicitly considered and included in tourism plans (McArthur, per. comm., 2000). To-date, it has not been integrated into an area management plan. VERP and VAMP have both been designed to integrate with management planning processes but their value is uncertain given their very low levels of application.

Sixth, is a published document based on the framework a desired outcome of applying the framework? Applications of TOMM, VIM and LAC have culminated in stand-alone published documents, making them accessible to others beyond the immediate natural area to which they have been applied. Although generally LAC and VIM, as well as ROS applications, are not published. Documents describing the application of VAMP or VERP are not widely available; however, this may be due to their low levels of application as much as anything else.

In terms of the values used to construct Table 4.3, TOMM and LAC appear to be the 'best' frameworks. However, they are only so if those applying them are intending to plan to achieve the outcomes/approaches listed across the top of the table. For example, if regional planning (column 2) taking into account impacts and their associated management needs (column 3) and including stakeholders (column 4) is required then TOMM is a good choice. If, however, a planning process directed toward regional allocation of zones and integration with other forms of planning is needed then ROS is the best choice. Table 4.3 makes clear these trade-offs and choices. There is no one 'best' framework.

Reasons for lack of implementation

Given all the work on frameworks it seems odd that implementation has not been more widespread. There are a number of explanations (Lipscombe, 1993). In the United States, Australia and Canada, park managers have been highly focused on preparing management plans for their parks. These are usually general documents prepared to meet legal requirements and covering a plethora of resource issues. The recreation/tourism frameworks outlined in this chapter are much more specific and managers have struggled with incorporating this level of specificity in management plans and associated planning processes. Another reason for low levels of adoption is the confusion regarding the purpose of each framework and deciding which to choose. This is not helped by imprecise and vague language, and confusion regarding the terms 'opportunity class' and 'zone' (Nilsen & Tayler, 1997). The extensive use of acronyms such as LAC and VAMP also tends to alienate those unfamiliar with the frameworks.

Lack of resources for managing natural areas is a problem worldwide. In developing countries, this problem is particularly evident. All of the frameworks have been initiated and applied in developed countries, primarily the United States, Canada and Australia. Few applications in developing countries exist, the exceptions being applications to marine areas in the eastern Carribean (Suba) and Belize (McCool, per. comm., 2000). Many natural areas in developing countries have only recently been protected, meaning management efforts are directed toward park or reserve establishment. Reservation and management, not planning, are seen as the priorities (Wallace, 1993).

Lack of resources is also a problem for these frameworks with their reliance on biophysical and social data. Data needed ranges from information on the recreation opportunities offered by an area (for ROS) to measures of indicators such as vegetation loss or size of visitor groups (LAC, VIM, TOMM). Many land management agencies have apparently more pressing concerns than data collection; to many it seems an unaffordable luxury. Additionally, many have histories of biophysical data collection but little expertise or practice in the social sciences (Lipscombe, 1993). Also managers may be concerned about how to select the 'right' indicator, a problem that can thwart applying LAC, VIM and TOMM (McArthur, 2000a).

Although there may be sufficient resources to apply the planning elements of the framework to a natural area, its implementation and subsequent monitoring can be thwarted by lack of commitment to implementation. Senior bureaucrats who allocate budgets within agencies may be unconvinced regarding the benefits of planning frameworks. Additionally, they may be concerned about the costs of ongoing monitoring and collecting data that may indicate their agency is performing poorly. Stankey (1997) suggested that compartmentalisation within land management agencies, with managers remote from planners and scientists, has impeded the application of LAC. Certainly, unless managers have ownership of a planning framework and associated processes they will not make its implementation their highest priority.

Conclusion

Planning is crucial if natural area tourism is to be sustainable. Such planning allows impacts to be recognised and managed. This chapter has described six visitor planning frameworks, all offering viable alternatives to carrying capacity, a previously popular concept but increasingly acknowledged as unsuitable for sustainable tourism. All focus on determining how much change is acceptable rather than trying to determine how much use is too much. They all follow the stages of rational planning – objective setting, data collection, collation and analysis, development of alternatives and a final plan, and recognition of implementation as a crucial last step. For most of them, stakeholder involvement is an integral part. There is no one 'right' framework with the choice depending on a number of factors such as the desired level of stakeholder involvement, whether information on the impacts of visitor use is needed and the extent to which visitor planning is to be integrated with other forms of planning.

This chapter plays a crucial, bridging role in this book. It provides, through the planning frameworks, a systematic means of linking the impacts detailed in Chapter 3 with possible management strategies especially interpretation in Chapters 5 and 6, and monitoring in Chapter 7. Several of the planning frameworks, such as VIM and TOMM, explicitly require planners to develop and assess a range of management strategies as part of the planning process. Both these frameworks also require analysis of the cause of impacts before management strategies are considered. Cause can only be determined if the ecology of the natural area is understood (Chapter 2). Most of the frameworks, for example LAC, VIM and TOMM, also require the identification of indicators and standards for monitoring conditions. Chapter 7 describes monitoring visitor impacts on the natural environment and on each other.

Further Reading

It is well worth reading the various reports in which each planning framework is first described or applied. For ROS, refer to Clark and Stankey (1979), for LAC Stankey *et al.* (1985) describes the framework and Forest Service (1985) its application to the Bob Marshall Wilderness Complex in the Northern Rocky Mountains of the United States. VIM is described by Graefe *et al.* (1990) and Manidis Roberts Consultants (1995) provides a good example of its application to Jenolan Caves in Eastern Australia. The development of TOMM, and its application to Kangaroo Island off the southern coast of Australia, is covered in Manidis Roberts Consultants (1997). An excellent overview of current issues associated with LAC is provided by McCool and Cole (1997). Simon McArthur's doctoral dissertation (McArthur, 2000a) provides a wealth of detailed information on these frameworks and their implementation. A useful comparison of the frameworks is given in Nilsen and Tayler (1997).

Several more general references are also valuable. Dowling (1993) provides a clear approach to environmental planning integrating the management of visitors and the natural environment. Hall and McArthur (1998) has several useful chapters on stakeholder involvement, while Bramwell and Lane (2000b) provides recent thoughts on collaboration and partnerships in tourism.

Chapter 5
Management Strategies and Actions

Introduction

There are a wealth of strategies and actions available for managing tourism in natural areas. Very often, the difficulty is knowing, and then choosing, which to employ. This chapter seeks to address this difficulty by describing the suite of possible management strategies, initially in the order they are likely to be implemented, and then the plethora of site and visitor management actions. Here, strategies are defined as the mechanisms and processes by which objectives are achieved. In this chapter an example of a strategy is reserving and/or zoning an area as a protected area (e.g. as a national park). They are general approaches to management. Actions are more specific; they are what must be done (Hall & McArthur, 1998). Examples of actions are providing educational materials and closing campsites for restoration.

For the majority of natural areas being reserved as a protected area is the crucial first management strategy. Zoning generally follows. Managers then have many possible actions to choose from. In this chapter these actions are discussed as either site or visitor management. Site management actions rely on manipulating infrastructure and the natural environment to influence where visitors go and what they do. Campsite and trail design and management are the most well known of these actions. Visitor management, on the other hand, relies on managing visitors themselves through regulating numbers, group size and length of stay, providing information and education, and enforcing regulations. A number of factors influence the actions chosen by managers, including the cause, location and extent of the impact of concern, the cost and ease of implementation of actions and their effectiveness, and the preferences of visitors and managers. A brief comment on and example of how actions are usually implemented in combination concludes this part of the chapter.

The chapter then goes on to describe current strategies being used to manage the tourism industry in natural areas. Voluntary strategies include codes of conduct, accreditation and best practice. Strategies employed by government organisations, more regulatory approaches, include licensing and leases. A brief mention of environmental management systems, not yet widespread in natural area tourism but increasingly being considered as part of managing other aspects of natural resource management, concludes the chapter.

Reasons for managing natural areas

When human populations were small with limited mobility, large parts of the world remained relatively untouched and ecological processes continued uninterrupted. In recent times, and particularly over the last 40 years, humans have travelled to and interacted with even the most remote and inhospitable parts of the world. Peaks in the Himalayas have been scaled numerous times, the Antarctic is becoming a popular tourism destination and tropical rainforests attract visitors in increasing numbers. Therefore, if we want some areas to be predominantly natural, then the impacts resulting from human use (see Chapter 3) must be managed with naturalness as a central goal (Cole, 2000).

The other crucial reason is the advocacy of natural area tourism as a sustainable industry. This appeal lies in its perceived ability to use natural and cultural environments without degradation while making sure such opportunities are available to both present and future generations. For developing countries, natural area tourism is viewed as a means for generating much needed foreign currency without degrading the environments on which the industry depends. This form of tourism is also favoured by environmental organisations who believe that it will increase support and the value attributed to natural areas, particularly in developing countries.

Creating Protected Areas

Protected areas as a recent phenomenon

For many natural areas, the crucial, first management strategy is designation as a protected area. A protected area is an 'area of land and/or sea especially dedicated to the protection and maintenance of biological diversity, and of natural and associated cultural resources, and managed through legal or other effective means' (IUCN, 1994). When countries such as the United States, Canada and Australia were initially colonised, Europeans occupied very small areas and the remainder of the country was occupied by the original inhabitants – indigenous people, plants and animals. By the late 19th century it was becoming apparent that most of the land would eventually be occupied by Europeans and used for resource production, such as agriculture and timber production, mining, fishing and urban settlement. This concern led to national parks being created. The first, Yellowstone in the United States (Figure 5.1), was set aside for its recreation and landscape values in 1872. Banff Hot Springs in Canada followed in 1885 and Yosemite in the United States in 1890. The purpose of Banff was 'public park and pleasure ground for the

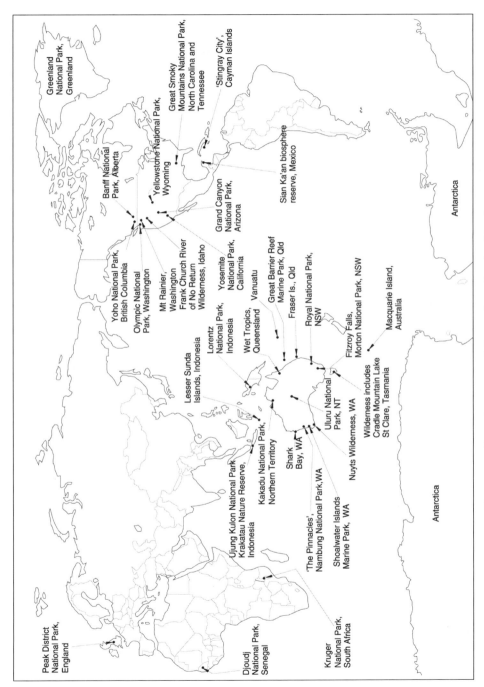

Figure 5.1 Location map of sites referred to in this chapter

benefit, advantage and enjoyment of the people of Canada'. All three included recreation as a major focus. Royal National Park, on the eastern coast of Australia, was declared in 1879.

For many parts of the world, however, establishing protected areas is a relatively recent phenomenon. In North Africa and the Middle East, China, South and South-East Asia, the former republics of the Soviet Union, Central America and the Caribbean, more than 50% of the area protected has been established since 1982 (McNeely *et al.*, 1994). Interestingly, Sub-Saharan Africa, currently the focus of extraordinarily high levels of wildlife tourism, had almost half of its current protected area system in place by 1962. This early adoption has been attributed to concerns centred on watershed protection and erosion control (Burnett & Butler Harrington, 1994).

Over the last two decades protecting biological diversity has become important to many people. Given that most species, and therefore biological diversity, exist in the wild, the best way to protect them is by protecting habitats in the wild. One of the most widely accepted ways is by establishing protected areas. Agardy (1993) noted that ecotourists are more inclined to visit well-managed protected areas where landscapes look natural, water quality is good and biodiversity is high, rather than degraded, poorly kept areas. Reservation and associated management by a government agency, such as a national parks service, and purchase and management by a private conservation organisation are the two most common approaches. Reservation is usually achieved by legislation.

The objective behind reservation is protecting the biological or recreational resources of an area from exploitation by a few, for enjoyment by broader society. This is the reason for government ownership in many cases. It is generally recognised that governments are responsible for helping to meet the needs of society at large in the face of a few individuals gaining personally. Once reserved, an area can then be managed by a government agency for the values that led to its reservation. In developed nations there is far greater involvement by private organisations, such as The Nature Conservancy in the United Kingdom, than in other less developed countries.

Designing protected areas

Protected areas are often created where lands or waters are not regarded as useful for other purposes such as agriculture or forestry. Often, such areas are opportunistically added to protected area systems when they become available. In the face of this haphazard approach, considerable knowledge now exists regarding how such areas should be selected and protected area systems designed. Many of these ideas are drawn from MacArthur and Wilson's (1967, in Primack, 1998) theory of island biogeography.

One of the most important design questions is what size should a protected area be. Is one single large reserve better than several small ones? This is known as the SLOSS debate (single large or several small). A single large area has the advantage of providing for large, wide-ranging, low-density species such as the large carnivores. It also has lower extinction rates than smaller reserves and lesser edge effects. On the other hand, creating more reserves, even if they are small, reduces the possibility of a single catastrophic event, such as a fire or disease, destroying a species because all individuals are located in one large reserve. Finally, although a single large reserve will contain more species than a single small one, several small reserves are more likely to contain more species than a single large one because they are more likely to contain more habitat types. Also, a large number of small reserves is more likely than a single large one to preserve diversity among smaller species such as invertebrates, fungi and bacteria (Jordon, 1995).

Another way of thinking about the optimal size for a protected area is to consider the size of the population(s) the area is required to support. Protected areas should be sufficiently large to conserve large populations of important species such as rare and endangered ones, and keystone and economically important species. Generally, populations of at least several hundred reproductive individuals are needed to ensure the long-term viability of a vertebrate species with several thousand individuals being preferable (Primack, 1998).

The other important elements of design, in addition to size, are shape and connectivity. Protected areas should be shaped so as to minimise the distances over which species have to disperse as well as minimising harmful edge effects, including weed invasion and fertiliser drift into the area (Caughley & Gunn, 1996). Protected areas should be round-shaped to minimise the ratio of circumference (edge) to area, thereby minimising external influences. Fragmentation of protected areas, by roads, farming and other human activities, should be avoided as it can separate populations, reduce their ability to disperse, and create undesirable edge effects.

Connectivity, achieved by creating or maintaining vegetated corridors between protected areas, has been a popular notion for decades, but the empirical evidence supporting its value is still limited. Corridors may be valuable in facilitating the movement of wide-ranging species, such as the panther and wolf in the United States. They may also assist in providing habitat for migratory species, for example those using riparian corridors. Some ecologists suggest that corridors to higher elevations and latitudes will prove useful for species migrating in the face of climate change. Drawbacks associated with corridors include their role in facilitating the movement of pests and diseases and their attractiveness to predators including humans because of the wildlife they contain (Primack, 1998).

Landscape ecology provides advice on reserve design at a regional scale. A landscape with large patches of protected habitat and minimal edge effects is favoured by many ecologists because such a pattern minimises habitat disturbance and protects species that rely on long-undisturbed (i.e. old growth) or 'interior' habitat. Take, for example, two landscapes each with an area of 100 ha of which half is forested and the other half cleared. One landscape has an alternating chequerboard of 1 ha patches of fields and forest. The other landscape has four patches, each 25 ha in area with two of the four forested. The latter landscape would be favoured by these ecologists as it provides large patches and minimises the length of edge.

Most recently, three objectives – comprehensiveness, adequacy and representativeness (CAR) – have been espoused to guide the design of reserve systems. Comprehensiveness means including the full range of ecosystems across a region or a country, at an appropriate scale, in the reserve system. Adequacy requires that sufficient areas are reserved to ensure the ecological viability and integrity of populations, species and communities. Representativeness refers to selecting areas for inclusion to reflect the biotic diversity of all the ecosystems across the areas being considered (ANZECC TFMPA, 1998).

Extent and types of protected areas

As of 1996, 8.8% of the world's land surface was in government-designated protected areas. This figure excludes the now-considerable natural areas protected by private individuals and organisations. The largest protected area, Greenland National Park, Greenland (Figure 5.1), covers 972,000 km^2. Based on available spatial data, 12 times more land than sea is protected. Rough calculations about the extent to which this system of protected areas represents the world's biomes have been made. Most biomes remain under-represented, based on the 10% of all ecosystems target set by the International Union for Conservation of Nature and Natural Resources (IUCN). Least well represented are temperate grasslands and lake systems, with only 1% protected. Evergreen eucalypt, temperate and needle-leaf forests also fall short of the 10% target (Green & Paine, 1997).

Once land or water comes under government control, it is then a matter of determining how it will be managed. A key concern is managing human disturbance, including tourism. How an area is managed depends on how much disturbance and use have occurred in the past, the biological values at stake and their vulnerability, and visitor numbers and activities. The IUCN has developed a system of classification for protected areas that ranges from minimal to intensive human use (Table 5.1) (IUCN, 1994).

National parks, the oldest and best-known form of protection for natural ecosystems, account for 57% of the world's protected areas (Green & Paine, 1997). Managed resource protection areas is another category making a significant contribution, with 27% of the world's protected areas. Included in this category are production forests and marine parks with commercial fishing. How these categories are implemented and match current practice varies from country to country. Box 5.1 describes the protected area systems in Australia.

Other forms of protection

There are a number of other ways in which areas are protected in addition to reservation. The most significant are international designations, such as World Heritage, Ramsar wetlands and biosphere reserves.

World Heritage Convention

The United Nations Educational, Scientific and Cultural Organisation (UNESCO) World Heritage Convention and World Heritage Trust aims to identify, protect and

Table 5.1 IUCN protected area categories

Category	Description
Category I:	Strict nature reserve/wilderness area
Category Ia:	*Strict nature reserve* managed for scientific research and/or monitoring; an area possessing some outstanding or representative ecosystems or features and/or species
Category Ib:	*Wilderness area* managed to preserve its natural condition; a large unmodified area without permanent or significant habitation
Category II:	*National park* managed for ecosystem protection and recreation/visitor enjoyment; natural areas; exploitation or occupation jeopardising the designated purposes are excluded
Category III:	*Natural monument* managed for conservation of specific natural features; area containing outstanding or unique natural (and sometimes cultural) features
Category IV:	*Habitat/species management area* managed for conservation through intervention
Category V:	*Protected landscape/seascape* managed for conservation and recreation; area where traditional interaction between people and the land/sea needs safeguarding to maintain the area's distinct character
Category VI:	*Managed resource protection area* managed for sustainable use of natural resources while protecting and maintaining biological diversity; area of predominantly unmodified natural systems

Derived from IUCN (1994)

preserve natural and cultural heritage sites worldwide. It does this via world heritage sites – natural areas and culturally significant structures, settlements and places with outstanding universal value (Anon., 1997). The Convention was adopted by UNESCO in 1972. Sites may be listed as natural, cultural or mixed properties having both natural and cultural values. There are currently 630 listed properties, comprising 128 natural, 480 cultural and 22 mixed sites (UNESCO, 2000).

Natural properties should:

- be outstanding examples representing major stages of the earth's history, significant ongoing geological processes influencing landform development, or significant geomorphic or physiographic features; or
- be outstanding examples representing significant ongoing ecological and biological processes in the evolution and development of terrestrial, freshwater, coastal and marine ecosystems and communities of plants and animals; or
- contain superlative natural phenomena or areas of exceptional natural beauty and aesthetic importance; or

---

Box 5.1 Government-managed protected areas in Australia

In Australia state governments are responsible for managing the majority of protected areas. This is in contrast to countries such as the United States, where these responsibilities rest mainly with the federal government. National parks occupy 3.3% of Australia's land area.[1] They are managed to provide recreation and tourism opportunities while ensuring that natural ecosystems are protected. Including all types of terrestrial protected areas – nature reserves, Aboriginal sites, wilderness areas, state recreation areas as well as national parks – places 7.8% of Australia's land mass in protected areas. Marine parks, a recent phenomenon, occupy 5.2% of Australian waters.[2] The Great Barrier Reef Marine Park (Figure 5.1), with an area of 334,800 km^2, is one of the largest protected areas in the world (Green & Paine, 1997). Marine parks include commercial fishing, although mining and oil and gas production are currently excluded. They are managed as multiple use reserves. The total percentage of Australian waters in marine protected areas, which includes marine parks and marine nature reserves, is 5.7%.[3]

1. The area is 768,308,153 ha, that of terrestrial Australia excluding external territories such as Norfolk Island, Heard Island and so on.
2. The area is 681,400, 500 ha, that of Australia's Economic Exclusion Zone.
3. The data on protected areas, and the areas of terrestrial Australia and its Economic Exclusion Zone were provided by the National Reserves System Section, Environment Australia, Canberra (as of June 2000).

- contain the most important and significant natural habitats for *in situ* conservation of biological diversity, including those containing threatened species with outstanding universal value for science or conservation (Anon., 1997).

The intention of listing is to protect outstanding areas by preventing them from falling into disrepair, as well as influencing development projects so they do not jeopardise a site's heritage values. If a site is in danger, the World Heritage Committee can place the site on the List of World Heritage in Danger. If a country does not fulfil its obligations under the Convention, it risks having its sites removed from the world heritage list (Anon., 1997). Recreation, tourism and interpretation are usually provided for at world heritage sites; however, some may be of such significance and fragility that such uses are prohibited.

To give an indication of the types of natural properties on the world heritage list, a brief description of the sites in Australia and Indonesia follows. Australia has 13 world heritage sites ranging from the largest monolith in the world in inland Australia (Ayers Rock at Uluru), to the wet tropics of Queensland, Tasmanian wilderness, offshore islands such as Macquarie Island, to Shark Bay in the west with its outstanding marine and terrestrial ecosystems. Australia's first world heritage site, the Great Barrier Reef, was listed in 1981. Indonesia has three sites, the most recent, Lorentz National Park in Irian Jaya province and including Indonesia's highest mountain, listed in 1999. The other two are Ujung National Park, on the extreme south-western tip of Java and the last viable natural refuge for the Javan rhinoceros, and Komodo National Park including the Lesser Sunda Islands and surrounding waters (WCMC, 2000a, 2000b, 2000c) (Figure 5.1).

Ramsar Convention on wetlands

The Convention on Wetlands, signed in Ramsar, Iran in 1971, is an international treaty providing for the conservation and wise use of wetlands. It relies entirely on goodwill and has no means of penalising countries that fail to conserve protected sites (Hollis & Bedding, 1994). A total of 122 countries are signatories, with 1035 wetland sites designated for inclusion in the Ramsar List of Wetlands of International Importance. The number of wetlands designated by individual countries is highly variable. For example, the United Kingdom has 147 designated sites, Australia has 52 and Cambodia 3 (Ramsar Convention Bureau, 2000).

Two sets of criteria are used to select Ramsar wetlands: the site must contain representative, rare or unique wetland types and/or be of international importance for conserving biological diversity (Ramsar Convention Bureau, 2000). Wetlands are defined by the Convention as areas of marsh, fen, peatland or water, whether natural or artificial, permanent or temporary, with water that is static or flowing, fresh, brackish or salt, including areas of marine waters, the depth of which at low tide does not exceed six metres (McNeely *et al.*, 1994).

Biosphere reserves

The Man and the Biosphere Programme (MAB) was initiated by UNESCO in Paris in 1968 (Batisse, 1982). Provisions for biosphere reserves were strengthened in 1995 at the International Conference on Biosphere Reserves held in Seville, Spain, where attendees agreed that sites be reviewed every 10 years and if they do not fulfil certain criteria they may no longer be recognised (Green & Paine, 1997). These reserves are intended as places where interdisciplinary science provides a basis for conservation and rational human use. They are connected as a worldwide network of representative natural areas where monitoring, research, management, training and education are undertaken (Batisse, 1982).

Each biosphere reserve is intended to fulfil three complementary and mutually reinforcing functions:

- a conservation function, contributing to the conservation of landscapes, ecosystems, species and genetic variation;
- a development function, fostering economic and human development which is socio-culturally and ecologically sustainable;
- a logistic function, providing support for research, monitoring, education and information exchange related to local, national and global issues of conservation and development (UNESCO MAB, 2000).

Biosphere reserves ideally consist of a protected core surrounded by buffers including a managed use area and a broader zone of cooperation (Figure 5.2). The managed use area may contain grazing, fishing, recreation and tourism, and settle-

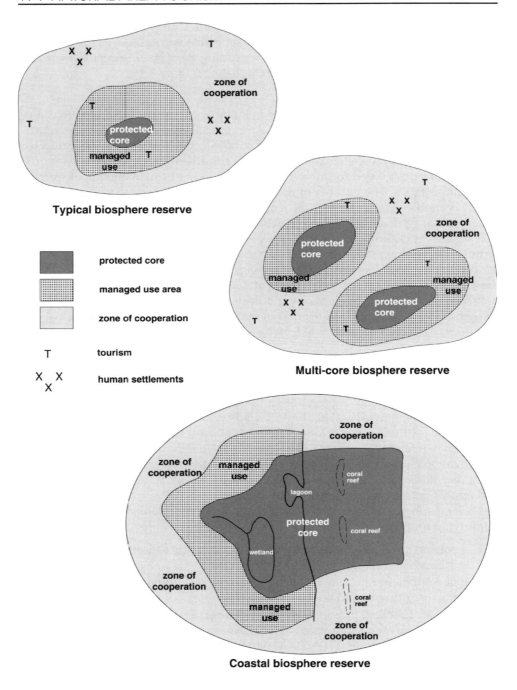

Figure 5.2 Zoning of international biosphere reserves. (Derived from Batisse, 1982)

ments. The zone of cooperation is the larger region where local residents, economic interests, scientists, and managing agencies work together linking conservation and economic development, guided by the cultural values of local communities (UNESCO MAB, 2000).

There are 352 biosphere reserves in 87 countries, with many of these reserves providing for tourism. For example, Sian Ka'an biosphere reserve in Mexico, regarded as one of the flagships of the UNESCO MAB programme, is beginning to accommodate ecotourism (Box 5.2). To give some indication of numbers of these reserves in various countries – Australia has 12, Canada 6, Indonesia 6, the United Kingdom 13 and the United States 47 (UNESCO MAB, 2000).

Box 5.2 Sian Ka'an biosphere reserve and natural area tourism

Sian Ki'an on the eastern shore of the Yucatan Peninsula in Mexico (Figure 5.1) was officially dedicated as a biosphere reserve in 1985. It encompasses coastal dry forest, extensive shallow water lagoons, part of the second largest barrier reef in the world, Mayan temples and other ruins, and numerous limestone sinkholes with associated biota (Agardy, 1993). Within the boundaries live about 800 Mayan people. The reserve has a core area where extractive uses of the forest and coastal areas are banned while buffers accommodate the needs of fishers, snorkellers and sightseers.

Tourism in the state of Quintana Roo in which Sian Ka'an is located is booming. Sian Ka'an has only recently developed facilities for tourists, with the Mayan residents building several visitor centres and running nature tours. Mayans are being trained to build and maintain park infrastructure, to guide visitors and market their crafts. They are also involved in sea turtle conservation, through guarding nesting turtles and their young from natural predators and human poachers (Agardy, 1993).

Joint Management

Joint management is the sharing of responsibility for managing a protected area and is an increasingly popular management strategy. It generally refers to the government agency responsible for managing a protected area entering into an arrangement with indigenous people living within or alongside the area. They may derive their living or have long-standing spiritual links with it. Such arrangements show formal recognition by government agencies of the relationships between indigenous people and protected areas.

Joint management may or may not rely on a formal agreement between the involved parties. For example, joint management of Kakadu and Uluru National Parks in northern Australia (Figure 5.1) is based on the park management agency formally leasing the land from the traditional Aboriginal owners. Joint arrangements also include a board of management with majority membership from the

Aboriginal owners and a jointly developed statutory management plan. Cooperation is sought in both longer-term planning and day-to-day management (De Lacy, 1994).

Joint management may also be a multi-way venture, as is the case with the Integrated Conservation and Development Projects (ICDPs) in Indonesia. Agenda 21-Indonesia (State Ministry for Environment Republic of Indonesia and United Nations Development Programme, 1997) noted that such projects were needed to gain support from local communities. These communities either live within the reserve boundaries or rely on its natural resources for part, or all, of their livelihood. Three main strategies form the basis of ICDPs: strengthening reserve management and/or creating buffer zones; providing compensation or substitution to local people for lost access to resources; and encouraging local social and economic development. For a number of ICDPs, joint management includes national and local government, international non-government organisations and local communities. During the 1990s, ICDPs became Indonesia's main approach to conserving biological diversity (McCarthy, 2001).

Joint management may also be employed where lands within a national park are privately owned, as is the case in England and Wales. Here, national parks have been designated in landscapes used for agriculture and forestry, with long histories of human occupancy and private ownership. Joint management involves fostering partnerships between national agencies responsible for conservation (e.g. Countryside Commission), individual national park authorities, national agricultural interests (e.g. Ministry of Agriculture), and individual farmers and landowners. The intent is managing changing agricultural practices to maintain the 'wildness' of these parks and thus their appeal to visitors (Swinnerton, 1995).

Although not strictly joint management, many examples exist worldwide of cooperation between protected area managers and adjacent landowners to both improve the conservation status of the protected area and the livelihoods of those living next to it. For example, Djoudj National Park in Senegal in west Africa (Figure 5.1) is managed cooperatively with people living nearby (Beintema, 1991). The park's fish stock will help maintain fish numbers in village ponds to the north of the park, part of the park will be opened for grazing, and park staff are using their equipment to help villagers construct rice fields and in reafforestation. Additionally, the park service intends to build a visitor centre and start activities in schools.

Zoning

It is generally insufficient to reserve an area of land and then hope its values will automatically be protected. The next crucial stage is management. Many parks in developing countries are at this point where they have been reserved but are still vulnerable to exploitation (Wallace, 1993). One of the key strategies for managing protected areas is zoning. This involves recognising smaller units or zones within the area, each with prescribed levels of environmental protection and certain levels and types of public use. Most of the planning frameworks described in the previous chapter include identifying and managing zones. Zoning for protected areas generally has two purposes – protecting the natural environment and providing a range of recreation/tourism opportunities.

Providing a choice of experiences for visitors through zoning is fundamental to the Recreation Opportunity Spectrum planning framework and subsequent approaches such as the Limits of Acceptable Change. Zones range from primitive with few to no facilities and little likelihood of encountering others through to developed areas with extensive facilities, such as resorts, and numerous interactions with others (Box 5.3). Zoning also clarifies future intentions. The management actions explored in the following sections are employed to maintain existing levels and types of use, manipulate use to return a zone to a more pristine state or conversely develop it further.

Another reason for zoning, in addition to providing choice, is separating incompatible visitor uses in space and time (i.e. spatial and temporal zoning). Spatial zoning is often used to separate hikers from motor vehicles, and motorised and non-motorised water craft. At a finer scale, cliffs may be zoned to separate abseilers and climbers. Zoning is also used to protect the natural environment from damaging use by visitors. It can be used to exclude people or strictly regulate them at fragile geological formations, such as the Burgess Shales in Yoho National Park, Canada (Figure 5.1). Or, as happens more frequently, types of use may be regulated. For example, spear fishing may be prohibited from areas with vulnerable species or ones of special interest.

Zoning may also be applied temporally. For example, Fairy Terns (*Sterna nereis*), a seabird breeding on beaches, are highly susceptible to disturbance. Colonies can be zoned to exclude people during the bird's breeding season. Seasonal closures have also been used in south-western Australia to prevent the spread of dieback fungus (*Phytophthora cinnamomi*), a soil-borne fungus affecting many native plant species. Wet conditions enable the fungus to be transported in mud attached to vehicles and shoes and introduced into previously disease-free areas. Zoning is used to close areas in wet conditions so the fungus is not introduced or spread.

Site Management Actions

Rationale for approach taken

In this book, we classify and describe management actions as being either site or visitor management, similarly to the approach taken by Hammitt and Cole (1998) (Figure 5.3). Site management seeks to control visitors through actions at the sites where the use occurs. Sites include linear transport corridors, such as roads and walk trails, and terminus points, such as resorts and lodges, campgrounds and individual campsites, picnic areas, water bodies and coastlines. Site management relies on locating use in the more durable parts of the landscape and designing and managing sites and associated facilities to minimise visitor impacts. Visitor

Box 5.3 National park and marine park zoning in Western Australia

National park zoning (terrestrial)

Five zones are applied to national park planning in Western Australia – three with very little development and two emphasising facilities and services. This approach was developed in the 1980s, based on the approach taken by Parks Canada (CALM, n.d.). The special preservation zone contains unique, rare or endangered features or the best examples of natural features. Access and use are strictly controlled and may be prohibited. No motorised access or built facilities are permitted. Areas zoned wilderness must be extensive, minimally disturbed by humans and with no motorised access. Natural environment zones can support low-density outdoor activities with minimum facilities. Non-motorised access is preferred, although in many parks access by four-wheel-drive vehicle will continue. Recreation zones can accommodate a broad range of recreation activities while protecting the natural environment. Motorised access is permitted. Park services zones may include visitor centres, park head-quarters and/or towns. Not all zones are used in every park.

Marine park zoning (marine)

Marine park zoning in Western Australia is a more recent development, a product of the late 1980s and 1990s and influenced by zoning of the Australian Great Barrier Reef Marine Park (Figure 5.1). The purpose, similarly to zoning terrestrial parks, is protecting sensitive habitats and providing a range of recreational opportunities. Equity and minimising conflict are emphasised. Four zones are delineated. The first, general use, provides for commercial and recreational uses, so both commercial and recreational fishing where they are consistent with conserving the natural resources. In the recreation zone, commercial fishing is not permitted; however, commercial activities associated with recreational uses are allowed, for example, commercial whale-shark viewing and game fishing. Sanctuary zones provide for total protection – fishing and removing other organisms are not permitted. This zone is usually specified to cover areas with vulnerable or special interest biota requiring the highest level of protection. Also, this zone preserves representative areas of the park's ecosystems free from disturbance. Special purpose zones are specified if the other zones are not appropriate. Uses may include a combination of commercial and/or recreational uses. Each special purpose zone has a stated purpose that is legally recognised. For example, in Shark Bay Marine Park, on the north-west coast of Australia (Figure 5.1), Cape Peron special purpose zone has the stated purpose of 'wildlife viewing and protection'. The area has abundant wildlife including dugongs, dolphins, humpback whales, manta rays and many fish species. Commercial and recreational fishing, diving, and non-motorised water sports are allowed; spear fishing and motorised water sports are not.

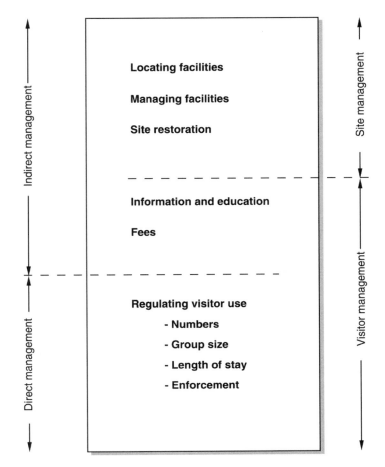

Figure 5.3 Common ways of classifying approaches to managing visitors to natural areas. (Derived from Hammitt & Cole, 1998; Lucas, 1990a)

management (covered later, see p. 212) focuses on managing visitors themselves through regulating use, communicating with them and providing education.

Three broadly different purposes in organising and describing management practices are apparent (Table 5.2). The most common is detailing and grouping actions so they are readily accessible to managers. The related classifications, numbered 1–6 in Table 5.2, typify this grouping and are described by Manning *et al.* (1996) as focusing on tactics. Possible actions are described and grouped to make the wealth of information digestible and accessible to managers. Within this group, the most widely used classification has been the direct–indirect approach. Direct actions restrict individual choice (e.g. by regulating visitor numbers) while indirect actions seek to influence visitors (e.g. by education) leaving them greater freedom

Table 5.2 Ways of classifying approaches to managing visitors to natural areas

Classification	Classification purpose	Description of approach
1. Management actions grouped as site or visitor management (Hammitt & Cole, 1998)	Actions grouped to make them accessible to managers and according to *what* is to be managed	Site management seeks to influence visitor activities by manipulating the natural environment and infrastructure, while visitor management relies on regulating visitors and information and education. The classification system adopted in this book.
2. Management actions grouped as direct and indirect (Lucas, 1990a)	Actions grouped to make them accessible to managers	Direct techniques, such as limiting visitor numbers, restrict individual choice while indirect techniques, such as education, seek to influence visitors leaving them free to choose. The most widely used classification system.
3. Management actions grouped as containment or dispersal approaches (Cole, 1981b)	Actions grouped to make them accessible to managers	Containment limits where activities occur while dispersal reduces the frequency of use at each site so that permanent impacts are avoided.
4. Management actions organised into five groups (Anderson *et al.*, 1998)	Actions grouped to make them accessible to managers	The five groups are site management, rationing and allocation, regulations, deterrence and enforcement, and visitor education. Developed for US National Park Service managers.
5. Management actions organised according to eight strategies (Cole *et al.*, 1987)	Actions grouped (within eight strategies) to make them accessible to managers	The eight strategies are reduce use of entire wilderness, reduce use of problem areas, modify location of use within problem areas, modify timing of use, modify type of use and visitor behaviour, modify visitor expectations, increase resistance of the resource, and maintain/rehabilitate the resource.
6. Management actions listed in general groupings (Hall & McArthur, 1998)	Actions listed to make them accessible to managers	Management actions loosely grouped as regulatory, fees-based, site modification, research, marketing, interpretation and education, profile management, and assisting alternative providers.
7. Grouping of actions according to impact location and source (Cole, 1990b)	Actions grouped according to the location and source of visitor impacts	Management actions organised as responses to campsite, trail, and pack and saddle stock impacts.
8. Strategies based on supply and durability of resources used by visitors (Manning, 1979)	Strategies described and organised	The four strategies are increasing supply, reducing the impact of use, increasing resource durability, and limiting use.
9. Typology of spatial strategies (Leung & Marion, 1999b)	Strategies described and organised	The four strategies are spatial segregation, spatial containment, spatial dispersal, and spatial configuration. The classification is spatially based.

Derived from Anderson *et al.* (1998); Cole (1990b); Cole *et al.* (1987); Hall & McArthur (1998); Hammitt & Cole (1998); Leung & Marion (1999b); Lucas (1990a); Manning (1979)

to choose. We adopted Hammitt and Cole's (1998) site-visitor management classification, rather than the more widely known indirect–direct classification, because it makes clear at the outset *what* is to be managed, whether it is a site or visitors themselves.

The two other ways of grouping management practices are either according to the location and source of visitor impacts (Classification 7 in Table 5.2) or to describe and categorise management strategies (Classifications 8–9). Neither of these purposes matches the needs of this book as well as the site–visitor management approach. Organising actions based on the location of impacts, for example grouping actions for locations such as campgrounds and trails, is potentially useful to managers. However, there are significant areas of overlap and repetition because an action such as managing visitor numbers applies to all locations. The last grouping focuses more broadly on strategies (Classifications 8–9) so is not directly comparable or relevant to the suites of actions covered by the other classifications.

Managing roads and trails

Locating roads and trails

Natural area tourism relies on major highways, such as the Interstate 1 traversing Banff National Park in Alberta, Canada, four-wheel-drive tracks in the desert nature reserves of central Australia, paved walk trails such as those along the edges of the Grand Canyon, and unmarked routes in remote wilderness areas such as the Frank Church River of No Return in Idaho, USA (Figure 5.1). Although it is difficult to generalise across this diversity, some guidance is possible regarding locating these linear features to minimise their adverse impacts. Through careful siting, construction and maintenance they can support substantial visitor traffic while at the same time protecting off-road and trail areas (Leung & Marion, 1999b).

Constructing roads and trails results in environmental impacts. Minimising the area cleared is the simplest management measure. Also, minimising changes to natural drainage patterns is important. This is best achieved by selecting a well-drained location, assisted by engineering if necessary. Using materials that blend with the colours of the existing landscape is another way of reducing the potentially intrusive appearance of such developments.

One of the most common ways in which soil pathogens such as dieback are spread is through road and trail construction and maintenance. Dieback spreads through the movement of infected soil as well as in water and by root contact with infected plants. Infected soil may be spread either attached to earthmoving equipment or in soil brought on-site for construction purposes. The introduction of infected material can be minimised by washing earthmoving equipment and making sure infected soil is not moved to uninfected sites.

If a choice is available, selecting positions in the landscape sufficiently robust to support use is preferable. Highways and major roads can be located almost anywhere with careful design and construction, although they may be very intrusive. As such, many of the following comments are not applicable. Where roads are mentioned, they should be read as being unsealed/unpaved.

The key influences in selecting a durable route are slope and soil characteristics such as soil moisture and erodibility (Hammitt & Cole, 1998). The degree of slope of the linear development itself and the extent to which it intercepts runoff are critical. Ideally, trails and roads should have gentle grades so that they do not erode but have some slope to prevent water pooling on them. Steep grades can be avoided by using switchbacks. Where this is not possible, engineering works are necessary.

In many places, especially in mountainous and tropical settings, muddy roads and trails caused by excessive soil moisture are a concern. Very often users skirt around muddy parts leading to trail widening and braiding. Locating these developments where they will not collect water from upslope or intercept high water tables is a useful preventative measure. High water tables can usually be identified by characteristic vegetation types. Trails and roads that have eroded below the surrounding ground level can become *de facto* streamlines.

Erodibility is also a key soil characteristic in deciding where to locate linear developments. Trails and vehicle tracks that are not hardened or engineered into the landscape are best located on well-drained soils such as loams with a substantial organic matter component (Hammitt & Cole, 1998). Clays tend to pond water while sands rapidly disperse when the vegetation is removed. Linear developments over clays and sands generally require engineering attention.

Stream banks with their steep slopes and high moisture content are best avoided as are coastal dunes with their sandy, poorly consolidated soils subject to wind erosion. Cole (1990b) drew on studies reporting that trail erosion and trampling led to increased iron and phosphorus levels in lakes. As such, trails should be set back from the edges of water bodies and runoff filtered by fringing vegetation. Erosion of stream banks can be minimised by locating trails where the banks are low and stable. The same applies to coastal dunes with the added proviso that where possible, trails should be aligned at right angles to prevailing winds. Trails used by stock are best located on rocky substrates, such as ridges, rock scree and bedrock, to minimise soil erosion.

Multiple or 'braided' trails are the result of conditions where it is difficult for visitors to walk or drive. Walking and driving are difficult in muddy, sandy, rocky or slippery conditions. The best solution is relocating where possible. Short-cutting switchbacks, another problem created by visitors leaving the designated trail, can be effectively managed by minimising the number used, locating them out of sight of each other, building barriers between them, and using wide turns. Informal use, that is visitors using non-designated areas resulting in environmental damage, is difficult to control. The best approach is to provide designated trails to features of interest (Cole, 1990b; Hammitt & Cole, 1998).

The safety of visitors and agency staff using roads and trails is a fundamental concern in managing natural areas. Safety can be enhanced by attention to road and trail design, construction and maintenance. Good design includes managing user speeds, sight distances, and road and trail surfaces and widths. Safety may be compromised by conflicts between users. Conflict within a single user group may occur, for example when passing areas on four-wheel-drive tracks are not provided.

The different requirements of mountain bikers, hikers and horse riders, for example, may compromise user safety on multiple-use trails (North Carolina State University, 1994). Providing crossings for wildlife, such as underpasses, protects them from vehicles as well as reducing accidents from drivers swerving to avoid them.

Where roads and trails are located and not located in natural areas is a powerful management tool. Road and trail location is an acceptable, unobtrusive way to influence visitor use. Areas deliberately kept free of roads and trails will remain little used. Trails can be built or rebuilt to be gentle or steep, short or long, navigationally easy or difficult. Each permutation will support different numbers and types of visitors. Roads and trails can take visitors past vistas or through monotonous landscapes, with them lingering at the former and passing rapidly through the latter. Trails can be routed through varied vegetation, to water points and into areas where there are increased chances of seeing wildlife. Trail design allows managers to heavily programme the experience that visitors have (Lucas, 1990a).

Despite the usefulness of trail and road design as a management tool, its application for this purpose has been limited. Most roads and trails follow routes pushed through the landscape for fishing or hunting access, resource extraction such as minerals or timber, or to reach other destinations. Many walk trails follow vehicle tracks constructed for fire management or the earliest routes followed by hikers, usually traversing the highest points in the landscape. Limited money is allocated by management agencies to trail construction and maintenance, with most going to relocating poorly located short sections of existing trails. Roads are relocated to reduce maintenance costs by moving them to a more durable part of the landscape, improve the available vistas, and ensure the road can be safely traversed at designated speeds.

Visitor use of areas accessible by non-motorised means only (usually by foot or horse) can also be strongly influenced by road locations. Use can be changed by closing, shortening, lengthening, and upgrading access roads. Closing or shortening roads makes non-motorised access deep into the area less likely and may decrease day use. Reducing use can increase the opportunities for solitude. Improving or extending roads has the opposite effect. Upgrading and constructing new roads provides greater access and levels of use and makes day use more likely. Improving access should be undertaken with great care as new problems due to increased numbers and types of visitors may be created (Lucas, 1990a).

The last way design can be used to influence how visitors use an area is the facilities provided at access points. For example, horse facilities such as loading ramps and corrals encourage horse riders. Where there are water bodies, launching ramps encourage use by larger trailer-based boats. Where visitors have to carry their boats from their motor vehicles to the water, canoe-sized vessels are more likely. The size of parking areas influences the number of users at one time, although people will park somewhere even if the area is full. However, parking areas should not be expanded where increased use is not wanted.

Managing roads and trails

Engineering is often an essential tool for managing roads and trails. In many instances it may not be possible to locate or relocate a linear development to improve its durability or the levels of use may be such that engineering actions become essential. Cole (1990b) listed erosion and muddiness as the common trail impact problems amenable to engineering solutions. Additional problems with roads in natural areas include safety concerns, such as poor visibility, tight corners and deterioration in surface conditions. Management becomes necessary when the safety of users or staff is jeopardised, the linear feature becomes difficult to use, maintenance becomes expensive, or the natural environment is being obviously damaged. Cole (1990b) advocated, where naturalness is the primary goal, keeping engineering to a minimum because of the intrusiveness of human structures.

To prevent erosion, walk trails can be aligned on the contour and built to slope slightly away from hillsides. They can have a rolling grade of dips and rises to prevent water building up speed and eroding the trail (Cole, 1990b). Water bars are a common tool, comprising rocks, logs, boards or mounded soil, angled across the trail, usually at 20–40 degrees, and securely anchored to prevent them being washed away. Steps, oriented perpendicular to the slope, can also be used to slow down water and soil movement. To prevent water getting onto trails and roads in the first place, earth or rock ditches, culverts of concrete, metal or other materials, or drains parallel to the linear feature are all engineering options. All this work must be carefully planned and maintained otherwise it can be intrusive and ineffectual (Cole, 1990b; Hammitt & Cole, 1998).

Muddiness can be addressed by 'hardening' the site using decking/boardwalks, forming up using earth and gravel, or sealing using asphalt or bitumen. Board-walks, slightly elevated across the landscape, are common in valley bottoms and in alpine areas subject to prolonged waterlogging (Plate 5.1). Another option is raising the trail or road using earth and gravel. This work is usually accompanied by some form of drainage to ensure the formed trail or road is not washed away. For high use roads and even trails, forming up and permanent sealing with asphalt/bitumen, although expensive, may be the best way to provide a durable, low-maintenance surface. All of these approaches are intrusive and show clear evidence of humans in the landscape. Box 5.4 gives examples of trail management from England and Australia.

Another engineering solution for muddiness is bridge construction. Bridges can prevent bank erosion and also improve the safety of river crossings (Hammitt & Cole, 1998). The bridge may be nothing more than a series of stepping stones. Or it may be a raised gravel walkway with culverts to shed the water downstream. A more elaborate approach is laying boards across a timber base. For major roads, steel and concrete fabrication will be required. In all cases, the structure must be sufficiently well anchored to prevent it washing away.

Signs are another built element associated with trails and roads. Directional, warning and interpretive signs are expected along major roads. Warning signs may be the only ones found on four-wheel-drive tracks. Visitors to wilderness areas in

Plate 5.1 Walking track in Tasmanian Wilderness World Heritage Area, Australia. (*Photo*: Grant Dixon, Parks and Wildlife Service, Tasmania)

the United States and Canada prefer a limited number of simple signs, whereas in an Australian study visitors were more tolerant of such structures (Morin *et al.*, 1997). Most managers of wilderness areas try to provide only limited, simple directional signs at confusing intersections (Lucas, 1990a). Generally, the less developed an area, the fewer signs should be provided.

Managing built accommodation, campgrounds and other facilities

Locating facilities

Built accommodation, campgrounds, campsites and other facilities are ideally located in durable parts of the landscape, in a similar manner to trails and roads. Durability is influenced by the soil's erodibility, drainage and depth, and the site's dominant vegetation type (Hammitt & Cole, 1998). Soils should be well-drained loams. Deep soils are preferred because many human waste disposal systems require on-site disposal. Because regeneration of vegetation around built accommodation and heavily used campsites is unlikely, such sites should be located in stands of relatively young, long-lived trees or tall shrubs (Hammitt & Cole, 1998). Species known to shed limbs should be avoided because of overhead safety risks.

Another essential consideration in locating facilities is visual impacts. Such facilities should blend with the landscape and, where possible, should not be visible from vista points, roads and trails. Building sizes and shapes should be in scale with, and borrow from, natural landforms while materials should blend with the

Box 5.4 Management to improve trail conditions: examples from England and Australia

The Pennine Way, Peak District National Park, England
The Peak District National Park (Figure 5.1) through which the Pennine Way passes receives 18.5 million visits annually. The Way is intensively used by long-distance walkers and day-trippers. In some places the bare area spanning the Way has grown to 7.8 m with trample widths approaching 70 m in places. To improve visitors' experiences as well as reducing trampling and disturbance by keeping people on the trail, part of the Way has been resurfaced using flagstones. This management action has reduced the number of walkers straying off the trail from 30% before resurfacing to 3.8%. Although the number of visitors has increased, probably because of the easier surface for walking, the concentration of this use on the paved Way means large areas of the adjacent moorland are relatively undisturbed (Pearce-Higgins & Yalden, 1997).

Tasmanian Wilderness World Heritage Area, Australia
This world heritage area occupies 1.38 million ha in south-west Tasmania (Figure 5.1), encompassing alpine vegetation, especially low-growing buttongrass plains, temperate rainforest and eucalypt forests (WCMC, 2000d). The alpine areas are popular for walking, while at the same time being vulnerable to damage because of water ponding and low-growing vegetation making it easy for visitors to stray off paths and create new ones. A dramatic increase in numbers over the last 25 years has led to escalating biophysical and social impacts (Hawes, 1996). Issues of concern are deterioration of existing tracks and development of new ones in formerly trackless areas.

Management actions included assessment, regulating use, site works and monitoring. Assessment has been used to describe the current condition of 960 km of track and to determine current and future supply (i.e. recreational opportunities) and demand. The management options of relocating and constructing walk trails, education, regulating the use of certain areas, and a mandatory permit system for access were also assessed. Track stabilisation through construction was considered cautiously because of the associated costs, the inappropriateness of construction in wilderness areas and the likelihood of it increasing use. Education was also treated with caution as it cannot solve the problems of unplanned track development and crowding. All four options, in combination, were regarded as the solution (Hawes, 1996).

Tracks have been relocated in preference to upgrading existing ones. This approach has successfully reduced erosion while minimising maintenance costs. Boardwalks have been used where erosion and trampling effects are severe and relocation is not possible or will not solve the problem (Plate 5.1). Education seeks to inform walkers about management problems of the area, safety and appreciating the natural environment. Materials include magazine articles, pamphlet and video. Restricting access to certain areas and an access permit system are proposed (Hawes, 1996).

colours and textures of the natural environment. The area cleared during construction should also be kept to a minimum, as should changes to natural drainage patterns.

Leung and Marion (1999b) noted the importance of design in reducing visitor impacts. For example, campgrounds can be designed to prevent short cuts between campsites and between sites and facilities such as toilets. They can also be designed to accommodate a variety of group sizes so large groups do not need to damage vegetation to fit in.

Managing facilities

Site management concentrates use by providing facilities wanted by visitors. Such facilities include day use areas, campgrounds and campsites, shelters, huts, horse-camps, interpretive centres, lodges and resorts. Although concentrating use significantly impacts on the site itself, surrounding natural areas receive greater protection. A plethora of accommodation types is now offered in natural areas ranging from resorts and lodges through to unmarked campsites in wilderness areas. For example, hotels are provided in Grand Canyon National Park, wilderness cabins in Cradle Mountain – Lake St Clare National Park, tent platforms in Great Smoky Mountains National Park and unmarked campsites in Kakadu National Park (Figure 5.1). Suggestions for managing built accommodation, such as resorts, are given later in this chapter (see 'Best practice', p. 231).

The most common form of site management in non-wilderness areas is hardening, using gravel, paving or asphalt/bitumen and channelling use into these hardened areas. Surfacing facility areas and associated trails minimises muddy areas and soil compaction. It can also be used to improve site durability around built accommodation, interpretive facilities and across campgrounds.

Managing vegetation to prevent site deterioration from trampling, erosion and muddiness, maintain the site's visual attraction, provide a visual and sound buffer between different activities and protection from the weather, and for educational purposes is also common (Van Riet & Cooks, 1990). Vegetation management at sites other than the most pristine can include introducing hardy vegetation, overstorey thinning, watering and fertilising (Hammitt & Cole, 1998). The most common example of introduced hardy vegetation is lawns. Many picnic areas use lawn to increase durability and it often provides the surrounds for built accommodation. In many parts of the world it also provides a food source for grazing animals, such as deer in the United States and kangaroos in Australia. These animals appeal to natural area tourists. Trees may be planted to provide shade and windbreaks for built accommodation, campgrounds and day use areas.

Hammitt and Cole (1998) suggested thinning overstorey trees to encourage more vigorous growth of ground covers, especially grasses. Grasses are more resistant to impacts than other plant types and hence their presence increases the robustness of a site. A study of campgrounds in the southern Appalachians found that reducing canopy cover from 90 to 60% doubled grass cover, and reducing the canopy cover to 30% more than tripled grass cover (Cordell et al., 1974).

Watering and fertilising can be important if lawns or shade/screening vegetation are planted in dry climates. Either flood or sprinkler-based systems can be used. Hammitt and Cole (1998) referred to flood irrigation being used to maintain trees and shrubs in the developed campgrounds at the bottom of the Grand Canyon. Van Riet and Cooks (1990) commented that a permanent irrigation system is required to ensure the endemic plants survive at Berg-en-Dal, a new camp in Kruger National Park (Figure 5.1).

The value of fertilising depends on the soil conditions. Soil testing is essential to determine what nutrients are limiting. Also, it is critical not to over-apply phosphorus or nitrogen as these can leach out of the soil and lead to nutrient enrichment of nearby waters. Although watering and fertilising individually lead to increases in ground cover, when both are applied the results may prove twice as effective as either one by itself. Both approaches are only effective when combined with careful site design and hardening of higher-use trails and facilities (Hammitt & Cole, 1998).

Other elements of sites that can be managed to protect the natural environment are toilets, fireplaces and rubbish disposal. All three concentrate use where the facilities are located, with the level of facilities provided depending on visitor numbers and the experience visitors are seeking. For example, wilderness visitors prefer not to see or have built toilets which are regarded as human intrusions (Lucas, 1990a). However, Hammitt & Cole (1998) noted that toilets are standard in developed natural areas and increasingly common in heavily used wilderness areas. Table 5.3 lists alternative methods of managing this form of human waste, associated levels of use and visitor acceptability.

For built accommodation such as resorts and lodges a permanent, enclosed human waste disposal system is essential. Septic systems are most common. However, in areas where water is scarce or leach fields and ponds are environmentally unacceptable, waterless systems are a possibility. For example, the Fitzroy Falls Visitor Centre in New South Wales, Australia (Figure 5.1) has a large experimental composting toilet facility which copes with 8000–16,000 visitors per week using both conventional composting toilets and worm-boosted ones.

Enjoying a campfire in natural areas is a contested practice. Campfires are integral to many people's overnight experience. However, there are safety concerns regarding fires escaping and becoming wildfires as well as the ecological and aesthetic effects of fuel collection and burning. Solutions include not allowing campfires in some areas, using loose rock rings that are pulled apart following use, providing wood for established fireplaces, and gas-fired, designated fireplaces/cookers. As with other facilities, the choice depends on levels of use, maintenance requirements, visitor preferences and environmental consequences. For example, gas cookers are most likely to be found where there are high levels of use, regular maintenance is possible and visitors are comfortable with human-built structures at the site. At the more primitive end of the recreation spectrum, a 'no campfires' approach seems more likely where signs of human intrusion are unwanted and managers aim to minimise the ecological effects of human use.

The disposal of solid rubbish and littering are both concerns. In wilderness areas,

Table 5.3 Methods for managing human wastes in natural areas

Method	Level of visitor use	Visitor acceptability
No facilities – individual's responsibility:		
Buried in a shallow hole (American 'cat hole') dug by the visitor, at least 60 m from water	Low; dispersed recreation areas with light use and soil cover	Good with educated users
Carried out in bag or container	Low; river-rafting and climbing settings	Compliance can be difficult
Direct ocean disposal	Low; infrequently visited areas	Fair with educated users
Pit toilet (Australian 'long-drop dunny') – hole at least several metres deep covered by a toilet seat and structure. Pit is covered with dirt and the structure moved when the hole is full	Low to moderate; available sites may be limited by water tables close to the surface and shallow soils	Fairly good, although flies and smell may be a concern to users
Transportable toilet – toilet seat and structure are placed over a transportable, replaceable drum	Low to moderate; as use levels increase the frequency of drum replacement increases; suitable where soils, water tables or risks of water contamination preclude using pit toilets	High, although use of vehicles for maintenance may not be accepted by users in wilderness areas
Compost (inc. worm-boosted) toilet – waste decomposes in digester tank to which a carbon source, such as wood chips must be regularly added; waste can be reduced in volume by as much as 80%	Moderate to high; requires frequent maintenance	High
Dehydrating toilet – waste is deposited in a tank and water evaporated; when full the waste must be dug out and removed	Moderate to high; suitable in low-humidity climates; requires frequent maintenance	High
Hybrid system – waste drops into tank partly filled with water; sludge is pumped out and liquid goes to leach field / pond	Moderate to high; requires frequent maintenance	High, where leach fields / ponds are acceptable (i.e. at the more developed end of the recreation spectrum)
Flush toilet – is flushed down toilet into septic system which is pumped regularly into a leach field / pond	High; requires maintenance and regular pumping of septic system	High, where plumbing systems and leach fields / ponds are acceptable

Derived from CALM (2000a); Cilimburg *et al.* (2000); Land (1995 in Hammitt & Cole, 1998)

visitors are expected to pack out their rubbish and dispose of it elsewhere. Many national parks now have bin-free sites, instead providing rubbish disposal facilities at a central location. This approach reduces the amount of time staff devote to rubbish collection, freeing them for other activities. For built accommodation and interpretive centres with large numbers of visitors often over extended periods, waste management must be multi-pronged. Purchasing goods with little packaging and recycling are two possible waste minimisation strategies. Ideally, solid waste can be disposed of outside the protected area. If this is not possible, the site should be located to avoid contaminating surface or ground waters and managed to prevent scavenging by wildlife.

Managing riverbanks, lakes and coastlines

Water bodies such as lakes, rivers and the sea hold a deep attraction for humans. Visitors enjoy vistas including water and preferably picnic and camp near water. Water bodies also have functional uses for visitors as sources of drinking water and for washing and swimming. About 30% of all wilderness areas in the United States prohibit camping close to streams and lakes (Washburne & Cole, 1983). Setbacks in wilderness and backcountry range from 2 m to 1 km, the most common being 30 m (Marion *et al.*, 1993; Washburne & Cole, 1983).

Setbacks reduce the risk of pollutants moving from the site into the water, protect fringing vegetation from trampling and other damage, and prevent erosion of steep banks and edges. There are also social reasons for setbacks, especially in relation to camping. Camping on shorelines effectively means that those who do not get one of these premier sites may not be able to access the water because to do so entails walking through someone else's camp. Also, campsites on shorelines are highly visible, decreasing perceptions of naturalness for other visitors. Because the social reasons are more compelling than the ecological ones, setbacks are more appropriate in high rather than low use natural areas (Hammitt & Cole, 1998). Setbacks stop visitors camping or visiting where they most want to. As such, they should only be undertaken when necessary for ecological and/or social reasons. Ecological outcomes can often be accomplished through education about not damaging shorelines or polluting waters.

Several other strategies can also be employed to reduce the movement of pollutants into water bodies. Maintaining or planting fringing vegetation between facilities and water bodies can filter out pollutants such as nutrients and pesticides. Locating toilets away from water bodies or ensuring that a closed system is installed, where warranted by visitor numbers, also minimises the flow of nutrients and pathogens into the water body.

Given the mobility of dunes and active erosive processes of coastlines, facilities should be located where they are not susceptible to wave or wind erosion or sand inundation (Oma *et al.*, 1992). Location should be where some protection from the wind is achieved – in low areas such as dune swales and deflation areas and next to vegetation if available (Box 5.5). Planting shrubs or trees, preferably those native to the area, is also a way of achieving some protection at sites. Plantings are not appropriate at primitive or semi-primitive sites where signs of humans are undesirable. Raised walkways are often used in coastal areas to enable visitors to access beaches (Hammitt & Cole, 1998). Plants can still grow underneath; however, on the downside, structures are often damaged or removed by storms.

Box 5.5 Locating and managing facilities in coastal settings: Fraser Island World Heritage Area, Australia

Fraser Island, located off the coast of south-east Queensland (Figure 5.1) and connected to the mainland by ferry, provides some of the best coastal four-wheel-driving and camping opportunities in Australia. About 100 km of beaches are used by 42,000 visitors per annum for camping. Over the period 1974 to 1994 this zone degraded markedly due to camping use (Hockings & Twyford, 1997).

Management actions that have improved the Island's coastal zone are improved signage, closure and rehabilitation of sites, and public education. Hockings and Twyford (1997) suggested that rationalisation and rehabilitation of tracks would improve foredune areas. They also recommended confining and concentrating camping to foredunes and swales.

Site restoration

Some sites do not have the capability to support visitors while others need temporary closure to allow regeneration. Sites may be permanently closed to ensure setbacks from water bodies, because they are poorly located or to reduce the number of sites. A total of 37% of wilderness areas in the United States and the same percentage of national parks with backcountry have closed campsites, with 16% and 27% respectively having active revegetation programmes (Marion *et al.*, 1993; Washburne & Cole, 1983). Another reason for site closure is rare or vulnerable plants or animals. Hammitt & Cole (1998) use the example of the endangered flowering plant, the sentry milk vetch (*Astragalus cremnophylax cremnophylax*) at Grand Canyon National Park (Figure 5.1). Managers rerouted walk trails and placed a fence around the population because of concerns regarding its viability.

Sites may be temporarily closed to allow them to recover. Temporary campsite closures have and can be used in both developed and primitive parts of natural areas. For this approach to work, managers need to know the relationship between the time it takes for impacts to occur, the threshold beyond which they become 'unacceptable', and the required recovery period. Also crucial is realising that most impact occurs in the first few years a site is used. Hammitt and Cole (1998) and others have described how impacts at wilderness campsites, canoe-accessed campsites and car camping sites increased dramatically for the first year or two and then levelled out. As such, a two-year use period followed by a recovery period of uncertain length has been suggested. The length of the rest period depends on moisture availability and growing season length, with active revegetation helping shorten this period. Rest-rotation is not generally recommended but if used, works best in resilient environments where active revegetation is feasible (Hammitt & Cole, 1998).

Several general comments can be made about restoration actions; however, site-specific approaches are usually required (Cole, 1990b). The first crucial step is effectively closing the site to all use. Barriers to access and information often work. All evidence of human use should be removed – fire rings, site furniture and litter. The site may then be left to regenerate naturally. Alternatively, active restoration through scarifying and / or direct seeding, planting seedlings or transplanting from adjacent areas can be pursued. Locally collected and propagated material should be used. At Olympic National Park in the United States, for example, approximately 25,000 plants are propagated annually for restoration projects. Rocks are dug in like 'icebergs' and dead wood placed vertically in closed areas to make the site unappealing and uncomfortable-looking (Scott, 1998).

Visitor Management Actions

Visitor management seeks to influence the amount, type, timing and distribution of use as well as visitor behaviour. Actions include regulating visitor numbers, group size and length of stay, using deterrence and enforcement, communicating with visitors and providing education (Figure 5.3). Charging fees as a means of regulating numbers is also discussed.

Regulating visitors

Until recently, managers have been encouraged to use light-handed management approaches such as communicating with visitors and education programmes rather than restricting visitor numbers or activities (Shindler & Shelby, 1993). These approaches were assumed to work and to be preferred by visitors. Minimal regulation was regarded as essential to satisfactory experiences by visitors to natural areas, especially more primitive places (Hendee et al., 1990b). Cole (1990b) has suggested that effectiveness should be a primary consideration in selecting actions. He noted that education and restoration efforts at campsites have been ineffective in many places. Regulation of numbers, regarded by managers as a last resort, may be more effective and better initiated earlier rather than later – taking regulatory action only after significant physical damage has occurred is like relying on bandages until the situation becomes so bad that surgery is required (Cole, 1993).

These researchers have questioned the assumption that visitors prefer education and communication efforts and will be opposed to more restrictive approaches, such as limiting numbers or activities within natural areas. In recent years, increases in ecological damage and visitor encounters at popular sites have increased visitor support for more direct approaches such as use limits (Shindler & Shelby, 1993). Their recent study of frequent visitors to three wilderness areas in Oregon found that setting limits on the number of users was generally supported. Watson and Niccolucci (1995) in a similar survey found that only 14% of campers thought there should never be use limits.

Visitor numbers

Although there is evidence that regulating access is supported by visitors, such an approach conflicts with one of the central objectives of management for most natural areas – that of providing opportunities for visitors. As such, other options should be considered first. Also, because the relationship between amount of use and impact is not linear, reducing use may not necessarily reduce impacts. In most situations, a little use causes considerable impact and further increases in use levels have less and less additional effect on the natural environment (Hammitt & Cole, 1998).

Most of the controversy associated with use limits is centred on determining how and when use levels should be implemented and much of the debate concerns whether empirical data can be directly translated into use limits. Use limits are actually subjective judgements made by managers and should be based on two factors: stakeholders' perceptions of impacts and scientists' understanding of the ecological impacts (Cole *et al.*, 1997). The planning frameworks outlined in the previous chapter provide the best way of determining the levels of impact acceptable to stakeholders. Cole and Landres (1996) suggested that ecological impacts are a function of the impact's intensity, its areal extent, and the rarity or irreplaceability of the attributes being impacted.

Scientists can then assess the relationships between amount of use and impacts, allowing the maximum levels of use that can be supported without exceeding the acceptable level to be determined. Once maximum levels have been decided, simulation models and computer programs can be used to set entry limits for individual trailheads. More sophisticated programmes allow travel routes to be determined, linking the availability of a number of sites with a visitor's route preference (Hammitt & Cole, 1998).

Other approaches have also been used as summarised by Hammitt and Cole (1998). In Yosemite National Park (Figure 5.1) use limits are based on the number of acres in a zone, the miles of trails it contains, and its ecological fragility based on ecological rarity, vulnerability, recuperability and repairability (Van Wagtendonk, 1986). In nearby Sequoia and Kings Canyon National Parks, existing campsites are assessed to determine if they are acceptable or unacceptable. Unacceptable ones were those within 8 m of water or 30 m of another heavily impacted site. The total number of acceptable sites was used to determine the maximum number of groups to be permitted at any one time (Parsons, 1986).

Hammitt and Cole (1998) and Cole (1990b) suggested there is little point in restricting visitor numbers in high use areas unless it is accompanied by confining use to certain sites. Otherwise, the reduced numbers of visitors will continue using all available sites, none of which will recover. Reduced numbers will improve the quality of the experience by being less crowded, but there will be no ecological benefits as all sites will still be impacted. Cole *et al.* (1997) cautioned that reducing use levels will deny access to many people as well as increase visitor impacts in nearby natural areas. At higher levels of use only large changes in visitor numbers have an effect on impact levels.

In lightly used areas, given that at low use levels differences in amount of use can have significant effects on the amount of impact, use limits can contribute substantially to keeping impact levels low. Use needs to be kept low at all sites, with visitors avoiding fragile sites and not undertaking destructive behaviours. To encourage

Table 5.4 Ways of allocating visitor access to natural areas

Allocation system	Equity outcome	Visitor acceptability
Advance reservation	Benefits those able to plan ahead	Generally high
Queuing/ First-come first-served	Favours those with lots of time and who live nearby	Low to moderate
Lottery	No group obviously benefited or disadvantaged	Low
Fees	Favours those able to pay	Low to moderate
Eligibility requirements	Favours those with time (and money) to meet requirements	Not known

Derived from Stankey and Baden (1977, in Hammitt & Cole, 1998)

these types of suitable behaviour use limits in such areas need to be accompanied by communication and education programmes on low impact use.

Having decided to limit visitor numbers, the issue then becomes one of equity and allocation. With restrictions, some people get to visit the area and others do not. For those permitted to enter, they can enjoy greater solitude. For those who are excluded, they do not get to enjoy the natural area (Lucas, 1990a). Table 5.4 summarises ways of allocating access, who benefits and acceptability to visitors. Access is usually allocated via a permit. A mixture of approaches may be used to manage access to a protected area. For example, as described by Lucas (1990a), for the seven allowed float trips per day down the Middle Fork of the Salmon River, Idaho (Frank Church River of No Return Wilderness), three permits are allocated to commercial guides and four are available to private parties through a lottery.

Fees are generally used to raise revenue although they are also a means of rationing use. Many protected areas have entrance fees. Ideally, fees would encourage those who place a low value on protected areas to go elsewhere. Unfortunately, however, those who value these areas but have low incomes may also be discouraged. Variable fees have been widely discussed, with higher fees for heavily used areas and lower or no fees for seldom-used sites. The hope with this approach is that higher fees would discourage use and vice versa.

Most wilderness users in the United States object to fees although these objections are quelled somewhat when the income from the fees is clearly used to manage the area (Lucas, 1990a). More recent research, however, suggests wilderness users generally support fees, with strongest support when the fees are used to restore human-damaged sites, remove litter and provide information (Vogt & Williams, 1999). These users preferred their fees going to maintenance of wilderness conditions rather than to developing new facilities and services.

Visitor numbers can be managed in other ways in addition to simply regulating the numbers entering an area (Table 5.5). In many places, overnight use is limited

Table 5.5 Nature and extent of restrictions on visitor use in natural areas

Restriction method	Description
1. Limit entry to an area:	May apply to day use or overnight visitors, more often the latter.
Whole area	Number of visitors to the whole area is regulated. Applications include the number of parties floating a wild river, number of visitors entering all trailheads, number of groups/individuals camping overnight.
Entry points – all or specified ones	Use managed through individual trailhead quotas with visitors free to travel and camp where they want once they have entered.
2. Limit activities once in the area:	Most likely to apply to overnight visitors.
Campsites/zones specified	Visitors must indicate where they intend to camp each night – either a site or within a specified area (e.g. travel zone). There may be restrictions on how long they can stay at one site/within one zone.
Travel routes specified	Permits may be issued for itineraries linking campsites, rather than for individual campsites in isolation. This allows itineraries to be adjusted and alternative routes selected if space is not available at sites on the preferred route.

Derived from Hammitt and Cole (1998), Lucas (1990a)

but day use is not. Marion *et al.* (1993) noted that in two-thirds of US national parks that limit backcountry use, limits apply only to overnight users. Also, overnight limits may be set in different ways. The number of visitors entering an area may be restricted, but once in they are free to travel and stay where they want. Alternatively, where they go within an area may be regulated by permits being issued to camp at certain campsites on specified nights (Hammitt & Cole, 1998). Stewart (1989) argued that trailhead entry quotas may be as efficient, simpler to implement and found by visitors to be easier to apply for and comply with than travel route and campsite quotas.

Restrictions can be developed and applied in various, apparently endless combinations. Tables 5.4 and 5.5 summarise different allocation systems and their varying nature and extent. Other elements that can be manipulated include times of year an area is available or rationing is in place, group size (see below), cost of acquiring an access permit, length of stay at one site or within one travel zone (see below), use of campfires, and number of access permits issued per person per season (Lucas, 1990a). Box 5.6 provides an example of combined restrictions applied to regulating visitor numbers and use.

Box 5.6 Regulating visitor use: Michaelmas Cay and Reef, Great Barrier Reef Marine Park, Australia

The Cay, with an area of 1.8 ha, provides a breeding site for seven species of bird and is one of the premier nesting islands for the Great Barrier Reef (Figure 5.1). It is also a popular and accessible destination for tourist boats, both commercial and private, operating from Cairns, a major tourism centre in north Queensland. Six tour operators with combined visitor numbers of 550 per day use the Cay (Muir & Chester, 1993).

The 1986 management plan for Michaelmas Cay and Reef gives conservation of natural resources as the most important objective, followed by tourism, recreation and education. Regulations to achieve these objectives include:

- not more than 100 people on the beach at one time;
- access available to all the reef and specified parts of the Cay;
- access is for quiet activities only, with no seaplanes or helicopters permitted;
- vessel speed is not to exceed 4 knots within 300 m of the Cay edge;
- no commercial instruction, such as scuba instruction, to be conducted on the Cay or its shallows;
- no fires or waste disposal in the area;
- groups of more than 10 visitors on the Cay must be supervised by the operator;
- vessels must anchor in sand, not coral, or use an established mooring (Muir & Chester, 1993).

These authors noted that since the introduction of the management plan, tourism demand for the area has increased beyond expectation. The number of visitors on the Cay at any one time frequently exceeds the 100-person prescribed limit. Although annual visitation is only 90,000 with a maximum permitted of 180,000, at peak use times the Cay is already at capacity. The above regulations seem likely to need revision based on these increases and patterns of use.

Completely excluding or spatially separating different types of visitor use are other ways managers seek to control impacts. Horses are excluded from 14% of wilderness areas in the United States (McClaran & Cole, 1993) and many Australian national parks. Spatial separation can be achieved by designating trails for different kinds of use. For example, at Yellowstone National Park (Figure 5.1), snowmobilers are restricted to roadways while cross-country skiers may go off-road. In the United States, 12% of national parks designate different trail uses. Managers have also segregated campsites by type of use, with separate sites for general visitors, groups, stock users, commercial outfitters, and even llama users (Leung & Marion, 1999b).

Visitor group size

Common sense and some research suggest that limiting the size of groups visiting wilderness areas has ecological and social benefits (Hammitt & Cole, 1998; Lucas, 1990a). Larger groups occupy and impact larger areas than a small group, especially in less-developed sites or where sites are designed for small groups. Most visitors to wilderness areas in the United States support limits on group size (Cole, 1990b). Group size, regulated in almost half the wilderness areas in the United States, ranges from 5–60, with a median size of 15 and most common limit of 25 (Washburne & Cole, 1983). Lucas (1990a) suggested a group size of 6–12 is reasonable, while Hammitt and Cole (1998) noted that visitors preferred groups of 10 or less.

Limits on group size are most effective in lightly used natural areas, such as wilderness, where use levels are low and camping is dispersed (Cole, 1990b). In more developed natural areas, catering for larger groups may be possible and desirable. Picnic areas and beach access points, for example, need to provide for larger groups. With careful site planning some geological features, such as The Pinnacles in south-western Australia (Figure 5.1), may be able to cater for hundreds of visitors per day. Wildlife viewing opportunities, such as whale watching from built platforms or headlands, may also be able to cater for larger groups so long as the viewing structures are designed with larger numbers in mind.

In many natural areas, limits have been placed on the number of horses, and other pack stock such as mules and llamas, in a group. Horses are used in many wilderness areas in the United States and in some protected areas in other parts of the world. Research is confirming that packstock have greater impacts on natural areas than hikers (De Luca *et al.*, 1998). Stock limits for US wilderness areas range from 5–50 head (McClaran & Cole, 1993; Washburne & Cole, 1983), with a median of 10 (Marion *et al.*, 1993). Hammitt and Cole (1998) suggested that one approach could be limiting the total number of bodies, say to 15. This would mean say six humans and nine head of stock and allow composite limits to be set.

Visitor length of stay

Length of stay generally does not contribute significantly to overuse (Lucas, 1990a). Additionally, in heavily used popular areas limiting length of stay is unlikely to reduce impacts (Hammitt & Cole, 1998). However, such limits at popular sites may allow more people to use them, while maintaining the existing levels of use and associated impacts (Cole, 1990b). In lightly used areas, length of stay limits can reduce ecological impacts. Hammitt and Cole (1998) suggested visitors should stay no more than a night or two at an individual site in remote areas. Additionally, sleeping and eating at different places can significantly reduce impacts (Cole, 1990b).

Washburne and Cole (1983) reported length of stay limits for 53% of US wilderness areas. National parks in the United States also commonly have stay limits. A 14 day limit is most common in national forest wilderness areas, with 1–3 nights for national parks (Lucas, 1990a).

Deterrence and enforcement

Field staff including wilderness rangers have a multitude of roles, one of which is deterring inappropriate behaviour and if necessary enforcing the law. A study of visitor behaviour at Mount Rainier in the United States (Figure 5.1) showed that the main deterrent to visitors wandering off trails was the presence of a uniformed employee. Most people knew what they were supposed to do, but chose to do otherwise unless regulated (Swearingen & Johnson, 1995). Visitor surveys indicate rangers are well accepted by wilderness users (Lucas, 1990a).

Visitor communication and education

Education is regarded as crucial to reducing impacts by visitors to natural areas, for all sites from primitive through to the most developed (Cole, 1990b; Hammitt & Cole, 1998; Lucas, 1990a). It is particularly important in addressing illegal, careless, unskilled and uninformed actions (Hammitt & Cole, 1998). Education is a widely accepted management approach because it does not overtly regulate or seek to directly control visitors. Visitors retain the freedom to choose, plus receive information that potentially makes their experience more rewarding. More than half of US wilderness areas have an educational programme (Washburne & Cole, 1983), while Marion *et al.* (1993) noted that 91% of backcountry areas in the national park system educated visitors about 'pack-it-in, pack-it-out'. Given the importance of education, communication and the associated process of interpretation, the following chapter is devoted to the latter.

Visitors to natural areas provide a good audience for communication-education programmes (Lucas, 1990a). Most studies agree that wilderness users have high education levels (Morin *et al.*, 1997). Lucas (1990b) noted that 60–85% of visitors to US wilderness areas have some form of tertiary education, while Morin *et al.* (1997) noted the same for 70% of those visiting an Australian wilderness (Nuyts Wilderness in south-western Australia, Figure 5.1).

The effectiveness of providing education and information compared with other actions is poorly known; however, Cole (1995) believes they have been preferentially favoured because of their palatability to visitors. He noted that managers believe they should try education and communication before restricting access even though the comparative efficacy is unknown. Education efforts at campsites to address deteriorating conditions have been found ineffective in many places. Also, recent research has shown that regulatory actions, such as site closures and restricting visitor numbers, are generally supported by visitors (Shindler & Shelby, 1993; Watson & Niccolucci, 1995).

The values of communication and education in impact management are four-fold: they support other more direct actions such as restricting access; can be applied from the most primitive to most developed settings; enable managers to start being proactive rather than reactive; and visitors have the opportunity to make informed choices. Education should not be expected to solve problems in the short term (Cole, 1995). Rather, specific problems may require immediate, direct responses while education is used as a longer-term, complementary strategy. Lucas

Table 5.6 Principles of Leave No Trace low impact education programme

Principle	Description
1. Plan ahead and prepare	Travel in small groups, with appropriate equipment
2. Camp and travel on durable surfaces	In *high use areas*, concentrate use on impacted/hardened surfaces (so the next group finds a clean and attractive site)
	In *low use areas*, disperse use and impacts (so the next group does not recognise the campsite)
	In *all situations*, stay off lightly impacted sites – they are the most vulnerable to further damage
3. Dispose of waste properly	Dispose of human waste in toilets or buried
	Pack out litter and food waste
4. Leave what you find	Avoid tree damage, moving soil, building rock cairns or marking trees or rock surfaces
5. Minimise campfire impacts	Cook on stoves and minimise use of, or do not use, campfires
6. Respect wildlife	Avoid scaring or harassing wildlife
7. Be considerate of other visitors	Respect solitude experiences being sought by others

Derived from Hammitt and Cole (1998), Cole (pers. comm., 2000)

(1990a) cautioned that unless used with care, information may stimulate over-use and create problems that might not have occurred.

Communication and education can be used to reduce impacts through redistributing use and providing information on minimum impact use (Lucas, 1990a). Redistribution may be within or to natural areas outside the area of concern. If managers can provide descriptive materials on a range of sites then they can make sure that particular sites are not overused. Visitors can also select the sites most closely matching their needs. Use redistribution is most likely to occur when visitors have access to previsit trip information (Roggenbuck & Lucas, 1987).

The other main use of communication and education is encouraging minimum impact use of natural areas. In the United States, most wilderness areas have minimum-impact education programmes. These are provided through schools and colleges, at wilderness access points, and on wilderness trails and campsites. Educational materials include brochures, staff in agency offices, agency-run community education programmes, maps, signs, field staff such as rangers in the backcountry, and trailhead displays. Most of these materials focus on resource impacts but some relate to effects on other visitors' experiences (Lucas, 1990a).

The international Tread Lightly Programme encourages minimum impact use of natural areas. Very similar is the Leave No Trace Programme with its seven guiding principles (Table 5.6). This programme recognises individual places and user groups as having different requirements and needing different approaches. Six ecoregions across the United States, with different requirements, are recognised. Similarly, river floating, horse use, rock climbing, snow camping, caving and sea kayaking are addressed as specialised activities (Hammitt & Cole, 1998).

Choosing Management Actions

Making the choice

A number of factors influence the selection of management actions by managers (Figure 5.4). If an unacceptable impact is identified, it is essential to determine whether visitors were the cause. Not all impacts in natural areas are due to visitors. Fluctuations in wildlife populations, for example in an elk population, may be due to variations in food availability, predation patterns or disease occurrence. Impacts can also result from outside influences. Poor water quality, for example, may be due to activities upstream of an area rather than within it. Although a complete understanding of the underlying causes may not be possible (Graefe *et al.*, 1990), if a relationship exists between visitor use and impacts it can usually be identified. Having determined visitors as the source of the impact, a wide range of actions is available as outlined in the preceding sections.

The location and extent of impacts influences the choice of management actions. At the primitive end of the spectrum in wilderness, engineering, extensive environmental modification and even restrictions on where visitors can go are undesirable. The wilderness experience is based on freedom, solitude and little evidence of humans. The available actions are then limited to restricting the number of visitors and communication and education. Towards the developed end of the spectrum, site engineering, buildings and extensive environmental modifications are more appropriate. Here, using communication and education is still useful. For example, managers of a lodge may rely on extensive engineering and site management as well as communicating with visitors about protecting wildlife and waste minimisation.

The extent of impacts also influences the actions chosen. Cole (1995) suggested that where impact problems are widespread at particular locations or require rapid attention and amelioration, then direct actions such as regulating visitor numbers and where they go are needed. For example, a campsite denuded of vegetation, increasing in size and showing signs of erosion requires direct intervention as well as educating visitors. Interventions could include site closure, redesign or hardening, and limiting visitor numbers.

Cost and ease of implementation are crucial considerations. Natural area managers worldwide face declining budgets and increasing visitor numbers. Management actions must be cost-effective both in terms of the initial action taken and the associated maintenance required. Engineering solutions, such as bridges and boardwalks, are expensive to construct and maintain. Also, undertaking work requiring moving materials into or out of remote locations is expensive and time-consuming. In the United States helicopters are routinely used to service cabins and toilets in wilderness areas, as

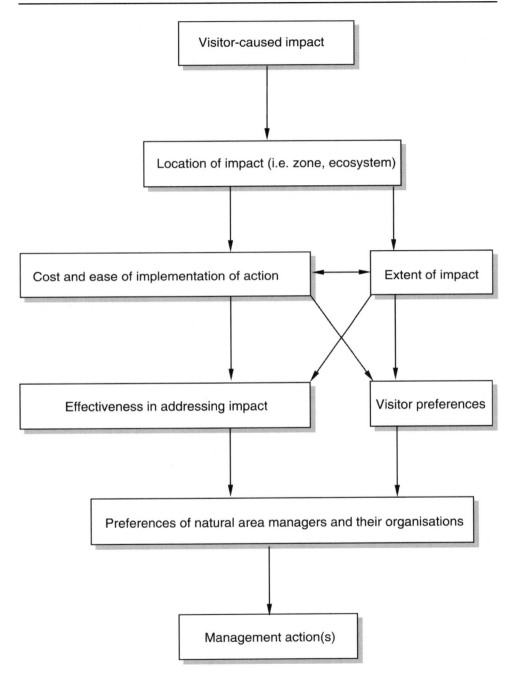

Figure 5.4 Factors influencing the choice of management actions by managers

well as moving trail-building materials. The associated cost would be prohibitive for natural area managers in many other countries.

The ease of implementation is influenced both by the initial and ongoing time commitment managers must make. Introducing a permit system, for example, necessitates time spent informing visitors it is in place and for its administration. Site engineering requires design skills as well as staff to do the construction work. Communication and education require an initial commitment of time; however, once materials are prepared little ongoing input from managers is necessary.

Managers' interpretations of visitor preferences have been highly influential in selecting management actions. Managers and researchers have generally believed that visitors prefer information and education to direct actions such as restricting access and rationing use (Cole, 1995). Research suggests this is not always the case. Shindler and Shelby (1993), in their survey of visitors to three wilderness areas in Oregon, found that regulating visitors through restricting access and site closures was generally supported. A survey of wilderness users in Western Australia showed that although educating visitors was the most strongly supported management action, more than two-thirds of visitors supported limiting use, length of stay during peak times, number of people in a group, and temporarily closing areas (Morin et al., 1997). A similar survey in Borneo by Chin et al. (2000) showed substantial support for regulatory actions such as limiting forest use and the number of people, as well as for indirect actions such as education.

Hammitt and Cole (1998) cautioned that in selecting a management strategy, visitor satisfaction must be considered equally with concerns for protecting the natural environment. Both are important, although their relative importance will vary from area to area. For example, in a nature reserve, resource protection will take priority, whereas in a national park with a substantial facilities area, visitor satisfaction may be of equal if not greater importance.

There is little point in undertaking management unless it is effective in ameliorating the impact. Generally, restricting and rationing use are more effective than information and education (Cole et al., 1995). Regulating use, if enforced, should change the behaviour of most visitors, whereas providing information only increases the likelihood of people behaving as desired. Lucas (1990a) also noted that regulation and trying to directly control visitors may result in confrontations and conflict. Thus, such approaches need to be accompanied by communication programmes.

An influential, but little discussed, element is how the preferences of protected area managers and their organisations guide the choice of management actions (Figure 5.4). Managers who see their role as a policing one are likely to prefer regulating. Those who see their role as educational are likely to prefer communicative and educative approaches. Others with training and experiences in site design and engineering are likely to prefer these approaches. Similarly, past preferences and practices of organisations will influence current preferences. For example, managers in organisations with few resources and limited political support may favour softer, inoffensive approaches such as education.

These preferences will also be shaped by the actions managers regard as being effective in protecting the natural area and visitors' experiences. Surveys of wilderness area managers in the United States by Marion *et al.* (1993) and Manning *et al.* (1996) showed that site design, management and facilities provision (e.g. designating campsites, using a formal trail system and plan, providing toilets), as well as regulating use (e.g. limiting group sizes, implementing quotas), are regarded by managers as highly effective practices. Education was only regarded as highly effective in managing impacts on wildlife. These views are likely to have been influenced by the policing background of a number of these managers. In an earlier study, Washburne and Cole (1983) noted that the majority of wilderness managers in the United States thought the most effective management was education through personal contact with the visitor, leading to increased dispersal and improved camping actions.

Management actions are generally used in combination (Box 5.7). Site design and education/communication are widely used. In marine environments where facilities are limited or absent, management is generally through regulation, and communication and education programmes.

A combined approach

Tourism management in most natural areas relies on a combination of various management strategies and actions. Where there are few resources for management, the main management thrusts are reservation followed by zoning. Such is the case for many protected areas in developing countries (Wallace, 1993). For protected areas in developed countries, reservation, zoning and often co-management are accompanied by a suite of management actions, including site design, regulating visitors and education. Box 5.8 describes the management of Kakadu National Park in northern Australia where many of the strategies and actions outlined in this chapter have been applied.

Managing the Tourism Industry

Managing natural area tourism relies on three parties – land managers, visitors and the tourism industry. This industry includes those operating tours through natural areas as well as the owners/managers of built accommodation and other facilities, such as interpretative centres. The previous two sections have been devoted to management strategies and actions available primarily to land managers. This section explores strategies focusing on the tourism industry. These may be voluntary, such as codes of conduct, or they may be licences and associated conditions administered by management agencies.

Voluntary strategies

A range of means are available for assisting tour operators and those who own or manage tourism facilities, such as resorts or interpretive centres, to conduct their business in ways that minimise its environmental consequences.

Codes of conduct and guidelines

A code is a set of expectations, behaviours or rules written by industry members,

Box 5.7 Management strategies for the marine environment: two examples

Example One. Managing tourist–stingray interactions at Stingray City in the western Caribbean

Stingrays congregating off the coast of Grand Cayman in the western Caribbean (Figure 5.1) are beginning to show major behavioural changes, such as shoaling behaviour, skin abrasion from handling and altered feeding habits (Shackley, 1998). This population now receives about 80,000–100,000 visitors per year with up to 500 divers in the water with them on a busy day. Visitors feed and touch the rays from within the water and rays are lifted out of the water for photographs. Most operators give a pre-dive briefing in which they explain how to handle the rays and give information on their ecology.

Shackley (1998) suggested several actions for better managing these interactions. Currently Stingray City is not part of a protected area. Making it part of one would enable some quota-based restrictions on tourist access if ecological studies show that current levels of use are environmentally damaging. Another possible strategy is visitor fees. Such a user-pays approach might reduce demand and the level of impacts on the stingrays. A user-fee is unlikely to be popular with tour operators as it would most likely be collected through increased tour prices and members of this industry compete on price. User-fees have hardly ever been used to manage marine resources (Shackley, 1998). A visitor education programme, beyond the *ad hoc* approaches currently taken by individual operators, coupled with management guidelines are also recommended.

These actions are directed predominantly at managing the visitors themselves, through education, fees and quotas on numbers. The only site-based strategy, in the most general sense, is making Stingray City a protected area.

Example Two. Scuba diving at Vanuatu in the western Pacific Ocean

Vanuatu is a sought-after diving destination because of its diversity of marine life and relaxed lifestyle. Howard (1999) noted in a recent study that most divers felt they had no impact on the reefs when they dived at Vanuatu. Buoyancy problems, that is, inadvertently sinking onto the reef, was the main reason given for contacting the reef and damaging it. Only 8% of divers noted this as a problem. Whether or not divers contacted the reef was strongly influenced by the instructor. If the instructor stayed above the reef, contact by the group was low.

Unlike the example above, in Vanuatu some actions are in place to reduce visitor impacts. Operators attempt to reduce the impact of divers by rotating sites, teaching buoyancy, and trying to educate divers. Several aspects of the operator–diver relationship could be improved, namely brochure content, courses conducted, pre-dive briefings and educational resources. Howard (1999) also suggested diver education programmes aimed at minimal impact and greater understanding of the environment.

The operators have a preference for site (e.g. rotating sites) rather than visitor (e.g. education) management because they feel they have more control over the former.

Box 5.8 A combined approach to management: Kakadu National Park, Northern Australia

Kakadu National Park is one of only 22 World Heritage sites listed for both its natural and cultural values. Located in northern Australia (Figure 5.1), with an area of almost two million hectares, it contains both ancient and modern landforms. The ancient Arnhem land plateau contains numerous spectacular cliffs, waterfalls and caves. The park covers most of the catchment of the South Alligator River, a major tropical monsoonal system regarded as a recent landform. The park's wetlands are internationally recognised under the Ramsar Convention. Additionally, Kakadu has one of the most important rock art collections in the world, dating back 18,000 years (Ryan, 1998).

Many tourists are attracted to Kakadu: visitor numbers average about 230,000 per year (Kakadu Board of Management and Parks Australia, 1998). Major reasons for visiting include appreciating the scenery, viewing wildlife and rock art, and learning about the area's ecological and cultural heritage (Wellings, 1995) (Plate 5.2). Tourist facilities include roads, a range of accommodation, boat launching facilities, walking tracks, viewing platforms and picnic areas (Commonwealth of Australia, 1991).

Kakadu National Park is regarded as a successful example of joint management by the Aboriginal traditional owners and the Commonwealth government through Parks Australia (De Lacy, 1994; Press & Hill, 1994). Approximately 300 Aboriginal people live in the park. The Kakadu Board of Management, established in 1989 and with an Aboriginal majority (10 out of 15 members), determines policy and is responsible along with the Director for preparing management plans for the park.

Joint management is achieved through enabling legislation, lease agreements with the Aboriginal traditional owners, and general management arrangements between the traditional owners and Parks Australia staff. The legislation allows traditional Aboriginal owners to claim land and lease it to the Director of National Parks as well as providing for boards of management for parks on Aboriginal lands. The lease agreements provide for the rights and protect the interests of traditional owners, employment and training for Aboriginal people in park management, public education and information services, lease payments, and a share in park revenue (Kakadu Board of Management and Parks Australia, 1998). General management arrangements include the Board of Management, the plan of management and day-to-day liaison. Day-to-day liaison is an informal but nevertheless crucial element and includes local meetings, employing senior traditional owners as cultural advisers, day-to-day working contact with traditional owners, and employing young Aboriginal people (Press & Hill, 1994; Press & Lawrence, 1995).

Four management zones are identified in the 1999 Plan of Management (Kakadu Board of Management and Parks Australia, 1998). These are Zone 1, including all major roads and major infrastructure development, Zone 2 with moderate levels of development such as designated camping areas, Zone 3 which has minimum development and low visitor numbers, and Zone 4 with opportunities for solitude and wilderness experiences. This zoning scheme provides a progression of recreation opportunities from a high level of facilities and social interactions in Zone 1 through to no facilities and solitary experiences in Zone 4. About one-third of the park, in the remote south-east, is Zone 4 (Chaffey, 1996).

Site management includes roads and tracks, built accommodation, safari camps and campgrounds. To improve site management, the 1999 Plan requires that area plans are prepared and implemented for a number of specified sites. The park has two major and many minor sealed roads providing all-weather access, and several unsealed roads and four-wheel-drive tracks. These will only be improved to protect the environment or to make the road safer, not to make access easier. For some roads, weight and/or vehicle limits will apply to protect them from damage.

Accommodation facilities have the potential to significantly impact on the park environment. Three hotels collectively accommodate about 870 guests a night while a lodge provides 120 moderately priced beds. There is also a youth hostel. The 1991 Plan recommended no further hotel development during the life of that plan (Commonwealth of Australia, 1991). The 1999 Plan expresses a preference for backpacker rather than hotel accommodation and expansion of existing rather than constructing new facilities. Safari camps, semi-permanent camps with basic facilities used by commercial tour operators, are approved in the 1999 Plan. They are to take up no more than 20% of a campground and have no adverse effects on the natural environment or other users.

A range of other camping opportunities is also provided, from highly developed and maintained sites to bush camping outside designated areas (Commonwealth of Australia, 1991). A number of the developed campsites are landscaped, the ablution blocks have hot water and lighting, and picnic tables and benches are provided. Other sites, accessible on unsealed rather than sealed roads, have pit toilets and a rubbish service only. The least developed option is bush camping with no facilities, primarily for hikers who must hold a permit. Several camping areas are recommended for relocation or at least redesign. Up to two new camping areas are proposed in the southern part of the park. A booking system is proposed, if necessary, for some areas (Kakadu Board of Management and Parks Australia, 1998).

Visitors are charged a fee to enter the park and to use the major developed camping areas. Revenue from fees now provides over a quarter of Kakadu's annual budget. Traditional owners also receive a share of this revenue. Interpretation is a focus of the 1999 Plan of Management where the importance of promoting the park as a cultural landscape, an Aboriginal place, is recognised. Associated actions include preparing guidelines with the traditional owners on appropriate promotional images and messages and working closely with tourist commissions and tour companies to ensure only appropriate imagery is used. Previsit information, regarded as a neglected area, will be made widely available. Park staff will help Aboriginal people to become more involved in face-to-face interpretive programmes (Kakadu Board of Management and Parks Australia, 1998).

More than 150 tour operators are licensed to operate in Kakadu, with about half of the tours consisting of up to 12 people travelling in small buses or four-wheel-drive vehicles (Commonwealth of Australia, 1991). About 50% of park visitors rely on commercial package tours to see Kakadu. Tours include boat cruises at Yellow Water and the South Alligator River, scenic flights, visits to art sites, four-wheel-drive excursions, birdwatching and general sightseeing. The 1999 Plan precludes non-Aboriginals or companies without Aboriginal involvement from developing new commercial tourism activities in the park (Kakadu Board of Management and Parks Australia, 1998).

Aboriginal people are both directly and indirectly involved in tourism. The Gagudju Aboriginal Association jointly owns the famous crocodile-shaped Gagadju Crocodile Hotel in Jabiru, the Gagudju Lodge Cooinda Hotel Motel and associated camping grounds, and the Yellow Water boat tours. The second of the three main Aboriginal associations in the park, the Djabulukgu Association, owns and operates the Marrawuddi Gallery and Guluyambi Cruise on the East Alligator River. The third, the Jawoyn Association, also have commercial interests. About 34% of the 75 officers working in the park are Aboriginal people (Ryan, 1998).

Management of Kakadu provides an excellent example of the strategies and actions that can be combined to manage a protected area. These begin with international agreements, here the World Heritage and Ramsar Conventions, and culminate in site design and management. Joint management by the Aboriginal traditional owners and the Australian Commonwealth government is a key feature.

Plate 5.2 Sunset viewing area at Ubirr Rock in the north east part of Kakadu National Park, Australia. (*Photo*: Greg Miles, Environment Australia)

government or non-government organisations (Holden, 2000). Their principal aim is to influence the attitudes and behaviour of tourists or the tourism industry. A code may be informal and adopted by a group, or more formal and instituted for industry members and/or tourists. The former are often referred to as codes of ethics and tend to be philosophical and value-based whereas the latter are usually known as codes of practice or conduct and are more applicable and specific to actual practice in local situations. Guidelines are also used to direct how tourism activities are undertaken and similarly to codes may be written by industry members, government or non-government organisations.

A code of ethics provides a standard of acceptable performance, often in written form, that assists in establishing and maintaining professionalism (Jafari, 2000). The Pacific Asia Tourism Association's code for environmentally responsible tourism is an example of such a code (PATA, 1991). This code urges its members and their industry partners to use resources sustainably, conserve flora and fauna habitats, recognise community beliefs and aspirations in planning, comply with all environmental laws and policies, remediate and correct the environmental impacts of tourism development, regularly audit environmental practices, and enhance the understanding by staff and visitors of the natural environment. More recently, the World Tourism Organisation has adopted a global code of ethics for tourism (WTO, 1999). The code includes nine principles outlining a sustainable approach to tourism development for destinations, governments, tour operators, developers, travel agents, workers and travellers themselves. A tenth principle focuses on implementation.

Many codes of conduct and guidelines exist for tourism in natural areas. Some have been developed for specific places such as Antarctica (Box 5.9), and others for activities such as river rafting or kayaking. Destination-specific codes recommend how tour operators and/or visitors should behave at a destination. Codes or guidelines for specific activities are intended to help tour operators and visitors improve their environmental management and minimise their impacts. Guidelines for whitewater rafting and kayaking note that environmental management is important because most rafting rivers have limited campsites, and minimal impact techniques are essential for client satisfaction as well as environmental protection (Buckley, 1999a). Such guidelines suggest that tourists plan ahead, tread lightly, camp with care, carry out their litter and continue learning about the environment.

Accreditation and certification

Accreditation and certification are other means of assisting industry members to act responsibly. Accreditation involves an agency or organisation evaluating and recognising a programme of study or institution as meeting certain predetermined standards or qualifications. Certification is testing an individual to determine their mastery of a specific body of knowledge. Thus, accreditation concerns programmes and institutions whereas certification applies to professionals such as tour operators (Morrison *et al.*, 1992). Despite this definitional difference, these words are used

Box 5.9 Antarctica: guidelines for the conduct of tourism and tourists

Antarctica, the last continent to be 'discovered' and the most isolated, occupies almost 10% of the world's land surface (Splettstoesser, 1999) (Figure 5.1). Nearly all of the continent is ice-bound (98%) although its extreme aridity means some areas of coast are permanently free of ice. In contrast to the limited extent and biological diversity of its land, the Antarctic waters are rich in wildlife including whales, seabirds, seals, squid and fish (Dingwall, 1998; Mason & Legg, 1999). Unlike the countries of the Arctic, the Antarctic has no indigenous inhabitants.

Antarctica has become a tourist destination relatively recently, with the first tourist aircraft in December 1956 and the first tourist ship in 1958. Seaborne tourists account for more than 95% of all tourists (Stonehouse, 1994). Antarctic tourism is growing rapidly. In the 1995–6 season about 9000 tourists visited the continent, more than double the number in 1990–91. There are now more tourists than scientists and support staff (Mason & Legg, 1999). Because of the extreme climate, tourism is limited to the Austral summer between late October and early March (Hall & Wouters, 1995). Attractions include the remoteness, extreme climate, beauty of the physical setting and abundant wildlife (Plate 5.3). The remains of explorers' huts as well as the scientific bases are also of great interest.

Expedition cruising, coupled with education, is the main form of seaborne tourism. Cruise ships vary in size from 40 to 400 passengers, with most carrying between 100 and 250 people. Cruise length also varies, although most last 12–15 days with 4–5 days spent landing at different sites using inflatable boats. A typical itinerary includes penguin rookeries, scientific bases, historic sites and trips in inflatable boats to scenic areas and to see seals on icebergs. Most ships provide educational briefings on history, geology, wildlife and scientific research (Enzenbacher, 1992).

Management responsibility for Antarctica is shared by more than 40 countries and is guided by the international Antarctic Treaty, which came into force in 1961. The Treaty freezes sovereignty claims (seven nations have territorial claims), demilitarises the area, guarantees free access and gives pre-eminence to scientific research. Industry guidelines, along with the Treaty, play an important role in managing tourism in the Antarctic.

The most widely known guidelines are those produced by the International Association of Antarctic Tour Operators (IAATO), an organisation founded in 1991. IAATO has two sets, one for tour operators and the other for visitors. The operator guidelines aim to increase environmental awareness, promote tourist safety, and establish a code of behaviour that minimises environmental impacts. The number of passengers ashore at one time and place is limited to 100 and one qualified naturalist/lecturer guide is requested for every 15–20 passengers when ashore. The guidelines for visitors emphasise wildlife and environmental protection, the value of historic huts, the vulnerability of protected areas and research activities, and ensuring safety by staying in groups (Enzenbacher, 1995). Both sets of guidelines are voluntary and seek to influence behaviour, there is no recourse to punitive action if they are not followed as is the case with regulations and associated penalties under the law of a country (Mason & Legg, 1999).

Plate 5.3 Tourists from the Kapitan Khlebnikov at Mill Island, Scott Glacier (near Bunger Hills), Antartica. (*Photo*: Rod Ledingham, Australian Antarctic Division) © Commonwealth of Australia, 1992/3

interchangeably and most often with an emphasis on accreditation of operators (which is really certification).

The Australian National Ecotourism Accreditation Program (NEAP) is an example of an implemented accreditation (certification) scheme. There is little published evidence of successful accreditation elsewhere (Blamey, 1997). This programme was launched in 1996 by the Ecotourism Association of Australia and the Australian Tour Operators Network. In 2000 it was broadened to include nature based tourism and renamed the Nature and Ecotourism Accreditation Program. The programme distinguishes bonafide ecotourism products on the basis of eight principles including best practice environmental management, education, contribution to local communities, sensitivity to different cultures, consistency of product delivery and ethical marketing. Accreditation can be given to ecotourism accommodation, tours or attractions.

At the time of writing, 300 products have been assessed and accredited. Assessment and administration of NEAP is done voluntarily by the Association. Accreditation is beginning to result in marketing benefits to accredited operators, including special promotions and more lucrative marketing positions than non-accredited counterparts, from organisations such as the Australian Tourism Commission, Queensland Tourism and Travel Bureau, Tourism NSW and regional tourism associations (McArthur, 1998b).

In early 1999, the World Travel and Tourism Council's Green Globe Program announced an environmental certification programme, Green Globe 21. It sets international standards for travel companies and communities for good environmental performance. Companies must agree to achieve certification within a fixed time frame, probably 18 months or more (Southgate, 1999). Objectives include protecting culture, tradition, wildlife and natural resources. The programme covers hotels, airlines, tour operators, travel agents, airports, visitor attractions, cruise ships and car rental companies. Of most relevance to natural area management is certification of tour operators, visitor attractions and hotels if they are located within or adjacent to natural areas (Anon., 1999a).

Accreditation and certification can benefit both the tourism industry and the natural environment (Dowling, 1996). Accredited / certified tourism companies can gain a market advantage over other market segments. A certification system allows tourists to identify those companies operating to achieve sustainable tourism. It is also a way of exposing those who purport to be providing sustainable tourism but are not. Environmental impacts can be reduced and the efficiency of natural resource use increased by certification and the associated improvements in practice.

More recently, a certification programme for guides has been established, the Australian National Ecotour Guide Certification Program (EAA, 2000). Key components of the programme are interpretation and education, and ecologically sustainable minimal impact techniques, operations and awareness. This is a voluntary industry qualification designed to recognise and reward best practice nature and ecotour guiding. Guides are assessed on their skills, knowledge, attitudes and actions. The assessment takes place through on-the-job assessment and in simulated settings. Guides who complete the programme are rewarded with an industry certificate and are provided with a pathway to formal, nationally recognised qualifications.

Best practice

Best practice, similarly to accreditation, certification and codes of conduct, is another means of encouraging responsible, self-motivated behaviour by members of the tourism industry. Best practice in this industry involves minimising environmental impacts, particularly through careful use of resources and their disposal. Such approaches may very often reduce costs, although not always (DOT, 1995). They may add to a company's market advantage if it is apparent that best practice approaches have been adopted.

In 1995 the Australian government produced *Best Practice Tourism: A Guide to Energy and Waste Minimisation* which provided suggestions for improving energy and waste management of specific activities (DOT, 1995). Included are transport, energy use, heating and cooling buildings, heating water, recovering heat, lighting, toilets, cooking, clothes washing and drying, dishwashing, washing and bathing, refrigeration, office equipment and paper, solid materials, newspaper and cardboard, glass, plastics, metal containers, building materials, food and garden materials, and pumping water. For example, guidance on heating and cooling includes using efficient heating and cooling equipment with timer controls and thermostats. The areas to be heated or cooled should be divided into separately managed zones. Heating or cooling should be switched off when a zone is unoccupied. Open fires are generally very inefficient; a properly designed wood heater is better. Solar is the preferred energy source followed by wood (DOT, 1995).

Best practice can also apply to government agencies managing protected areas. A review conducted by Biosis Research in 1997 found there was very little material on best practice in natural resource management in national parks although there was considerable interest in it within some agencies (Meredith, 1997). The emphasis in this sector is on best practice as work methods, processes or initiatives that improve organisational effectiveness, service delivery and employee satisfaction (DOT, 1995). This is a focus on best practice in organisational activities rather than on-ground actions for minimising environmental impacts.

In the general tourism industry, such approaches are referred to as greening programmes (Todd & Williams, 1996). Industry leaders are the accommodation, transport and restaurant sectors. Hotel sustainability programmes have addressed waste reduction, energy conservation and water conservation. Zinkan and Syme (1997) noted that Canadian Pacific Hotels, with several properties in Banff National Park (Figure 5.1), helps hotel guests join guided tours and evening lectures on the park's ecology. The airline industry has been active in greening programmes through addressing noise and emissions reductions and fuel efficiency. Restaurant programmes have focused on solid waste and energy reduction as well as broader community conservation issues (Todd & Williams, 1996). Conservation groups are becoming involved with hotel chains such as Sheraton and ACCOR to improve environmental practice. For example, Sheraton is working with the Worldwide Fund for Nature to conserve local areas surrounding resorts in Africa and Asia (McArthur, 1998b).

Regulatory strategies

Several regulatory strategies are widely used by government agencies managing protected areas. Licences with associated conditions are issued to tour operators, while leases are issued to tourism businesses occupying fixed premises for longer periods. Both provide legally based guidance to tourism companies as to how they must conduct their business within protected areas.

Licences

A licence is a certificate or document giving official permission to undertake an activity. Licences are often mandatory for tourism on government lands and waters to ensure the natural environment is conserved and managed. Licences allow the governing agency to monitor access and use of the areas under its control and to ensure that conservation values are maintained. It is self-evident that by protecting these values, tour operators will be able assure themselves of continued use of these natural locations over the longer term. Licence holders agree to abide by a set of rules and regulations in regard to the natural areas in which they operate. The rules are both general, for example, protecting plants and animals, obeying road rules, prohibiting firearms, and removing rubbish, and specific, for example, in regard to camping and specialised activities such as abseiling and caving.

Licences usually but not always apply to non-exclusive activities, where the activities of one operator do not preclude or exclude the activities of another. For example, wildflower tours and birdwatching can support a number of operators. Where the resource is potentially susceptible to damage from over-use and/or a significant level of capital investment is required, some agencies such as the Department of Conservation and Land Management (CALM) in Western Australia have the capacity to issue an exclusive licence to one operator only. An example is the licence for tours and a ferry service provided in Shoalwater Islands Marine Park off the Western Australian coast (Figure 5.1). The operator has significant capital invested in boats as well as the market being too small to support more than one operator. Also, the associated marine and coastal environment is not robust enough to support more than one operator.

McArthur (1998b) commented that the problems with licensing tour operators remains one of the disappointments in visitor management in protected areas. He noted licensing as bureaucratic, meaning that the benefits of such a process for the natural environment, visitors and the operators themselves was not the primary consideration; rather licensing was being done to satisfy bureaucratic needs. Another problem he noted was lack of coordination. In Australia there is no coordinated approach nationwide to licensing, creating problems for operators who work across state boundaries. There is also no justification of differences in fees between states. A further problem is lack of incentives within current licensing systems to improve performance.

Leases

Leases are generally issued where operators require exclusive rights to land or waters. Such rights are likely when the operator intends to construct or manage a substantial facility such as a lodge, restaurant or visitor centre. Such leases usually involve major capital investment over an extended period of time.

Environmental Management Systems

Environmental management systems are 'the organisational structure, responsibilities, practices, procedures, processes, and resources for determining and implementing environmental policy' (British Standards Institute, 1994). Every individual in the organisation accepting responsibility for environmental improvements is an associated ideal (Standards Australia and Standards New Zealand, 1996). To date they have not been widely used by protected area managers or the tourism industry. Todd and Williams (1996) noted, however, that many practitioners believe that they could be used in this sector.

Environmental management systems are a recent development, coming out of concerns in the 1990s regarding implementation of environmental policy. By this stage many companies in the mining and manufacturing sectors had developed environ-

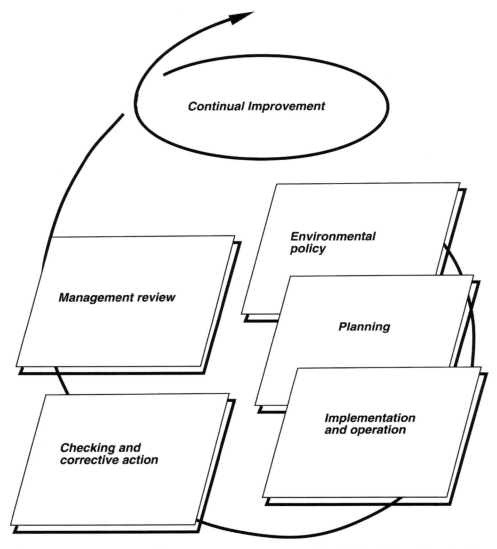

Figure 5.5 Environmental management system model. (Derived from Standards Australia, 1997)

mental policies and reviewed their practices but were unable to implement the necessary changes. Quality systems, such as BS 5750 and ISO 9000, were developed as possible solutions. Both assisted organisations to conform to specified quality standards. The philosophy behind quality systems, that of continual improvement of performance, underpins environmental management systems (Figure 5.5).

Today the most widely recognised environmental management system is the

International Standard ISO 14001, published in 1995. This standard describes five principles for a complying organisation: commitment and policy, planning, implementation, measurement and evaluation, and review and improvement (Standards Australia and Standards New Zealand, 1996). These principles are an integral part of the continuous improvement process, as illustrated in Figure 5.5. The success of such a system depends heavily on training employees so they understand the key issues and their roles and responsibilities (Netherwood, 1996). A number of earlier management systems, such as the British Standard BS 7750, the International Organisation for Standardisation ISO 9000 and ISO 9001, and the community-run eco-management and audit scheme EMAS, contributed to the formulation of ISO 14001 (Kuhre, 1995; Starkey, 1996).

If an environmental management system was developed for natural area tourism, what would it look like? Todd and Williams (1996) provided a possible application to the North America ski areas (Box 5.10). Their proposal is potentially applicable to other types of natural area tourism given that ski areas worldwide sit predominantly in natural areas and very often in national parks.

Conclusion

This chapter describes the wealth of approaches available to manage natural area tourism. Management generally begins with some form of protection, whether it is designation as a protected area such as a national park, or through an international convention such as the Ramsar Convention. Such designation, although a crucial starting point, is generally insufficient for sustainable management of a natural area as a tourist destination. Development of joint management arrangements, usually between local people and external parties such as national park agencies, and/or zoning, often follow.

This chapter then described the plethora of actions from which a manager can choose. Site management relies on designing and then managing linear features such as roads, tracks and trails and terminus points such as campgrounds and parking areas to keep environmental impacts to acceptable levels. Visitor management focuses on visitors, with management either through direct regulation or communication and education. Education is emphasised in both research and practice as an essential element in managing natural area tourism. The next chapter explores in detail the importance of education and interpretation for the sustainable management of natural area tourism.

The tourism industry, as well as the destinations themselves, can be managed to protect the environment and the experiences of visitors. Such management can be through voluntary strategies including codes of conduct and accreditation/certification, regulatory approaches, for example licences and leases, and environmental management systems. Although such systems are not evident in the industry today, their systems approach and emphasis on continuous improvement could benefit both the industry and the natural environments on which it depends.

In all instances, effective management relies on managing with some objective in

Box 5.10 A proposed environmental management system for natural area tourism: the North America ski areas

A survey by Todd and Williams (1996) of the North American ski area industry indicated environmental management systems were not currently in place, although commitments to system elements, such as a formal environmental policy, were made by about half those surveyed. The benefits of environmental management systems for this industry are becoming obvious, with the industry realising its environmental effects and operators seeing the economic benefits accruing from sound environmental practices. As such, the authors suggested an environmental management system (EMS) with six components as follows.

Policy
Policy formulation is usually the first step in an EMS. Included should be the organisation's concerns and stakeholder requirements as well as guiding principles. Evidence of the organisation's commitment to environmental management is essential. The purpose of an environmental policy for the ski industry might be to reduce a ski area's legal or financial liability for environmental damage or improve its public image.

Planning
This is the step where the environmental effects of the ski area's operation are investigated and documented. The concerns of stakeholders, including employees, shareholders, suppliers, visitors, local communities, government and special interest groups, are also identified here. Current and likely regulations are listed and objectives and targets are also set here. An environmental target could be reducing waste by 50% over three years. The final part of this step is developing an implementation plan, including the objectives, targets and associated actions, estimates of funding required, and assigning responsibilities.

Procedures and controls
These are the 'nuts and bolts' of the EMS (Todd & Williams, 1996). First, environmental responsibility throughout the organisation needs assigning. All employees, from managers to ski lift operators and those grooming the slopes, are responsible for environmental outcomes. Second, performance must be measured either by quantitative measures such as laboratory tests or through subjective evaluation. Procedures must be in place to make sure the measurements are done regularly and properly. Site inspections and sign-off sheets could be used. Third, procedures need to be in place for accidents such as fuel spills.

Training and education
Training also includes education enabling ski area staff to understand the relevant environmental issues. Education of visitors is also important. The authors also note the importance of strategic research given the fragility of alpine ecosystems and

the increasing pressures for such industries to prove their practices are environmentally sound.

Communication

Communication for the ski industry means communicating within the organisation, including formal reporting to senior managers and shareholders, as well as communicating with stakeholders. One common means of communicating with stakeholders is through environmental performance reporting.

Assessment and improvement

This assessment step, described as management review in Figure 5.5, is where feedback occurs and makes EMS a system. The assessment includes reviewing that the systems of the EMS are in place and working. It also includes environmental audits, where the focus is often regulatory compliance. For the ski industry, such an audit could be used to assure investors that the organisation was properly complying with its licences, permits and regulations. Follow-up action on any system and compliance weaknesses is essential. Lastly, an EMS must be integrated with other management systems, especially budgetary ones.

mind. A fundamental management objective for many natural areas is offering experiences that satisfy visitor needs while at the same time protecting and maintaining natural systems and processes. Acceptable conditions provide a measure of how managers are performing against this objective. They are best determined using a planning framework, such as the Limits of Acceptable Change or Visitor Impact Management, as described in the previous chapter. The success or otherwise of management is then determined by monitoring and evaluation, the subject of Chapter 7. Cole (1993) emphasised that good management relies on adequate planning, knowledge, implementation and monitoring. Where management strategies are employed without planning and monitoring, these may be inefficient and ineffective.

Further Reading

Hammitt and Cole (1998) and Hendee *et al.* (1990a) provide a wealth of material on strategies and actions for managing recreational use of wilderness – all directly relevant to managing natural area tourism. Crucial to managing natural area tourism is understanding the effectiveness of possible management strategies, as well as associated visitor preferences. Useful references, again drawn from research and practice in wilderness management, are Marion *et al.* (1993), Shindler and Shelby (1993) and Washburne and Cole (1983).

For those interested in the selection and design of protected areas the books on conservation biology by Caughley and Gunn (1996) and Primack (1998) provide useful, readable starting points. Green and Paine (1997) provide an excellent, reasonably current overview of the state of the world's protected areas. Websites established by UNESCO and the Ramsar Convention Bureau provide current and historic information on forms of protection achieved through international designations, such as world heritage.

An important aspect of managing natural area tourism not considered in this chapter is wildlife management. Very often, it is wildlife that draws visitors to natural areas and brings them back again and again. There are a number of books and articles addressing wildlife tourism and its management. One of the most useful is *Wildlife Tourism* (Shackley, 1996).

Chapter 6
Interpretation

Introduction

There is an expanding literature on interpretation following a slow but increasing recognition of its significance and in the development of accreditation systems for tour guiding. The importance of interpretation lies in communicating ideas and enriching visitor experiences. It is considered by a number of writers to be an integral part of 'best practice' ecotourism. Despite this researchers in the field report that interpretation continues to be under-utilised as an effective means of promoting sustainable tourism and enhancing the tourism experience (e.g. McArthur, 1998a; Orams, 1996).

McArthur (1998a) goes on to state that much of the interpretation practised by the tourism industry is of poor quality and he recommends two actions to remedy the situation. The first is to value the significance of interpretation and secondly the deliverers of ecotourism need to understand how 'best practice' interpretation is achieved.

The objectives of this chapter are therefore to provide some background on the theory and application of interpretation and offer some discussion and examples of what comprises 'best practice' interpretation. Wearing and Neil (1999) describe the various situations in which interpretation can be applied. These include promotional, value adding, educational, economic and ecological contexts. This chapter is principally concerned with the last of these, that is the role of interpretation in management and conservation of the tourism resource. This is in keeping with the major focus of the book and completes the suite of planning and management strategies that are available for sustainable tourism.

Principles and Application

Interpretation can be defined in a number of ways but is generally described as being an educational activity that brings out meaning and enriches visitor experience (Figure 6.1). In a wildflower guided walk, for example, it is not simply informing people about plants by systematically providing a list of names. It is a 'hands on' involvement where visitors learn and self-discover the answers to questions like:

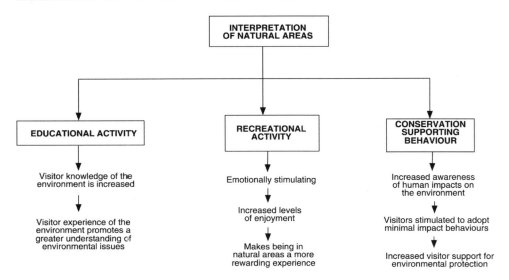

Figure 6.1 The education–knowledge–awareness relationship embodied within interpretation

- How do plants survive?
- Why does it look like this?
- How does it relate to the animal life around it?

Tilden's (1957) definition (Box 6.1) has been widely used but in recent years various other definitions have emerged reflecting the particular objectives of the organisations involved (McArthur, 1998a). These definitions, however, always embrace the fundamental principles presented by Tilden's original work. Tilden (1957) emphasised that interpretation is an art and techniques need to be designed to accommodate visitor needs, attitudes and expectations. For example, there needs to be varying approaches for adults and children. Moreover, visitors need to relate to what is being conveyed with interpretation being much more effective when it is directly relevant to the individual.

Principles

Following on from the concepts outlined by Tilden (1957) several basic principles have emerged as the mainstay of interpretation. They are variously outlined by McArthur (1998a), Wearing and Neil (1999) and Weiler and Ham (2000). The fundamental principles of interpretation can be summarised as follows:

1. Interpretation should centre on a theme and associated messages

Writers on interpretation frequently state that it is important to develop a theme that contains concepts and messages. Crabtree (2000) justifies the use of theme in that it allows interpretive ideas and information to be organised and easy to follow. Ham (1992) states that themes embrace entire ideas and all encompassing messages

---

Box 6.1 Definitions of interpretation

1. Tilden (1957)
'An educational activity which aims to reveal meaning and relationships through the use of original objects, by first hand experience, and by illustrative media, rather than simply to communicate factual information.'

Meaning is achieved through stimulation and revelation. Whereas education *per se* is generally a more formal provision of facts, interpretation is more concerned with concepts and messages.

2. McArthur (1998a)
'Interpretation is a coordinated, creative and inspiring form of learning. It provides a means of discovering the many complexities of the world and our role within it. It leaves people moved, their assumptions challenged and their interest in learning stimulated.'

It has been shown that visitors actually like to hear minimal impact messages and learn of the various strategies to protect various natural areas (McArthur & Hall, 1996).

3. Moscardo (2000)
'Interpretation is any activity which seeks to explain to people the significance of an object, a culture or a place. Its three core functions are to enhance visitor experiences, to improve visitor knowledge or understanding, and to assist in the protection or conservation of places or cultures.'

---

that a visitor can reflect on after the interpretive experience. McArthur (1998a) uses the idea of natural disturbance in Australian forests to show how theme, concept and message relate to one another. The theme being that forests are subject to natural disturbance by fire. The concept of naturally changing forests, that contain fire-adapted plants, can then be subsequently developed from this theme. The final interpretive message being that the structure and composition of such forests is shaped by fire. Various techniques can then be applied in delivering this message (see 'Techniques and Examples', p. 250).

2. Interpretation entails active involvement and the engagement of first-hand experiences

Getting actively involved and 'doing', rather than just passively listening to straightforward instruction, makes the interpretive activity easier to appreciate and a more enjoyable experience. In continuing the theme of naturally changing forests participants could be asked to look for evidence of disturbance. Such active involvement is more likely to engage the audience in a sense of discovery in the field situation.

3. Interpretation facilitates maximum use of the senses

Encouraging use of the senses is an approach that is likely to bring the interpretive experience 'alive' and make it more enjoyable and satisfying. By analogy simply looking at food is not as satisfying as smelling it, feeling its texture in the mouth and then tasting it! Similarly, the smells (oils and resins in leaves) texture (bark and spiny vegetation) and even the taste (various fruits) of a forest will deepen visitor experience by forging a greater connection with the forest.

4. Interpretation seeks to foster self-discovered insights

Such insight comes from active involvement and maximum use of the senses. A guided walk or elephant trek in a rainforest clearly leaves more scope for insight than a vehicle excursion. This is because of the opportunity to use all of ones senses in discovering the forest. Walking in the humid environment also brings the visitor closer to the specific environmental conditions that characterise rainforests. Good trail design maximises the opportunities to see specific features in a self-discovered fashion. Wild animals are difficult to see in the rainforest environment and good interpretation will build on this and develop a thrill of anticipation. Active participation in searching for wildlife and learning about forest ecology then provides the scope for self-discovered insight.

5. Interpretation is of relevance to the visitor and clients find the imparted knowledge and insights useful

Crabtree (2000) recommends asking the audience about their interests and motivations and suggests that this can be achieved by talking to a group for a few minutes before the activity commences. Making the whole visitor experience relevant to the chosen site or particular activity through self-discovered insight is also important. In this way people can appreciate the importance of a particular theme and link the interpretive experience to the situation and site in which it takes place. Most people are seeking accurate information in relation to the interpretive experiences they are having and this is best achieved through personal face-to-face interpretation.

Crabtree (2000) also maintains that the experience can be made unique by layering what is delivered to accommodate both adults and children with different backgrounds. In this way everyone can become involved with technical information supplied to some people while children are involved in some other activity. Such layering is the approach taken in the design and operation of many visitor centres. Features listed by Crabtree (2000) can be seen in the Scottish Seabird Centre (see Box 6.2). The centre contains material for children (simple bird identification, colouring and drawing), opportunities for people to use the centre at their own pace, static displays, interpretive displays, photographs, a touch table and even the provision of research methodologies and data. All of this provides for variety and the different levels of visitor interest.

Visitors generally like to learn about a particular area or wildlife situation and develop some understanding of what it means to them. Realising why they have to keep to footpaths and understanding why animals should not be fed makes

Box 6.2 Scottish Seabird Centre

The Scottish Seabird Centre is a 'state of the art' interpretation centre situated close to the Bass Rock Gannet (*Sula bassana*) colony at North Berwick, Scotland (Figure 6.2). The centre contains educational and interpretive features (e.g. photographs, diagrams, specimens and interactive displays) that are common to visitor and education centres around the world (Plate 6.1). The materials are arranged in a series of themes that are designed to capture the attention of all age groups and account for different levels of interest. Displays titled 'What is a seabird?'; 'The shore'; 'Survival'; 'Built for the job' and 'High rise living' provide information and inter - pretation on the biology and ecology of seabirds.

Plate 6.1 Static and interactive displays at the Scottish Seabird Centre, North Berwick, Scotland. (*Photo*: David Newsome)

There is also a multimedia show that focuses on the gannets themselves and a viewing deck with telescopes that can be trained on to Bass Rock and the island of Fidra where Puffins (*Fratercula arctica*) are visible particularly during April and May. Furthermore, the most up-to-date interactive technology has been used in order to provide visitors with a unique view of birds on otherwise restricted access seabird breeding islands. From inside the centre the 'seabirds live' exhibit video screens provide people with the opportunity to see birds going about their normal and breeding activities on the two islands. This is achieved by the use of remote cameras positioned on the islands with zoom, pan and rotate facilities that allow visitors in the centre to scan the islands for birds and focus in on nests and chicks during the breeding season. Trained volunteers who are present to assist and answer questions support all of this. A theatre is also present in which films about seabirds are screened. In addition to this there is a website as well as the traditional boat trip that circumnavigates Bass Rock.

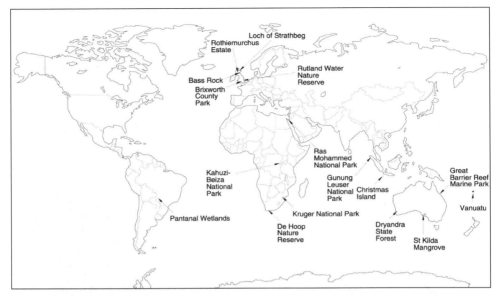

Figure 6.2 Map of important nature-based tourism destinations referred to in this chapter

management relevant to them. Keeping to footpaths and using a sensitive approach to wildlife engages the audience and allows them to appreciate its relevance. The public is also interested in learning about why natural areas are important and what efforts are being made to preserve what remains. The major goal of interpretation is to make people aware of the natural world, enhance their sense of wonder and capacity to enjoy nature and stimulate an interest in environmental protection.

Stages of the interpretive experience

From a psychological standpoint it is recognised that visitor experience can exist in several cognitive states during a particular interpretive experience. Cognition relates to the processes of perception and reasoning in acquiring knowledge. Particular cognitive states, as they apply to a nature-based tourism experience, have been explained in the Forestall and Kaufman model as pre-contact, contact and post-contact phases (Orams, 1995).

The first cognitive state or pre-contact phase is where the visitor lacks knowledge of a particular tourism experience and in doing so a number of questions can be generated. Fennell (1999) provides the example of whale watching where participants need to learn about and then carefully observe whales on a whale-watching trip. The dearth of information at the commencement of the interpretive process can be satisfied long before a participant gets on a boat or travels to a designated viewing spot. It is usually achieved through pamphlets and information boards that also frequently include wider information about marine ecosystems. It can also be obtained from natural history books, conversations with friends and from web sites.

Most visitors will then have been stimulated through this initial phase to seek further information. People are left with a desire for more knowledge. This then provides the appropriate conditions for the second or contact phase which is the real essence of interpretation. It is here that the fundamental principles of interpretation, as already described, can be applied in answering questions. The particular approach is clearly dependent on the situation. In the case of whale watching participants may want to know how to identify individual whales, require information on whale behaviour and have their own knowledge-base verified (Fennell, 1999). Encouraging a questioning approach, allowing visitors to talk more and posing return questions creates the conditions for interaction with guides and results in greater visitor satisfaction.

The post-contact phase is where the imbalance between the initial pre-contact phase and the new state of awareness is realised and can be followed through and built on. A successful interpretive experience will have engaged people's emotions. Moreover, a successful emotional involvement can be powerful in leaving the visitor with a long-lasting experience and a desire to take a deeper interest. The motivation to return and re-live the experience is fostered. It is also here that the opportunity for participants to contribute and become involved in conservation related activities could be discussed.

Orams (1995) nevertheless points out that there will be many situations where interpretation cannot take place within the framework of pre- and post-contact activity. This can be especially so in the case of pre-contact information. Despite this potential deficiency interpretive staff need to be aware of, and sensitive to, the different stages of the interpretive experience so that interpretation can be tailored accordingly (Fennell, 1999).

Application

The immense scope of interpretation is indicated by the set of objectives developed by the US National Park Service. These objectives include providing information and orientation of visitors; educating visitors in relation to park resources and the national park system; bringing about understanding and appreciation of the natural world; fostering environmental protection and opening up dialogue between the public and park management (Sharp, 1999). Moreover, there are a number of situations where interpretation is particularly critical in ensuring sustainable tourism and fostering visitor satisfaction. These include the case of fragile environments such as caves and the situation with sensitive species such as in Whale Shark and gorilla tourism and situations where the public feeds animals. In cases such as these ignorance and lack of awareness can be a major problem and can lead to accidental and unwitting negative impact.

Various approaches have been prescribed in planning for interpretation (e.g. Bradley, 1982; McArthur & Hall, 1996). McArthur (1998a) identifies three important components in planning for interpretation. These are target audience definition, pre-planned content and structure and the selection of a technique that suits the audience. He stresses that it is important to define the target audience because of the values and interests that people of contrasting ages, origins and various levels of education have. For example, the requirements of a local school group will be quite different from that of a group of adults from an overseas country.

This initial stage would be followed by a consideration of interpretive structure and content based on target audience characteristics and followed by utilisation of the theme and message approach. The development of a theme focuses attention onto a particular aspect of the area being visited. This allows an interpretive activity to be completed in a particular time slot, provides scope for including aspects of management and the interests of the interpreter.

The final step in planning for interpretation is the selection of an appropriate technique to deliver the interpretive experience. McArthur (1998a) maintains that many interpreters make the mistake of selecting techniques before understanding the target audience or developing themes. Techniques can be personal, as in guided walks, or non-personal where the reliance is on a visitor centre or signage. The effectiveness of any particular technique will depend on group size, the age and interests of participants and their level of education. Different techniques can be utilised to cater for these different visitor characteristics.

A general approach that contains five main elements in the application of interpretation is discussed by Orams (1995). This consists of establishing objectives, developing a specific theme, selecting appropriate techniques, engaging aspects of the psychological theory behind interpretation and then evaluating its effectiveness at the end. Establishing objectives consists of determining whether the focus is to be a combination of visitor orientation, enhancing awareness and increased understanding of management issues or a specific topic such as a birdwatching guided walk. As discussed by McArthur (1998a) themes and messages need to be developed.

A range of techniques are available and the most important of these are discussed later under 'Techniques and Examples', p. 250. Orams (1995) also highlights the importance of utilising the psychological theory behind the Forestall and Kaufman Model in providing answers to visitor questions and providing opportunities for motivated individuals to become involved in a particular environmental issue. Finally, interpretation plans and activities need to be evaluated. The costs and effectiveness of interpretation need to be monitored for evidence of success or failure so that modifications can be made.

The Role of Interpretation

Guided tours in order to reduce impacts and educate visitors about wildlife have been in progress for some time. There would be many examples of these from around the world that commonly include guided walks around bird reserves, national park trail walks and supervised visits to areas of concentrated wildlife and wildlife breeding areas. Despite this there is much scope for the application of interpretation and in particular 'best practice' approaches.

The need for such an approach is illustrated by two examples of uncontrolled and poorly planned ecotourism and where interpretation is pivotal in providing for a more enriching experience. A third example illustrates the case of where interpretation is vital in reducing negative impact. The first is a case study of ecotourism in the Brazilian Pantanal (Figure 6.2) by Trent (1991) who reported on the behaviour and attitudes of guides and tourists towards wildlife. The second is the case of Orang utan (*Pongo pygmnaeus*) tourism at Gunung Leuser National Park in Indonesia which further indicate the problems associated with a poorly thought out tourism operation and the urgent need for appropriate interpretive programmes. The third example explores the role of interpretation in reducing the transmission of human diseases to gorillas in Africa.

The Pantanal: a tour operator's perspective

The Pantanal is a large wetland and a major habitat for migratory birds, endemic species and species threatened with extinction. Spectacular and enigmatic species include the Hyacinth Macaw (*Anodorhynchus hyacinthinus*), Giant Anteater (*Myrmecophaga tridactyla*), Jaguar (*Panthera onca palustris*), Maned Wolf (*Chrysocon brachyurus*) and Yellow Anaconda (*Eunectes notaeus*). Trent (1991) considered the effects of uncontrolled visitation, ignorance and a lack of sensitivity towards wildlife. Littering was a widespread problem and its effects on wildlife was reflected in observations of birds that had swallowed plastic netting and cigarette butts.

The lack of interpretation and ignorance about Pantanal ecology and potential impacts of tourism was lamented. A tour operator himself, Trent observed visitors attempting to drive over snakes, approaching colonies of breeding birds too closely and deliberately putting birds to flight. In addition to these problems he noted the illegal collection of wildlife for the pet trade and hunting carried out by so-called tourists. Besides the obvious impacts on wildlife many visitors at the time would have found such behaviour offensive as well as reducing the effectiveness of their tourism experience.

This may seem a particularly bad example and it is hoped that the situation has now improved. Documenting the case study here serves to illustrate the results of uncontrolled and poorly planned tourism. Obviously wider management problems are evident but Trent (1991) clearly highlighted the problems associated with ignorance. He maintained that many of the problems stemmed from a lack of education about the Pantanal as an ecosystem and the natural history of its wildlife.

The tours conducted by Trent aimed to provide such information. Furthermore, the company developed policies on waste disposal, recorded the presence of species, conducted population counts, reported on illegal activities and fostered environmental education. Clients were educated on the value of tropical habitats, wildlife and rainforests. A percentage of company profit was also donated to conservation projects. The example provided by Trent (1991) clearly demonstrates

the contribution that private tour operators can make in enhancing visitor experience and in fostering sustainable tourism.

Orang utan rehabilitation centres as tourist attractions

The Indonesian Gunung Leuser National Park (Figure 6.2) has already been
considered in the context of tourism impacts on wildlife. Cochrane (1996), in a
discussion on the sustainability of tourism in Indonesia, spelt out some of the problems associated with poorly planned and organised ecotourism development at
Gunung Leuser. A major problem was the attitude of poorly paid and educated
park wardens at the Orang utan rehabilitation station at Bohorok. Here park
wardens ignored regulations and allowed visitors to feed and hold Orang utans.
Cochrane (1996) maintained that there was sufficient evidence that animals
constantly subjected to close contact with humans become or remain habituated,
thereby hindering successful rehabilitation. Such activities also increase the risk of
disease transmission from humans to the animals as discussed in the case of gorilla
tourism in the following section.

There was also the issue of wardens and guides at Gunung Leuser being igno-
rant of wider conservation issues such as environmental quality and the need for
'natural experiences'. One line of evidence for this is the extent of littering that
degrades natural qualities. When the rehabilitation centre was first opened some
30 years ago a forest trek had to be undertaken in order to reach the centre.
Cochrane (1996) notes that since then the pathway to the centre has been sealed
and is now accessible to coaches. Furthermore, there have been no building
controls with tourist accommodation increasing from three to 14 guesthouses
within only a four-year period.

Cochrane (1996) cautions that all of the work on Orang utan rehabilitation indicates that it should not be carried out as part of a tourist attraction. She goes on to
emphasise that the tourism succession and resultant crowding that develops from
such approaches is not sustainable because tourists are increasingly looking for
more natural and less crowded ecotourism experiences.

Instead of overcrowded, unsatisfying knowledge-deficient situations such wildlife tourism needs informed guided forest walking. It is here that the self-discovered
insights explained earlier can be applied. Negative views (leech infested!) about the
rainforest habitat of Orang utans need to be managed so that walking is the
preferred means of access. There needs to be a sense of anticipation that compen-
sates for the elusive nature of many rainforest species. Listening for calls, checking
spoor and searching for footprints will add a sense of adventure and excitement.
This is the real contribution that interpretation can make in eliciting visitor interest.
Wildlife tourism that is conducted with trained guides and in a variety of situations,
such as tree top walkways, trails with views, visits to hides and salt licks and trails
that contain variable distance walks lead to greater visitor satisfaction and therefore
sustainable ecotourism activities.

The case of reducing impacts on rare and endangered species

Ecotourism features as a motivating factor in justifying the conservation of habitats that are under pressure from expanding and economically poor human populations in Africa. For example, primates are another group of mammals that are in high demand by the ecotourism industry. In recent decades the viewing of wild chimpanzees and gorillas has been developed in a number of central and east African countries.

The endangered Mountain Gorilla (*Gorilla gorilla berengei*) continues to remain under threat from habitat loss and poaching and illustrates the role of, and problems associated with, tourism in attempting to conserve this species. Continued clearing for agriculture and grazing is gradually forcing the animals into higher and less favourable habitat (Barnes, 1994). Tourism, which is promoted as an argument for conserving the gorillas, has been successfully developed in Rwanda, Uganda and in the Democratic Republic of Congo. In these countries various gorilla groups have been deliberately habituated so that tourists can gain close access. Previously there was a high demand to see gorillas but in recent years the number of visitors has declined in response to human disease epidemics, terrorist activity and military conflict. Nevertheless, five gorilla tourism programmes have been developed and visitation is now increasing due to the greater protection of tourists from undesirable political events (Butynski & Kalina, 1998).

Some of the early gorilla tourism in Kahuzi-Beiga National Park in the Democratic Republic of Congo (Figure 6.2) started with no controls over tourist group size and behaviour. It was reported that some groups numbered up to 40 people and that guides provoked displays in order to impress and entertain tourists (Butynski & Kalina, 1998).

Because park staff and guides are poorly paid they can be easily pressured to ignore rules and allow visitors to closely approach the animals. There is also evidence that, once again, larger groups of tourists are being taken to view the animals. This, coupled with extended and twice daily visits, disrupts social activity and increases the risk of physical contact between tourists and gorillas.

The importance of informing visitors and reducing contact with the gorillas is emphasised by Butynski and Kalina (1998), because of the animals' susceptibility to human disease. In 1988 six gorillas died as a result of respiratory disease. In addition to this 27 individuals were successfully treated with antibiotics. Moreover, these infections took place in three out of four habituated tourist groups. Because of the threat and susceptibility of gorillas to measles a vaccination programme was implemented and 65 gorillas were vaccinated. Vaccination and treatment with antibiotics are however only responses to the disease risk problem and not always successful. This was evident during the 1990 bronchopneumonia outbreak in a group of 35 gorillas visited by tourists. The disease affected 26 animals, four of which were given antibiotics but still two gorillas died.

The impact of disease is a significant issue where isolated populations of a rare animal occur. Human-sourced infection from tourists is potentially a serious problem and can lead to local extinction where animals exist under stressed conditions due to habitat fragmentation and frequent contact with humans. Butynski and Kalina (1998) maintain that this is the biggest threat to tourist-habituated gorilla populations. Sustainable gorilla tourism in the future, besides depending on socio-political stability, will require research and monitoring. Such work would need to answer questions relating to the effectiveness of current management strategies. Sustainable tourism will also depend on adequately paid and trained interpretive guiding. Moreover, interpretation needs to start at the pre-contact phase so that tourists are fully aware of the disease risk posed by humans before they visit the park.

Techniques and Examples

Various approaches and techniques can be applied in delivering interpretation. The major techniques include visitor centres and displays; publications; lecture programmes on cruise ships; self-guided trails and guided tours. Interpretation can also be delivered to individuals, small groups (4–8 people) and much larger groups (10–20 people). It can last for only several minutes or be part of a much longer tourism experience that lasts for up to two weeks. The most widely used and important techniques (Table 6.1) are now considered in turn.

Publications and websites

Publications and websites provide the important role of orientating visitors to a natural area. They also frequently contain visitor impact minimisation and wider environmental conservation messages. Many contain site maps on which footpaths are marked which is the first stage in advising visitors where they can go to discover the area for themselves.

In most cases published material takes the form of brochures, pamphlets and information sheets which provide information on access, major site characteristics and wildlife. A typical example would be the pamphlet produced by the Royal Society for the Protection of Birds (RSPB) reserve at Loch of Strathbeg Nature Reserve in Scotland (Figure 6.2). It describes the importance of the reserve, facilities that are available, the location of observation hides, its wildlife, elements of management, the seasonal occurrence of birds and contains environmental conservation messages.

While many pamphlets are essentially just two pages of information, others take more of a booklet form. The Rothiemurchus Estate (Figure 6.2) Visitor Guide, for example, contains 20 pages of information about the area. Besides the usual visitor orientation and map, all of the recreational options for the area are described for the visitor. These include guided walks, off-road vehicle tours, fishing activities, birdwatching, cycling and mountain bike riding. The specific management objectives and activities of the estate are explained in addition to information on educational activities for schools. The location and nature of tourism facilities such as the Rothiemurchus Visitor Centre, camping and accommodation sites are also included.

Table 6.1 Summary of major interpretation techniques

Technique	Application	Strengths/ Advantages	Weaknesses/ Disadvantages
Publications and websites	Supply of pre-contact information. Visitor orientation and trip planning. Support for visitor centres and self-guided trails. Information on landscape, fauna and flora.	Cost effective and portable information. Many possible distribution/access points with wide dissemination.	There is no active visitor involvement. Does not necessarily cater for different visitor needs. Can be expensive if subject to frequent updates and alterations.
Visitor centres	Information on landscape, fauna, flora and management. Opportunity for face-to-face contacts with staff. Located at the entrance gates to national parks and within popular nature-based recreation areas.	Recognisable sites where visitors can obtain information. Scope for the application of a wide range of techniques (e.g. audiovisual, verbal interpretation, interactive displays and original objects).	Can be expensive to set up. May not be designed to cater for different audiences (e.g. focus may be entirely on school groups).
Self-guided trails	Focus of attention for visitors in various natural settings. Opportunities to provide messages through signage.	Always available and visitors can explore trails at their own pace.	Signs and displays subject to vandalism. Signage may contain too much information. Generally not suitable for children.
Guided touring	Wide application in all environments. Especially important in forests, wildflower tourism and during wildlife observation. Time frames can be from only 1 hour up to 2 weeks duration.	Very powerful and highly effective if applied properly. Interpreter can respond to client needs and deal with various levels of complexity. Information can be constantly updated. Interpreter can facilitate active involvement.	Requires the availability of well-trained and effective interpreters. Requirement of audience attention and commitment to be entirely successful.

Published material can also take the form of booklets and more substantial guides and books as can be seen in visitor centres in many North American national parks and wildlife refuges. Well established tourism destinations elsewhere, such as the Kruger National Park in South Africa (Figure 6.2), have maps and 'where to find' guides that contain ecological information. The 'where to find' guides are designed to assist with self-discovery about the park and its wildlife. They are important resources that visitors can use in the largely self-drive wildlife-viewing situation that the Kruger National Park provides for. Specific field guides to wildlife that occur in the park through to larger, more expensive, books that contain numerous colour photographs also support the 'where to find' guides.

Websites are becoming increasingly important as providers of information and as a means of orientating potential visitors to various national park systems around the world. Information provided includes facilities available, activities undertaken and information on key attractions. Many of them provide maps that can be downloaded and contain suggested trip plan itineraries.

Visitor centres

Visitor centres (Box 6.3) provide a focal point for the tourist to obtain information, find out about walks and commence a sense of discovery about a particular area. They contain site maps, static and interactive displays, brochures and sometimes live exhibits. The visitor centre at Brixworth Country Park in England (Figure 6.2) for example has a live tank pond life exhibit which provides an example of the sorts of organisms that can be found in the ponds that occur within the park. This display is supplemented by the opportunity to borrow a magnifying glass, tray and net. Visitors can then go to a nearby artificially created pond and sweep for aquatic organisms. Identification charts and books are also available and in this way visitors are able to engage in, identify, and find out about pond life for themselves. An excellent example of a 'state of the art' visitor centre is the Scottish Seabird Centre in Scotland which is described in Box 6.2.

Self-guided trails

A self-guided trail usually involves following a designated route in which various items of interest are indicated by signage at numerous points along the trail (Plate 6.2). Such trails are often supported by pamphlets that explain, in further detail, features such as specific plants, geological characteristics and plant–animal interactions. Besides walking, such tours can also be completed on horseback or in a vehicle. Self-guided trails have been developed in various settings such as in underwater coral reef trails, riverbank walks and in many forest environments around the world.

The St Kilda Mangrove trail near Adelaide, Australia (Figure 6.2) is a 1.7 kilometre boardwalk which has been constructed within a mangrove system with the aim of developing a wider understanding of mangroves. Although guided walking does take place there is a self-guiding visitor map for those who wish to

---

Box 6.3 Bird watching at Rutland Water Nature Reserve, England

Rutland Water (Figure 6.2) has become one of the most important birdwatching sites in the British Isles. Originally developed as a water supply reservoir the site now supports significant populations of birds and was designated a RAMSAR site in 1991. The conservation area consists of two reserves comprising woodlands, ponds and extensive lagoons juxtaposed with open grassy areas and adjacent agricultural land. The two reserves are actively managed to create a range of habitats in order to maximise the number and diversity of winter visiting and breeding birds. So far, up to 248 bird species have been recorded. During winter the area supports up to 20,000 waterfowl and comprises an important over-wintering site for various species of ducks, geese and swans.

Facilities include two visitor centres, 19 birdwatching hides, walkways and nature trails. The main visitor centre at Egleton Reserve sells field guides and educational material and contains an indoor observation gallery from which woodland and water birds can be observed. There is an environmental interpretation section containing displays about birds and information on how and why the reserve is managed as it is. There is also an interpretation centre on the south side of Rutland Water at Lyndon. The reserve has its own website containing information on bird sightings, meetings and educational programmes. An interactive migration trail, which highlights the difficulties faced by migrating birds, is also planned for the Lyndon Reserve. Facilities such as these play a significant role in public education, environmental interpretation and reducing impacts on wildlife.

---

undertake a walk without a guide. The map contains information on flora and fauna and arrows highlight various aspects of the mangrove ecosystem along the boardwalk.

The Christmas Island (Figure 6.2) nature trail is 1 kilometre long and serves to interpret the Christmas Island rainforest. There is a supporting booklet that describes 22 stops and visitors are urged to walk slowly and look carefully at and into the forest. Illustrated descriptions are used to assist in observation and help describe aspects of forest ecology, the nature of individual plants and wildlife. In this way the visitor can, for example, search the forest for buttress roots and locate them and then read the necessary text by referring to the appropriate illustration.

An audio drive trail has been developed in the Dryandra Woodland in Western Australia (Figure 6.2). Dryandra is one of the best sites in Western Australia to view rare mammals and this, in combination with extensive woodland, flora and landscape values, results in a visitation rate of 30,000 people a year. The trail, described by Moncrieff and Lent (1996), consists of six radio transmitters which have been placed along the 25 kilometre road trail. Commentary points are indicated with a drive trail logo and a brochure provides additional information. A radio broadcast band is indicated in order to access the commentary about conservation and various aspects of forest management at Dryandra. The commentaries have been recorded

Plate 6.2 Information sign, Sherwood Forest, England (*Photo*: Trevor Hall)

onto microchips and concealed transmitters are powered by 60-watt solar panels. However, batteries provide backup should there be a period of cloudiness and reduced sunshine. Such approaches provide an additional dimension to the concept of self-guided trails. Moncrieff and Lent (1996) speculate on various possibilities associated with audio trails such as visitors actually having to complete an activity, like crawling through a cave, in order to activate the transmitter.

Guided touring

A guided tour requires the services of a guide and, although usually undertaken on foot, can also involve the use of pack animals, boats, off-road vehicles and even coaches. They take place in all kinds of settings and involve a range of activities such as birdwatching, wild flower appreciation, whale watching, tracking mammals, spotlighting and snorkelling. Wearing and Neil (1999) assert that guided touring is 'one of the most powerful and worthwhile interpretation techniques'. This is achieved according to the principles of interpretation described earlier in this chapter.

An excellent example of guided touring (Box 6.4) is provided by tour guides at the Buchu Bushcamp which is situated close to the De Hoop Nature Reserve on the southern coastline of South Africa (Figure 6.2). De Hoop offers opportunities to observe rare mammals, undertake bird and whale watching as well as being an

Box 6.4 Buchu Bushcamp: interpreting the South African fynbos vegetation

Fynbos means fine leaved bush and is characterised by plants belonging to the plant families Proteaceae, Ericaceae and Restionaceae. These particular plant associations are very diverse and unique to South Africa. The reduced leaf size has evolved to reduce water loss under dry windy conditions. Fynbos is also adapted to cope with periodic fire which helps to maintain species richness. These aspects of fire adaptation and diversity provide ideal themes for interpretive guiding.

The approach taken by Buchu Bushcamp Tours is considered within the framework discussed earlier in this chapter by Wearing and Neil (1999), namely that of active involvement, use of the senses, self-discovered insights and usefulness of knowledge.

Active involvement consists of walking through the vegetation, feeling its texture, noticing colours, smelling flowers and leaves and interacting with the tour guide. Use of all senses is encouraged. Visitors are asked to look for detail in the vegetation. The leaves of different members of the Rutaceae are crushed so different odours can be appreciated. The reason why the vegetation smells the way it does is discussed. The question of plant chemical defence is raised and participants are given the opportunity to taste various crushed leaves. Other leaves and plant structures are then handled for their textural characteristics. Aspects of herbivory and the grazing preferences of various animals follow on from this. The interpretation naturally moves on to plant animal interactions and visitors are asked to listen for birdcalls. The different birdcalls are discussed and any observations noted.

An exploration of fynbos diversity provides for self-discovered insights. Participants are asked to take a straight-line drop point from where they are standing down to soil level. They are asked to look at the detail and consider what is in the fynbos. People are asked to compare their observations. How many different plants did they see? The guide then discusses the different drop points and the number of plants that they did not see is revealed to them. Questions as to why the fynbos is so diverse and has so many endemic plants are raised.

All of these approaches provide for first-hand experiences of the fynbos. Examining pollination mechanisms and considering why plants have been given their scientific names supports this further. The handling of *Heteropogon contortus* provides a striking example of the latter because the contorted nature of the grass can be readily appreciated in the hand. The importance of conserving fynbos and the role that diverse ecosystems have to play in our lives provides for the 'usefulness of knowledge' component discussed by Wearing and Neil (1999). Visitors are shown what constant trampling can do to fynbos vegetation and the importance of minimising impact is emphasised. Allardice (2000) further maintains that the public education benefits derived from walking through a designated area, crushing leaves and picking flowers, so that their structure can be fully appreciated, far outweighs the pruning damage to the vegetation along the trail.

important flora reserve. These activities can be achieved on foot, by self-drive touring or through mountain biking.

Buchu Bushcamp Tours cater for small groups of 1–5 and up to 60 people at a time. Large coach tour groups will have been given previsit information as to what books and equipment (hand lens, binoculars) to bring. On arrival they are split into smaller groups and leaders are assigned to each group. On a coastal tour visitors are asked to state what they can see, questions are posed as to why an animal 'is here and not there?' The sensitivity of coastal environments is discussed and explanations given as to why it is important to remain on footpaths. People are asked to feel and smell various plants and animals. There is an overall philosophy of active involvement and visitors are encouraged to contribute what they think about what has been covered in the tour.

A Case Study in the Use, Application and Effectiveness of Interpretation

The purpose of this section is to highlight the importance of interpretation in visitor impact management. This again is a feature that corresponds with the ecological focus of this book. Interpretation is a vital component in managing tourism in sensitive environments such as caves, at many geological sites and in wildlife tourism situations. This case study covers the contribution that interpretation can make in the protection of coral reef ecosystems from increasing tourism pressure.

Howard (1999) has recently highlighted the need for interpretation. Vanuatu (Figure 6.2) is a popular snorkelling and scuba diving destination with some 50,000 tourists visiting in 1997. Howard (1999) reports on a survey where divers were asked whether their activities had any impact on the coral reef. It was found that 90% of respondents listed that there was no impact on the coral reef. Howard (1999) nevertheless found that when divers were observed in the water they frequently made contact with the coral while trying to counter buoyancy problems. It was also observed that the number of contacts depended on the approach taken by the instructor leading the dive.

As it is clear that appropriate diver behaviour can reduce impacts on coral reefs, then interpretation can play a role in visitor impact management. The study found that although divers were originally attracted to diving for social reasons and a sense of adventure, the major stimulus in recent years was to appreciate the reef as a natural area. Howard (1999) also noted that divers tended to make contact when moving through narrow spaces or while examining a particular coral feature. The study concluded that dive operators could do much more in interpreting the natural history of the coral reef, raise a greater awareness of potential impact and educate divers in minimising their impacts on the coral. Moreover the influence of group leaders in these situations is clear evidence of the effectiveness of interpretation that can delivered by a tour leader.

A logical question that emerges from the work and recommendations of Howard

(1999) is 'Do expanded and appropriate interpretive programmes work?' An indication of this is provided by work carried out by Medio *et al.* (1997) in the Ras Mohammed National Park system along the Egyptian Red Sea coastline (Figure 6.2). These authors report that reservation as a national park alone is not sufficient to protect the coral reef from damage. A visitation rate of around 500,000 tourists a year, that includes some 20,000 dives, now constitutes a major pressure on the reef.

Medio *et al.* (1997) set out to show how briefings about coral sensitivity and awareness about diver impacts on the reef actually reduced damage. Diver behaviour and activity was observed and the number of contacts divers made with coral was recorded over an eight-week period. During this period environmental briefings were delivered to divers with the aim of testing whether they had any effect on diver behaviour. The briefings consisted of the same points raised by Howard (1999) – that of coral biology and impacts as well as ideas about the role of protected areas in conserving coral.

Recordings of diver behaviour after the briefings showed that the rate of contact with coral substrate decreased from 1.4 to 0.4 per diver for every 7-minute observation period. While there was increased and allowable contact with non-living coral, contact with living coral declined from 0.9 to 0.15 instances per diver per 7-minute period. Medio *et al.* (1997) calculated that there is a large potential impact from the many dives that take place. Moreover such potential impact can be significantly reduced by the use of environmental briefings and interpretation delivered by instructors and guides.

Earlier work by Hockings (1994) suggested that tour operators are in the best situation to deliver the full range of interpretation about marine ecosystems and tourism. Given that the Great Barrier Reef Marine Park Authority in Australia views education as a major process in managing tourism in the park, the development of a well-established and widespread interpretive programme is essential. Hockings (1994), however, found at the time the level of interpretive activity conducted by tour operators in the Great Barrier Reef Marine Park (Figure 6.2) to be unsatisfactory. In particular it was found that although large operators offered a wide range of interpretive experiences, the interpretation offered by small operators was considerably lower.

In recent years Weiler and Ham (2000) have advocated the importance of staff training in interpretation so that visitor satisfaction is improved and impacts are reduced. This has been actively embraced by the Ecotourism Association of Australia as part of training programmes and in the development of accreditation systems for tour operators. McCawley and Teaff (1995) have also emphasised the importance of interpretation in informing visitors about marine biology, reducing potential impacts on coral reefs and in gaining compliance with other management techniques that may be in place in marine environments. It would seem that the development of, and wide acceptance of, accredited tour guiding programmes will go a long way in supporting other forms of management and reducing impacts on coral reef and other ecosystems.

Conclusion

The value of interpretation in enhancing visitor experience and reducing impacts is being increasingly realised. Although some writers express caution as to the effectiveness of interpretation in managing natural area tourism the available evidence (e.g. Medio *et al.*, 1997) indicates that it is effective in reducing impacts.

Wearing and Neil (1999) highlight three important considerations as to where interpretation fits into the main scheme of natural area tourism:

(1) That it should be part of natural area management plans.
(2) Natural resource management is dependent on the interests and support of its users. This provides much scope for the role of interpretation in educating and inspiring the public. This in turn should foster further support for natural area conservation.
(3) Monitoring should take place so that the effectiveness of interpretation can be evaluated.

There is a global trend in tourists seeking out natural experiences, undisturbed conditions and authenticity. The interests of people will also be increasingly focused on the need for information and inspiration from nature. This, coupled with the need to manage ever-increasing visits to national parks and other natural areas, provides for much scope in the wider use and application of interpretation in the future.

Further reading

Sharpe (1982) provides a comprehensive account of interpretive techniques. McArthur and Hall (1996) and McArthur (1998a) provide useful overviews and discussion on planning for interpretation. Ham (1992) covers the principles and practice of interpretation and focuses in particular on the practicalities of conducted activities and self-guided tours. The important practice of tour guiding is discussed further in Weiler and Ham (2000).

Chapter 7
Monitoring

Introduction

Monitoring has long been a neglected element of natural area management. Today, however, monitoring is essential for managers who are increasingly being required to report on the outcomes of their activities. This chapter describes why and how monitoring must be an essential part of natural area management. It begins by defining monitoring and explaining the reasons for doing it before detailing guiding principles.

Most of the chapter is devoted to describing ways of monitoring the impacts of visitors on the natural environment and visitors' attributes, activities, needs and perceptions. Campsites, built facilities, roads, trails and water bodies are covered in the natural environment material. Water bodies are also taken to include marine environments. Ways of monitoring visitors are then described. Given the importance of setting standards against which changes can be assessed, the next section is devoted to this. Also included is environmental auditing, a facet of natural area management likely to become more common. The conclusion links this chapter to earlier ones, especially those on impacts and planning.

Definition

Monitoring is the systematic gathering and analysis of data over time. For natural area tourism, a comprehensive monitoring programmeme will collect data on the natural environment and its visitors. Information on the natural environment could include vegetation cover, damage to vegetation, weed invasion, soil properties (especially erosion), water quality, and wildlife populations (e.g. changes in breeding success, distribution). Such data can be used to identify and quantify site-specific impacts (Monz, 2000).

Four distinct components of visitor monitoring have been identified (Cope *et al.*, 2000; Pitts & Smith, 1993).

(1) Park use: quantitative data on total visitor use as well as mode of arrival (e.g. bus or car) and entry point.
(2) Site use: mainly quantitative information on sites visited, seasonal use

patterns, group size, length of stay, frequency of visits and activities undertaken.

(3) Visitor profiling (characteristics): quantitative and qualitative information on demographic and socio-economic attributes of individuals, reasons for visiting, attitudes, motivations, preferences, expectations and information needs.

(4) Visitor outcomes: quantitative and qualitative information on satisfactions, disappointments, suggestions and comments.

Reasons for monitoring

In many countries such as Australia the lack of monitoring the effects of visitors in natural areas has been lamented. Gardner (1994) commented that 'too few park managers in Australia have incorporated strategic visitor monitoring into their visitor management process'. Pitts and Smith (1993), when reflecting on the past 20 years of park management in Australia and overseas, said 'One of the most striking observations is the lack of representative, systematic and accurate visitor information'. When staff at Kakadu National Park, one of the most significant natural areas in Australia, were asked about the importance they assigned to visitor monitoring they placed it behind weed management and education/interpretation, but ahead of office administration, issuing permits and collecting fees (Pitts & Smith, 1993). In contrast (Cope *et al.*, 2000) observed that in the United Kingdom visitor monitoring by natural area managers is commonplace.

Numerous, sound reasons for monitoring the impacts of natural area tourism and of tourists themselves exist.

1. Management of natural areas – monitoring provides the information needed to ameliorate impacts and assess management effectiveness

Managing the impacts of visitor use is essential if the natural environment is to be protected and visitor experiences maintained. Monitoring provides information, not only on when management intervention is required, but can also improve managers' understanding of the cause–effect relationship between levels and types of visitor use and the resultant impacts (Cole, 1989; Marion, 1995; Pitts & Smith, 1993). Such understanding is essential if use is to be managed to prevent further impacts and in many cases, to reduce the existing levels of impact. Additionally, if an impact can be detected early, it is probably cheaper and easier to remedy before it reaches a 'threshold of irreversible change' (Buckley, 1999b).

Monitoring also allows managers to assess the effectiveness of management strategies once in place. The outcomes of different strategies, assessed by measuring changes in resource conditions and/or visitors' perceptions, can be compared. Data from one point in time are insufficient for this assessment, hence the need for monitoring rather than a single inventorying exercise.

2. Planning – monitoring provides the information needed for management plans, recreation/tourism planning frameworks and site design activities

Essential data for planning include visitor numbers and characteristics, activities, resource impacts, patterns of use, satisfaction and expectations. Such data can be provided by a one-off inventorying exercise or preferably from an ongoing monitoring programme. Monitoring also allows the success of these plans to be determined as well as indicating when revision is needed and assisting in the revision process. The planning frameworks outlined in Chapter 4 rely on monitoring for measurements of initial baseline conditions and then subsequent repeat measures of selected indicators to determine the amount of change.

3. Resource allocation – monitoring provides managers with a systematic basis for allocating funds and resources

Natural area managers need a systematic basis for allocating funds and resources, such as staff, within and between natural areas. Without reliable data on environmental impacts, visitation levels and patterns of use, allocation is based either on a manager's intuitions or external pressures such as financial availability, staff constraints and political directives (Marion, 1991; Pitts & Smith, 1993). Although managers' intuitions will often stand them in good stead, frequent staff turnover mean changes in the natural environment and visitors often go unnoticed. Using reliable data enables resources to be allocated where they are most needed, for example to a site where damage to vegetation or overcrowding needs management attention, rather than to a less impacted site that a manager intuitively believes needs attention. Such strategic allocation of resources improves the economic efficiency of natural area management.

Environmental impact and visitor monitoring data also have a crucial role to play at the corporate level in helping land management organisations seek funding from government and other sources (Pitts & Smith, 1993). Senior agency staff may use total visitor numbers, visitor satisfaction or total areas impacted (for example, kilometres of trail impacted by horses) to justify requests for financial support. Also at the corporate level these cumulative data, such as total visitor numbers to a state's national parks, may be used to develop community awareness by demonstrating the extent of use and support for such areas.

4. Public accountability – monitoring provides information to the corporate levels of land management agencies to assist with accountability and transparency

Increasingly, the activities of natural area managers and their organisations are being subjected to public scrutiny. Performance reporting, where monitoring data are made publicly available, is one way of meeting public requests for accountability. In Australia, organisations such as the Western Australian Department of Conservation and Land Management (CALM) report annually to the state government on their performance. Examples of tourism performance measures include number of visits to CALM-managed sites and visitor satisfaction (CALM, 2000b).

Landres *et al.* (1994) emphasised the increasing importance of policy makers being able to assess the status and trends of the natural area system they manage. At a most basic level a description of the system is required; how many natural areas and their sizes. Objective data documenting the threats to this system would be useful. Trends in conditions and visitor demand are also potentially useful, reported via a few core indicators. Last, understanding how society values natural areas and the benefits of such areas to society are essential for political forums. 'State of the Park' reporting may become a regular feature of managing natural areas. Cope *et al.* (2000) reported on the North York Moors National Park Authority developing sustainability indicators and trend indices, recorded and reviewed through State of the Park reports.

5. Marketing and interpretation – monitoring provides the information needed to successfully market and interpret natural areas

Understanding who visitors are and what they want is fundamental to successfully marketing a natural area. And increasingly, natural area managers are trying to meet the needs of specific user groups each with their own particular information and interpretation requirements. Such an approach requires information on the characteristics and expectations of different segments of the user population (Pitts & Smith, 1993).

6. Legislative and legal requirements – monitoring may be legally required

For many land managers, the legislation guiding their operations (for example the United States National Park Service is guided by the National Park Service Organic Act of 1916) requires that visitor experiences are to be provided, but only to the extent that the natural environment is unimpaired. Monitoring shows when 'impairment' has occurred and is needed to meet this legislative mandate. Management policies and guidelines may also explicitly require visitor impact monitoring. Marion (1995) noted that in several places in the United States National Park Service management policies, monitoring of resource impacts is prescribed.

Monitoring may also be legally prescribed as part of the approval of tourism developments subject to environmental impact assessment (EIA). A recent study of tourism developments in Australia by Warnken and Buckley (2000) noted that of the 175 developments subject to EIA from 1980 to 1993, only 13 had formal resource monitoring. Obviously, such a requirement is not widespread. Most of the projects requiring monitoring were coastal resorts and day visit pontoons on the Great Barrier Reef (Figure 7.1). Parameters included reef fish and coral communities, mangrove and seagrass communities, water quality and a wetland filter system (for a ski resort).

Principles

The following principles should guide the development of a monitoring programme for natural area tourism.

1. Clear objectives are integral to the success of a monitoring programme

The objectives will vary depending on the reasons for monitoring. Monitoring should never be an end in itself. Reasons range from managing the impacts of visitor use through to legal requirements accompanying approval of tourism developments. Objectives must be clearly identified before commencing activities, otherwise important information may not be collected and time and money could be wasted on collecting unnecessary data (Marion, 1991). Cope *et al.* (2000), from

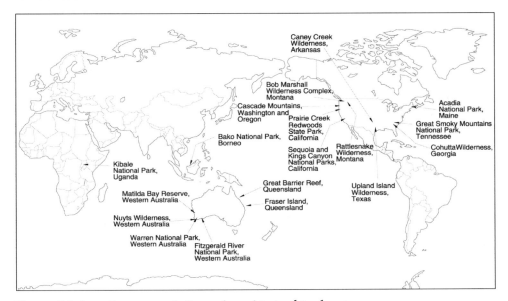

Figure 7.1 Location map of sites referred to in this chapter

their study of visitor monitoring by resource management organisations in the United Kingdom, concluded that the value of data is greatest when monitoring objectives are explicitly clear at the outset and remain the focus throughout data collection.

2. A well-planned and managed information storage and retrieval system is an essential element of a monitoring programme

Monitoring requires comparing repeat measures of the same parameters. As such, data need to be stored somewhere they are safe but accessible so that new data can be compared with the old. It is also desirable that the form of storage allows simple manipulations and analysis so that comparisons between data collected at different times can be readily made. Such information systems need not be grandiose and expensive so long as the system is based on a systematic, standardised process for data collection, a structured filing system, preferably computer-based, and clear instructions and simple procedures for manipulating and retrieving information (Pitts & Smith, 1993).

3. A sampling strategy providing cost-effective, robust data is crucial for successful monitoring

Careful consideration of where and how much data are collected is crucial to the success of a monitoring programme. Such considerations must take place during the design phase. Environmental impacts may be monitored by census, with all sites surveyed, or by sampling only a subset of sites (Marion, 1991). With sampling a subset, the sites must be selected in such a way that the results are generalisable to all sites and measurements can be repeated over time. For trails, for example, if a description of the condition of the whole trail is the objective, then either the whole trail can be censused or a subset of randomly located points sampled and the results generalised to the whole trail (Leung & Marion, 2000; Marion & Leung, 2001). The first approach will be much more expensive and accurate than the second. The choice depends on the objectives of monitoring and available resources. Visitor monitoring generally relies on sampling where inferences about the whole visitor population are drawn from a subset of this larger population (Pitts & Smith, 1993). Sampling strategies are discussed further later in this chapter.

Ideally, environmental monitoring associated with natural area tourism would involve measurements before and after a development takes place, as well as records from the impacted site and a similar, nearby, undisturbed control site. This before, after, control, impact, paired sampling approach (BACIP) is widely applied in ecology (Bernstein & Zalinski, 1983). Unfortunately, such an approach has few opportunities for application in natural area tourism because most of the sites requiring monitoring have been in use for many years. However, this does not preclude managers using control sites where possible and when major developments are proposed ensuring that predevelopment monitoring is done.

4. Quality assurance is critical to the success of a monitoring programme

Quality assurance must be a key element of any monitoring programme. It is achieved by training staff involved in data collection, entry and analysis, calibration and regular checking of counting devices (e.g. traffic counters), regular feedback to staff and regular reviews of performance (Marion, 1991). Performance reviews could include regular checks of how surveys are conducted, completed data sheets or visitor questionnaires, overall system performance, and the information needs, objectives and priorities of the whole monitoring programme (Pitts & Smith, 1993).

Quality is also improved by providing standardised means for conducting monitoring and recording the data obtained. Field data forms can be used to collect information on environmental parameters such as vegetation and visitor information such as activities and numbers at a particular site. Questionnaires are a common means of collecting information from visitors themselves. Computer databases are the best way of providing a standardised data storage, manipulation and retrieval system. A manual to guide monitoring, such as the one produced by Marion (1991), also assists in quality control.

5. Skilled managers must lead and take responsibility for designing and implementing monitoring programmes for their natural area

The responsibility for monitoring generally rests with managers, as part of their suite of management responsibilities. Marion (1991), in his manual on monitoring visitor impacts in US national parks, noted that the usefulness of monitoring programmes is entirely dependent on the managers who initiate and manage them and that programmes developed in isolation from other resource protection decision making will be short-lived. To help managers cope with limited resources, seasonal staff or students may be contracted so long as they are adequately trained and supervised. Roles for scientists could include assistance in designing a monitoring programme and periodic reviews to ensure that the quality of data is being maintained and programmes are scientifically defensible. Scientists may also have ongoing research interests that could form part of a programme.

Any new monitoring programme should build on what already exists. Existing data may include direct counts from traffic counters or entry tickets or indirect counts from permits, trail registration or records of interpretive programme attendance. Building on and modifying such systems recognises years of practical experience by field staff and should help them adopt the 'new' programme (Pitts & Smith, 1993).

Developing a monitoring programme

Many of us would like to get straight out into the field and start measuring environmental impacts or interviewing visitors. However, to make sure resources are used efficiently and effectively and that the measurements taken are useful and repeatable, pre-fieldwork planning is necessary. This thinking is best guided through developing a monitoring programme based on the principles above and the steps outlined in Table 7.1. Key steps include evaluating the need for such a programme and establishing explicit objectives and documenting the data collection methods. Such documentation is essential if data are to be consistently and reliably collected, given that repeat measures over time will be made, probably by different people.

In the past, monitoring programmes have been regarded as the responsibility of managers. Recently, contributions by tour operators and volunteers have been recognised through monitoring programmes developed for coral reefs worldwide (Hodgson, 1999), the Great Barrier Reef (Anon., 1998; Anon., 1999b) (Figure 7.1) and the Western Australian marine environment (CALM & AMCS, 2000). These programmes rely on training, guidelines and protocols for survey techniques and data collection to ensure that accurate and useful data are collected (Anon., 1998).

Monitoring Visitor Impacts on Natural Areas

A wealth of research on monitoring visitor impacts on the natural environment in the backcountry areas of national parks and wilderness areas in the United States exists (Leung & Marion, 2000). Most of this work is directly applicable to natural area tourism, with some modifications and additions to cover the monitoring of facilities at the developed end of the spectrum, such as lodges and resorts. Techniques are grouped according to whether they are used for terminus points, such as resorts, campgrounds and campsites, or linear features, such as roads and walk trails. Techniques for monitoring visitor impacts on water bodies are also briefly reviewed. For each grouping, comments are made on sampling strategies, the techniques themselves, indicators and assessment procedures.

Table 7.1 Steps in a monitoring programme for resource impacts and visitors in natural areas

Step	Description
1. Evaluate need for monitoring programme and determine objectives	• Review of legislative, legal and policy reasons for monitoring; often critical in enlisting organisational support • Determine agreed objectives
2. Review existing approaches	• Examine what has been done elsewhere and previously in the area to be monitored
3. Develop monitoring procedures	• Select techniques (e.g. photo points, visitor surveys) based on considerations of accuracy, precision, sensitivity and cost • Test techniques, including pilot testing of any visitor survey forms, and modify as needed
4. Document monitoring protocols and provide training	• Produce monitoring manual, field data forms, survey forms for visitors, computer database • Provide staff training
5. Conduct monitoring fieldwork	• Plan fieldwork – for resource impacts, best conducted by a small number of evaluators working full-time for a short period towards the middle or end of the recreation season; for visitor monitoring decide where and when to survey (surveys based on personal contact give the best response rate)
6. Develop analysis and reporting procedures	• Use computer, if possible, to store, analyse and retrieve data
7. Apply monitoring data to management	• Establish priorities based on data • Undertake actions

Derived from Cole (1989); Marion (1991)

Built facilities, campgrounds and campsites

Campsites in wilderness and backcountry areas have been the focus of much of the monitoring effort in the United States. This work is relevant to natural area tourism, both in wilderness areas and more developed natural areas including large campgrounds with built facilities. Unfortunately, widely accepted and used techniques are not currently available for monitoring the environmental impacts of facilities such as resorts. A brief mention is made later in this chapter, in the section on water bodies, of some limited monitoring underway for resorts in marine environments (Warnken & Buckley, 2000).

Four general approaches to monitoring campsites exist. These approaches and their advantages and disadvantages are summarised in Table 7.2. All aim to provide

Table 7.2 Summary of campsite monitoring techniques

Monitoring technique	Advantages	Disadvantages	Application
Photographs – taken of the site from a fixed point, through 360° to create a panorama, or of vegetation quadrats	Quick, relatively low cost; visually documents extent and location of impacts	Does not provide accurate quantitative measures of changes in indicators; comparisons between photos are often impossible due to differences in cameras, lens and film	Best used as a supplement to other data collected in the field
Condition class rating – a single rating (1–5) is given to each site based on the degree of vegetation loss, tree damage, bare mineral soil and erosion See Frissell (1978) for original rating system and Marion (1995) for system based on ground cover conditions only as many sites lack trees	Quick, relatively low cost; provides a rapid survey approach when large numbers of campsites are spread over large areas; rapidly provides data on which campsites are most seriously impacted	Does not provide accurate quantitative measures of changes in indicators; the single rating does not provide information on the severity of each impact type (e.g. is vegetation loss or erosion more serious) and thus selection of appropriate management response is difficult; rating classes are so broad that major changes may occur before allocation to another class occurs	Best used for assessing large natural areas where there are numerous sites and the resources are not available to spend more than a few minutes at each site; may be used in combination with multiple indicator approaches
Multiple indicator ratings – ratings for individual indicators recorded and then summed to give a summary impact score* for each site See Parsons and MacLeod (1980), Cole (1983a)	Quick – a campsite can be evaluated in 5–10 minutes – as well as providing a lot of information at relatively low cost; accuracy is sufficient to detect changes over time in campsites as well as categorising the status of existing sites; can identify the most serious impacts	Information on individual indicators is not very precise (large variations in ratings for an indicator made by different evaluators) although the overall score does not vary greatly between different evaluators	Particularly useful for rapidly assessing a large number of sites
Multiple indicator measurements – measures taken of multiple indicators See Cole (1989), Marion (1991)	Provides a large amount of precise information; amenable to statistical analysis (e.g. multivariate techniques)	Time-consuming – 30 minutes to 2 hrs per site; vegetation quadrat and soil sampling skills may be required	Useful for checking if rapid assessment measures are accurate; feasible only where there are small numbers of campsites

* Such summing is regarded as a statistically improper procedure because of the wide variation in assessment units between indicators (e.g. number of trails versus m^2 of site area)

Derived from Cole (1983a, 1989), Frissell (1978), Hammitt and Cole (1998), Leung and Marion (1999c, 2000), Marion (1991), Monz (2000), Parsons and MacLeod (1980)

information for managers so they can take action before impacts become unacceptable. As these approaches were developed for backcountry sites in North America, some of the indicators will not be suitable or will need modifying before they can be applied elsewhere. For example, for many national parks in Australia bare ground is a natural state. As such, it will not be a useful indicator of impact in these situations.

Photographs

The first approach, taking photos, provides a visual record of the site. Photos may be taken from a fixed point, and then subsequent photos used to determine changes over time. Another approach is to take a 360° panorama of the site by rotating a camera located at fixed point. Repeat photos may also be taken of vegetation quadrats (usually a square 1 m × 1 m, laid over the top of the vegetation) to determine changes in vegetation cover. Photographs are recommended as a supplement to other forms of data collection rather than as a technique used on its own (Hammitt & Cole, 1998; Marion, 1991).

Condition class rating

The second approach, as developed by Frissell (1978), is determining the condition class that best describes the campsite being surveyed. The five classes range from Class 1 with vegetation flattened but not permanently injured through to Class 5 with obvious soil erosion (Table 7.3). This system is quick and easy to apply and provides a useful single value for each site (Marion, 1991). This value can be used to compare the levels of impacts for campsites across an area. Repeat monitoring can be used to indicate movements from one condition class to another. Because of the inaccuracy of this approach and information lost through aggregating impact information into a single rating, condition class ratings are generally only used to complement other forms of data collection.

Multiple indicator ratings

The third approach, variously referred to as a multiple-indicator approach (Leung & Marion, 1999c), multiparameter systems (Marion, 1991) and multiple

Table 7.3 Condition classes for monitoring campsites in natural areas

Class	Description
1	Ground vegetation flattened but not permanently injured. Minimal physical change except for possibly a simple rock fireplace.
2	Ground vegetation worn away around fireplace or centre of activity.
3	Ground vegetation lost on most of the site, but humus and litter still present in all but a few areas.
4	Bare mineral soil widespread. Tree roots, where present, exposed on the surface.
5	Soil erosion obvious, as indicated by exposed tree roots and rocks (where present), and/or gullying.

Derived from Frissell (1978) and Marion (1995)

parameter systems (Hammitt & Cole, 1998), is collecting information on a number of indicators. A widely used indicator rating system is that developed by Parsons and MacLeod (1980) for Sequoia and Kings Canyon National Parks in the United States (Figure 7.1) and subsequently modified by Cole (1983a). Both assign ratings to a suite of indicators. Cole (1983a) used ratings of 1–3 for nine indicators – campsite area, bare core area, condition of ground cover vegetation, exposed bare mineral soil, damage to trees, exposed tree roots (i.e. a measure of erosion), extent of development, site cleanliness, and number of associated trails ('social' trails) (Table 7.4). A raw value and rating are recorded for each indicator. For example for campsite area, the rating categories were (1) 0–50 m^2, (2) 51–100 m^2 and (3) >100 m^2. For a campsite area of 60 m^2, this area and a rating of '2' are recorded.

A summary impact score is then obtained by summing the raw or weighted ratings for the nine indicators. Parsons and MacLeod (1980) used raw individual ratings while Cole (1983a) weighted his ratings. Although it is simpler to have equal weightings, this implies that all types of change are of equal importance. For example, bare mineral soil and camp area might be much more important than cleanliness of the site. As such, they should be weighted more heavily. A weight for each indicator should be decided by managers, in consultation with stakeholders. When applied to the Bob Marshall Wilderness Complex (Figure 7.1), scores ranged from 20 to 60. This range was divided into four impact classes: light (ratings of 20–29), moderate (30–40), heavy (41–50) and severe (51–60) (Hammitt & Cole, 1998). This system has been used to quantify the impacts of natural area tourism in Kibale National Park in Africa (Box 7.1, Figure 7.1).

When using this monitoring system it is essential to adapt it to the specific setting. Modifying rating descriptions and the range of each summary impact score category may be necessary to ensure that approximately equal numbers of sites fall into each category. If these changes are not made then differentiation of sites for different levels of management attention will not be possible. For example, if all the sites fall into the severe impact category then it will be impossible to prioritise management actions. Also, for developed sites such as an 80 bay campground, the rating choices for campsite area will need to be very different to those for a backcountry campsite.

Multiple indicator measurements

Taking individual measurements of a number of indicators is the best way to get accurate, replicable data for individual campsites. Table 7.5 lists and describes the most commonly used indicators. Recording visual indicators, plus measuring the campsite area, takes two workers 10–15 minutes per site (Marion, 1991). Although more time-consuming than the multiple indicator ratings system, it is still feasible to apply this approach to a reasonably large number of sites. Leung and Marion (1999c) surveyed 195 campsites in the Great Smoky Mountains National Park using this approach.

More comprehensive vegetation quadrats and soil measurements can also be added but such work is generally reserved for research or monitoring of a small

Table 7.4 Indicators commonly used in multiple indicator ratings systems

Indicator	Description	Rating
Campsite area	Estimation (by tape, pacing or eye) of the total area trampled	(1) 0–50 m^2 (2) 51–100 m^2 (3) >100 m^2
Barren core area	Estimation (by tape, pacing or eye) of the area denuded of vegetation	(1) 0–5 m^2 (2) 6-50 m^2 (3) >50 m^2
Condition of ground cover vegetation*	Relative measure (from walking around) of the extent of vegetation cover within the campsite compared with a nearby, similar, unimpacted area	(1) site and control belong to the same coverage class[+] (2) coverage on site is one class less than on control (3) difference in coverage is two or more classes (e.g. 51–75% at control and 6–25% at site)
Exposed bare mineral soil*	Relative measure (from walking around) of the extent of bare soil within the campsite compared with a nearby, similar, unimpacted area	Rate as for condition of ground cover vegetation (above)
Damage to trees	Number of lower branches broken, boles hacked, carvings and nails	(1) no damage/a few broken lower branches (2) 1–7 mutilations (e.g. axe marks, carvings, cut stumps) (3) >7 mutilations
Exposed tree roots (i.e. a measure of erosion)	Number of exposed roots as a simple measure of soil erosion	(1) no trees with exposed roots (2) 3 trees or less with exposed roots (3) >3 trees with exposed roots
Extent of development	Number of human 'improvements' such as fire rings, seats, tent pads and windbreaks	(1) nothing more than a scattered fire ring (2) nothing more than 1 fire ring and rudimentary seats (3) more than 1 fire ring or seats, tables, windbreaks, levelled tent pads or other developments
Site cleanliness	Amount of charcoal, blackened logs, litter, human waste and horse manure	(1) nothing more than scattered charcoal from 1 fire site (2) either scattered charcoal from >1 fire site or some litter (3) horse manure, human waste, widespread litter, remnants of campfires
Number of associated trails ('social' trails)	Number of trails radiating from the campsite and their degree of development to provide a measure of impact on surrounding areas	(1) no trails discernible (2) 1-2 discernible trails, no more than 1 well-developed trail (3) either >2 discernible trails or >1 well-developed trail

*Relies on measures of a nearby, similar, unimpacted site (i.e. a 'control' site); [+]coverage classes are 0–5, 6–25, 26–50, 51–75, 76–100%
Derived from Cole (1983a); Parsons & MacLeod (1980)

Box 7.1 Applying a multiple indicator ratings system to monitoring campsites in Kibale National Park, Uganda

Kibale is one of nine national parks in Uganda. It covers about 560 km^2 of high forest, grassland and swamps. The forest has a rich diversity of trees and animals, with 11 primate and 325 bird species. Ecotourism commenced in 1992 following the establishment of campsites and nature trails (Obua & Harding, 1997). Since then the number of visitors has increased from 1300 to about 5000 in 1996.

A multiple indicator ratings system, as developed by Parsons and MacLeod (1980) and modified by Cole (1983a), was used to assess the extent of campsite degradation by visitors (Table 7.4). The nine indicators were vegetation loss, mineral soil increase, tree damage, root exposure, development, cleanliness, social trails, camp area, and barren core area. All the ratings were based on visual estimates. Assessing vegetation loss and increase in mineral soil involved comparing the campsite (S_0) with nearby undisturbed forest (S_1). Five classes (0–5, 6–25, 26–50, 51–75 and 76–100%) were used to describe cover. Ratings were then allocated as follows: both the site (S_0) and control (S_1) belong to the same coverage class – 1; coverage on S_0 is one class lower than on S_1 – 2; the difference in coverage on S_0 and S_1 is two or more classes – 3.

A rating of 1–3 was given to each indicator depending on the severity of the impact. Each rating was then multiplied by a weighting before being summed to give an overall impact score for each campsite. The ratings and weightings were those developed by Cole (1983a). For example, a campsite where the trees had no exposed roots was given a rating of 1, from a choice of 1–3. This rating was multiplied by 3, the weight assigned to exposed tree roots, before being summed with the other weighted ratings to give an overall impact score. The summary impact score for this campsite was 24, described by Obua and Harding (1997) as a low level of impact. This designation was based on the following categories: 0–29 low, 30–40 moderate, 41–50 high and 51–60 severe.

Obua and Harding (1997) concluded that more than three-quarters of the campsites had experienced some form of degradation. This finding is supported by work elsewhere showing that even low levels of use cause noticeable impacts (Hammitt & Cole, 1998).

number of sites due to the substantial field time required. This comprehensive assessment, plus collecting data on visual indicators, can take up to two hours per site (Hammitt & Cole, 1998). About 15–20 vegetation quadrats at each campsite and an adjacent control are sampled to determine groundcover loss, species composition and exposed soil. Soil parameters, such as organic matter and soil compaction, are similarly measured at the campsite and control, with multiple samples taken (Cole, 1989; Cole & Marion, 1988). Skilled, experienced staff are needed.

Of importance for measures of most indicators and repeat monitoring of a site is accurately measuring its area. The variable radial transect method is accurate

Table 7.5 Indicators commonly used in multiple indicator measurement systems

Indicator (including measurement unit)	Measured visually	Descriptions and comments
Campsite size (m^2)	No	Measured using the variable transect or geometric figure method (Fig. 7.2)
Groundcover loss (%)*	Yes/No	Determined using six cover classes (e.g. Class 1: 0–5%) and derived by subtracting from the value for a nearby, similar, unimpacted control site to give percentage loss OR 15–20 1 × 1 m permanent quadrats on site and nearby control – infrequently used because of time involved
Exposed soil (%)*	Yes	Determined using six exposure classes (e.g. Class 1: 0–5%) and derived by subtracting from the value for a nearby, similar, unimpacted control site OR 15–20 1 × 1m permanent quadrats on site and nearby control – infrequently used because of time involved
Trees with exposed roots (#,%)	Yes	Number of trees with exposed roots or as a percentage of all trees on the site
Tree stumps (#,%)	Yes	Number of tree stumps or as a percentage of all trees on the site
Damaged trees (#, %)	Yes	Number of damaged trees or as a percentage of all trees on the site
Fire sites (pits or rings) (#)	Yes	Number of fire sites
Visitor-created social trails (#)	Yes	Number of visitor-created social trails
Cleanliness (rating #)	Yes	Determined by categorising the amount of charcoal, blackened logs, litter, human waste and horse manure – not widely used
Campsite development (rating #)	Yes	Determined by categorising the number of human 'improvements' such as fire rings, seats, tent pads and windbreaks – not widely used
Impacts to soil organic horizons(#)*	No	Measures include organic horizon cover, organic horizon depth and degree of disturbance of litter and duff from site and control; take 1 sample from each of the vegetation quadrats established to measure groundcover loss – infrequently used because of time involved
Impacts to mineral soil (#)*	No	Measures include soil compaction (bulk density or resistance of the soil to penetration), water infiltration rates, moisture content, organic matter content and chemical composition; more than 5 samples from site and control needed – infrequently used because of the time involved in field work and laboratory analyses

*Relies on measures of a nearby, similar, unimpacted site (i.e. a 'control' site)
Derived from Cole (1989), Hammitt and Cole (1998), Leung and Marion (1999c), Marion (1991), Marion (1995), Smith (1998)

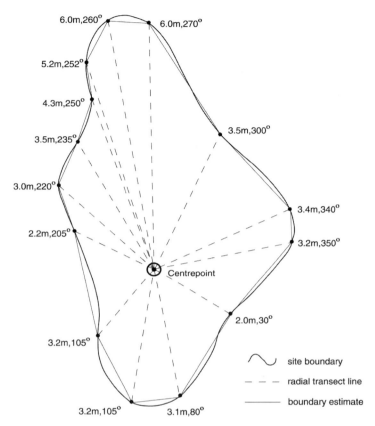

Figure 7.2(a) Variable radial transect method for measuring site area. (Derived from Marion, 1991)

(Figure 7.2a), although more time-consuming than other methods such as the geometric figure method (Figure 7.2b). The former is based on flagging as many points on the campsite boundary as are necessary to define a polygon approximating the area. The distance from a marked, fixed centrepoint to each point, plus the associated compass bearing is then recorded. The result could be a list of as many as 15–20 lengths and bearings. Computerised arithmetic procedures can then be used to calculate the area (Marion, 1991). The geometric figure method is based on approximating the area of the campsite to common geometric figures and calculating its area accordingly. Although it is more rapid it is less accurate.

Combined systems

A combined approach using ratings and multiple indicator measurements has been developed and applied by Marion (1991, 1995) (Box 7.2). The visual indicators

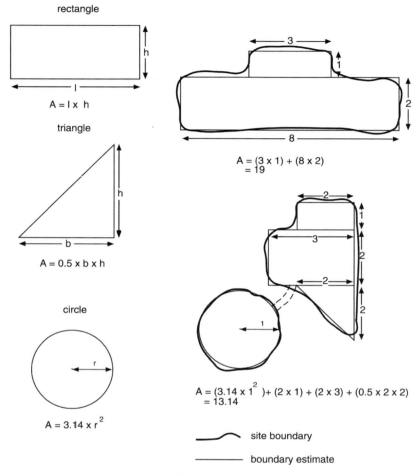

rectangle

$A = l \times h$

triangle

$A = 0.5 \times b \times h$

circle

$A = 3.14 \times r^2$

$A = (3 \times 1) + (8 \times 2)$
$= 19$

$A = (3.14 \times 1^2) + (2 \times 1) + (2 \times 3) + (0.5 \times 2 \times 2)$
$= 13.14$

site boundary

boundary estimate

Figure 7.2(b) Geometric figure method for measuring site area. (Derived from Marion, 1991)

are quickly measured, with vegetation cover and exposed soil estimated for the site and a control rather than using quadrats. Soils are not sampled.

Choosing a monitoring strategy

Choice of a monitoring approach involves considering accuracy, precision, sensitivity and cost. Accuracy refers to how close a measurement is to its true value while precision refers to how close repeated measures are to each other. Both are important and generally improved by using more time-consuming techniques. Sensitivity refers to how large a change must be before it can confidently be identified as a real change in conditions. A system using a small number of broad

Box 7.2 A combined system for monitoring campsites in Great Smoky Mountains National Park, USA

Great Smoky Mountains National Park, with an area of 209,000 ha and located along the border of Tennessee and North Carolina (Figure 7.1), is one of the most visited national parks in the United States. About 470,000 overnight stays were reported in 1998 with backcountry camping restricted to 87 designated campgrounds and 18 shelters. Each designated campground typically consists of 2–4 individual campsites. The following study was conducted to improve assessment procedures and under-standing of backcountry impacts (Leung & Marion, 1999c).

A total of 377 backcountry campsites were assessed, 308 legal and the remainder illegal. Site size, number of fire sites and damaged trees and stumps were assessed for all sites. A ratings system was used to give each site a condition class: Class 1 sites are barely evident while Class 5 sites have lost most vegetation and litter cover and are eroding.

To reduce field assessment time, only campsites rated Class 3 or above were assessed further (195 sites). For these sites, eight indicators were selected and measured based on their ecological and managerial significance, use in other studies and their level of measurement being suitable for multivariate analysis. They were grouped as area disturbance indicators, including campsite size (ft^2), fire sites (number of pits or rings) and visitor-created social trails (number); soil and ground cover damage indicators, including trees with exposed roots (%), absolute groundcover loss (%) and exposed soil (%); and tree-related damage indicators, including tree stumps (%) and damaged trees (%). The groundcover and exposed soil indicators required measure-ments at the site and an environmentally similar but undisturbed nearby site.

Leung and Marion (1999c) concluded that two aspects of impact, spatial extent (areal measures) and intensity (percent measures), could be used to differentiate four campsite types. The first type, low impact campsites (38% of campsites), had minimal areas and levels of vegetation and soil disturbance. These sites are generally remote from trails and water sources such as streams. Moderately impacted sites (24%) had low to medium areas and levels of impact. Intensively impacted campsites (21%) had high levels of soil and ground cover damage but the area disturbed was relatively small compared to extensively impacted campsites. The area of these sites appeared to be constrained by topography and dense vegetation. Extensively impacted campsites (8%), while only showing intermediate levels of soil and ground cover damage, had large areas of disturbance. For these sites there were no topographic or vegetative barriers restricting site expansion or proliferation of new campsites in adjacent areas.

In this study, the combination of a rapid but standardised set of field procedures with statistical analysis provided a useful assessment tool for a large number of campsites. For managers it seems more effective to design management strategies based on the campsite types differentiated in this study rather than individual impact indicators (Leung & Marion, 1999c). For example, strategies for intensively and extensively impacted sites are likely to be different. For the former the focus will be controlling soil erosion and site restoration. For extensively impacted sites, the priorities are more likely to be controlling the expansion and proliferation of sites.

categories will have low sensitivity. If a system for campsite size has three categories, with the third described as '>100 m^{2}', a site of 150 m^2 could triple in size without the site moving to another impact category. The last consideration is cost with staff time often being the limiting factor.

Deciding which approach to take also depends on the objectives of the monitoring programme as well as the resources and time available. How many sites to survey is an important consideration. Generally, managers want an inventory and then repeat monitoring of all sites, usually to provide data on total number of sites, their distribution and levels of impact. Cole (1983a) recommended inventorying all sites: 'If funding is insufficient to take measurements on all sites, it would be better to use an estimate system on all sites than to only take measurements on some of the sites'. Such an approach is a census rather than sampling process so concerns regarding selection of a representative sample of sites are largely irrelevant.

The only time when sampling will be a concern is when quadrat-based measurements at a few sites are used to supplement less precise rapid estimates at all sites (Cole, 1989). To make sure that the findings from this sub-set can be generalised to all sites in the area of interest, a sufficient number of sites need to be sampled. Little guidance is available as to what this number should be.

If resources are very limited, a rating system may be the best approach. More preferable is a combined ratings and multiple indicator measurement system as employed by Marion (1995) and Leung and Marion (1999c). Little can be saved in time or money by collecting data on a small, rather than large number of indicators, given that most of the time spent on monitoring in natural areas is devoted to travelling between sites. Most programmes seem to rely on eight or more indicators. From Leung and Marion's (1999c) work it appears that indicators of both the spatial extent (e.g. campsite area) and intensity (e.g. number of tree stumps) of impacts are needed.

Roads and trails

Much research effort has been directed to developing and applying monitoring techniques to trails in backcountry and wilderness areas, similarly to campsite monitoring. The techniques are equally as relevant to other natural areas, although will need modification before they can be applied to sealed and gravel roads and four-wheel-drive tracks. Most of the following is directed toward monitoring trails because limited information on monitoring roads and tracks used for natural area tourism is available, although a brief description of a monitoring system for gravel roads concludes this section.

A number of techniques are available, with the choice depending on the objectives guiding monitoring and the resources available. Two rapid survey approaches have been developed and used: sampling- and problem-based rapid surveys (Farrell & Marion, 2001; Marion & Leung, 2001). In rapid surveys substantial time is saved by not relocating points. A third survey approach relies on establishing and surveying fixed points (Table 7.6).

All of the survey approaches include some measure of erosion, usually recorded

Table 7.6 Summary of trail monitoring techniques

Trail monitoring technique*	Advantages	Disadvantages	Application
Sampling-based rapid surveys – evaluator records trail condition at systematically-located but non-permanent points, aiming for generalisation to the whole trail system See Cole (1983b)	Permits rapid assessment of general trail conditions	May not accurately reflect trail problems unless a large number of sample points are used	Most common survey approach, specifically the approach of taking measurements at points located at a constant interval along a trail
Problem-based rapid surveys – evaluator searches for and documents the location and extent of trail problems in a trail system, usually based on searching the whole trail system (a census approach) See Leung & Marion (1999a)	Permits rapid assessment of trail problems; allows description of the condition of the whole trail system	Not able to provide information on average conditions, e.g. no statement can be made about the average level of muddiness for the system	Recently used to advise managers on extent and location of trail problems as well as the efficacy of current erosion control measures
Permanent point surveys – evaluator locates and marks sites to sample either the trail system so generalisations to the whole trail system can be made, or purposively samples portions of interest (e.g. to assess management actions) See Cole (1983b)	Provides accurate and precise data on changing trail conditions for sample sites; permits subtle changes to be detected	Very time-consuming because of the need to document and relocate measurement sites; does not document overall trail condition	Less useful to managers than rapid survey techniques; can be used to provide advice to managers on the effectiveness of management actions

* All three techniques use multiple indicators
Derived from Cole (1983b), Cole *et al.* (1997), Hammitt and Cole (1998), Leung and Marion (1999a), Leung and Marion (2000), Marion and Leung (2001), Monz (2000), Williams and Marion (1992)

as trail depth. The most accurate and time-consuming approach is measuring the cross-sectional area between the trail surface and a taut line stretched between two fixed points on each side of the trail (Leonard & Whitney, 1977 in Hammitt & Cole, 1998) (Figure 7.3). Cross-sectional area is determined by measuring the distance between the two fixed points (L) and then taking at least 20 vertical measurements

($V_1 - V_{n+1}$). The formula following Figure 7.3, with these measurements included, gives the cross-sectional area.

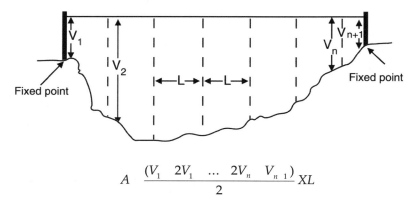

$$A = \frac{(V_1 + 2V_1 + \cdots + 2V_n + V_{n+1})}{2} \times L$$

Where A = Cross-sectional area
$V_1 - V_{n+1}$ = Vertical distance, with V_1 measured at the first fixed point, through to V_{n-1} measured on the other side of the trail at the other fixed point
L = Length of the horizontal line

Figure 7.3 Method for measuring trail cross-sectional area to determine trail erosion (derived from Hammitt and Cole 1998)

A far simpler and more rapid, but less accurate, way of measuring trail depth is to record the depth a trail has eroded below its construction level. Leung and Marion (1999a) used a range to describe the depth of each trail segment measured – 30–60 cm, 61–90 cm and so on. In his rapid survey work, Cole (1983b) measured the maximum depth of the trail every 0.32 km.

Sampling-based rapid surveys

In sampling-based rapid surveys, data on trail condition are collected at points a predetermined, set distance apart, a distance of 50–500 m being most common. The minimum number of sampling points is usually 100. The indicators most commonly used are trail width, width of bare ground, and maximum trail depth. Determination of the average width and depth of the trail system sampled and the portion with problems should be possible using these data. And, if the standard for the system is 'no more than 1% of all trails will be more than 30 cm deep', this can be easily monitored using this approach (Hammitt & Cole, 1998).

Problem-based rapid surveys

Problem-based rapid surveys let managers know where the problems are and can guide trail location, design and maintenance (Cole, 1983b). Such surveys require recording of the starting and end points of problems such as soil erosion/

trail depth, excessive root exposure, excessive trail width, wet soil, running water on the trail and multiple trails (Cole, 1983b; Leung & Marion, 1999a). Features of the site such as slope, the type of use (usually pedestrians and less often horses), track surface and drainage measures are also noted. Generally this approach relies on censusing the whole trail system. Recently however, Leung and Marion (1999a) sampled a representative portion and then extrapolated their findings to the whole trail system (Box 7.3).

Permanent point surveys

In contrast to rapid surveys is permanent point surveys (Table 7.6). They are time-consuming because of the need to locate, permanently mark and relocate each survey point. These points may be randomly distributed throughout the trail system or purposively located on portions of the trail where managers want to closely watch active erosion or where some new trail design (e.g. a new trail surface or drainage structure) is being tried. The results from surveying the randomly distributed points can be generalised to the whole trail system if a sufficient number of points are sampled. For purposive sampling this is not the case as only trail portions with features of interest have been surveyed. Cole (1983b) recommended measuring, at each survey point, the cross-sectional area between the trail surface and a taut line between two fixed points on either side of the trail (Figure 7.3). An increase in cross-sectional area between successive surveys indicates that soil loss has occurred.

Choosing a monitoring strategy

The choice depends on the objectives of the survey and the resources available. Generally, the choice will be between sampling- and problem-based rapid surveys (Table 7.6). The sampling-based approach requires a large number of sample points, which is potentially resource-intensive; however, to be meaningful, the problem-based approach requires a search of the whole trail system which also takes time. The latter approach seems more useful for managers as it provides details on where problems begin and end and can also record information on the effectiveness of management actions, such as dips and banks for controlling water movement.

Marion and Leung (2001) noted that point sampling and problem assessment methods yield distinctly different types of quantitative information. Point sampling provides more accurate and precise measures of trail characteristics that are continuous and frequent (e.g. tread width or exposed soil). The problem assessment method is a useful approach for monitoring trail characteristics that can be easily predefined and are infrequent (e.g. excessive width or secondary treads), particularly where information on the location of specific trail impact problems is needed. However, Leung and Marion (2000) have recently raised concerns that the usefulness of these data may be offset by their reduced precision due to subjectivity in defining where impact problems begin and end on a trail.

Surveying roads and vehicle tracks

Gravel roads and other unsealed vehicle tracks can be monitored, similarly to walk trails, using rapid survey approaches. Walker (1991) developed a monitoring

Box 7.3 A rapid monitoring system for trails in Great Smoky Mountains National Park, USA

As described in Box 7.2, Great Smoky Mountains National Park, on the border of Tennessee and North Carolina (Figure 7.1), is one of the most visited national parks in the United States. The park has 1496 km of official trails, with two-thirds of this system open for horse use. Permit data indicate more than 10,000 animals annually are part of groups on overnight stays. In 1985 the number of day hikers was estimated at 700,000 (Leung & Marion, 1999a).

Leung and Marion (1999a) used a problem-based rapid survey approach, the trail problem-assessment method (TPAM), to document the locations and extent of various trail problems, in particular excessively muddy, wide or eroded trails. They surveyed 35% of the park's total trail length, arguing this was a sufficiently large and representative sample to allow conclusions to be drawn of relevance to the whole trail system. A total of 23 'indicators' were assessed, grouped in three categories – inventory indicators (e.g. use type such as horse riding and trail width), resource condition indicators (e.g. soil erosion, root exposure and wet soil) and design and maintenance indicators (e.g. grades > 20% and the effectiveness of water bars).

The data from TPAM provided managers with locational information on all trail problems and maintenance features such as drainage dips and water bars. Trail maintenance crews can now be directed to sections with erosion and/or wet soil. The most common impact was soil erosion, with 4.6% of the trails surveyed with erosion exceeding 30 cm in depth. Running water, wet soil and rutted tracks were the main contributors to excessive trail width (affecting 0.7% of surveyed trails) and multiple trails (1.8% of trails).

The TPAM also allowed several other simple assessments. Lineal measurements of the extent of a problem could be used to determine for an indicator whether its standard had been exceeded. For example, if the standard for wet soil is 'no wet segment to exceed 30 m in length', then this monitoring system can give the number of segments where this value has been exceeded. This method also allowed comparison between different trails and lengths of trail by converting the number of occurrences of a problem to m/km or a percentage.

By standardising the data, different trail lengths can be characterised and compared in terms of user type, trail width, erosion problems, and design and maintenance conditions. Such information is vital for planning and managing trails. From this characterisation it was apparent that the eastern portion of the Great Smoky Mountains National Park had the poorest trails, with the most prevalent problems being wet soil and excessive width. Both problems were a result of poorly designed trails located close to streams on poorly drained soils. Poor trail conditions such as these lead to trail widening and multiple parallel tracks as hikers attempt to avoid wet areas. High horse use of the area has also exacerbated the problems (Leung & Marion, 1999a).

Table 7.7 Rating scale for monitoring gravel roads in natural areas

Class	Description
5 (Excellent)	Excellent surface condition and ride.
4 (Good)	Slight corrugations.
3 (Fair)	Good crown (7.5–15 cm). Ditches present on >50% of roadway. Moderate corrugations (2.5–7.5 cm) over 10–25% of the area. None or slight rutting.
2 (Poor)	Little or no crown (<7.5 cm). Adequate ditches on <50% of roadway. Culverts partly full of debris. Moderate to severe corrugations (>7.5 cm deep) over 25% of the area. Moderate rutting (2.5–7.5 cm) over 10–25% of the area. Moderate potholes (5–10 cm) over 10–25% of the area.
1 (Failed)	No crown or road is bowl-shaped with extensive ponding. Little if any ditching. Filled or damaged culverts. Severe rutting (>7.5 cm) over 25% of the area. Severe potholes (>10 cm) over 25% of the area.

Derived from Walker (1991)

system for gravel roads in Wisconsin. First, he divided the roadway system into segments of one mile or more (i.e. at least 1.6 kilometres) based on similar function, traffic volume and surface thickness. Each segment has its geometry (e.g. road width) and maintenance history recorded and a rating is generated based on the major factors likely to influence road performance – road crown, drainage and adequacy of the gravel layer. A road with a good crown falls 1–2 cm per 30 cm from its centre to its edges. Poor drainage is characterised by ponding, flooding, erosion and collapsed or silted culverts and bridges. Evidence of an inadequate gravel layer is rutting, corrugations (washboarding) and potholes. If the time and skills are available, the thickness of the gravel layer can be measured.

A simple 5-point rating scale is used to assign a value to each road segment (Table 7.7). The information and ratings can then be used to assign maintenance priorities to road segments. This system can easily be used to assess 30 to 65 kilometres of gravel roads per day (Walker, 1991).

Water bodies

Water, whether lakes, streams, estuaries or the ocean, attract people resulting in facilities such as resorts, campgrounds, roads and trails being located on their edges and in some instances over the top of them (e.g. pontoons over coral reefs). These environments also provide habitat for a wealth of plants and animals. Water quality can be adversely affected by nutrients, pathogens and sediments moving into the water (see Chapter 3 for details on impacts). Monitoring is essential for human and ecosystem health.

Design of the sampling programme is an important consideration. From the data collected managers need to be able to accurately measure, and differentiate from other causes, changes due to natural area tourism. For most natural area tourism developments, the impacts are likely to be localised. For a resort or floating pontoon over a coral reef, for example, sampling should be conducted in the immediate vicinity. An undisturbed but environmentally similar site should also be sampled to provide a control. Warnken and Buckley (2000) make a strong case for resource monitoring at the impact and control site before the development occurs, during construction and then once the facility is operational. Very often lack of money, forethought or time precludes predevelopment monitoring.

Hammitt and Cole (1998) noted that the frequency of sampling and the number of samples taken can only be decided once some idea of data variability has been obtained. For example, bacterial contamination from human waste varies greatly depending on the time of year and the flushing effects of precipitation. Sampling must be frequent enough to pick up these variations.

Monitoring techniques and standards for drinking water and for swimming are known and widely used. The usual measure is the number of coliform bacteria. These bacteria are found in human faeces and are regarded as a good indicator of bacterial contamination. Numerous physical and chemical water quality indicators can be measured including phosphorus, nitrogen, pH and dissolved oxygen. Other aquatic elements that may be sampled include plankton, algae, macroinvertebrates and fish. Where road or trail construction and use may lead to increased sedimentation, monitoring of aquatic fauna to determine the impacts of suspended solids may be useful (Box 7.4).

Box 7.4 Monitoring stream amphibians in California's redwood reserves, Humboldt County, California

Road construction activities accompanied by a storm resulted in a large volume of sediments moving into pristine streams of the redwood forests of Prairie Creek Redwoods State Park in northern California (Figure 7.1). Road construction and maintenance are often a central feature of managing natural area tourism. Welsh Jr and Ollivier (1998) selected amphibians as an indicator of environmental stress because their populations remain stable in stable environments and yet their dual life histories, highly specialised physiological adaptations and specific microhabitat requirements mean they are highly vulnerable to disturbance.

Following the large intrusion of sediments into the Prairie Creek system, resulting from construction of the Redwood National Park highway bypass, Welsh Jr and Ollivier (1998) sampled five of the seven streams affected and five unimpacted streams interspersed among the impacted ones. Three species of amphibians were present in sufficient numbers to provide useful data – tailed frogs (*Ascaphus truei, larvae*), Pacific giant salamanders (*Dicamptodon tenebrosus, paedomorphs and larvae*) and southern torrent salamanders (*Rhyacotriton variegatus, adults and larvae*).

To sample the amphibians, these researchers identified five stream habitat types – pools, glides and runs, riffles, step runs, and step pools. Fine sediment depths were measured for pools in both impacted and unimpacted streams to determine if sediment loads had changed following the storm. They then randomly sampled within each of these types, counting the number of amphibians in numerous 'belt transects' 0.6 m wide from bank to bank.

In total, 3.6 km of impacted streams, using 137 belt transects, and 3.2 km of unimpacted streams, using 130 belt transects, were sampled. A total of 540 amphibians were captured. Welsh Jr and Ollivier (1998) found that fine sediment depths in the impacted pools ranged from 0.1 to 25.0 cm compared with 0.0 to 4.0 cm in the unimpacted pools. All three species were found in significantly lower densities in the impacted streams. The authors concluded that amphibians provide a useful and reliable indicator of environmental disturbances.

Although little has been written about monitoring the effects of tourism on marine environments, several marine monitoring programmes of relevance to natural area tourism exist. The Reef Check programme aims to document human impacts, including those originating from natural area tourism, on coral reefs worldwide (Hodgson, 1999). Data collection by recreational divers trained and led by marine scientists centres on three belt transects 20 m long by 5 m wide. Information is collected on the site; fish species, especially those targeted by spearfishers and aquarium collectors; invertebrates, particularly those taken for food or collected as curios; and reef substrate types (Global Coral Reef Monitoring Network, 2000). Transects are surveyed at two depth contours, 3 and 10 m. Photographing and/or videoing the length of each transect is recommended.

Several similar monitoring programmes have been developed in Australia. Eye on the Reef, developed for use by marine tourist operators on the Great Barrier Reef (Figure 7.1), collects data on distinctive marine mammals such as dugongs and whales and ecological disturbances like coral bleaching and algal blooms (Anon., 1999b). Again, it has not been specifically developed to monitor natural area tourism but could reveal the impacts of such use.

The Western Australian Marine Community Monitoring Manual (CALM & AMCS, 2000) as well as guiding monitoring of the physical and biological environments, prescribes several ways of monitoring the social environment. Their approach relies on volunteers, trained to ensure that monitoring is undertaken effectively and safely (CALM & AMCS, 2000). Elements of the physical and biological environments to be monitored include beaches, water clarity and temperature, seagrasses, mangroves, algal blooms, fish, marine mammals, seabirds and marine pests. Their approaches to social monitoring are briefly covered below in visitor monitoring.

Monitoring Visitors to Natural Areas

To re-cap from earlier in this chapter, monitoring of visitors to natural areas can provide information on use of a natural area, use of specific sites, visitor characteristics and visitor outcomes (Table 7.8). Such monitoring provides data for management, planning, resource allocation, public accountability, and interpretation and

Table 7.8 Summary of uses of visitor monitoring data

Monitoring focus	Data required	Main uses of data*	Data collection technique
Visitor use of an area	Visitor numbers, mode of arrival, entry and exit points	• Making resource allocation decisions • Public accountability	Automated counters, guesstimates, entrance records (e.g. ticket sales), manual counts, visitor books, tour records, aerial photos
Site use by visitors	Sites visited, seasonal use patterns, group size, length of stay, frequency of visits, activities undertaken	• Planning – management plans, planning frameworks (e.g. LAC) and site design • Making resource allocation decisions • Routine management, especially ameliorating impacts	Questionnaires, telephone surveys, personal interviews, field observations
Visitor profiling (characteristics)	Demographic and socio-economic attributes of visitors, reasons for visiting, attitudes, motivations, preferences, expectations, information needs	• Marketing and interpretation • Planning (as given above)	Questionnaires, telephone surveys, personal interviews, focus groups and other interactive techniques
Visitor outcomes	Satisfactions, disappointments, suggestions and comments	• Routine management, especially ameliorating impacts • Planning (as given above)	Questionnaires, telephone surveys, personal interviews, focus groups and other interactive techniques

* For 'Main uses of the data', only the most important uses for each monitoring focus are given, to make the information in this table as accessible and meaningful as possible, while recognising that visitor use of an area through to visitor outcomes all need data for planning and resource allocation.
Derived from CALM (2000c), Cope *et al.* (2000), Pitts and Smith (1993)

marketing. Although visitor monitoring provides a wealth of information, managers regularly place the natural environment and its management ahead of visitor management (McArthur, 1994). The reasons are both philosophical and practical. Often, managers find it is easier to manage natural resources rather than visitors, especially as most of their training has centred on the natural environment. Also, managing visitors is difficult because of the lack of information on the relationships between visitors and the natural environment. Practically, visitor monitoring may not be done as it generally has a lower priority than other activities, such as replacing old facilities or building new ones.

Sampling design is an important consideration, as it is in monitoring resource impacts. The design chosen depends on the objectives of the monitoring programme. Generally, the population of concern will be all visitors to the natural area. Visitor monitoring then relies on sampling part of this population and drawing conclusions about the whole population from this sample. Pitts and Smith (1993) regarded the lack of scientific sampling strategies as the greatest weakness of Australian visitor monitoring efforts. However, this problem is unlikely to be restricted to Australia. They also emphasised that sampling must represent the full diversity of the user population, while acknowledging that selecting representative samples is notoriously difficult. This difficulty stems from users being widely dispersed, mobile and engaged in diverse activities.

If more general information from non-users as well as users of natural areas is required, then the population of interest will be much larger. Again, the same principle as outlined above applies; sampling must be designed to represent the diversity of the whole population. To assess future demand and the community's perceived benefits of natural areas, it is critical to sample non-users as well as users. The remainder of this section focuses on visitors themselves. Specific attention is paid to the monitoring required to determine visitors' perceptions of their and others' impacts on the natural environment.

Visitor monitoring techniques

Visitor monitoring techniques range from counting visitors, through questionnaires, telephone surveys and personal interviews, to focus groups and other interactive techniques. Table 7.9 summarises and discusses these techniques in four groups: counting visitors; questionnaires and personal interviews; observing visitors; and focus groups and other interactive techniques.

Counting visitors

Counting visitors is the most widespread form of visitor monitoring in natural areas. Automated infrared, photoelectric and seismic pad counters have been used on walk trails (Cope *et al.*, 2000; Watson *et al.*, 1998). On roads and vehicle tracks, counters are triggered by vehicle wheels passing over an air-filled tube (pneumatic tube counters) or an inducted loop (inducted loop axle counters). More recently, traffic classifiers have been used. These have double pneumatic tubes and record and classify vehicle types, speeds, direction of travel, time and date (CALM, 2000c). All automated counters require careful calibration and frequent checking. Also, deductions must be made for management staff otherwise visitor numbers can be over-estimated.

Other less sophisticated methods of counting visitors are in widespread use. Numbers may be guesstimated by staff or volunteers, or extrapolated from entry passes purchased or numbers self-registering at trailheads. Manual counts by staff or

Table 7.9 Summary of visitor monitoring techniques

Visitor monitoring technique	Advantages	Disadvantages	Application
Counting visitors – includes automated counters, guesstimates, entrance records (e.g. ticket sales), manual counts, visitor books, tour records, aerial photos	Provides simple measure of extent of use of a natural area; automated counters are one of the most reliable ways of estimating numbers	Most methods provide estimates only; automated counters are expensive to purchase and some may have significant margins of error	Traffic counters can be used on most roads used by vehicles; aerial photos useful for marine areas and difficult-to-access locations such as beach dunes
Questionnaires and personal interviews – includes site-based, mail and/or telephone data collection	Questionnaires provide comprehensive information on visitors, their activities and expectations; they are widely used making results comparable with those obtained elsewhere	Can be expensive to design, administer and analyse	Best used where detailed information on visitors and their visit characteristics, preferences and expectations are required for planning and impact management
Observing visitors – used to count numbers and observe behaviour	Useful for counting numbers when other means are not available; observing behaviour can be correlated with other techniques, especially self-reporting by visitors	Counts of numbers approximate only; observing behaviour is expensive, training of observers is essential	Best used where information on numbers and behaviour is unavailable via other means
Focus groups and other interactive techniques – users brought together to provide data, often on more than one occasion	Efficient means of accessing a range of ideas at one time (focus group) or seeking determination and agreement over time on indicators and standards (task force)	Extremely time-consuming to organise and administer, data may be difficult to analyse if consensus is not reached	Using task forces only warranted for large complex natural areas with multiple stakeholders

Derived from CALM (2000c), Cole (1997)

volunteers are another possible approach, although usually this is only done on selected occasions. Cavana and Moore (1988) manually counted the numbers, and recorded the plates, of cars entering and leaving the entrances/exits of Fitzgerald River National Park (Figure 7.1). Their objective was determining total visitor numbers over the busy Easter long weekend, as well as mapping visitor movement patterns.

Data can also be collected from tour operators through logbooks and receipts. Information on numbers of visitors accessing certain sites or engaged in activities such as whale watching as part of an organised tour can then be collated. Similar data on sites used and numbers involved can be obtained from associations and clubs where permits are required for using natural areas. In Western Australia for example, clubs using natural areas for orienteering (a cross-country navigational sport) require approval from land management agencies. This gives managers information on the areas accessed, plus they can estimate numbers knowing the levels of club membership.

For marine areas and difficult-to-access places like sand dunes and beaches, aerial photography or visual observations from a small plane allows visitor numbers to be counted. Usually, numbers are extrapolated from the number of vehicles or vessels recorded. In marine parks aerial surveys can give rapid estimates of the number of boats and where boat use is concentrated. Aerial photography has routinely been used to monitor camping activity adjacent to the beaches of Fraser Island off the eastern coast of Australia (Hockings & Twyford, 1997) (Figure 7.1).

Questionnaires and personal interviews

Questionnaires are widely used to collect information on visitors, their activities and expectations in relation to natural areas. Personal interviews are less common, primarily because they are more time-consuming. Attention to sampling design is important in both approaches because conclusions are usually being drawn for the whole population of users. To make these conclusions as robust as possible a large sample size is needed as well as equally representing all groups within the population. Babbie (1992) suggested if we want to be 95% confident that the results are within 5% of their values for the population, then a sample size of at least 400 should be the aim. If a response rate of only 50–60% is likely, as is often the case with questionnaire-based surveys (Neuman, 1994), then at least 670–800 questionnaires should be distributed.

A variety of means of distributing questionnaires exists. Cole *et al.* (1997) surveyed visitors on-site, asking two members from each group leaving wilderness areas in the Cascade Mountains of Washington and Oregon to fill out a short 10-minute questionnaire. Roggenbuck *et al.* (1993) interviewed all parties entering and leaving four wilderness areas (Cohutta, Georgia; Caney Creek, Arkansas; Upland Island, Texas; Rattlesnake, Montana; Figure 7.1) and having obtained contact names and addresses sent party members a mailback questionnaire. Chin *et al.* (2000), in their survey of visitors to Bako National Park in Borneo (Figure 7.1), handed out questionnaires at the park office, accommodation areas and canteen, areas most frequented by visitors and then collected them once completed (Box 7.5).

Box 7.5 Using questionnaires to monitor visitors to Bako National Park, Borneo

Bako National Park, 37 km east of the capital city of Kuching (Figure 7.1), was the first national park gazetted in Sarawak. Attractions include its diverse coastal and forest ecosystems and abundant wildlife. Three species of monkey are found in the park – the proboscis monkey (*Nasalis larvatus*) inhabiting mangrove swamps and found only in Borneo, and the silver leaf monkey (*Presbytis cristata*) and common long-tailed macaque (*Macaca fascicularis*). Facilities include the park office, information centre, canteen, accommodation and camping ground, and the jetty where visitors arrive by longboat. Visitor activities include enjoying nature, hiking, sightseeing, observing wildlife, relaxing and photography (Chin *et al.*, 2000).

Visitors were surveyed using a questionnaire handed out and returned in the park. It sought information on visitor and visit characteristics, activities undertaken, and visitor perceptions of impacts and management strategies. Visitors were young – most were aged between 16 and 40 – and their activities centred on enjoying nature. The environmental conditions of greatest concern to visitors were litter, damage to natural vegetation and erosion along walk trails. Very few visitors were concerned about visitor numbers or the size of groups encountered. These results suggest that suitable indicators, all of them environmental rather than social, could be litter, damage to natural vegetation and erosion along walk trails. In terms of management strategies to address these problems, those surveyed favoured most of the strategies suggested, from education to limiting the overall number of visitors (Chin *et al.*, 2000). Least favoured was providing more visitor facilities, probably because visitors to natural areas prefer little to no development (Buckley & Pannell, 1990).

Morin *et al.* (1997) used trailhead registration details from Nuyts Wilderness in Western Australia (Figure 7.1) to mail out questionnaires. Cavana and Moore (1988) provided boxes at entrances/exits to Fitzgerald River National Park where questionnaires could be collected and returned.

For questionnaires and interviews, the more personalised the level of contact, the higher the response rate. Personal interviews have the highest response rate, followed by questionnaires handed out and back on-site, while mail-out mail-back questionnaires are much lower. Telephone surveys have an intermediate response rate between interviews and questionnaires. Surveys should be designed and conducted to get the highest possible response rate, given the resources available. A higher response rate gives a larger sample, meaning that the survey findings can be more confidently generalised to the whole visitor population. It also means that one or more groups are unlikely to have been omitted, with omissions potentially biasing the results. Response rates of 50–60% are regarded as acceptable, although a higher rate is preferable (Neuman, 1994).

How questionnaires and interviews are conducted, presented and worded all affect visitor responses. Many useful social research texts exist, such as Frankfort-Nachmias and Nachmias (1992) and Neuman (1994), that should be consulted before commencing this type of work. A number of design choices need to be made, an important one being whether questions are open- or close-ended. Open-ended questions often provide more information, but they can be more difficult to analyse than close-ended ones. Close-ended questions are easier to analyse but may bias the results by limiting the choice of responses visitors have. Also, if questions are not carefully worded, they can lead or even threaten respondents.

Questionnaires and personal interviews place strong reliance on visitors' perceptions as a data source. Using perceptions must be accompanied by several understandings. First, they are a valid data source given that a central part of natural area management is addressing visitors' perceptions regarding the experiences they have and are seeking. Second, differences may exist between managers and visitors regarding the perceived acceptability of impacts. Martin and McCool (1989), working in the United States, found that managers were more sensitive than visitors to bare ground, while visitors found tree damage and fire rings more objectionable than managers. These findings suggest that if managers choose indicators in isolation from visitors they may chose the wrong ones or ones of lesser importance to visitors. Therefore data on visitor preferences and perceptions are an essential input to natural area management.

Observing visitors

Visitor numbers and behaviour at specific sites and along walk trails are most often the focus of this monitoring technique (Table 7.9). Visitor numbers at the popular Matilda Bay Reserve on the Swan River in Perth, Western Australia, were estimated at 400,000 per year using observation surveys by rangers (Hammond, pers. comm., 2000) (Figure 7.1). Observations can also be conducted by other trained observers and visitors themselves. Cole *et al.* (1997), in studying trail monitoring, found trained observers to be more accurate in their estimates of the number of encounters between groups of visitors than visitors themselves. It appeared that self-reporting under-estimated the number of encounters.

For marine areas, observing and counting the number of people at a site has been recommended as part of marine monitoring programmes. The Marine Community Monitoring Manual (CALM and AMCS, 2000) gives details on monitoring boat use by counting and recording the number of boat trailers near boat ramps and the number of boats at popular sites such as anchorages, fishing and scuba diving spots, and islands. Monitoring is suggested during peak use times.

Focus groups and other interactive techniques

Focus groups bring people together to 'focus' on an issue. Trained facilitators guide, record and analyse discussions within the group. A focus group made up of users of a natural area could be convened to determine indicators and standards for monitoring. Experience with groups involved in providing input to environmental management suggests they need to meet on a number of occasions if consensus is to be reached (Moore & Lee, 1999).

A widely used means of developing indicators and standards is through task forces established as part of Limits of Acceptable Change planning activities (Watson & Cole, 1992). Often these groups work together over a number of years. Important products of their interactions are indicators and standards agreed to and supported by the group. Further details on task force activities are provided in a later section on setting standards for indicators.

Combined systems

To provide the complex array of information on visitors and their activities needed to manage natural area tourism, a combination of techniques is likely to be used by managers. Data are needed to prepare management plans, design campgrounds and other facility areas, demonstrate outcomes, arrange budgets, schedule maintenance, provide interpretation, evaluate performance and undertake business planning (CALM, 2000c). Box 7.6 overviews the integrated approach taken by CALM to visitor monitoring, as an example of applying a suite of visitor monitoring techniques.

Box 7.6 Vistat: An integrated approach to visitor monitoring by the Department of Conservation and Land Management, Western Australia

The Department of Conservation and Land Management (CALM) in Western Australia manages over 22.5 million ha of land and water, including many of the state's premier natural area tourism attractions. Over 800 sites, attracting in excess of 9 million visits annually are managed for tourism and recreation. The aim of the Visitor Information Statistics (VISTAT) programme is to provide the visitor information needed to make strategic decisions in all facets of planning, funding, developing, managing and monitoring nature-based tourism and recreation (CALM, 2000c).

Because CALM reports annually on visitor numbers and satisfaction to the State Parliament, collection of these data is a central concern of the VISTAT programme. Total annual visitor numbers are obtained from automated traffic counters/classifiers and where these devices are not yet in place, from estimates based on observations and entry tickets. Visitor numbers from individual areas are summed to give total number of visitors. A long-term aim of VISTAT is to have every visited site automatically monitored using traffic classifiers.

Visitor feedback forms provide information on levels of satisfaction derived by visitors, and visitor characteristics and activities. These forms are handed out annually at 21 tourism/recreation sites selected as representative of the recreation opportunities offered by CALM: 10% of these sites are primitive, 30% intermediate and 60% developed. These percentages reflect the proportional levels of use of CALM areas, with most visitors being recorded at developed sites. A visitor satisfaction index is calculated for each site, based on the responses to a subset of questions from the feedback form. The indices are averaged to give an overall visitor satisfaction index for the Department.

VISTAT also describes observation studies as an additional, optional monitoring activity. The guidelines for VISTAT also include personal contact and interviews, telephone surveys, aerial photographs, visitor books and logbooks, and other recorded data as possible visitor monitoring techniques (CALM, 2000c).

Data collected can be entered locally or centrally to CALM's recreation and tourism information system (RATIS). Data collection and entry are standardised through provision of data collection forms and data entry screens. Data are then processed and collated within RATIS.

Choosing a monitoring strategy

As with other forms of monitoring, the choice of techniques depends on the objectives guiding the monitoring programme. The combined approach of recording visitor numbers by automated means and questionnaires focusing on issues of management concern, whether they be visitor satisfaction or impacts and their management, seems an efficient and effective way of monitoring visitors. The choice of technique can influence the information obtained. Cole *et al.* (1997) noted from their work on six high-use wilderness destinations in the Cascade Mountains of Washington and Oregon (Figure 7.1), that estimates of encounters with other groups varied between visitors, trained observers in the field and wilderness rangers. If perceptions of the number of groups encountered by visitors are of central interest, then the visitors' data are most useful. Otherwise, the most accurate measures are from trained observers. They found rangers' reports less useful because they measured their encounters not those of visitors.

Setting Standards for Indicators

Having standards is a crucial aspect of managing natural areas for tourism. Without standards it is impossible to tell if impacts have reached unacceptable levels jeopardising the values that attracted visitors in the first place. The planning frameworks detailed in Chapter 4 rely on standards for the indicators identified. It is only when these standards have been exceeded and the impacts become unacceptable, that the management strategies detailed in Chapter 5 become necessary.

Managers are often loath to set standards, generally because data on impacts and their causes are lacking and they are concerned about the political consequences of poorly informed management decisions. As with many aspects of environmental management, it reasonable to make a 'best guess', selecting a standard based on the best available information and then modifying it as new information becomes available. The political dimension can be managed by ensuring standards are determined with visitor input. It is also important to consult visitors because they may have different standards to managers (Martin & McCool, 1989). To help deal with uncertainty, the Tourism Optimisation Management Model relies on an acceptable range for indicators, rather than a single standard. For example, for the indicator 'proportion of visitors who were very satisfied with their overall visit' the acceptable range is 95–100% of respondents (Manidis Roberts Consultants, 1997).

The role of perceptions

Visitors' perceptions play a key role in setting standards as well as identifying indicators. Resource and social indicators can be selected by asking visitors what conditions contributed to their experience. Indicators can then be derived to measure these conditions. Once indicators have been identified, visitors can be asked about potential standards. Questionnaires are a common approach used to elicit this information, as well as deliberations by task forces convened as part of Limits of Acceptable Change (LAC) planning processes for natural areas. Brief descriptions of these two approaches follow.

Questionnaires can be used to identify what resource and social conditions influenced the quality of visitors' experiences (Roggenbuck *et al.*, 1993). The answers to these questions give possible indicators, such as the amount of litter, vegetation loss and the number of people in other groups. Visitors can then be asked to provide maximum acceptable levels, before their experience would be changed, for a list of indicators. Box 7.7 describes this approach as applied in Nuyts Wilderness Area in south-western Australia (Morin *et al.*, 1997) (Figure 7.1). These authors used one questionnaire, others, such as Manning *et al.* (1996), used two; the first to collect information on conditions and possible indicators and the second to determine standards for the indicators identified in the first phase.

Box 7.7 Using a questionnaire to identify indicators and standards for Nuyts Wilderness Area, Western Australia

Nuyts Wilderness, with an area of only 4500 ha, lies on the south coast of Western Australia (Figure 7.1). It is used for day trips and overnight stays, with activities including appreciating nature, walking for exercise, solitude, viewing wildlife and photography. A questionnaire was mailed to visitors who had filled in the logbook at the trailhead. Included were questions seeking information on visit and visitor characteristics, preferences regarding current conditions and management strategies, and maximum levels of acceptable impact for a number of environmental and social indicators (Morin *et al.*, 1997).

Most visitors were aged 26–60, with activities centring on enjoying nature. The environmental conditions of greatest concern were the amount of litter, inadequate disposal of human waste, presence of wildlife, erosion of trails leading to the beaches, vegetation loss at the beaches, and tree damage at the campsite. Visitors were less concerned about visitor numbers or the size of groups encountered than environmental conditions such as vegetation loss and tree damage. These results suggest a number of potential indicators. Most management strategies were supported, with education and rehabilitation of degraded areas most favoured.

Standards were requested for a list of impacts including trees damaged by humans, vegetation loss/bare ground, number and size of groups encountered, litter, human-made structures (e.g. signs) and fire rings. Standards acceptable to 50% of visitors were calculated from the results (Roggenbuck *et al.*, 1993). The standard for trees damaged, acceptable to 50% of visitors, was two trees. Therefore, if damage to more than two trees occurred this would be an unacceptable impact and warrant management intervention. The standard for group size was six people or less per group. For several indicators the standard given by respondents varied depending on location. For the area of bare ground, up to 11 m² was acceptable at the campsite but only up to 3 m² was acceptable at the beaches (Morin *et al.*, 1997). These data provided managers with indicators and standards for an ongoing monitoring programme.

Manning *et al.* (1996) and Manning *et al.* (1998) used photographs in their questionnaires to help people visualise different standards. Manning *et al.*'s (1998) work in Acadia National Park in Maine (Figure 7.1) focused on use of carriage roads built in the early 1990s and today enjoyed by thousands of hikers and bikers. Their research had two phases – the first to identify indicators and the second, where photographs were used, to determine standards. The two indicators identified in the first stage were numbers of visitors on the carriage roads and problem behaviours such as bikes passing without warning. A series of photographs showing different numbers of visitors, from zero to 30, along a 100 m section of the carriage way was used to determine the standard for visitor numbers. Visitors were shown the photographs in random order and asked to rate their acceptability on a scale from minus 4 (very unacceptable) to plus 4 (very acceptable). The results indicate that visitors find it acceptable to see up to 14 people in the 100 m section.

Task forces are another means of setting standards for indicators. Such groups can work together over time to identify not only indicators but standards as well. This approach is extremely time-consuming and resource-intensive but does allow managers to access visitor knowledge on what conditions are important as well as the standards that can potentially maintain conditions at levels regarded as acceptable. For the Bob Marshall Wilderness Complex (Figure 7.1), the Limits of Acceptable Change Task Force worked together for five years and developed a suite of indicators and standards applicable to four zones / opportunity classes across the area (Box 7.8, Table 7.10). Part of the process involved field trips enabling indicators and standards to be visualised and discussed in the field. Such an approach helps address Williams *et al.*'s (1992) concern that assigning numerical standards is problematic because it is often too abstract or hypothetical to be meaningful.

One of the problems with setting standards is the great variations in levels of visitor use throughout the year. In temperate southern Australia, peak use of natural areas occurs at long weekends and over Easter, predominantly in late summer, autumn and spring. In the United States, the summer months see peaks in visitor numbers to natural areas, although some areas peak in winter with the onset of snow-based activities. To address these peak use periods and numbers, which are nevertheless limited in duration, standards with an attached probability have been used, for example three parties or less will be encountered per day on a trail for 80% of the time. This allows that, for 20% of the time during peak use periods, this standard will be exceeded but the level of encounters will not be regarded as unacceptable. Table 7.10 provides examples of these probability-based standards for the Bob Marshall Wilderness Complex.

Box 7.8 Using a task force to identify indicators and standards for the Bob Marshall Wilderness Complex, Montana

As noted in Chapter 4, the Bob Marshall Wilderness Complex is the most often used example of the Limits of Acceptable Change planning process. A central feature of this process was defining indicators and standards. This wilderness complex covers 682,000 ha of the Rocky Mountains in the north-western United States (Figure 7.1). Further details on the area are provided in Box 4.2 in Chapter 4. In the early 1980s a task force was convened representing visitors and other stakeholders as well as land managers from the US Forest Service (Stokes, 1987, 1990). A central task for the group was determining indicators and standards.

The task force's choices were influenced by field trips, lengthy discussions within meetings and members' personal experiences. Members agreed that both biophysical and social indicators were important. Area of bare soil, number of damaged trees and number of human impacted sites per 290 ha (640 acres) were the indicators chosen for campsite conditions. Number of trail encounters and others camped within site and sound were the social indicators. To determine standards and set a baseline for ongoing monitoring, the indicators were surveyed by stakeholders and the US Forest Service.

The standards selected vary between opportunity classes, with higher standards for more remote and pristine areas (Table 7.10). These differences reflect visitors' perceptions that impacts are less acceptable at more pristine/remote sites. For example, in the most pristine zone (Opportunity Class I) the standard is 1 human impacted site per 290 ha compared to 6 sites in the most developed zone (Opportunity Class IV).

To allow for short periods with high levels of visitor use, a probability was attached to the social standards. For example, an 80% probability was attached to the trail encounters standard. For a moderately used zone, for example Opportunity Class II, the standard was an 80% probability of 1 or fewer encounters per day. This can be interpreted as, if more than 1 encounter was experienced for up to 20% of the time, such as over peak use periods, then the indicator was still regarded as within standard.

Standards will also vary depending on the zone or opportunity class. They will be more relaxed in more developed zones where more signs of human presence are accepted. The task of monitoring is made easier if the same set of indicators can be measured across a natural area or system of natural areas, although the standards will vary between zones. Box 7.8 and Table 7.10 use the Bob Marshall example to illustrate variations in standards between opportunity classes.

Environmental auditing

Environmental auditing is monitoring and evaluating the environmental performance of agencies and companies. Most commonly, the focus is determining

Table 7.10 Standards for social and biophysical indicators for the Bob Marshall Wilderness Complex

Indicator	Opportunity Class I	Opportunity Class II	Opportunity Class III	Opportunity Class IV
Social				
Number of trail encounters with other parties	80% probability of 0 encounters per day	80% probability of 1 or fewer encounters per day	80% probability of 3 or fewer encounters per day	80% probability of 5 or fewer encounters per day
Number of other parties camped within sight or continuous sound	80% probability of 0 parties per day	80% probability of 0 parties per day	80% probability of 1 or 0 parties per day	80% probability of 3 or fewer parties per day
Biophysical				
Area of barren core (ft^2)	100	500	1000	2000
Number of damaged trees or trees with exposed roots	5	15	25	30
Number of human impacted sites per 640 acre area	1	2	3	6

Derived from Forest Service (1985)

compliance with regulatory requirements and environmental policies and standards (Ding & Pigram, 1996). As a self-regulatory initiative, such auditing contributes to environmental management by providing feedback about overall environmental performance as well as specific problems requiring action. Environmental audits/eco-audits are not yet widely applied in the tourism industry (Ding and Pigram, 1996; Trauer, 1998).

Ding and Pigram (1996) outlined an audit process for monitoring and evaluating the environmental performance of beach resorts which is also applicable to natural area tourism. Their process has 12 steps: (1) preparing to audit; (2) determining objectives, scope and foci; (3) understanding the management system; (4) determining regulations, policy requirements and standards; (5) surveying and assessing; (6) identifying key environmental issues; (7) identifying key environmental impact areas; (8) gathering and evaluating evidence; (9) determining compliance; (10) reviewing findings; (11) developing actions; and (12) preparing report. Unlike much of the monitoring discussed in this chapter, environmental auditing is at an organisational rather than a site or individual visitor level. It is monitoring how administrative systems and managers are performing rather than changes in the field. The hope is that if organisations and their staff are complying with environmental policies and standards then natural areas and the tourists using them will also benefit.

Integrated Approaches

An integrated approach to monitoring natural area tourism includes monitoring visitor impacts and visitors themselves. Integrated approaches have been used in wilderness areas in the Cascade Mountains in the Washington and Oregon (Cole, 1997; Cole *et al.*, 1997) and Warren National Park in Western Australia (Smith, 1998) (Figure 7.1). The Cascade Mountains study focused on six high-use destination areas. Rapid survey methods were used to quantify the areal extent and degree of impact of recreation on trails, campsites and lakeshores. Visitors leaving each wilderness were asked to fill in a short questionnaire about their characteristics, expectations and responses to conditions as well as the number of other parties they had encountered. In the Warren National Park study both rapid and detailed impact measurements were made, plus a detailed questionnaire distributed to visitors (Box 7.9).

Integrated approaches are not widespread, with either visitor impacts or less often visitors themselves the focus of data collection. An integrated approach seems essential if standards are to be provided for environmental and social conditions of importance to visitors and managers. Monitoring of environmental impacts is crucial to understand and make explicit changes in the natural environment resulting from visitor use. Standards are then needed to advise managers when actions are needed to ameliorate impacts. Meaningful standards, and an understanding of the desired conditions that underpin them, can be obtained by asking visitors. Such standards should also include recognition of the ecological significant of an impact, especially in relation to the rarity or irreplaceability of the attribute being impacted (Cole & Landres, 1996). Visitor monitoring over time provides access to visitors' perceptions regarding standards and a ready means of revising them as more information becomes available.

Conclusion

This chapter has comprehensively reviewed monitoring for natural area tourism, moving from general considerations such as the reasons for monitoring and guiding principles, through to the plethora of techniques available. Techniques for monitoring impacts on the natural environment, as well as monitoring visitors themselves, were outlined. Depending on the objectives for resource monitoring and the resources available, either rapid or more time-consuming measurement-based approaches can be applied. Visitor monitoring can range from simple counts of numbers to personal interviews and task forces. For all the approaches outlined, sampling considerations were given as well as ways of assessing the data obtained. Suggestions for choosing between techniques were also made.

The last part of the chapter describes setting standards for indicators, a process

Box 7.9 Developing an integrated monitoring programme for Warren National Park, Western Australia

Warren National Park, including old growth eucalypt forest and the picturesque Warren River, occupies 3000 ha in south-western Australia (Figure 7.1). Activities include appreciating nature, viewing wildlife, walking, picnicking, camping, swimming and fishing. Visitor numbers are estimated at 126,000 a year. The Park has three designated and nine informal campsites, all on the Warren River. Other facilities include three picnic areas, a lookout and numerous walk trails.

Smith (1998) developed and conducted a monitoring programme for resource impacts and visitor use. Resource impacts were determined using multiple indicator rating and measurement systems (Table 7.2). Her work focused on the 12 campsites, plus associated walk trails and the nearby river bank. Photographs were taken to record campsite condition and obvious deterioration along trails and the river bank. A questionnaire was used to gain information on visitors, their use of the area and associated expectations.

Smith (1998) based her campsite work on the multiple indicator rating system developed by Parsons and MacLeod (1980) and modified by Cole (1983a) (Table 7.4). Indicators included human damage to trees, root exposure, development, cleanliness, social trails and campsite area. Each was given a rating of 1–3 depending on the level of impact and then weighted. Indicators of greater concern to managers, such as campsite area and root exposure (a default measure of erosion), were weighted more heavily. The weighted ratings were then summed to give a summary impact score for each site. Half the campsites were identified as high to severely impacted.

The multiple indicator measurement system, drawing on the approaches taken by Marion (1991) and Cole (1989), relied on detailed measurements as well as visual counts of a number of features, such as number of damaged trees (Table 7.5). The area of each campsite was measured using the variable radial transect method (Figure 7.2). A variable number of transects were run out from a fixed centre point (the campfire) to the campsite boundary and their length and compass bearing recorded. The campsite area was then calculated. For vegetation and soils, detailed measurements were made using 1 × 1 m quadrats at each campsite and a nearby, similar, unimpacted, control site. For each campsite, quadrats were located along four predefined linear transects at 90° to each other, with four quadrats 1–2 m from the campsite centre and the remaining four on the perimeter. In the control sites, four randomly placed quadrats were sampled. Other information recorded from the quadrats included soil compaction as measured by bulk density and penetrometry, percentage understorey and overstorey cover, and percentage weed vs native species coverage.

The vegetation data showed a 61% reduction in cover at designated campsites and a 51% reduction at the informal sites compared to the control sites. Weed invasion of campsites was also noted, with informal sites averaging 11% weed cover and designated sites 5%. Virtually no weeds were recorded from the control sites. Measurements of soil bulk density and penetration resistance showed increased soil compaction at campsites, with bulk density measurements of $1.4\,gcm^{-3}$ for campsite centres and $0.7\,gcm^{-3}$ or less for perimeters and control sites.

Two other indicators measured were loss of overstorey and removal of material for firewood. A spherical densiometer was used to measure canopy cover at the campsite, the main access point to the river bank and two randomly placed controls in unimpacted, nearby forest. Measurements showed the canopy cover was significantly lower at the campsites than in unimpacted, nearby areas.

To determine the extent of firewood collection, three survey lines each 25 m long and laid out to form an equilateral triangle, were placed at selected sites, including designated, informal and control sites. The diameter of each piece of wood, allocated to a size class (25–70 mm, 71–300 mm, 301–600 mm and >600 mm), intercepting the line was recorded. Campsites had much less coarse woody debris than the control sites. For size classes >70 mm diameter, designated sites had 64% less coarse woody debris than control sites, while informal sites had 27% less.

Because all the campsites were near the Warren River, Smith (1998) wanted to measure the environmental effects on the river's bank. She measured the width and depth of walk trails, described erosion features such as root exposure and bank collapse, and sampled vegetation quadrats in disturbed and similar, undisturbed sites. The data showed that the greatest amount of degradation of the river bank is associated with designated campsites.

Walk trails associated with campsites were also studied. These trails have developed informally as people have accessed the river for swimming and fishing. Measurements of trail length, width and depth and visual observations of litter, erosion, exposed roots, and numbers of river access trails and trails radiating from the campsite provided a useful overview. For example, several of the popular campsites have up to 18 trails, with moderate levels of erosion, radiating from them.

Information on visitor use was obtained from a questionnaire completed by 117 respondents. The questionnaire was handed out at sites throughout the park as well as a nearby café. Questions addressed visitor and visit characteristics, reasons for visiting, visitor perceptions regarding existing environmental conditions and management preferences. Reasons for visiting focused around appreciating nature and enjoying the scenery. The conditions most often mentioned as contributing to visitors' experiences all related to the biophysical environment – litter, wildlife, number of trees damaged, amount of vegetation loss and bare ground, and erosion of banks. Social conditions such as the number of walk trails, size of other groups camped within sight or sound and the number of people camping on the river were regarded as important by less than half of those surveyed. Standards for indicators were sought by asking visitors to give the maximum level of change they would accept. Most visitors supported high standards, for example, 81% of visitors would accept only 0–5 pieces of litter before this impact became unacceptable.

The results of this study show that a combined monitoring programme collecting data on biophysical and social parameters can provide useful information on the status of campsites and associated walk trails in a popular national park. These techniques, largely developed and applied in the United States, appear equally as suitable for application in other countries such as Australia.

central to the planning frameworks of Chapter 4. The key role of visitors' perceptions in this process is emphasised. Brief mention is then made of environmental auditing, where the performance of an organisation rather than an individual site or visitor is monitored. Lastly, an integrated monitoring programme for Warren National Park, Western Australia, is included as a case study of an integrated approach to monitoring to draw the chapter together and to a close.

As noted in this chapter's introduction, monitoring has long been neglected in the management of natural areas. In reality, it is a crucial element of the sustainable management of such areas for tourism. It is needed to identify impacts and is especially important in determining when such impacts become unacceptable and require management action. Monitoring is also crucial for accountability, with society becoming increasingly interested in knowing how public agencies, including land management ones, are performing. Monitoring provides the data needed to assess such performance. Finally, both managers and visitors increasingly want to know how effective management actions have been. For example, does providing information to visitors reduce their impacts on campsites? Again monitoring, both of impacts and visitors themselves, can provide the much-needed answers.

Further reading

Cole (1983a, 1989), Marion (1991), and Leung and Marion (1999c, 2000) provide a wealth of material on monitoring campsites in backcountry areas – all directly relevant to inventorying and monitoring the impacts of tourists in natural areas. Cole (1983b), Leung and Marion (1999a) and Marion and Leung (2001) similarly provide a wealth of material on trail monitoring. Hammitt and Cole (1998) and Monz (2000) are also valuable for their advice on campsite and trail monitoring. Leung and Marion (2000) provide a useful state-of-knowledge review of recreation impacts and management in wilderness; also directly relevant to managing natural area tourism.

Two thoughtful papers – Leung et al. (1997) and Marion and Leung (2001) – encourage readers to consider how different ways of collecting trail information determine the standards that can be set. They suggest that data from point sampling (Table 7.6) are best used to estimate the percentage of a trail affected by an impact, such as erosion, and then base the standard on that percentage measure. On the other hand, for data from problem-based surveys, standards are best based on the frequency of occurrence of an impact, for example, the number of times erosion occurs in a kilometre.

Cope et al. (2000) provides an excellent overview, for natural areas in the United Kingdom, of the reasons for and types of visitor monitoring. Other articles, for example those by Chin et al. (2000), Manning et al. (1998), Morin et al. (1997) and Roggenbuck et al. (1993) are useful because they provide clear examples of visitor monitoring programmes from a number of different countries, based on the widely used approach of visitor questionnaires. Frankfort-Nachmias and Nachmias (1992) and Neuman (1994) are examples of general social research texts useful for designing visitor surveys and questionnaire construction.

Chapter 8
Conclusion

Introduction

Tourism in natural areas is a rapidly growing area of tourism and one that is also of immense interest to students, scholars, developers and managers. Central to this interest lies the question: 'Can tourism be beneficial to the natural environments in which it takes place?' The answer is not simple, but after reviewing the ideas and case studies presented in this book it is clearly possible to argue for the affirmative, that is, tourism in natural areas can be symbiotic with tourism development feeding off its environmental resources whilst being conservation supporting in orientation. The key to this relationship lies in understanding its foundations and for natural area tourism the primary foundation is the natural environment.

Thus it is essential that we understand the various forms and processes of the environment, as displayed through its myriad landscapes and ecosystems. Overlying this outward expression of the natural world is the tourism system, with its destination components of attractions, accommodations and tours. Through the intersection of tourism and the environment the resultant outcome is a range of impacts from negative (adverse) to positive (beneficial) as well as from small (negligible) to large (significant). In order to minimise the negative impacts and maximise the positive ones, appropriate planning, management and monitoring is required. However, it is only through the active pursuit of these things that natural area tourism will flourish and benefit both the environment as well as humanity. Finally, given that it is advocated that tourism and the environment may be beneficial for both elements, then it is instinctive to suggest that the key benefit of tourism in natural areas is its sustainable approach. This represents the future of tourism in natural areas, that is, tourism that is truly economically viable, socially compatible and conservation supporting.

The Centrality of Ecology

McNaughton (1989) states that:

> As we look forward to conservation in the twenty-first century, it is well to remember how recent and fragile is the idea that humans should preserve as well as conquer nature.

Formal conservation of natural resources is a relatively recent phenomenon and understanding the forms and processes of the natural environment is even newer. Founders of ecology such as Forbes (1925) in the USA and Tansley (1935) in Britain, fostered the notion of the ecosystem concept as a central idea in ecology. But unlike many physical and chemical systems, these ecosystems are 'open' systems, which may be impacted for good or bad. Thus a central tenet in conservation is the preservation of whole ecosystems of sufficient size and diversity to maintain their forms and processes and especially their critical species.

Alongside this advocacy for *in situ* conservation are a number of other tools, which can be utilised to help conserve and protect natural areas. These include combining conservation and economics through sustainable development, undertaking restoration ecology to reconstitute ecosystems, and fostering environmental ethics through aesthetic and moral reasoning. In all of these components, tourism can play an important role but it will never be fully realised until the tourism developers, planners and managers embrace an understanding of ecology and its importance to humanity. This is the principal message of this text.

Thus this book unashamedly champions the notion that an understanding of ecology predetermines the success of tourism in natural areas. While whale watching or geological tours may follow sound ecotourism principles, without a wider appreciation of the environment, these specific foci are limited in their usefulness. If instead, these tours are couched in more holistic terms, than the jigsaw of the natural environment would be more complete, and provide the visitor (tourist) with the backdrop or environmental fabric with which to more fully understand the significance of the species or rocks under scrutiny.

Ecosystems need to be better understood if natural area tourism is to bring about environmental benefits. Their structure and functions should be more fully understood by tour guides, and then better interpreted for the tourists themselves. Visitors to natural areas should leave the areas with clear understandings of their abiotic, biotic and cultural attributes. The interaction of plants and species should be shared and understood. Symbiotic relationships should be noted and habitats identified. In addition dominant and keystone species should be identified as well as rare and endangered ones. Ecosystem disturbance and succession should also be described along with the overarching landscape mosaics comprising matrices, patches and corridors.

If the steps outlined above are followed then tourism in natural areas can be justified in terms of its fostering of environmental understanding, ethics and values. Implicit in such values are not only its instrumental or anthropocentric values but also its intrinsic or ecocentric ones. If these are adhered to and espoused them tourism to natural areas will bring about a significant interest in, and support for, our natural environment, and the promise of ecotourism will be realised.

Understanding Impacts

Impacts occur wherever tourism takes place in natural areas. Whilst tourism is often 'sold' to communities as being a better environmental alternative to farming, logging or mining, in reality it may be just as detrimental in the long term (Weaver, 2000). The sources of impact are numerous and include infrastructure development and tourism activities in relation to transport, accommodations and attractions. Impacts can also be classified according to the vulnerability of the ecosystem. Some environments are inherently more fragile than others which have greater resistance. The impacts can also be described in a range of ecosystems from reefs to rainforests.

Central to our understanding of the impacts of tourism in natural areas is the idea that it is often rare and endangered species or particularly fragile habitats which are attractive for tourists. Allied to this concept is the fact that scores of minimal impacts can be imperceptibly cumulative. Thus an understanding of the cause and types of environmental impacts caused by tourism is essential in the planning, development and management of natural area tourism.

Emerging Views on Management

One of the most urgent problems facing national parks and protected areas today is how to cope with the increasing number of tourists (Sowman & Pearce, 2000). While a common trend is to focus on visitor management issues, as outlined in Chapter 5, it is also important to implement appropriate management for the environment as well as for visitors. Therefore, an integrated approach to environmental/visitor management is advocated since it cannot be assumed that one automatically includes the other. It is contended that in actual fact environmental management often excludes the inclusion of human visitation or use, and visitor management often minimises the significance of the natural environment. Conservation management is about knowing when and how to intercede as the case for doing so becomes more compelling (Western, 1989). An interesting point to dwell on is that it was human enjoyment, not biological conservation, that was the driving force behind the establishment of national parks. This has led to a preoccupation with forms (objects) in national parks, rather than processes (Hales, 1989). Thus few parks embrace entire ecosystems and instead focus on the natural environment's tourist icons such as Mount Fuji (Japan), Iguazu Falls (Argentina and Brazil) or the Great Barrier Reef (Australia).

Thus maybe there is a place for an integrated holistic approach to the management of natural areas, which not only embraces the management of natural areas including their form (features) and process, but also the overlying component of visitors. However, we would not like to be so prescriptive that management models do not allow for individual differences. We are advocating the management of natural areas for tourism and as such, are merely suggesting that the management of the natural environment for the natural environment is not overlooked in the debate about which visitor management system or model is best for a particular area.

Alongside all of this is the move towards the establishment of 'protected landscapes', which are characterised by the harmonious interaction of people and the land (Lucas, 1992). Such landscapes complement national parks and other protected areas through their inclusion of people as part of the natural environmental fabric of the landscape. The values of protected landscapes are that they conserve nature and biological diversity, buffer more strictly protected areas, conserve human history in structures and land-use practices, maintain traditional ways of life, offer recreation and inspiration, provide education and understanding, and demonstrate durable systems of use in harmony with nature.

The management of natural areas for tourism is thus influenced by both the management approach (e.g. for the environment or visitors) and the type of area (e.g. national park or protected landscape). These factors present many challenges for managers seeking to bring about an integrity of environmental protection combined with a quality visitor experience. However, based on the recognition of the importance of ecosystem protection the underlying principle of management should be that the basic ecological and cultural features of the natural area should be recorded, examined and protected. At the same time, the area should be managed in such a way as to provide visitors with a sound understanding of, and experience in, the natural environment so that the participants are empowered to return to their home environments keen to act as environmental ambassadors.

The Importance of Sustainability

According to Hall and Lew (1998) defining and achieving sustainable development has become one of the major policy debates of our generation. The adoption of the principles of sustainable development to tourism has become widely accepted as embracing environmental, cultural and economic elements. However, more often than not, it has been the economic component only that has been championed, leaving the other two elements languishing under a lip service mentality. Therefore, an underlying theme of this book has been the notion of equity amongst the three major platforms of sustainable tourism and the challenge is to ensure that this equity is achieved in the future. As Stabler (1997) contends the challenge facing the industry is how to translate principles into practices and to attain the seemingly irreconcilable objectives of tourism development with ecological conservation.

Yet these are the very challenges which have been addressed, in part, by this book through its advocacy of the dependence of natural area tourism on its ecological foundations intersecting with stakeholder involvement. When these two are integrated then tourism in natural areas will foster sustainable development in its truest sense.

Future Research

Tourism in natural areas is an exciting area of study and research and over the next decade a lot more will be written about it. However, there are a number of emerging research trends as identified by this text. The number of tourism and recreation planning frameworks will increase but there is a need to ensure that they are integrated with broader environmental protection and tourism development planning models designed for natural areas. Self-management practices introduced by the tourism industry will increase through the adoption of codes of practice and certification schemes. It is predicted that there will be a move towards greater research in providing simple, rapid, cost-effective means of monitoring natural area visitors including their numbers, satisfactions, activities and impacts. This research is already well progressed for campsites and walk trails but is less so for more developed sites such as wilderness lodges and ecoresorts. Allied to this research will be the need to determine standards for tourist accommodation sites in natural areas given that the accommodation standards combined with the need to retain naturalness often presents unrealistic tourist expectations.

In the whole field of natural area tourism the significance of planning for sustainable outcomes cannot be overemphasised. Tourism in such areas relies on strategic planning which can only be achieved through the setting and evaluation of a range of sustainable options. These options should be presented to all stakeholders for their consideration and comment well before any final decisions are made. This is a crucial element in order to strive towards a more sustainable future for tourism in natural areas. When this high level of environment – tourism planning is achieved, then it will also need to be followed by sustainable management practices in the operational phase. Finally, the importance of monitoring is stressed as the monitoring of practices against performance indicators is an increasingly influential component in the sustainability discourse. Thus when adequate and appropriate planning, practice and monitoring occurs then tourism in natural areas will provide a sustainable future for many of the world's great natural ecosystems.

References

Acott, T.G., La Trobe, H.L. and Howard, S.H. (1998) An evaluation of deep ecotourism and shallow ecotourism. *Journal of Sustainable Tourism* 6(3), 238–53.

Adams, J.A., Endo, A.S., Stolzy, L.H., Rowlands, P.G. and Johnson, H.B. (1982) Controlled experiments on soil compaction produced by off-road vehicles in the Mojave Desert, California. *Journal of Applied Ecology* 19, 167–75.

Adams, L.W. and Geis, A. (1983) Effects of roads on small mammals. *Journal of Applied Ecology* 20, 403–15.

Agardy, M.T. (1993) Accommodating ecotourism in multiple use planning of coastal and marine protected areas. *Ocean and Coastal Management* 20, 219–39.

Ahmad, A. (1993) Environmental impact assessment in the Himalayas: An ecosystem approach. *Ambio* 22(1), 4–9.

Allan, N.J.R. (1988) Highways to the sky: The impact of tourism on South Asian mountain culture. *Tourism Recreation Research* 13(1), 11–16.

Allardice, R. (2000) *Environmental Conservationist*. Bredasdorp, Western Cape, South Africa: Buchu Bushcamp.

Allison, W.R. (1996) Snorkeler damage to coral reefs in the Maldive Islands. *Coral Reefs* 15, 137 and 215–18.

Anders, F.J. and Leatherman, S.P. (1987) Effects of off-road vehicles on coastal foredunes at Fire Island, New York, USA. *Environmental Management* 11(1), 45–52.

Anderson, D.H., Lime, D.W. and Wang, T.L. (1998) Maintaining the quality of park resources and visitor experiences (*Report No. TC-777*). St Paul, Minnesota: Cooperative Parks Studies Unit Department of Forest Resources University of Minnesota.

Anderson, D.W. and Keith, J.O. (1980) The human influence on seabird nesting success: Conservation implications. *Biological Conservation* 18, 65–80.

Anon. (1997) What is the World Heritage? *UNESCO Courier*, September, 1–5.

Anon. (1998) Guide for volunteer divers to monitor coral reefs. *Reef Research* 8(3&4), 24.

Anon. (1999a) Green Globe 21 is new certification program for tourism sector. *Business and the Environment*, November, 10.

Anon. (1999b) Tour operators keep an eye on the reef. *Reef Research* 9(1), 10–11.

ANZECC TFMPA (Australia and New Zealand Environment and Conservation Council Task Force on Marine Protected Areas) (1998) *Guidelines for Establishing the National Representative System of Marine Protected Areas*. Australia and New Zealand Environment and Conservation Council, Task Force on Marine Protected Areas, December. Canberra, ACT: Environment Australia.

Ap, J. (1990) Residents' perceptions research on the social impacts of tourism. *Annals of Tourism Research* 17(4), 610–16.

Arnstein, S.R. (1969) A ladder of citizen participation. *American Institute of Planners Journal* 35(4), 216–24.

Ashley, C. and Roe, D. (1998) *Enhancing Community Involvement in Wildlife Tourism: Issues and Challenges.* IIED Wildlife and Development Series No. 11. London: International Institute for Environment and Development.

Australian Department of Tourism (1994) *National Ecotourism Strategy.* Canberra: Commonwealth Government Publishing Service.

Babbie, E. (1992) *The Practice of Social Research.* Belmont, CA: Wadsworth Publishing Company.

Baker, A. and Gentry, D. (1998) Environmental pressures on conserving cave speleothems: Effects of changing surface land use and increased cave tourism. *Journal of Environmental Management* 53, 165–75.

Bannister, A. and Ryan, B. (1993) *National Parks of South Africa.* London: New Holland Publishers.

Barnes, D.J., Chalker, B.E. and Kinsey, D.W. (1986) Reef metabolism. *Oceanus* 29(2), 20–6.

Barnes, R.F.W. (1994) Sustainable development in African game parks. In G.K. Meffe and C.R. Carroll (eds) *Principles of Conservation Biology* (pp. 504–11). Sunderland, MA: Sinauer Associates, Inc.

Batisse, M. (1982) The biosphere reserve: A tool for environmental conservation and management. *Environmental Conservation* 9(2), 101–11.

Batten, L.A. (1977) Sailing on reservoirs and its effects on water birds. *Biological Conservation* 11, 49–58.

Bayfield, N.G. (1986) Penetration of the Cairngorms Mountains, Scotland, by vehicle tracks and footpaths: Impacts and recovery. In *National Wilderness Research Conference: Current Research* (pp. 121–8). USA: US Department of Agriculture Forest Service.

Beckwith, J.A. and Moore, S.A. (2001) The influences of recent changes in public sector management on biodiversity conservation. *Pacific Conservation Biology* 7 (1), 45–54.

Beeton, S. (1999) Visitors to national parks: Attitudes of walkers toward commercial horseback tours. *Pacific Tourism Review* 3, 49–60.

Begon, M., Harper, J.L. and Townsend, C.R. (1996) *Ecology: Individuals, Populations and Communities.* London: Blackwell Scientific.

Beintema, A.J. (1991) Management of Djoudj National Park in Senegal. *Landscape and Urban Planning* 20, 81–4.

Bernstein, B.B. and Zalinski, J. (1983) An optimum sampling design and power test for environmental biologists. *Journal of Environmental Management* 16, 335–43.

Bilsen, F. (1987) Integrated tourism in Senegal: An alternative. *Tourism Recreation Research* 13(1), 19–23.

Blamey, R.K. (1997) Ecotourism: The search for an operational definition. *Journal of Sustainable Tourism* 5(2), 109–30.

Blane, J.M. and Jackson, R. (1994) Impact of ecotourism boats on the St.-Lawrence Beluga Whales. *Environmental Conservation* 21(3), 267–9.

Boniface, B.G. and Cooper, C.P. (1987) *The Geography of Travel and Tourism.* Oxford: Heinemann Professional Publishing.

Boucher, D.H., Aviles, J., Chepote, R., Dominguez, O.E. and Vilchez, B. (1991) Recovery of trailside vegetation from trampling in a tropical rain forest. *Environmental Management* 15(2), 257–62.

Bowen, L. and Van Vuren, D. (1997) Insular endemic plants lack defences against herbivores. *Conservation Biology* 11(5), 1249–54.

Boyd, S.W. and Butler, R.W. (1996) Managing ecotourism: An opportunity spectrum approach. *Tourism Management* 17(8), 557–66.

Bradley, G.A. (1982) The interpretive plan. In G.W. Sharpe (ed.) *Interpreting the Environment.* New York: John Wiley.

Brady, N.C. (1990) *The Nature and Properties of Soils.* New York: Macmillan.

Bramwell, B. and Lane, B. (2000a) Collaboration and partnerships in tourism planning. In B. Bramwell and B. Lane (eds) *Tourism, Collaboration and Partnerships: Politics, Practice and Sustainability* (pp. 1–19). Clevedon: Channel View Publications.

Bramwell, B. and Lane, B. (eds) (2000b) *Tourism, Collaboration and Partnerships: Politics, Practice and Sustainability* (Vol. 2). Clevedon: Channel View Publications.

Brennan, E.J., Else, J.G. and Altmann, J. (1985) Ecology and behaviour of a pest primate: Vervet monkeys in a tourist lodge habitat. *African Journal of Ecology* 23, 35–44.

British Standards Institute (1994) *British Standard for Environmental Management Systems: BS7750*. London: British Standards Institute.

Broadhead, J.M. and Godfrey, P.J. (1977) Off-road vehicle impact in Cape Cod national seashore: Disruption and recovery of dune vegetation. *International Journal of Biometeorology* 21(3), 299–306.

Brunson, M.W. (1997) Beyond wilderness: Broadening the applicability of limits of acceptable change. In S.F. McCool and D.N. Cole (eds.) *Proceedings from a Workshop on Limits of Acceptable Change and Related Planning Processes: Progress and Future Directions, University of Montana's Lubrecht Experimental Forest, Missoula, Montana, May 20–22, 1997* (pp. 44–8). Ogden, UT: US Department of Agriculture Forest Service, Rocky Mountain Research Station.

Buchy, M. and Ross, H. (2000) *Enhancing the Information Base on Participatory Approaches in NRM* (Report No. 5). Canberra: LWRRDC SIRP Programme, The Australian National University.

Buckley, R. (1999a) *Green Guide for White Water: Best Practice Environmental Management for Whitewater Raft and Kayak Tours*. Queensland, Australia: CRC for Sustainable Tourism, Griffith University.

Buckley, R. (1999b) Tools and indicators for managing tourism in parks. *Annals of Tourism Research* 26(1), 207–9.

Buckley, R. and Pannell, J. (1990) Environmental impacts of tourism and recreation in national parks and conservation reserves. *Journal of Tourism Studies* 1(1), 24–32.

Buckley, R.C., Pickering, C.A. and Warnken, J. (2000) Environmental management for alpine tourism and resorts in Australia. In P.M. Godde, M.F. Price and F.M. Zimmermann (eds) *Tourism and Development in Mountain Regions*. Oxford: CABI Publishing.

Budowski, G. (1976) Tourism and environmental conservation: Conflict, coexistence, or symbiosis? *Environmental Conservation* 3(1), 27–31.

Burger, J. and Gochfeld, M. (1993) Tourism and short-term behavioural responses of nesting Masked, Red-footed and Blue-footed Boobies in the Galapagos. *Environmental Conservation* 20(3), 255–9.

Burger, J., Gochfeld, M. and Niles, L.J. (1995) Ecotourism and birds in coastal New Jersey: Contrasting responses of birds, tourists and managers. *Environmental Conservation* 22(1), 56–65.

Burnett, G.W. and Butler Harrington, L.M. (1994) Early national park adoption in sub-Saharan Africa. *Society and Natural Resources* 7(2), 155–68.

Bury, R.B., Luckenbach, R.A. and Busack, S.D. (1977) *Effects of Off-road Vehicles on Vertebrates in the California Desert* (Wildlife Research Report No. 8). United States Fish and Wildlife Service.

Bush, M.B. (1997) Ecosystems: Getting to the root of productivity. In M.B. Bush (ed.) *Ecology of a Changing Planet* (pp. 60–77). New Jersey: Prentice Hall.

Butler, E.A. and Knudson, D.M. (1977) *Recreational Carrying Capacity* (Element No. 16). Indiana: Indiana Outdoor Recreation Planning Program.

Butler, R.W. and Waldbrook, L.A. (1991) A new planning tool: The tourism opportunity spectrum. *The Journal of Tourism Studies* 2(1), 2–14.

Butynski, T.M. and Kalina, J. (1998) Gorilla tourism: A critical look. In E.J. Milner-Gullard and R. Mace (eds) *Conservation of Biological Resources*. Oxford: Blackwell.

Cabelli, V.J., Dafour, A.P., McCabe, L.J. and Levin, M.A.A. (1982) Swimming associated gastroenteritis and water quality. *American Journal of Epidemiology* 115, 606–16.

CALM (WA Department of Conservation and Land Management) (undated) *Zoning for National Parks in Western Australia* (Discussion Paper). Perth, Western Australia: Department of Conservation and Land Management.

CALM (WA Department of Conservation and Land Management) (1992) Biological diversity in Western Australia. In *A Nature Conservation Strategy for Western Australia* (Draft). Perth, Western Australia: Department of Conservation and Land Management.

CALM (WA Department of Conservation and Land Management) (1996) *Stirling Range and Porongorup National Parks* (Draft Management Plan). Perth, Western Australia: Department of Conservation and Land Management.

CALM (WA Department of Conservation and Land Management) (2000a) *Sewerage Treatment Analysis: Information Exchange L6[00]*, Report dated October 2000. Como, Western Australia: WA Department of Conservation and Land Management, Recreation, Planning and Site Design Branch.

CALM (WA Department of Conservation and Land Management) (2000b) *Annual Report 1999–2000*. Kensington, Western Australia: Department of Conservation and Land Management.

CALM (WA Department of Conservation and Land Management) (2000c) *VISTAT 2000: Guidelines for the Collection of Visitor Information Data on CALM-managed Lands and Waters* (Guidelines). Kensington, Western Australia: Department of Conservation and Land Management.

CALM (WA Department of Conservation and Land Management) and AMCS (Australian Marine Conservation Society, WA) (2000) *Marine Community Monitoring Manual*. Fremantle, WA: Department of Conservation and Land Management.

CALM and NPNCA (Department of Conservation and Land Management and National Parks and Nature Conservation Authority) (1995) *Dryandra Woodland: Management Plan, 1995–2005*. Perth, Western Australia: Department of Conservation and Land Management.

Camp, R.J. and Knight, R.L. (1998) Rock climbing and cliff bird communities at Joshua Tree National Park, California. *Wildlife Society Bulletin* 26(4), 892–8.

Cater, E. (1993) Ecotourism in the third world: Problems for sustainable tourism development. *Tourism Management* 85, 90.

Cater, E. (1994) Introduction. In E. Cater and G. Lowman (eds) *Ecotourism: A Sustainable Option?* (pp. 3–17). Chichester: John Wiley.

Caughley, G. and Gunn, A. (1996) *Conservation Biology in Theory and Practice*. Cambridge, MA: Blackwell Science.

Cavana, M. and Moore, S.A. (1988) *Fitzgerald River National Park Visitor Survey: November 1987 – April 1988*. Perth: Western Australian Department of Conservation and Land Management.

Ceballos-Lascurain, H. (1996) Impact of tourism vehicles on wildlife in Masai Mara National Reserve Kenya. In H. Ceballos-Lascurain (ed.) *Tourism, Ecotourism and Protected Areas* (pp. 64–5). Gland, Switzerland: The World Conservation Union.

Ceballos-Lascurain, H. (1998) Birdwatching and ecotourism. *The Ecotourism Society Newsletter* 1, 1–3.

Cessford, G.R. and Dingwall, P.R. (1994) Tourism on New Zealand's sub-Antarctic islands. *Annals of Tourism Research* 21(2), 318–32.

Chaffey, J. (1996) *Managing Wilderness Regions*. London: Hodder & Stoughton.

Chalker, L. (1994) Ecotourism: On the trail of destruction or sustainability? A minister's view. In E. Cater and G. Lowman (eds) *Ecotourism: A Sustainable Option?* (pp. 87–99). Chichester: John Wiley.

Charman, P.E.V. and Murphy, B.W. (2000) *Soils: Their Properties and Management*. Melbourne: Oxford University Press.

Chin, C.L.M., Moore, S.A., Dowling, R.K. and Wallington, T.J. (2000) Ecotourism in Bako National Park, Borneo: Visitors' perspectives on environmental impacts and their management. *Journal of Sustainable Tourism* 8(1), 20–35.

Christ, C. (1998) Taking ecotourism to the next level. In K. Lindberg, M. Epler Wood and D. Engeldrum (eds) *Ecotourism: A Guide for Planners and Manager* Vol. 2 (pp. 183–95). Vermont: The Ecotourism Society.

Christiansen, D.R. (1990) Adventure tourism. In J.C. Miles and S. Priest (eds) *Adventure Education*. Pennsylvania: Venture Publishing.

Churchill, S. (1987) The conservation of cave fauna in the top end. *Australian Ranger Bulletin* 4(3), 10–11.

Cigna, A.A. (1993) Environmental management of tourist caves. *Environmental Geology* 21, 173–80.

Cilimburg, A., Monz, C. and Kehoe, S. (2000) Wildland recreation and human waste: A review of problems, practices and concerns. *Environmental Management* 25(6), 587–98.

Clark, R.N. and Stankey, G.H. (1979) *The Recreation Opportunity Spectrum: A Framework for Planning, Management, and Research* (General Technical Report PNW-98). Portland, Oregon: Department of Agriculture, Forest Service, Pacific Northwest Forest and Range Experiment Station.

Cochrane, J. (1996) The sustainability of ecotourism in Indonesia: Fact or fiction. In M.J.G. Parnwell and R.L. Bryant (eds) *Environmental Change in South-East Asia: People, Politics and Sustainable Development*. London: Routledge.

Cole, D.N. (1981a) Vegetational changes associated with recreational use and fire suppression in the Eagle Cap Wilderness, Oregon: Some management implications. *Biological Conservation* 20, 247–70.

Cole, D.N. (1981b) Managing ecological impacts at wilderness campsites: An evaluation of techniques. *Journal of Forestry* 79, 86–9.

Cole, D.N. (1983a) *Monitoring the Condition of Wilderness Campsites* (Research Paper, INT-302). Ogden, UT: United States Department of Agriculture Forest Service Intermountain Forest and Range Experiment Station.

Cole, D.N. (1983b) *Assessing and Monitoring Backcountry Trail Conditions* (Research Paper, INT-303). Ogden, UT: United States Department of Agriculture Forest Service Intermountain Forest and Range Experiment Station.

Cole, D.N. (1989) *Wilderness Campsite Monitoring Methods: A Sourcebook* (General Technical Report, INT-259). Ogden, UT: United States Department of Agriculture Forest Service Intermountain Research Station.

Cole, D.N. (1990a) Trampling disturbance and recovery of cryptogamic crusts in Grand Canyon National Park. *Great Basin Naturalist* 50(4), 321–5.

Cole, D.N. (1990b) Ecological impacts of wilderness recreation and their management. In J.C. Hendee, G.H. Stankey and R.C. Lucas (eds) *Wilderness Management* (pp. 425–66). Golden, CO: North American Press.

Cole, D.N. (1992) Modelling wilderness campsites: Factors that influence amount of impact. *Environmental Management* 16(2), 255–64.

Cole, D.N. (1993) Wilderness recreation management: We need more than bandages and toothpaste. *Journal of Forestry* 91(2), 22–4.

Cole, D.N. (1995) Wilderness management principles: Science, logical thinking or personal opinion? *Trends* 32(1), 6–9.

Cole, D.N. (1997) Visitors, conditions, and management options for high-use destination areas in wilderness. Making protection work. *Proceedings of the Ninth Conference on Research and Resource Management in Parks and on Public Lands, Albuquerque, New Mexico, March 17–21, 1997* (pp. 29–35). Albuquerque, NM: The George Wright Society Biennial Conference.

Cole, D.N. (2000) Paradox of the primeval: Ecological restoration in wilderness. *Ecological Restoration* 18(2), 77–86.

Cole, D.N. and Landres, P.B. (1995) Indirect effects of recreation on wildlife. In R.L. Knight and K.J. Gutzwiller (eds) *Wildlife and Recreationists: Coexistence through Management and Research*. Washington, DC: Island Press.

Cole, D.N. and Landres, P.B. (1996) Threats to wilderness ecosystems: Impacts and research needs. *Ecological Applications* 6(1), 168–84.

Cole, D.N. and Marion, J.L. (1988) Recreational impacts in some riparian forests of the eastern United States. *Environmental Management* 12(1), 99–107.

Cole, D.N. and McCool, S.F. (1997) The limits of acceptable change process: Modifications and clarifications. In S.F. McCool and D.N. Cole (eds) *Proceedings of a Workshop on Limits of Acceptable Change and Related Planning Processes: Progress and Future Directions, University of Montana's Lubrecht Experimental Forest, Missoula, Montana, May 20–22, 1997* (pp. 61–8). Ogden, UT: US Department of Agriculture Forest Service, Rocky Mountain Research Station.

Cole, D.N. and Stankey, G.H. (1997) Historical development of limits of acceptable change: Conceptual clarifications and possible extensions. In S.F. McCool and D.N. Cole (eds) *Proceedings from a Workshop on Limits of Acceptable Change and Related Planning Processes: Progress and Future Directions, University of Montana's Lubrecht Experimental Forest, Missoula, Montana, May 20–22, 1997* (General Technical Report INT-GTR-371) (pp. 5–9). Ogden, UT: US Department of Agriculture Forest Service, Rocky Mountain Research Station.

Cole, D.N., Petersen, M.E. and Lucas, R.C. (1987) *Managing Wilderness Use: Common Problems and Potential Solutions* (General Technical Report INT-230). Ogden, UT: United States Department of Agriculture Forest Service Intermountain Research Station.

Cole, D.N., Watson, A.E. and Roggenbuck, J.W. (1995) *Trends in Wilderness Visitors and Visits: Boundary Waters Canoe Area, Shining Rock, and Desolation Wildernesses* (Research Paper, INT-RP-483). Ogden, UT: United States Department of Agriculture Forest Service Intermountain Research Station.

Cole, D.N., Watson, A.E., Hall, T.E. and Spildie, D.R. (1997) *High-use Destinations in Wilderness: Social and Biophysical Impacts, Visitor Responses, and Management Options* (Research Paper INT-RP-496, INT-RP-496). Ogden, UT: United States Department of Agriculture Forest Service Intermountain Research Station.

Colinvaux, P.A. (1993) *Ecology*. New York: John Wiley.

Collins, M. (1990) *The Last Rain Forests*. London: Mitchell Beazley.

Commonwealth of Australia (1991) *Kakadu National Park Plan of Management* (Plan of Management). Canberra: Australian National Parks and Wildlife Service.

Cooke, K. (1982) Guidelines for socially appropriate tourism development in British Columbia. *Journal of Travel Research* 21(1), 22–8.

Cope, A., Doxford, D. and Probert, C. (2000) Monitoring visitors to UK countryside resources: The approaches of land and recreation resource management organisations to visitor monitoring. *Land Use Policy* 17, 59–66.

Cordell, H.K., James, G.A. and Tyre, G.L. (1974) Grass establishment on developed recreation sites. *Journal of Soil and Water Conservation* 29, 268–71.

Crabtree, A. (2000) Interpretation: Ecotourism's fundamental but much neglected tool. *The International Ecotourism Society Newsletter*, Third Quarter, 1–3.

Crabtree, B. and Bayfield, N. (1998) Developing sustainability indicators for mountain ecosystems: A study of the Cairngorms, Scotland. *Journal of Environmental Management* 52, 1–14.

Craven, S.A. (1996) Carbon dioxide variations in Cango Cave, South Africa. *Cave and Karst Science* 23(3), 89–92.

Craven, S.A. (1999) Speleothem deterioration at Cango Cave, South Africa. *Cave and Karst Science* 26(1), 29–34.

Daily, G.C., Ehrlich, P.R. and Haddad, N.M. (1993) Double keystone bird in a keystone species complex. *Proceedings National Academy Science* 90, 592–4.

Dale, D. and Weaver, T. (1974) Trampling effects on vegetation of the trail corridors of North Rocky Mountain Forest. *Journal of Applied Ecology* 11, 767–72.

Davis, P.B. (1999) Beyond guidelines: A model for Antarctic tourism. *Annals of Tourism Research* 26(3), 516–33.

Dasmann, R.F., Milton, J.P. and Freeman, P.H. (1973) *Ecological Principles for Economic Development*. London: John Wiley.

De Kadt, E. (ed.) (1979) *Tourism: Passport to Development*. Oxford: Oxford University Press.

De Lacy, T. (1994) The Uluru/Kakadu model-Anangu Tjukurrpa: 50,000 years of Aboriginal law and land management changing the concept of national parks in Australia. *Society and Natural Resources* 7(5), 479–98.

Deacon, A. (1992) People pressure threatens rivers. *Custos* 21(4), 18.

Dell, B., Hopkins, A.J.M. and Lamont, B.B. (1986) *Resilience in Mediterranean-type Ecosystems*. Boston: Kluwer Academic Publishers.

Dellue, B. and Dellue, G. (1984) Lascaux II: A faithful copy. *Antiquity* 58, 194–6.

De Luca, T.H., Patterson, W.A. (IV), Freimund, W.A. and Cole, D.N. (1998) Influence of llamas, horses, and hikers on soil erosion from established recreation trails in Western Montana. *Environmental Management* 22(2), 255–62.

Deming, A. (1996) The edges of the civilized world: Tourism and the hunger for wild places. *Orion* 15(2), 28–35.

Department of Tourism (1995) *Best Practice Tourism: A Guide to Energy and Waste Minimisation*. Canberra, ACT: Commonwealth of Australia.

Dickinson, G. and Murphy, K. (1998) *Ecosystems*. London: Routledge.

Ding, P. and Pigram, J.J. (1995) Environmental audits: An emerging concept in sustainable tourism development. *The Journal of Tourism Studies* 6(2), 2–10.

Ding, P. and Pigram, J.J. (1996) An approach to monitoring and evaluating the environmental performance of Australian beach resorts. *Australian Geographer* 27(1), 77–86.

Dingwall, P.R. (1998) Implementing an environmental management regime in Antarctica. In A.E. Watson, G.H. Aplet and J.C. Hendee (eds) *Personal, Societal and Ecological Values of Wilderness: Proceedings of Sixth World Wilderness Congress on Research, Management and Allocation, 1997 October, Bangalore, India* (RMRS-P-4, pp. 1–5). Bangalore, India: Department of Agriculture Forest Service Rocky Mountain Research Station, Ogden, Utah.

Dowling, R.K. (1977) Environmental education. *New Zealand Environment* 16, 24–6.

Dowling, R.K. (1979) An introduction to environmental education. In R.K. Dowling (ed.) *Environmental Education Handbook: For New Zealand Secondary Schools* (pp. 6–14). Christchurch, New Zealand: Canterbury Environment Centre.

Dowling, R. (1993) An environmentally-based planning model for regional tourism development. *Journal of Sustainable Tourism* 1(1), 17–37.

Dowling, R.K. (1996) The implementation of ecotourism in Australia. *Proceedings of 2nd International Conference of the Ecotourism Asociation of Australia: The Implementation of Ecotourism: Planning, Developing and Managing for Sustainability, 18–21 July, 1996, Bangkok, Thailand* (pp. 1–19). Bangkok, Thailand: Srinakharinwirot University.

Dowling, R.K. (1999) Developing tourism in the environmentally sensitive North West Cape Region, Western Australia. In T.V. Singh and S. Singh (eds) *Tourism Development in Critical Environments* (pp. 163–75). New York: Cognizant Communication Corporation.

Driver, B.L. and Brown, P.J. (1978) The opportunity spectrum concept and behavioral information in outdoor recreation resource supply inventories: A rationale. In G.H. Lund, V.J. La Bau, P.F. Folliott and D.W. Robinson (eds) *Integrated Inventories of Renewable Natural Resources* (General Technical Report RM-55) (pp. 24–31). Fort Collins CO: United States Department of Agriculture Forest Service, Rocky Mountain Forest and Range Experiment Station.

Drumm, A. (1998) New approaches to community-based ecotourism management. In K. Lindberg, M. Epler Wood and D. Engeldrum (eds) *Ecotourism: A Guide for Planners and Managers*, Vol. 2 (pp. 197–213). Vermont: The Ecotourism Society.

EAA (Ecotourism Association of Australia) (2000) *EcoGuide Program Guide Workbook*. Brisbane: Ecotourism Association of Australia.

Eagles, P. (1984) *The Planning and Management of Environmentally Sensitive Areas*. London: Longman.

Eagles, P.F.J., Ballantine, J.L. and Fennell, D.A. (1992) Marketing to the ecotourist: Case studies from Kenya and Costa Rica. Unpublished paper. Department of Recreation and Leisure Studies, University of Waterloo, Canada.

Edington, J.M. and Edington, M.A. (1977) *Ecology and Environmental Planning*. London: Chapman and Hall.

Edington, J.M. and Edington, M.A. (1986) *Ecology, Recreation and Tourism*. Cambridge: Cambridge University Press.

Eldridge, D.J. and Rosentreter, R. (1999) Morphological groups: A framework for monitoring microphytic crusts in arid landscapes. *Journal of Arid Environments* 41, 11–25.

Enzenbacher, D.J. (1992) Antarctic tourism and environmental concerns. *Marine Pollution Bulletin* 25, 258–65.

Enzenbacher, D.J. (1993) Tourists in Antarctica: Numbers and trends. *Tourism Management*, April, 142–6.

Enzenbacher, D.J. (1995) The regulation of Antarctic tourism. In C.M. Hall and M.E. Johnston (eds) *Polar Tourism: Tourism in the Arctic and Antarctic Regions* (pp. 179–215). Chichester: John Wiley.

Etherington, J.R. (1975) *Environment and Plant Ecology*. New York: John Wiley.

Fa, J.E. (1988) Supplemental food as an extranormal stimulus in Barbary Macaques (*Macaca sylvanus*) at Gibraltar – its impact on activity budgets. In J.E. Fa and C.H. Southwick (eds) *Ecology and Behaviour of Food Enhanced Primate Groups*. Oxford: UK National History.

Farrell, T.A. and Marion, J.L. (2001) Identifying and assessing ecotourism visitor impacts at eight protected areas in Costa Rica and Belize. *Environmental Conservation* (submitted 21 November 2000).

Farris, M.A. (1998) The effects of rock climbing on the vegetation of three Minnesota cliff systems. *Canadian Journal of Botany* 76, 1981–90.

Fennell, D. (1999) *Ecotourism: An Introduction*. London: Routledge.

Forbes, B.C. (1992) Tundra disturbance studies 1: Long term effects of vehicles on species richness and biomass. *Environmental Conservation* 19(1), 48–58.

Forbes, S.A. (1925) The lake as microcosm. *Illinois Natural Historical Survey Bulletin* 15, 537–50.

Forman, R.T.T. (1995) *Land Mosaics: The Ecology of Landscapes and Regions*. Cambridge: Cambridge University Press.

Forest Service (Flathead National Forest) (1985) *Bob Marshall Great Bear Scapegoat Wildernesses Action Plan for Managing Recreation* (The Limits of Acceptable Change). United States Department of Agriculture, Forest Service, Flathead National Forest.

Fowler, G.S. (1999) Behavioral and hormonal responses of Magellanic penguins (*Spheniscus magellanicus*) to tourism and nest site visitation. *Biological Conservation* 90, 143–9.

Frangialli, F. (1998) Tourism: 2020 vision. *World Travel and Tourism Development* 3, 93–7.

Frankfort-Nachmias, C. and Nachmias, D. (1992) *Research Methods in the Social Sciences*. New York: St Martins Press.

Freedman, B., Zelazny, V., Beaudette, D., Fleming, T., Fleming, S., Forbes, G., Gerrow, J. S., Johnson, G. and Woodley, S. (1996) Biodiversity implications of changes in the quantity of dead organic matter in managed forests. *Environmental Review* 4, 238–65.

Frissell, S.S. (1978) Judging recreation impacts on wilderness campsites. *Journal of Forestry* 76, 481–3.

Frohoff, T.G. (2000) *Behavioral Indicators of Stress in Odontocetes During Interactions with Humans: A Preliminary Review and Discussion* (SC/52WW2). International Whaling Commission Scientific Committee.

Furley, P.A. and Newey, W.W. (1983) *The Geography of the Biosphere*. London: Butterworth.

Gabrielsen, G.W. and Smith, E.N. (1995) Physiological responses of wildlife to disturbance.

In R.L. Knight and K J. Gutzwiller (eds) *Wildlife and Recreationists: Coexistence through Management and Research*. Washington, DC: Island Press.

Gajraj, A.M. (1988) A regional approach to environmentally sound tourism development. *Tourism Recreation Research* 13(2), 5–9.

Gales, N. (2000) Presentation on wildlife tourism at Marine Tourism Conference, Notre Dame University, November 2000. Perth, Western Australia: Forum Advocating Cultural and Ecotourism Inc.

Galicia, E. and Baldassarre, G.A. (1997) Effects of motorised tour boats on the behaviour of non-breeding American Flamingos in Yucatan, Mexico. *Conservation Biology* 11(5), 1159–65.

Gardner, T. (1994) Visitor monitoring programs in urban parks and natural areas: Taking a strategic approach. *Australian Parks and Recreation*, Spring 1994, 27–31.

Garland, G.G. (1987) Rates of soil loss from mountain footpaths: An experimental study in the Drakensberg mountains, South Africa. *Applied Geography* 1, 121–31.

Garland, G.G. (1988) Experimental footpath soil losses and path erosion risk assessment in the Natal Drakensberg. Unpublished PhD Thesis. Durban, South Africa: University of Natal.

Garland, G.G. (1990) Technique for assessing erosion risk from mountain footpaths. *Environmental Management* 14(6), 793–8.

Garland, G.G., Hudson, C. and Blackshaw, J. (1985) An approach to the study of path erosion in the Natal Drakensberg, a mountain wilderness area. *Environmental Conservation* 12(4), 337–42.

Garrison R.W. (1997) Sustainable nature tourism: California's regional approach. In *World Ecotour '97 Abstracts Volume* (pp. 180–2). Rio de Janiero: BIOSFERA.

Getz, D. (1986) Models in tourism planning: Towards integration of theory and practice. *Tourism Management* 7(1), 21–32.

Gibeau, M.L. and Heuer, K. (1996) Effects of transportation corridors on large carnivores in the Bow River Valley, Alberta. In G.L. Evink, P.Garrett, D.Zeigler and J.Berry (eds) *Trends in Addressing Transportation Related Wildlife Mortality*. Tallahassee, FL: State of Florida Department of Transportation.

Giese, M. (2000) Polar wandering. *Wingspan* 10(1), 8–13.

Gillen, K. and Watson, J. (1993) Controlling *Phytophthora cinnamomi* in the mountains of south-western Australia. *Australian Ranger* 27, 18–20.

Gillieson, D. (1996) *Caves: Processes, Development, Management*. Oxford: Blackwell.

Giuliano, W. (1994) The impact of hiking and rock climbing in mountain areas. *Environmental Conservation* 21(3), 278–9.

Global Coral Reef Monitoring Network (2000) *Reef Check 2000* (8 April 2000). Online at http://www.ust.hk/~webrc/ReefCheck/ (Accessed 29 November 2000).

Goeft, U. and Alder, J. (2000) Mountain bike rider preferences and perceptions in the south-west of Western Australia. *CALM Science* 3(2), 261–75.

Gomez-Limon, F.J. and de Lucio, J. (1995) Recreational activities and loss of diversity in grasslands in Alta Manzanares Natural Park, Spain. *Biological Conservation* 74, 99–105.

Goodwin, H., Kent, I., Parker, K. and Walpole, M. (1998) *Tourism, Conservation and Sustainable Development: Case Studies from Asia and Africa* (Wildlife and Development Series No. 10). London: International Institute for Environment and Development.

Goosem, M. (2000) Effects of tropical rainforest roads on small mammals: Edge effects in community composition. *Wildlife Research* 27, 151–63.

Gordon, D.M. (1987) *Disturbance to Mangroves in Tropical-arid Western Australia: Hypersalinity and Restricted Tidal Exchange as Factors Leading to Mortality* (Technical Series 12). Perth, Western Australia: Environmental Protection Authority.

Graefe, A.R., Kuss, F.R. and Vaske, J.J. (1990) *Visitor Impact Management: The Planning Framework* Vol. 2. Washington, DC: National Parks and Conservation Association.

Graham, A.W. and Hopkins, M.S. (1993) Ecological prerequisites for managing change in tropical rainforest ecosystems. In N. McIntyre (ed) *Track to the Future: Managing Change in Parks and Recreation*. Queensland: Royal Institute of Parks and Recreation.

Great Barrier Reef Marine Park Authority (1997) *Guidelines for Managing Visitation to Seabird Breeding Islands*. Townsville: Great Barrier Reef Marine Park Authority.

Green, J.B. and Paine, J. (1997) State of the world's protected areas at the end of the twentieth century. In *IUCN World Commission on Protected Areas Symposium on 'Protected Areas in the 21st Century: From Islands to Networks', 24–29 November, 1997, Albany, Australia*.

Green, R.J. (1999) Negative effects of wildlife viewing on wildlife in natural areas. In K. Higginbottom and M. Hardy (eds) *Wildlife Tourism – Discussion Document* (unpublished report). Gold Coast, Australia: Cooperative Research Centre for Sustainable Tourism.

Green, R.J. and Higginbottom, K. (2000) The effects of non-consumptive wildlife tourism on free-ranging wildlife: A review. *Pacific Conservation Biology* 6 (3) 183–197.

Greeves, G.W., Leys, J.F. and McTainsh, G.H. (2000) Soil erodibility. In P.E.V. Charman and B.W. Murphy (eds) *Soils: Their Properties and Management*. Melbourne: Oxford University Press.

Greller, A.M., Goldstein, M. and Marcus, L. (1974) Snowmobile impact on three alpine tundra plant communities. *Environmental Conservation* 1(2), 101–10.

Griffiths, M. and Van Schaik, C.P. (1993) The impact of human traffic on the abundance and activity periods of Sumatran rain forest wildlife. *Conservation Biology* 7(3), 623–6.

Gunn, C.A. (1979) *Tourism Planning*. New York: Crane-Russak.

Gunn, C.A. (1987) Environmental designs and land use. In J.R.B. Ritchie and C.R. Goeldner (eds) *Travel, Tourism and Hospitality Research: A Handbook for Managers and Researchers* (pp. 229–47). New York: John Wiley.

Gunn, C.A. (1988a) *Tourism Planning* (2nd edn). New York: Taylor and Francis.

Gunn, C.A. (1988b) *Vacationscape: Designing Tourist Regions* (2nd edn). New York: Van Nostrand Reinhold.

Gunn, C.A. (1994) *Tourism Planning: Basics, Concepts, Cases* (3rd edn). Washington, DC: Taylor and Francis.

Gunther, K.A., Beil, M.J. and Robison, H.L. (1998) Factors influencing the frequency of road killed wildlife in Yellowstone National Park. In G.L. Evink, P. Garrett, D. Zeigler and J. Berry (eds) *Proceedings of the International Conference on Wildlife Ecology and Transportation*. Tallahasse, FL: State of Florida Department of Transportation.

Hales, D. (1989) Changing concepts of national parks. In D. Western and M. Pearl (eds) *Conservation for the Twenty-First Century* (pp. 139–144). New York: Oxford University Press.

Hall, C.M. (1991) *Introduction to Tourism in Australia: Impacts, Planning and Development*. Melbourne: Longman Cheshire.

Hall, C.M. (2000a) *Tourism Planning: Policies, Processes and Relationships*. Essex: Prentice Hall, Pearson Education Ltd.

Hall, C.M. (2000b) Policy. In J. Jafari (ed.) *Encyclopedia of Tourism* (pp. 445–8). London: Routledge.

Hall, C.M. and Kuss, F.R. (1989) Vegetation alteration along trails in Shenandoah National Park, Virginia. *Biological Conservation* 48, 211–27.

Hall, C.M. and Lew, A.A. (eds) (1998) *Sustainable Tourism: A Geographical Perspective*. Essex: Addison Wesley Longman.

Hall, C.M. and McArthur, S. (1998) *Integrated Heritage Management: Principles and Practice*. London: The Stationery Office.

Hall, C.M. and Wouters, M. (1995) Issues in Antarctic tourism. In C.M. Hall and M.E. Johnston (eds) *Polar Tourism: Tourism in the Artic and Antarctic Regions* (pp. 147–66). Chichester: John Wiley.

Hall, D. and Kinnaird, V. (1994) Ecotourism in Eastern Europe. In E. Cater and G. Lowman (eds) *Ecotourism: A Sustainable Option?* (pp. 111–37). Chichester: John Wiley.

Ham, S. (1992) *Environmental Interpretation: A Practical Guide for People with Big Ideas and Small Budgets*. Golden, CO: Fulcrum/North American Press.

Hamilton-Smith, E. (1987) Karst kreatures: The fauna of Australian Karst. *Australian Ranger Bulletin* 4(3), 9–10.

Hammitt, W.E. and Cole, D.N. (1998) *Wildland Recreation: Ecology and Management*. New York: John Wiley.

Harmon, M.E., Franklin, J.F., Swanson, F.J., Sollins, P., Gregory, S.V., Lattin, J.D., Anderson, N.H., Cline, S.P., Aumen, N.G., Sedell, J.R., Lienkaemper, G.W., Cromack, K. and Cummins, K.W. (1986) Ecology of coarse woody debris in temperate ecosystems. *Advances in Ecological Research* 15, 133–302.

Harrington, R., Owen-Smith, N., Viljoen, P.C., Biggs, H.C. Mason, D.R. and Funston, P. (1999) Establishing the causes of the roan antelope decline in the Kruger National Park, South Africa. *Biological Conservation*, 90, 19–78.

Harrison, D. (1997) Ecotourism in the South Pacific: The case of Fiji. In *World Ecotour '97 Abstracts Volume* (p. 75). Rio de Janiero, Brazil: BIOSFERA.

Harrison, L.C. and Husbands, W. (eds) (1996) *Practicing Responsible Tourism: International Case Studies in Tourism Planning, Policy, and Development*. New York: John Wiley.

Hawes, M. (1996) A walking track management strategy for the Tasmanian Wilderness World Heritage Area. *Australian Parks and Recreation*, Winter, 18–26.

Hawkins, J.P. and Roberts, C.M. (1993) Effects of recreational scuba diving on coral reefs: Trampling on reef flat communities. *Journal of Applied Ecology* 30, 25–30.

Hecnar, S.J. and M'Closkey, R.T. (1998) Effects of disturbance on Five-lined Skink, *Eumeces fasciatus*, abundance and distribution. *Biological Conservation* 85, 213–22.

Hendee, J.C. and Schoenfeld, C. (1990) Wildlife in wilderness. In J.C. Hendee, G.H. Stankey and R.C. Lucas (eds) *Wilderness Management* 2nd edn (revised) (pp. 215–39). Golden, CO: North American Press.

Hendee, J.C., Stankey, G.H. and Lucas, R.C. (1990a) *Wilderness Management* 2nd edn (revised). Golden, CO: North American Press.

Hendee, J.C., Stankey, G.H. and Lucas, R.C. (1990b) Managing for appropriate wilderness conditions: The carrying capacity issue. In J.C. Hendee, G.H. Stankey and R.C. Lucas (eds) *Wilderness Management* 2nd edn (revised) (pp. 215–39). Golden, CO: North American Press.

Henderson, J.C. (2000) The survival of a forest fragment: Bukit Timah Nature Reserve, Singapore. In X. Font and J. Tribe (eds) *Forest Tourism and Recreation*. Oxford: CABI Publishing.

Hockin, D., Ounsted, M., Gorman, M., Keller, V. and Barker, M.A. (1992) Examination of the effects of disturbance on birds with reference to its importance in ecological assessments. *Journal of Environmental Management* 36, 253–86.

Hockings, M. (1994) A survey of the tour operator's role in marine park interpretation. *Journal of Tourism Studies* 5(1), 16–28.

Hockings, M. and Twyford, K. (1997) Assesment and management of beach camping impacts within Fraser Island World Heritage Area, South-East Queensland. *Australian Journal of Environmental Management* 4, 26–39.

Hodgson, G. (1999) A global assessment of human effects on coral reefs. *Marine Pollution Bulletin* 38(5), 345–55.

Hof, M. and Lime, D.W. (1997) Visitor experience and resource protection framework in the national park system: Rationale, current status, and future direction. In S.F. McCool and D.N. Cole (eds) *Proceedings from a Workshop on Limits of Acceptable Change and Related Planning Processes: Progress and Future Directions, University of Montana's Lubrecht Experimental Forest, Missoula, Montana, May 20–22, 1997* (pp. 29–36). Ogden, UT: US Department of Agriculture Forest Service, Rocky Mountain Research Station.

Holden, A. (2000) *Environment and Tourism*. London: Routledge.

Hollis, T. and Bedding, J. (1994) Can we stop the wetlands from drying up? *New Scientist*, 2 July, 30–5.

Holmes, D.O. and Dobson, H.E. (1976) *Ecological Carrying Capacity Research: Yosemite National Park. (1). The Effect of Human Trampling and Urine on Subalpine Vegetation – A Survey of Past and Present Backcountry Use and the Ecological Carrying Capacity of Wilderness.* Springfield, Virginia, USA: Department of Commerce, National Technical Information Service.

Honey, M. (1999) *Ecotourism and Sustainable Development: Who Owns Paradise?* Washington, DC: Island Press.

Howard, J.L. (1999) How do scuba diving operators in Vanuatu attempt to minimise their impact on the environment? *Pacific Tourism Review* 3, 61–9.

Huntley, B.J. and Walker, B.H. (eds) (1982) *Ecology of Tropical Savannas.* Berlin: Springer-Verlag.

Huston, M.A. (1994) *Biological Diversity: The Coexistence of Species on Changing Landscapes.* Cambridge: Cambridge University Press.

Huxtable, D. (1987) *The Environmental Impact of Firewood Collection for Campfires and Appropriate Management Strategies.* Salisbury: South Australian College of Advanced Education.

Huyser, O., Ryan, P.G. and Cooper, J. (2000) Changes in population size, habitat use and breeding biology of Lesser Sheathbills (*Chionis minor*) at Marion Island: Impacts of cats, mice and climate change? *Biological Conservation* 92, 299–310.

Hvenegaard, G.T. (1994) Ecotourism: A status report and conceptual framework. *The Journal of Tourism Studies* 5(2), 24–35.

Hvenegaard, G. and Dearden, P. (1998) Ecotourism versus tourism in a Thai national park. *Annals of Tourism Research* 25(3), 700–20.

Hylgaard, T. and Liddle, M.J. (1981) The effect of human trampling on a sand dune ecosystem dominated by *Empetrum nigrum*. *Journal of Applied Ecology* 18, 559–69.

IFAW (International Fund for Animal Welfare) (1996) *Report on the Workshop on the Scientific Aspects of Managing Whale Watching, Montecastello di Vibio, Italy, 1995.* Crowborough: International Fund for Animal Welfare.

Industry and Environment (1986) *Carrying Capacity for Tourism Activities.* Special Issue of UNEP's Industry and Environment Newsletter Vol. 9(1). Paris: United Nations Environment Programme.

Inskeep, E. (1987) Environmental planning for tourism. *Annals of Tourism Research* 14(1), 118–35.

Inskeep, E. (1988) Tourism planning: An emerging specialisation. *Journal of the American Planning Association* 54(3), 360–372.

Iso-Ahola, E.S. (1980) *The Social Psychology of Leisure and Recreation.* Iowa: Wm C. Brown.

Ittleson, W.H., Franck, K.A. and O'Hanlon, T.J. (1976) The nature of environmental experience. In S. Wagner, B.S. Cohen and B. Kaplan (eds) *Experiencing the Environment* (pp. 187–206). New York: Plenum Press.

IUCN (International Union for the Conservation of Nature and Natural Resources) (1980) *World Conservation Strategy: Living Resource Conservation for Sustainable Development.* Gland, Switzerland: IUCN, United Nations Environment Programme and the World Wildlife Fund.

IUCN (International Union for the Conservation of Nature and Natural Resources) (1994) *United Nations List of National Parks and Protected Areas.* Prepared by WCMC and CNPPA. Gland, Switzerland: IUCN.

Iveson, J.B. and Hart, R.P. (1983) Salmonella on Rottnest Island: Implications for public health and wildlife management. *Journal of the Royal Society of Western Australia* 66, 15–23.

Jackson, I. (1986) Carrying capacity for tourism in small tropical Caribbean islands. *UNEP's Industry and Environment Newsletter* 9(1), 7–10.

Jacobs, M. (1981) *The Tropical Rain Forest.* Berlin: Springer-Verlag.

Jacobson, S.K. and Lopez, A.F. (1994) Biological impacts of ecotourism and nesting turtles in Tortuguero National Park, Costa Rica. *Wildlife Society Bulletin* 22(3), 414–19.

Jafari, J. (1987) Tourism for whom? Review of E. Hong (1985) See the Third World while it lasts: The social environmental impact of tourism with special reference to Malaysia. Consumers' Association of Penang, Malaysia. *Tourism Recreation Research* 12(2), 65–8.

Jafari, J. (ed.) (2000) *Encyclopedia of Tourism*. London: Routledge.

Jarvinen, O. and Vaisanen, R.A. (1977) Long term changes of North European land bird fauna. *Oikos* 29, 225–8.

Jim, C.Y. (1989) Visitor management in recreation areas. *Environmental Conservation* 16(1), 19–32 and 40.

Johannes, R.E. (1977) Coral reefs. In J. Clark (ed.) *Coastal Ecosystem Management* (pp. 593–4). New York: John Wiley.

Johnstone, I.M., Coffey, B. and Howard-Williams, C. (1985) The role of recreational boat traffic in interlake dispersal of macrophytes: A New Zealand case study. *Journal of Environmental Management* 20, 263–79.

Jordon, C.F. (1995) *Conservation: Replacing Quantity with Quality as a Goal for Global Management*. New York: John Wiley.

Kakadu Board of Management and Parks Australia (1998) *Kakadu National Park Plan of Management*. Jabiru, NT: Commonwealth of Australia.

Kariel, H.G. (1989) Tourism and development: Perplexity or panacea? *Journal of Travel Research* 28(1): 2–6.

Kelly, P.E. and Larson, D.W. (1997) Effects of rock climbing on populations of presettlement Eastern White Ceder (*Thuja occidentalis*) on cliffs of the Niagara escarpment, Canada. *Conservation Biology* 11(5), 1125–32.

Kevan, P.G., Forbes, B.C., Kevan, S.M. and Behan-Pelletier, V. (1995) Vehicle tracks on high Arctic tundra: Their effects on the soil, vegetation and soil arthropods. *Journal of Applied Ecology* 32, 655–67.

Khan, M. (1997) Tourism development and dependency theory: Mass tourism vs ecotourism. *Annals of Tourism Research* 24(4), 988–91.

Kiernan, K. (1987) Soils and cave management. *Australian Ranger Bulletin* 4(3), 6–7.

Kingsford, R.T. (2000) Ecological impacts of dams, water diversions and river management on floodplain wetlands in Australia. *Austral Ecology* 25, 109–27.

Kinlaw, A. (1999) A review of burrowing by semi-fossorial vertebrates in arid environments. *Journal of Arid Environments* 41, 127–45.

Kinnaird, M.F. and O'Brien, T.G. (1996) Ecotourism in the Tangkoko Duasudara Nature Reserve: Opening Pandora's Box? *Oryx* 30(1), 65–73.

Kirkby, M.J. (1980) The problem. In M.J. Kirkby and R.C.P. Morgan (eds) *Soil Erosion*. Chichester: John Wiley.

Knight, R.L. and Gutzwiller, K.J. (1995) *Wildlife and Recreationists: Coexistence through Management and Research*. Washington, DC: Island Press.

Krakauer, J. (1998) *Into Thin Air*. New York: Anchor Publishing.

Krebs, C.J. (1985) *Ecology: The Experimental Analysis of Distribution and Abundance*. New York: Harper & Row.

Krumpe, E. and McCool, S.F. (1997) Role of public involvement in the limits of acceptable change wilderness planning system. In S.F. McCool and D.N. Cole (eds.) *Proceedings from a Workshop on Limits of Acceptable Change and Related Planning Processes: Progress and Future Directions, University of Montana's Lubrecht Experimental Forest, Missoula, Montana, May 20–22, 1997* (General Techicnal Report INT-GTR-371, pp. 16–20). Ogden, UT: University of Montana's Lubrecht Experimental Forest, Rocky Mountain Research Station.

Kuhre, W.L. (1995) *ISO 14001 Certification*. Upper Saddle River, NJ: Prentice Hall.

Kuitunen, M., Rossi, E. and Stenroos, A. (1998) Do highways influence density of land birds? *Environmental Management* 22(2), 297–302.

Kuss, F.R. and Morgan, J.M. (1984) Using the USLE to estimate the physical carrying capacity of natural areas for outdoor recreation planning. *Journal of Soil and Water Conservation* 39, 383–7.

Kuss, F.R., Graefe, A.R. and Vaske, J.J. (1990) *Visitor Impact Management: A Review of Research* Vol. 1. Washington, DC: National Parks and Conservation Association.

Kutiel, P., Eden, E and Zheveley, Y. (2000) Effect of experimental trampling and off-road motorcycle traffic on soil and vegetation of stabilized coastal dunes, Israel. *Environmental Conservation* 27(1), 14–23.

Landres, P., Cole, D. and Watson, A. (1994) A monitoring strategy for the national wilderness preservation system. In J.C. Hendee and V.G. Martin (eds) *International Wilderness Alloca-tion, Management, and Research* (pp. 192–7). Fort Collins, CO: International Wilderness Leadership (WILD) Foundation.

Lawrence, T., Wickins, D. and Phillips, N. (1997) Managing legitimacy in ecotourism. *Tourism Management* 18(5), 307–16.

Leiper, N. (1981) Towards a cohesive, curriculum in tourism, the case for a distinct discipline. *Annals of Tourism Research* 8(1), 69–84.

Leonard, M. and Holmes, D. (1987) Recreation management and multi-resource planning for the Mt Cole Forest, Victoria. *Forest Management in Australia: Proceedings of the 1987 Conference of the Institute of Foresters of Australia, September 28 – October 2, 1987, Perth, Western Australia* (pp. 399–415).

Leslie, D. (1986) Tourism and conservation in national parks. *Tourism Management* 7(1), 52–6.

Leung, Y-F. and Marion, J.L. (1995) *A Survey of Campsite Conditions in Eleven Wilderness Areas of the Jefferson National Forest* (USDI National Biological Service Report). Blacksburg, VA: Virginia Tech Cooperative Park Studies Unit, Virginia Tech University.

Leung, Y-F. and Marion, J.L. (1996) Trail degradation as influenced by environmental factors: A state of the knowledge review. *Journal of Soil and Water Conservation* 51, 130–6.

Leung, Y-F. and Marion, J.L. (1999a) Assessing trail conditions in protected areas: Application of a problem assessment method in Great Smoky Mountains National Park, USA. *Environmental Conservation* 26(4), 270–9.

Leung, Y-F. and Marion, J.L. (1999b) Spatial strategies for managing visitor impacts in national parks. *Journal of Park and Recreation Administration* 17(4), 2–38.

Leung, Y-F. and Marion, J.L. (1999c) Characterizing backcountry camping impacts in Great Smoky Mountains National Park, USA. *Journal of Environmental Management* 57, 193–203.

Leung, Y-F. and Marion, J.L. (2000) Recreation impacts and management in wilderness: A state-of-knowledge review. In D.N. Cole, S.F. McCool, W.T. Borrie and J. O'Loughlin (eds) *Wilderness Science in a Time of Change Conference*. Vol. 5. *Wilderness Ecosystems, Threats, and Management, May 23–27, 1999, Missoula, MT* (pp. 23–48). Ogden, UT: USDA Forest Service Rocky Mountain Research Station.

Leung, Y-F., Marion, J.L. and Ferguson, J.Y. (1997) Methods for assessing and monitoring backcountry trail conditions: An empirical comparison. In D. Harmon (ed.) *Making Protection Work: Proceedings of the 9th Conference on Research and Resource Management in Parks and on Public Lands: The George Wright Society Biennial Conference, March 17–21, Albuquerque, New Mexico.*

Levinton, J.S. (2001) *Marine Biology: Function, Biodiversity, Ecology.* New York: Oxford University Press.

Liddle, M.J. (1975) A theoretical relationship between the primary production of vegetation and its ability to tolerate trampling. *Biological Conservation* 8, 251–5.

Liddle, M.J. (1997) *Recreation Ecology: The Ecological Impact of Outdoor Recreation and Ecotourism.* London: Chapman & Hall.

Liddle, M.J. and Kay, A.M. (1987) Resistance, survival and recovery of trampled corals on the Great Barrier Reef. *Biological Conservation* 42, 1–18.

Liddle, M.J. and Scorgie, H.R.A. (1980) The effects of recreation on freshwater plants and animals: A review. *Biological Conservation* 17, 183–206.

Lindberg, K. (1998) Economic aspects of ecotourism. In K. Lindberg, M. Epler Wood and D.

Engeldrum (eds) *Ecotourism: A Guide for Planners and Managers* Vol. 2 (pp. 87–117). Vermont: The Ecotourism Society.

Lindberg, K. (2001) Economic impacts. In D. Weaver (ed.) *The Encyclopedia of Ecotourism* (pp. 363–77). Wallingford: CABI.

Lindberg, K., Enriquez, J. and Sproule, K. (1996) Ecotourism questioned: Case studies from Belize. *Annals of Tourism Research* 23, 3 and 543–62.

Lindberg, K., McCool, S. and Stankey, G. (1997) Rethinking carrying capacity. *Annals of Tourism Research* 24, 461–5.

Lipscombe, N. (1993) Recreation planning: Where have all the frameworks gone? *Proceedings of Royal Australian Institute of Parks and Recreation, Cairns, Queensland, September 1993.* Cairns, Australia: Centre for Leisure Research, Griffith University.

Lipscombe, N.R. (1987) *Park Management Planning: A Guide to the Writing of Management Plans.* Wagga Wagga: Riverina-Murray Institute of Higher Education.

Liu, J.C., Sheldon, P.J. and Var, T. (1987) Resident perception of the environmental impacts of tourism. *Annals of Tourism Research* 14(1), 17–37.

Lucas, P.H.C. (1992) *Protected Landscapes: A Guide for Policy-Makers and Planners.* London: Chapman & Hall.

Lucas, R.C. (1990a) The wilderness experience and managing the factors that influence it. In J.C. Hendee, G.H. Stankey and R.C. Lucas (eds) *Wilderness Management* (pp. 469–99). Golden, CO: North America Press.

Lucas, R.C. (1990b) Wilderness use and users: Trends and projections and wilderness recreation management: An overview. In J.C. Hendee, G.H. Stankey and R.C. Lucas (eds) *Wilderness Management* (pp. 355–98). Golden, CO: North American Press.

Luckenbach, R.A. and Bury, R.B. (1983) Effects of off-road vehicles on the biota of the Algodunes, Imperial County, California. *Journal of Applied Ecology* 20, 265–86.

Lull, H.J. (1959) *Soil Compaction on Forest and Rangelands.* USDA Forest Service Miscellaneous Publication 768. Washington, DC.

Mabberley, D.J. (1992) *Tropical Rain Forest Ecology.* Glasgow: Blackie & Son.

MacKay, R. (1995) Visitor impact management: Determining a social and environmental carrying capacity for Jenolan Caves. In H. Richins, J. Richardson and A. Crabtree (eds) *Ecotourism and Nature-Based Tourism: Taking the Next Steps: Proceedings of the Ecotourism Association of Australia, National Conference, 18–23 November 1995, Alice Springs, Northern Territory* (pp. 223–8). Newcastle NSW: Department of Leisure and Tourism Studies, University of Newcastle.

Madej, M.A., Weaver, W.E. and Hagans, D.K. (1994) Analysis of bank erosion on the Merced River, Yosemite Valley, Yosemite National Park, California, USA. *Environmental Management* 18(2), 234–50.

Mader, S.S. (1991) *Inquiry into Life.* Dubuque: C. Brown Publishers.

Malanson, G.P. (1993) *Riparian Landscapes.* Cambridge: Cambridge University Press.

Manidis Roberts Consultants (1995) *Determining an Environmental and Social Carrying Capacity for Jenolan Caves Reserve: Applying a Visitor Impact Management System.* Sydney: Manidis Roberts Consultants.

Manidis Roberts Consultants (1997) *Developing a Tourism Optimisation Management Model (TOMM)* (Final Report). Sydney: Manidis Roberts Consultants.

Mann, J. and Barnett, H. (1999) Lethal Tiger Shark (*Gaeocerdo cuvier*) attack on a Bottlenose Dolphin (*Tursiops sp*) calf: Defense and reactions by the mother. *Marine Mammal Science* 15(2), 568–75.

Manning, R.E. (1979) Strategies for managing recreational use of national parks. *Parks* 4(1), 13–15.

Manning, R.E., Ballinger, N.L., Marion, J. and Roggenbuck, J. (1996) Recreation management in natural areas: Problems and practices, status and trends. *Natural Areas Journal* 16(2), 142–6.

Manning, R., Jacobi, C., Valliere, W. and Wang, B. (1998) Standards of quality in parks and recreation. *Parks and Recreation*, July, 88–94.

Manning, R.E., Lime, D.W. and Hof, M. (1996) Social carrying capacity of natural areas: Theory and application in the U.S. national parks. *Natural Areas Journal* 16(2), 118–27.

Marchant, S. and Higgins, P.J. (1990) *Handbook of Australian, New Zealand and Antarctic Birds* Vol. 1. Melbourne: Oxford University Press.

Marion, J.L. (1991) *Developing a Natural Resource Inventory and Monitoring Program for Visitor Impacts on Recreation Sites: A Procedural Manual* (Natural Resources Report, NPS/NRVT/NRR-91/06). Denver, CO: United States Department of Interior National Park Service.

Marion, J.L. (1995) Capabilities and management utility of recreation impact monitoring programs. *Environmental Management* 18(5), 763–71.

Marion, J.L. and Leung, Y.F. (2001) Trail resource impacts and an examination of alternative assessment techniques. *Journal of Park and Recreation Administration (Special Issue on Parks and Greenways)* 19 (in press).

Marion, J.L., Roggenbuck, J.W. and Manning, R.E. (1993) *Problems and Practices in Backcountry Recreation Management: A Survey of National Park Service Managers* (Natural Resources Report NPS/NRVT/NRR-93/12). USDI National Park Services.

Marron, C-H. (1999) The impact of ecotourism. *Flora and Fauna News* 11, 14.

Marsh, N.R. and Henshall, B.D. (1987) Planning better tourism: The strategic importance of tourist–resident expectations and interactions. *Tourism Recreation Research* 12(2), 47–54.

Martin, S.R. and McCool, S.F. (1989) Wilderness campsite impacts: Do managers and visitors see them the same? *Environmental Management* 13(5), 623–9.

Mason, P.A. and Legg, S.J. (1999) Antarctic tourism: Activities, impacts, management issues, and a proposed research agenda. *Pacific Tourism Review* 3, 71–84.

Mastran, T.A., Dietrich, A.M., Gallagher, D.L. and Grizzard, T.J. (1994) Distribution of polyaromatic hydrocarbons in the water column and sediments of a drinking water reservoir with respect to boating activity. *Water Research* 28, 2353–66.

Mathieson, A. and Wall, G. (1982) *Tourism: Economic, Physical and Social Impacts*. London: Longman.

May, V. (1990) Tourism, environment and development. *Tourism Management* 12(2), 112–18.

McArthur, S. (1994) Acknowledging a symbiotic relationship. Better heritage management via better visitor management. *Australian Parks and Recreation*, Spring, 12–17.

McArthur, S. (1996) Beyond the limits of acceptable change: Developing a model to monitor and manage tourism in remote areas. *Towards a More Sustainable Tourism Down Under 2 Conference, Centre for Tourism, University of Otago, Dunedin, New Zealand* (pp. 223–229). Otago: Centre for Tourism.

McArthur, S. (1998a) Introducing the undercapitalized world of interpretation. In K. Lindberg, M. Epler Wood and D. Engeldrum (eds) *Ecotourism: A Guide for Planners and Managers* Vol. 2 (pp. 63–85). North Bennington, VT: The Ecotourism Society.

McArthur, S. (1998b) Embracing the future of ecotourism, sustainable tourism and the EAA in the new millenium. *Proceedings of Sixth Annual Conference of the Ecotourism Association of Australia, 29 October – 1 November, 1998, Margaret River, Western Australia* (pp. 1–14).

McArthur, S. (2000a) Visitor management in Action: An analysis of the development and implementation of visitor management models at Jenolan Caves and Kangaroo Island. PhD thesis, University of Canberra, Canberra, ACT.

McArthur, S. (2000b) Beyond carrying capacity: Introducing a model to monitor and manage visitor activity in forests. In X. Font and J. Tribe (eds) *Forest Tourism and Recreation: Case Studies in Environmental Management* (pp. 259–78). Wallingford: CABI Publishing.

McArthur, S. and Hall, C.M. (1996) Interpretation: principles and practice. In C.M. Hall and S. McArthur (eds) *Heritage Management in Australia and New Zealand*. Melbourne: Oxford University Press.

McCarthy, J. (2001) The fourth circle: A political ecology of Sumatra's rainforest frontier. PhD thesis. The Asia Research Centre, Murdoch University, Murdoch, WA.

McCaw, L. and Gillen, K. (1993) Fire. In C. Thomson, G. Hall and G. Friend (eds) *Mountains of Mystery: A Natural History of the Stirling Range* (pp. 143–8). Perth: Department of Conservation and Land Management.

McCawley, R. and Teaff, J.D. (1995) Characteristics and environmental attitudes of coral reef divers in the Florida Keys. In S. F. McCool and A. E. Watson (eds) *Linking Tourism, the Environment, and Sustainability: Topical Volume of Compiled Papers from a Special Session of the Annual Meeting of the National Recreation and Park Association, 1994*. Minneapolis: US Department of Agriculture, Forest Service.

McClaran, M.P. and Cole, D.N. (1993) *Packstock in Wilderness: Use, Impacts, Monitoring, and Management* (General Technical Report INT-301). Ogden, UT: United States Department of Agriculture Forest Service Intermountain Research Station.

McCool, S.F. (1986) Putting wilderness research and technology to work in the Bob Marshall Wilderness Complex. *Proceedings from National Wilderness Research Conference: Current Research, July 23–26, 1985, Fort Collins, Colorado*, (General Technical Report INT-212, July1986). Fort Collins, CO: USDA Forest Service Intermountain Research Station.

McCool, S.F. and Cole, D.N. (1997) Experiencing limits of acceptable change: Some thoughts after a decade of implementation. In S.F. McCool and D.N. Cole (eds) *Proceedings from a Workshop on Limits of Acceptable Change and Related Planning Processes: Progress and Future Directions, University of Montana's Lubrecht Experimental Forest, Missoula, Montana, May 20–22, 1997* (General Technical Report INT-GTR-371) (pp. 72–8). Ogden, UT: US Department of Agriculture Forest Service, Rocky Mountain Research Station.

McCool, S.F. and Patterson, M. (2000) Trends in recreation, tourism and protected area planning. In D.W. Lime and W. Gartner (eds) *Trends in Outdoor Recreation, Leisure and Tourism* (pp. 111–20). Wallingford: CABI Publishing.

McNaughton, S.J. (1989) Ecosystems and conservation in the twenty-first century. In D. Western and M. Pearl (eds) *Conservation for the Twenty-First Century* (pp. 109–20). New York: Oxford University Press.

McNeely, J.A. (1990) The future of national parks. *Environment* 32(1), 16–20 and 36–41.

McNeely, J.A. and Thorsell, J.W. (1989) Jungles, mountains and islands: How tourism can help conserve the natural heritage. *World Leisure and Recreation* 31(4), 29–39.

McNeely, J.A., Harrison, J. and Dingwall, P. (1994) Introduction: Protected areas in the modern world. In J.A. McNeely, J. Harrison and P. Dingwall (eds) *Protecting Nature: Regional Reviews of Protected Areas* (pp. 1–28). Gland, Switzerland: International Union for Conservation of Nature and Natural Resources.

Medio, D., Ormond, R.F.G. and Pearson, M. (1997) Effect of briefings on rates of damage to corals by SCUBA divers. *Biological Conservation* 79, 91–5.

Meredith, C. (1997) *Best Practice in Performance Reporting in Natural Resource Management: ANZECC Working Group on National Parks and Protected Area Management Benchmarking and Best Practice Program* (Report). Port Melbourne: Biosis Research.

Merigliano, L., Cole, D.N. and Parsons, D.J. (1997) Applications of LAC-type processes and concepts to nonrecreation management issues in protected areas. In S.F. McCool and D.N. Cole (eds) *Proceedings from a Workshop on Limits of Acceptable Change and Related Planning Processes: Progress and Future Directions, University of Montana's Lubrecht Experimental Forest, Missoula, Montana, May 20–22, 1997* (General Technical Report INT-GTR-371) (pp. 37–43). Ogden, UT: US Department of Agriculture Forest Service, Rocky Mountain Research Station.

Mignucci-Giannoni, A.A., Monyoya-Ospina, R.A., Jimenez-Marrero, N.M., Rodriguez-Lopez, MA., Williams, E.H. and Bonde, R.K. (2000) Manatee mortality in Puerto Rico. *Environmental Management* 25(2), 189–98.

Mill, R.C. and Morrison, A.M. (1985) *The Tourism System: An Introductory Text*. New Jersey: Prentice-Hall.

Miller, Jr, G.T (2002) *Living in the Environment: Principles, Connections, and Solutions* (12th edn). Belmont, CA: Brooks/Cole.

Moncrieff, D. (1997) *A Tourism Optimisation Management Model for Dryandra Woodland* (unpublished report). Perth: WA Department of Conservation and Land Management.

Moncrieff, D. and Lent, L. (1996) Tune into the future of interpretation. *Ranger* 34, 10–11.

Monz, C. (2000) Recreation resource assessment and monitoring techniques for mountain regions. In P.M. Godde, M.F. Price and F.M. Zimmermann (eds) *Tourism and Development in Mountain Regions* (pp. 47–68). Oxford: CABI Publishing.

Moore, S.A. and Lee, R.G. (1999) Understanding dispute resolution processes for American and Australian public wildlands: Towards a conceptual framework for managers. *Environmental Management* 23(4), 453–65.

Morgan, J.M. and Kuss, F.R. (1986) Soil loss as a measure of carrying capacity in recreation environments. *Environmental Management* 10(2), 263–70.

Morin, S.L., Moore, S.A. and Schmidt, W. (1997) Defining indicators and standards for recreation impacts in Nuyts Wilderness, Walpole-Nornalup National Park, Western Australia. *CALM Science* 2(3), 247–66.

Morrison, A., Hsieh, S. and Wang, C.Y. (1992) Certification in the travel and tourism industry: The North American experience. *The Journal of Tourism Studies* 3(2), 32–40.

Morrison, R.J. and Munroe, A.J. (1999) Waste management in the small island developing states of the South Pacific: An overview. *Journal of Environmental Management* 6(4), 232–46.

Moscardo, G. (2000) Interpretation. In J. Jafari (ed.) *Encyclopedia of Tourism*. London: Routledge.

Mosisch, T.D. and Arthington, A.H. (1998) The impacts of power boating and water skiing on lakes and reservoirs. *Lakes and Reservoirs: Research and Management* 3, 1–17.

Muir, F. and Chester, G. (1993) Case study: Managing tourism of a seabird nesting island. *Tourism Management* April, 99–105.

Murphy, K.J., Willby, N.J. and Eaton, J.W. (1995) Ecological impacts and management of boat traffic on navigable inland waterways. In D.M. Harper and A.J.D. Ferguson (eds) *The Ecological Basis for River Management*. Chichester: John Wiley.

Murphy, P.E. (1985) *Tourism: A Community Approach*. New York: Methuen.

Murphy, P.E. (1986a) Tourism as an agent for landscape conservation: An assessment. *The Science of the Total Environment* 55, 387–95.

Murphy, P.E. (1986b) Conservation and tourism: A business partnership. In *Tourism and the Environment: Conflict or Harmony?* CSEB Proceedings of a Symposium sponsored by the Canadian Society of Environmental Biologists, Alberta Chapter, Calgary, Canada, 18–19 March 1986 (pp. 117–27). Alberta: CSEB, Alberta Chapter.

Naiman, R.J. (1988) Animal influences on ecosystem dynamics. *Bioscience* 38: 750–2.

Neale, G. (1998) *The Green Travel Guide*. London: Earthscan.

Nelson, B. (1980) *Seabirds: Their Biology and Ecology*. London: Hamlyn.

Netherwood, A. (1996) Environmental management systems. In R. Welford (ed.) *Corporate Environmental Management: Systems and Strategies* (pp. 35–58). London: Earthscan.

Neuman, W.L. (1994) *Social Research Methods: Qualitative and Quantitative Approaches*. Boston: Allyn & Bacon.

Newsome, D. (2001) The role of an accidentally introduced fungus in degrading the health of the Stirling Range National Park ecosystem in South Western Australia: Status and prognosis. In B. Lasley, D. Rapport, D. Rolston, O. Nielsen and C. Qualset (eds) *Managing for Biodiversity*, Vol. II *Issues and Methods: Managing for Biodiversity*. (In press.)

Newton, I. (1995) The contribution of some recent research on birds to ecological understanding. *Journal of Animal Ecology* 64, 675–96.

Nilsen, P. and Tayler, G. (1997) A comparative analysis of protected area planning and management frameworks. In S.F. McCool and D.N. Cole (eds) *Proceedings of a Workshop on Limits of Acceptable Change and Related Planning Processes: Progress and Future Directions, University of Montana's Lubrecht Experimental Forest, Missoula, Montana, May 20–22, 1997* (pp. 49–57). Ogden, UT: US Department of Agriculture Forest Service, Rocky Mountain Research Station.

North Carolina State University and Department of Parks, Recreation and Tourism Management (1994) Conflicts on multiple-use trails: Synthesis of the literature and state of the practice. Document produced by the Federal Highway Administration Intermodal Division, Washington, DC (2000). Sourced via the New Zealand Mountain Bike Website: http://www.mountainbike.co.nz/ on 13 July 2000).

Obua, J. and Harding, D.M. (1997) Environmental impact of ecotourism in Kibale National Park, Uganda. *Journal of Sustainable Tourism* 5(3), 213–23.

Oma, V.P.M., Clayton, D.M., Broun, J.B. and Keating, C.D.M. (1992) *Coastal Rehabilitation Manual*. South Perth: Department of Agriculture, Western Australia.

Ongerth, J.E., Hunter, G.D. and DeWalle, F.B. (1995) Watershed use and *Giardia* cyst presence. *Water Research* 29(5), 1295–9.

Onyeanusi, A.E. (1986) Measurements of impact of tourist off-road driving on grasslands in Masai Mara National Reserve, Kenya: A simulation approach. *Environmental Conservation* 13(4), 325–9.

Orams, M.B. (1995) Using interpretation to manage nature based tourism. *Journal of Sustainable Tourism* 4(2), 81–93.

Orams, M.B. (1996) A conceptual model of tourist-wildlife interaction: The case for education as a management strategy. *Australian Geographer* 27(1), 39–51.

Parsons, D.J. (1986) Campsite impact data as a basis for determining wilderness use capacities. *Proceedings from National Wilderness Research Conference: Current Research, July 23–26, 1985)* (General Technical Report INT-212, published July 1986). Fort Collins, CO: USDA Forest Service Intermountain Research Station.

Parsons, D.J. and MacLeod, S.A. (1980) Measuring impacts of wilderness use. *Parks* 5(3), 8–12.

PATA (Pacific Asia Tourism Association) (1991) *PATA Code for Environmentally Responsible Tourism: An Environmental Ethic for the Travel and Tourism Industry*. San Francisco, CA: Pacific Asia Tourism Association.

Pearce, D.G. (1985) Tourism and planning in the Southern Alps of New Zealand. In T.V. Singh and J. Kaur (eds) *Integrated Mountain Development* (pp. 293–308). New Delhi: Himalayan Books.

Pearce, D.G. (1989) *Tourist Development* (2nd edn). Harlow: Longman Scientific and Technical.

Pearce, D.G. and Kirk, R.M. (1986) Carrying capacities for coastal tourism. *UNEP's Industry and Environment Newsletter* 9(1), 3–7.

Pearce-Higgins, J.W. and Yalden, D.W. (1997) The effect of resurfacing the Pennine Way on recreational use of Blanket Bog in the Peak District National Park, England. *Biological Conservation* 82, 337–43.

Petts, G.E. (1984) *Impounded Rivers: Perspectives for Ecological Management*. Chichester: John Wiley.

Phillips, A. (1985) Opening address. In *Tourism, Recreation and Conservation in National Parks and Equivalent Reserves: A European Heritage Landscapes Conference, Peak National Park Centre* (pp. 9–14). Derbyshire: Peak Park Joint Planning Board.

Phillips, N. (2000) A field experiment to quantify the environmental impacts of horse riding in D'Entrecateaux National Park, Western Australia. Unpublished Honours thesis, School of Environmental Science, Murdoch University, Western Australia.

Pitts, D. and Smith, J. (1993) A visitor monitoring strategy for Kakadu National Park. In *Track to the Future: Managing Change in Parks and Recreation: National Conference of the Royal Australian Institute of Parks and Recreation, September 1993, Cairns* (12 pp.). Dickson, ACT: RAIPR.

Plog, S.C. (1974) Why destination areas rise and fall in popularity. *Cornell Hotel and Restaurant Administration Quarterly*, November, 13–6.

Poland, R.H.C., Hall, G.B. and Smith, M. (1996) Turtles and tourists: A hands-on experience of conservation for sixth formers from King's College, Taunton, on the Ionian island of Zakynthos. *Journal of Biological Education* 30(2),120–8.

Poon, A. (1993) *Tourism, Technology and Competitive Strategies.* Wallingford: CAB International.

Press, A.J. and Hill, M.A. (1994) Kakadu National Park: An Australian experience in comanagement. In D. Western, R.M. Wright and S.C. Strum (eds) *Natural Connections: Perspectives in Community-Based Conservation* (pp. 135–57). Washington, DC: Island Press.

Press, T. and Lawrence, D. (1995) Kakadu National Park: Reconciling competing interests. In T. Press, D. Lea, A. Webb and A. Graham (eds) *Kakadu: Natural and Cultural Heritage and Management* (pp. 1–14). Darwin: Australian Nature Conservation Agency and North Australia Research Unit, ANU.

Primack, R.B. (1998) *Essentials of Conservation Biology.* Sunderland, MA: Sinauer Associates.

Prosser, G. (1986) The limits of acceptable change: An introduction to a framework for natural area planning. *Australian Parks and Recreation* 22(2), 5–10.

Ramsar Convention Bureau (2000) *The Ramsar Convention on Wetlands: The List of Wetlands of International Importance* (14 September 2000). Online at http://www.ramsar.org/key_sitelist.htm#list (Accessed 30 October 2000).

Regel, J. and Putz, K. (1997) Effect of human disturbance on body temperature and energy expenditure in penguins. *Polar Biology* 18, 246–53.

Reijnen, R., Foppen, R., ter Braak, C. and Thissen, J. (1995) The effects of car traffic on breeding bird populations in woodland. III. Reduction of density in relation to the proximity to main roads. *Journal of Appied Ecology* 32, 187–202.

Rickard, W.E. and Brown, J. (1974) Effects of vehicles on Arctic tundra. *Environmental Conservation* 1(1), 55–62.

Ritter, D. (1997) Limits of acceptable change planning in the Selway-Bitterroot Wilderness: 1985 to 1997. In S.F. McCool and D.N. Cole (eds) *Proceedings from a Workshop on Limits of Acceptable Change and Related Planning Processes: Progress and Future Directions, University of Montana's Lubrecht Experimental Forest, Missoula, Montana, May 20–22, 1997* (General Technical Report INT-GTR-371, pp. 25–8). Ogden, UT: University of Montana's Lubrecht Experimental Forest, Rocky Mountain Research Station.

Roe, D., Leader-Williams, N. and Dalal-Clayton, B. (1997) *Take only Photographs, Leave Only Footprints: The Environmental Impacts of Wildlife Tourism* (Wildlife and Development Series No. 10). London: International Institute for Environment and Development.

Roggenbuck, J.W. and Lucas, R.C. (1987) Wilderness use and user characteristics: A state-of-knowledge review. *Proceedings of National Wilderness Research Conference: Issues, State-of-Knowledge, Future Directions* (General Technical Report INT-220), pp. 204–45. Ogden, UT: United States Department of Agriculture Forest Service Intermountain Research Station.

Roggenbuck, J.W., Williams, D.R. and Watson, A.E. (1993) Defining acceptable conditions in wilderness. *Environmental Management* 17(2), 187–97.

Romeril, M. (1985) Tourism and the environment: Towards a symbiotic relationship (introductory paper). *International Journal of Environmental Studies* 25(4), 215–18.

Romeril, M. (1989) Tourism and the environment: Accord or discord? *Tourism Management* 10(3), 204–8.

Rosen, P.C. and Lowe, C.H. (1994) Highway mortality of snakes in the Sonoran Desert of southern Arizona. *Biological Conservation* 68, 143–8.

Ryan, C. (1998) Kakadu National Park (Australia). In M. Shackley (ed.) *Visitor Management: Case Studies from World Heritage Sites* (pp. 121–38). Oxford: Butterworth-Heinemann.

Salm, R.V. (1986) Coral reefs and tourist carrying capacity: The Indian Ocean experience. *UNEP Industry and Environment* 1(9), 11–14.

Sautter, E.T. and Leisen, B. (1999) Managing stakeholders: A tourism planning model. *Annals of Tourism Research* 26(2), 312–28.

Scott, R.L. (1998) Wilderness management and restoration in high use areas of Olympic National Park, Washington, USA. In A.E. Watson, G.H. Aplet and J.C. Hendee (eds) *Personal, Societal, and Ecological Values of Wilderness: Proceedings Sixth World Wilderness*

Congress on Research, Management and Allocation, October 1997, Bangalore, India (pp. 144–7). Ogden, UT: United States Department of Agriculture Forest Service Rocky Mountain Research Station.

Shackley, M. (1996) *Wildlife Tourism*. London: International Thomson Business Press.

Shackley, M. (1998) 'Stingray City': Managing the impact of underwater tourism in the Cayman Islands. *Journal of Sustainable Tourism* 6(4), 328–38.

Sharp, D. (1999) Chief of Resource management, Wrangell-St Elias National Park and Preserve, Alaska, USA. [Personal communication.]

Sharpe, G.W. (1982) *Interpreting the Environment*. New York: John Wiley.

Shearer, B.L. (1994) The major plant pathogens occurring in the native ecosystems of south-western Australia. *Journal of the Royal Society of Western Australia* 77, 113–22.

Shelby, B. and Heberlein, T.A. (1984) A conceptual framework for carrying capacity determination. *Leisure Sciences* 6(4), 433–51.

Shindler, B. and Shelby, B. (1993) Regulating wilderness use: An investigation of user group support. *Journal of Forestry* 91(2), 41–4.

Sigal, L.L. and Nash, T.H. (1983) Lichen communities on conifers in southern California mountains: An ecological survey relative to oxidant air pollution. *Ecology* 64, 1343–54.

Singh, T.V. (1992) *Tourism Environment: Nature, Culture, Economy*. New Delhi: Inter India Publications.

Smith, A.J. (1998) Environmental impacts of recreation and tourism in Warren National Park, Western Australia and appropriate management planning. Unpublished Honours Thesis, Department of Environmental Science, Murdoch University, Western Australia.

Smith, R.H. and Neal, J.E. (1993) *Wood Residues in Regenerated Karri Stands* (CALM Internal Report). Manjimup, Western Australia: Science and Information Division, Department of Conservation and Land Management.

Smith. V.L. (ed.) (1977) *Hosts and Guests: The Anthropology of Tourism*. Pennsylvania: University of Philadelphia Press.

Smith, V. and Moore, S. (1990) Identifying park users and their expectations: A fundamental component in management plans. *Australian Parks and Recreation* 26(1), 34–41.

Smith,V.L. and Eadington, W.R. (eds) (1992) *Tourism Alternatives: Potentials and Problems in the Development of Tourism*. Philadelphia: International Academy for the Study of Tourism, University of Pennsylvania Press.

Smyth, D. (1999) *Economic Impact of National Park Visitor Spending – Gleaning Visitor Spending Patterns from Secondary Data, Glacier National Park – 1990*. East Lansing, MI: Department of Park, Recreation and Tourism Resources, Michigan State University.

Snowcroft, P.G. and Griffin, J.G. (1983) Feral herbivores suppress Mamane and other browse species on Mauna Kea, Hawaii. *Journal of Range Management* 36, 638–45.

Solbrig, O.T., Medina, E. and Silva, J.F. (eds) (1996) *Biodiversity and Savanna Ecosystem Processes: A Global Perspective*. Berlin: Springer.

Southgate, L. (1999) Green stamp of approval. In *The Australian* newspaper, 13 September 1999 (p.22). Sydney, Australia.

Sowman, P. and Pearce, D.G. (2000) Tourism, national parks and visitor management. In R.W. Butler and S.W. Boyd (eds) *Tourism and National Parks: Issues and Implications* (223–43). Chichester: John Wiley.

Splettstoesser, J. (1999) Antarctica tourism: Successful management of a vulnerable environment. In T.V. Singh and S. Singh (eds) *Tourism Development in Critical Environments* (pp. 137–48). New York: Cognizant Communication Corporation.

Stabler, M. J. (ed) (1997) *Tourism and Sustainability: Principles to Practice*. Oxford: CAB International.

Standards Australia (1997) *Integrating Quality and Environmental Management Systems ISO 9001 and ISO 14001*. Homebush, NSW: Standards Australia.

Standards Australia and Standards New Zealand (1996) *Environmental Management Systems:*

General Guidelines on Principles, Systems and Supporting Techniques. Homebush, NSW: Standards Australia and Standards New Zealand.

Stankey, G.H. (1997) Institutional barriers and opportunities in application of the limits of acceptable change. In S.F. McCool and D.N. Cole (eds) *Proceedings of a Workshop on Limits of Acceptable Change and Related Planning Processes: Progress and Future Directions* (pp. 10–15). Ogden, UT: University of Montana's Lubrecht Experimental Forest, Rocky Mountain Research Station.

Stankey, G.H. and Brown, P.J. (1981) A technique for recreation planning and management in tomorrow's forests. In *Proceedings of XVII IUFRO World Congress, Japan* (pp. 63–73). Japan.

Stankey, G.H., Cole, D.N., Lucas, R.C., Petersen, M.E. and Frissell, S. (1985) *The Limits of Acceptable Change (LAC) System for Wilderness Planning* (General Technical Report, INT-176). Ogden, UT: United States Department of Agriculture (Forest Service), Intermountain Forest and Range Experiment Station.

Stankey, G.H., McCool, S.F. and Stokes, G.L. (1990) Managing for appropriate wilderness conditions: The carrying capacity issue. In J.C. Hendee, G.H. Stankey and R.C. Lucas (eds) *Wilderness Management* (pp. 215–39). Golden, CO: North American Press.

Starkey, R. (1996) The standardization of environmental management systems. In R. Welford (ed.) *Corporate Environmental Management: Systems and Strategies* (pp. 59–91). London: Earthscan.

State Ministry for Environment Republic of Indonesia and United Nations Development Programme (1997) *Agenda 21: Indonesia.* Jakarta: State Ministry for Environment Republic of Indonesia and United Nations Development Programme.

Stattersfield, A.J., Crosby, M.J. and Long, A.J. (1998) *Endemic Birds of the World: Priorities for Biodiversity Conservation.* USA: Smithsonian Institute Press.

Steiner, A.J. and Leatherman, S.P. (1981) Recreational impacts on the distribution of ghost crabs (*Ocypode quadrata*). *Biological Conservation* 29, 11–122.

Stephenson, P.J. (1993) The impacts of tourism on nature reserves in Madagascar: Perinet: A case study. *Environmental Conservation* 20(3), 262–5.

Stewart, W.P. (1989) Fixed itinerary systems in backcountry management. *Journal of Environmental Management* 29, 163–71.

Stokes, G.L. (1987) Involving the public in wilderness management decision making: The Bob Marshall Wilderness Complex – A case study. *Economic and Social Development: A Role for Forests and Forestry Professionals, Proceedings of the 1987 Society of American Foresters National Convention Minneapolis, Minnesota, October 18–21* (pp. 157–61). Bethesda, MD: Society of American Foresters.

Stokes, G.L. (1990) The evolution of wilderness management: The Bob Marshall Wilderness Complex. *Journal of Forestry* 88(10), 15–21.

Stonehouse, B. (1994) Ecotourism in Antarctica. In E. Cater and G. Lowman (eds) *Ecotourism: A Sustainable Option?* (pp. 195–212). Chichester: John Wiley.

Stonehouse, B. and Crosbie, K. (1995) Tourism impacts and management in the Antarctic Peninsula area. In C. M. Hall and M. E. Johnston (eds) *Polar Tourism: Tourism in the Arctic and Antarctic Regions* (pp. 217–33). Chichester: John Wiley.

Storrie, A. and Morrison, S. (1998) *The Marine Life of Ningaloo Marine Park and Coral Bay.* Western Australia: Department of Conservation and Land Management.

Sun, D. and Liddle, M.J. (1993a) A survey of trampling effects on vegetation and soil in eight tropical and subtropical sites. *Environmental Management* 17(4), 497–510.

Sun, D. and Liddle, M.J. (1993b) Plant morphological characteristics and resistance to simulated trampling. *Environmental Management* 17(4), 511–21.

Sun, D. and Walsh, D. (1998) Review of studies on environmental impacts of recreation and tourism in Australia. *Journal of Environmental Management* 53, 323–38.

Swearingen, T.C. and Johnson, D.R. (1995) Visitors' responses to uniformed park employees. *Journal of Park and Recreation Administration* 13, 73–85.

Swinnerton, G.S. (1995) Conservation through partnership: Landscape management within national parks in England and Wales. *Journal of Park and Recreation Administration* 13(4), 47–60.

Tansley, A.G. (1935) The use and abuse of vegetational concepts and terms. *Ecology* 16, 284–307.

TAT (Tourism Authority of Thailand) (1995) *Policies and Guidelines: Development of Ecotourism (1995–1996) of the Tourism Authority of Thailand.* Bangkok: TAT.

TAT (Tourism Authority of Thailand) (1999) Development of Ecotourism Areas Project: Khao Sok National Park, Surat Thani Province. In C. Kandel and M. Marcolina (compilers). *Environment, Culture and Heritage: Best Practice Papers for 1999* (pp. 39–44). Bangkok: Pacific Asia Tourism Association Office of Environment and Culture.

Temple, K.L., Camper, A.K. and Lucas, R.C. (1982) Potential health hazard from human wastes in wilderness. *Journal of Soil and Water Conservation*, November/Decmber, 357–9.

The Ecotourism Society (TES) (1998) *Ecotourism Statistical Fact Sheet.* North Bennington, VT: The Ecotourism Society.

Thrash, I. (1998) Impact of water provision on herbaceous vegetation in Kruger National Park, South Africa. *Journal of Arid Environments* 38, 437–50.

Tilden, F. (1957) *Interpreting our Heritage.* Chapel Hill, NC: University of North Carolina Press.

Timothy, D.J. (1999) Participatory planning: A view of tourism in Indonesia. *Annals of Tourism Research* 26(2), 371–91.

Todd, S.E. and Williams, P.W. (1996) From white to green: A proposed environmental management system framework for ski areas. *Journal of Sustainable Tourism* 4(3), 147–73.

Trauer, B. (1998) Green tourism in the hotel and resort sector: International and New Zealand perspectives. *Australian Parks and Leisure*, December, 5–9.

Trent, D.B. (1991) Case studies of two ecotourism destinations in Brazil. In J.A. Kusler (ed.) *Ecotourism and Resource Conservation* Vol. 1. Miami Beach, FL: International Symposium: Ecotourism and Resource Conservation.

Tuite, C.H., Hanson, P.R. and Owen, M. (1984) Some ecological factors affecting winter wildfowl distribution on inland waters in England and Wales, and the influence of water-based recreation. *Journal of Applied Ecology* 21, 41–62.

Tyler, D. and Dangerfield, J.M. (1999) Ecosystem tourism: A resource based philosophy for ecotourism. *Journal of Sustainable Tourism* 7(2), 146–58.

UNESCO (United Nations Educational, Scientific and Cultural Organization) (2000) *The World Heritage List* (2 December 1999). Online at http://www.unesco.org/whc/heritage.htm (Accessed 15 June 2000).

UNESCO MAB (United Nations Educational, Scientific and Cultural Organization; Man and the Biosphere program) (2001) *Biosphere Reserve Information.* Produced by UNESCO Man and the Biosphere Program (MAB). Website: http://www.unesco.org.mab/ (Accessed 3 April, 2001).

Valentine, P.S. and Cassells, D.S. (1991) Recreation management issues in tropical rain forests. In *Proceedings of the Institute of Tropical Rainforest Studies* (pp. 9–14). Townsville, Australia.

Van der Zande, A.N., Berkhuizen, J.C., van Latesteijn, H.C., ter Keurs, W.J. and Poppelaars, A.J. (1984) Impact of outdoor recreation on the density of a number of breeding bird species in woods adjacent to urban residential areas. *Biological Conservation* 30, 1–39.

Van Riet, W.F. and Cooks, J. (1990) Planning and design of Berg-en-Dal, a new camp in Kruger National Park. *Environmental Management* 14(3), 359–65.

Van Vuren, D. and Coblentz, B.E. (1987) Some ecological effects of feral sheep on Santa Cruz Island, California, USA. *Biological Conservation* 41, 252–68.

Van Wagner, C.E. (1968) The line intersect method in forest fuel sampling. *Forest Science* 14, 20–6.

Van Wagtendonk, J.W. (1986) The determination of carrying capacities for the Yosemite Wilderness. *Proceedings from National Wilderness Research Conference: Current Research, July*

23–26, 1985) (General Technical Report INT-212, July 1986) (pp. 456–61). Fort Collins, CO: USDA Forest Service Intermountain Research Station.

Van Woesik, R. (1992). *Ecology of Coral Assemblages on Continental Islands in the Southern Section of the Great Barrier Reef, Australia*. Townsville: James Cook University of North Queensland, Department of Marine Biology.

Vaske, J.J., Decker, D.J. and Manfredo, M.J. (1995) Human dimensions of wildlife: an integrated framework for coexistence. In R.L. Knight and L.J. Gutzwiller (eds) *Wildlife and Recreationists: Coexistence Through Management and Research*. Washington, DC: Island Press.

Veron, J.E.N. (1986) Distribution of reef building corals. *Oceanus* 29(2), 27–32.

Vogt, C.A. and Williams, D.R. (1999) Support for wilderness recreation fees: The influence of fee purpose and day versus overnight use. *Journal of Park and Recreation Administration* 17(3), 85–99.

Wagar, J.A. (1964) *The Carrying Capacity for Wildlands for Recreation*, Forest Science Monograph 7). Washington, DC: Society of American Foresters.

Wagner, J.E. (1997) Estimating the impacts of tourism. *Annals of Tourism Research* 24, 592–608.

Walker, D.M. (1991) Evaluation and rating of gravel roads. *Transportation Research Record* 2, 120–5.

Wall, G. (1994) Ecotourism: Old wine in new bottles? *Trends* 31(2), 4–9.

Wallace, C.C., Babcock, R.C., Harrison, P.L., Oliver, J.K. and Willis, B.L. (1986) Sex on the reef: Mass spawning of corals. *Oceanus* 29(2), 38–42.

Wallace, G.N. (1993) Wildlands and ecotourism in Latin America. *Journal of Forestry* 91(2), 37–40.

Wardle, D.A. (1992) A comparative assessment of factors which influence microbial biomass carbon and nitrogen levels in soil. *Biological Reviews* 67, 321–58.

Warnken, J. and Buckley, R. (2000) Monitoring diffuse impacts: Australian tourism developments. *Environmental Management* 25(4), 453–61.

Washburne, R.F. and Cole, D.N. (1983) *Problems and Practices in Wilderness Management: A Survey of Managers* (Research Paper, INT-304). USDA Forest Service.

Watson, A. and Cole, D. (1992) LAC indicators: An evaluation of progress and list of proposed indicators. In L. Merigliano (ed.) *Ideas for Limits of Acceptable Change Process* (pp. 65–84). Washington, DC: US Department of Agriculture, Forest Service.

Watson, A.E. and Niccolucci, M.J. (1995) Conflicting goals of wilderness management: Natural conditions vs. natural experiences. *Proceedings of the Second Symposium on Social Aspects and Recreation Research, February 23–25, 1994, San Diego, CA* (pp. 11–5). San Diego, CA: United States Department of Agriculture Forest Service, Pacific Southwest Research Station.

Watson, A.E., Cronn, R. and Christensen, N.A. (1998) *Monitoring Inter-group Encounters in Wilderness* (Research Paper, RMRS-RP-14). Fort Collins, CO: United States Department of Agriculture Forest Service Rocky Mountain Research Station.

Watson, A.E., Niccolucci, M.J. and Williams, D.R. (1994) The nature of conflict between hikers and recreational stock users in the John Muir wilderness. *Journal of Leisure Research* 26(4), 372–85.

Watson, J. (1997) Regional planning and protected areas in south Western Australia. *Parks* 7(1), 2–8.

WCED (World Commission on Environment and Development) (1987) *Our Common Future: Report of the the WCED* (The Brundtland Commission). Oxford: Oxford University Press.

WCMC (World Conservation Monitoring Centre) (2000a) *Protected Areas Programme, World Heritage Sites (descriptions of Natural World Heritage Properties)*. Indonesia: Lorentz National Park. Online at http://www.unesco.org/whc/sites/955.htm (Accessed 13 July 2000).

WCMC (World Conservation Monitoring Centre) (2000b) *Protected Areas Programme, World Heritage Sites. Indonesia – Java and Bali: Ujung Kulon National Park and Krakatau*

Nature Reserve. Online at http://www.wcmc.org.uk:80/protected_areas/data/wh/ujungk.html (Accessed 13 July 2000).

WCMC (World Conservation Monitoring Centre) (2000c) *Protected Areas Programme, World Heritage Sites (descriptions of Natural World Heritage Properties). Indonesia – Lesser Sunda Islands*: Komodo National Park. Online at http://www.wcmc.org.uk:80/protected_areas/data/wh/komodo.html (Accessed 13 July 2000).

WCMC (World Conservation Monitoring Centre) (2000d) *Protected Areas Programme, World Heritage Sites (descriptions of Natural World Heritage Properties). Australia – Tasmania: Tasmanian Wilderness.* Online at http://www.wcmc.org.uk/protected_areas/data/wh/taswild.html (Accessed 13 July 2000).

Wearing, S. and Neil, J. (1999) *Ecotourism: Impacts, Potentials and Possibilities.* Oxford: Butterworth-Heinemann.

Weaver, D.B. (1991) Alternative to mass tourism in Dominica. *Annals of Tourism Research* 18(3), 414–32.

Weaver, D.B (2000) Tourism and national parks in ecologically vulnerable areas. In R.W. Butler and S.W. Boyd (eds) *Tourism and National Parks: Issues and Implications* (pp. 107–24). Chichester: John Wiley.

Weaver, D.B. (ed.) (2001) *The Encyclopedia of Ecotourism.* Oxford: CABI Publishing.

Weaver, T. and Dale, D. (1978) Trampling effects of hikers, motorcycles and horses in meadows and forests. *Journal of Applied Ecology* 15, 451–7.

Weaver, D. and Oppermann, M. (2000) *Tourism Management.* Brisbane: John Wiley.

Webb, R.H. (1982) Off-road motorcycle effects on a desert soil. *Environmental Conservation* 9(3), 197–208.

Webb, R.H. and Wiltshire, H.G. (1983*) Environmental Impacts of Off-road Vehicles: Impacts and Management in Arid Regions.* New York: Springer-Verlag.

Webb, R.H., Ragland, H.C., Godwin, W.H. and Jenkins, D. (1978) Environmental effects of soil property changes with off-road vehicle use. *Environmental Management* 2(3), 219–33.

Weiler, B. and Davis, D. (1993) An exploratory investigation of the nature-based tour leader. *Tourism Recreation Research* 18(1), 55–60.

Weiler, B. and Ham, S. (2000) Tour guides and interpretation in ecotourism. In D. Weaver (ed.) *The Encyclopedia of Ecotourism.* Oxford: CABI Publishing.

Weir, J., Dunn, W., Bell, A. and Chatfield, B. (1996) *An Investigation into the Impact of 'Dolphin Swim Ecotours' in Southern Port Phillip Bay.* Hampton, Victoria, Australia: Dolphin Research Project Inc.

Wellings, P. (1995) Management considerations. In T. Press, D. Lea, A. Webb and A. Graham (eds) *Kakadu: Natural and Cultural Heritage and Management* (pp. 238–70). Darwin: Australian Nature Conservation Agency and North Australia Research Unit, ANU.

Welsh, H.H. Jr and Ollivier, L.M. (1998) Stream amphibians as indicators of ecosystem stress: A case study from California's redwoods. *Ecological Applications* 8(4), 1118–32.

Western, D. (1989) Why manage nature? In D. Western and M. Pearl (eds) *Conservation for the Twenty-First Century* (pp. 133–7). New York: Oxford University Press.

Whinam, J. and Chilcott, N. (1999) Impacts of trampling on alpine environments in central Tasmania. *Journal of Environmental Management* 57, 205–20.

White, D., Kendall, K.C. and Picton, H.D. (1999) Potential energetic effects of mountain climbers on foraging Grizzly Bears. *Wildlife Society Bulletin* 27(1), 146–51.

Whitford, W.G., Rapport, D.J. and deSoyza, A.G. (1999) Using resistance and resilience measurements for 'fitness' tests in ecosystem health. *Journal of Environmental Management* 57, 21–9.

Whittaker, R.J. (1998) *Island Biogeography: Ecology, Evolution and Conservation.* Oxford: Oxford University Press.

Whittaker, D. and Knight, R.L. (1998) Understanding wildlife responses to humans. *Wildlife Society Bulletin* 26(2), 312–17.

Whyte, I., van Aarde, R. and Pimm, S.L. (1998) Managing the elephants of Kruger National Park. *Animal Conservation* 1, 77–83.

Wight, P.A. (1995) Sustainable ecotourism: Balancing economic, environmental and social goals within an ethical framework. *Tourism Recreation Research* 20(1), 5–13.

Williams, P.B. and Marion, J.L. (1992) Trail inventory and assessment approaches applied to trail system planning at Delaware Water Gap National Recreation Area. In G.A. Stoep (ed.) *Proceedings of the 1992 Northeastern Recreation Research Symposium, April 5–7, 1992, Saratoga Springs, NY* (pp. 80–3), General Technical Report NE-176. USDA Forest Service, Northeastern Forest Experiment Station.

Williams, D., Russ, G. and Doherty, P.J. (1986) Reef fish: Large scale distribution and recruitment. *Oceanus* 29(2), 76–82.

Williams, D.R., Roggenbuck, J.W., Patterson, M.E. and Watson, A.E. (1992) The variability of user-based social impact standards for wilderness management. *Forest Science* 38(4), 738–56.

Wills, R. (1992) Ecological impact of *Phytopthora cinnamomi* in the Stirling Range National Park. *Australian Journal of Ecology* 17, 145–59.

Wills, R. and Kinnear, J. (1993) Threats to the Stirling Range. In C. Thomson, G. Hall and G. Friend (eds) *Mountains of Mystery: A Natural History of the Stirling Range* (pp. 135–41). Perth: Department of Conservation and Land Management.

Wilson, R. (1999) Possums in the spotlight. *Nature Australia,* Autumn, 35–41.

Wilson, B.A., Newell, G., Laidlaw, W.S. and Freind, G. (1994) Impact of plant disease on animal communities. *Journal of the Royal Society of Western Australia* 77, 139–43.

Wilson, J.P. and Seney, J.P. (1994) Erosional impact of hikers, horses, motorcycles and off-road bicycles on mountain trails in Montana. *Mountain Research and Development* 14(1), 77–88.

Wischmeier, W.H. and Smith, D.D. (1978) *Predicting Rainfall Losses: A Guide to Conservation Planning* (Agriculture Handbook No. 537). Washington, DC: United States Department of Agriculture.

Wolcott, T.G. and Wolcott, D.L. (1984) Impact of off-road vehicles on macro-invertebrates of a Mid-Atlantic beach. *Biological Conservation* 29(3), 217 40.

Woodland, D.J. and Hooper, N.A. (1976) The effect of human trampling on coral reefs. *Biological Conservation* 11, 1–4.

World Resources Institute (1993) Cited in M. Honey (1999) *Ecotourism and Sustainable Development: Who Owns Paradise?* Washington, DC: Island Press.

WTO (World Tourism Organisation) (1998a) Ecotourism: Now one-fifth of market. *World Tourism Organisation News,* January-February, 6.

WTO (1998b) Protection: From the Amazon to Antarctica *World Tourism Organisation News,* July / August, 10–11.

WTO (World Tourism Organisation) (1999) *Sustainable Development of Tourism: An Annotated Bibliography.* Madrid: WTO.

WTTC (World Travel and Tourism Council) (1995) *Travel and Tourism's Economic Perspective (Global Estimates to 2005).* Madrid: WTTC.

Yalden, P.E. and Yalden, D.W. (1990) Recreational disturbance of breeding Golden Plovers (*Pluvialis apricarius*). *Biological Conservation* 51, 243–62.

Zabinski, C.A. and Gannon, J.E. (1997) Effects of recreational impacts on soil microbial communities. *Environmental Management* 21(2), 233–8.

Zinkan, C. and Syme, I. (1997) Changing dimensions of park management. *Forum for Applied Research and Public Policy* 12, 39–42.

Index

General index

Abiotic 13, 27, 28, 29, 31, 35, 39, 42, 44, 66, 90,104, 110, 301
Aboriginal 195, 196, 225, 226, 227
– owners 195, 196, 225
– people 225, 226, 227
– sites 192
Acceptable change 22
Acceptable range 171, 173, 178
Accommodation 22, 59, 75, 83, 101, 134, 158, 170, 172, 205, 207, 225, 230, 232, 248, 252, 288, 304
Accountability 151, 261, 284, 299
Accreditation 22, 186, 228, 230, 231, 235, 239, 257, 304
Aggression 54, 74, 75
Algae 33, 38, 52, 60, 115, 123, 282
Alien 37
– plants 37
Alpine 5, 28, 90, 121, 136, 205, 206, 236
Antarctic 5, 14, 53, 73, 167, 186, 229, 230
Anthropocentric 4, 9, 301
Arctic 5, 24, 28, 29, 95, 103, 138, 140, 142, 229
Arid 90, 91, 95, 103, 111, 113, 138, 142, 143
Assessment 23, 78, 83, 93, 100, 106, 127, 155, 178, 206, 231, 237, 260, 267, 269, 271, 275, 277, 279
– environmental impact 19, 20, 22, 82, 86, 102, 115, 138, 143, 144, 155, 201, 228, 231, 235, 262, 266, 302
– path erosion 48, 99
– trail condition 99, 155, 206, 277
Attitudes 9, 10, 72, 126, 135, 228, 240, 247, 260, 284
Attraction 55, 64, 73, 126, 128, 207, 248
Attractions 6, 8, 116, 172, 229, 230, 248, 252, 288, 290, 300, 302
Attributes 17, 21, 47, 71, 163, 213, 259, 284,
– socio-economic 260
Audio drive trail 253
Auditing
– environmental 23, 259, 294, 295
Australian Department of Tourism 17

Australian National Ecotour Guide Certification Program 231
Australian National Ecotourism Accreditation Program (NEAP) 230
Autotrophic 29, 32
Avoidance 73, 75, 76, 120, 126, 127, 128

Bacteria 38, 61, 90, 105, 106, 117, 189, 282
– soil 35
Barrier reef 56, 57, 195
Bats 52, 122, 123, 124, 126
Beach 51, 101, 111, 115, 128, 138, 173, 197, 210, 216, 283, 287, 292
Bear 97
Benchmark 171, 173
Benchmarking 173
Best practice 17, 186, 230, 231, 232, 239, 247
– energy conservation 232
– fuel efficiency 232
– noise and emissions reductions 232
– organisational activities 232
– waste management 209, 231
– waste reduction 232
– water conservation 232
Bike riding 83, 250
Biodiversity 1, 4, 14, 41, 48, 57, 71, 108, 142, 149, 188
– biological diversity 1, 6, 131, 140, 186, 188, 191, 196, 303
Biogeochemical 35, 36, 41, 90
Biomass 29, 31, 44, 49, 52, 54, 77, 87, 89, 104, 138, 141
– animal 29
– plant 29
Biome 35, 60
Biosphere
– reserve 5, 115, 190, 193, 194, 195
Biotic 13, 14, 27, 30, 35, 39, 41, 66, 73, 77, 91, 103, 108, 110, 190, 301

Location index